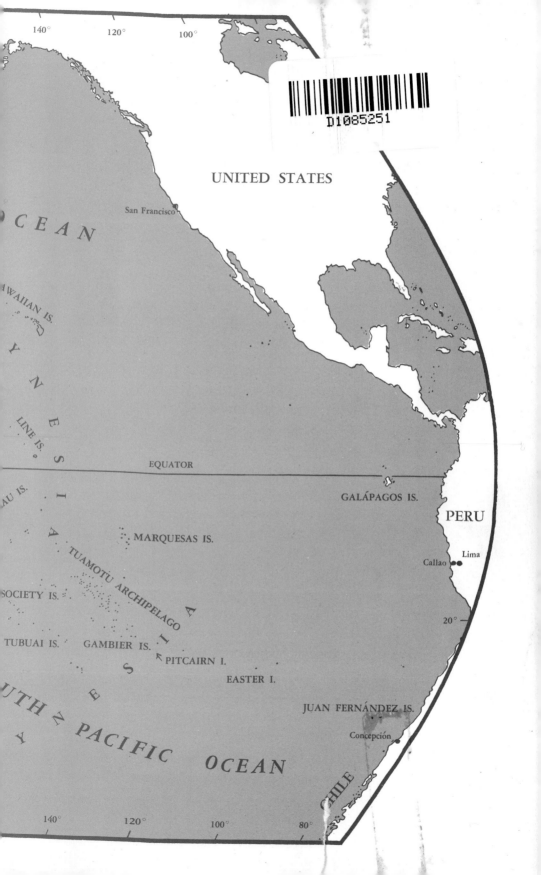

140°   120°   100°

UNITED STATES

San Francisco

OCEAN

AWAIIAN IS.

Y   N   E
S
LINE IS.

EQUATOR

GALÁPAGOS IS.

PERU

AU IS.

A   I   S

MARQUESAS IS.

TUAMOTU ARCHIPELAGO

Lima
Callao

SOCIETY IS.

TUBUAI IS.   GAMBIER IS.

PITCAIRN I.

20°

EASTER I.

JUAN FERNÁNDEZ IS.

UTH   PACIFIC   OCEAN

Concepción

CHILE

140°   120°   100°   80°

D1085251

A Dream of Islands

VOYAGES OF SELF-DISCOVERY
IN THE SOUTH SEAS

Also by Gavan Daws:

Shoal of Time: A History of the Hawaiian Islands
The Hawaiians (with Robert Goodman and Ed Sheehan)
Holy Man: Father Damien of Molokai

A Dream of Islands

VOYAGES OF SELF-DISCOVERY IN THE SOUTH SEAS

John Williams

Herman Melville

Walter Murray Gibson

Robert Louis Stevenson

Paul Gauguin

GAVAN DAWS

W. W. NORTON & COMPANY

New York   London

Published simultaneously in Canada by George J. McLeod Limited,
Toronto. Printed in the United States of America.

FIRST EDITION

Library of Congress Cataloging in Publication Data

Daws, Gavan.
  A dream of islands.

  1. Polynesia—Description and travel.
2. Polynesia—Social life and customs.
3. Travelers—Polynesia.   I. Title.
DU510.D26   1980   996   79–19301
ISBN 0–393–01293–X

1 2 3 4 5 6 7 8 9 0

To four friends across the Pacific:
Ron Stewart, who knew me before;
Bill Illerbrun and Denny Kull, who listened to me later;
Tony Hodges, who saw how it turned out.

Contents

List of Illustrations

The following illustrations appear between pages 148 and 149

Author's Note

THE PACIFIC OCEAN covers one third of the earth's surface. Across this vastness hundreds of islands are scattered, most of them in the tropics and subtropics, ranging in size from tiny coral atolls to mountain chains of volcanic origin. The scale of the ocean—seventy million square miles—reduces even the biggest of these island groups to insignificance. That is the geographic reality of the Pacific,* whose peoples inhabit a wave-lapped island world different in every way from the one we are used to, in which the continental civilization of the West has spread itself over extensive land masses.

European ships crossed the Pacific for the first time during the first circumnavigation of the world, accomplished by the Spanish expedition of Ferdinand Magellan in the early sixteenth century. Over the next two hundred years islands were sighted in mid-ocean, landings were made, new populations were discovered by the West, and European names were given to whole archipelagoes. But the white men who were sailing the Pacific in those days still had no accurate means of measuring distance from east to west at sea, so they did not know how big the Pacific was, just that it was enormous; and they could only guess at what it might hold.

A theory framed long before the age of exploration persisted into the late eighteenth century—that on the other side of the globe from Europe a Great Southern Continent existed as a sort of physical counterpoise to the land masses of the known world. This continent was what many exploring expeditions to the Pacific were sent to discover. What they found instead was a hemisphere that was mostly water.

Where the islands loomed infinitely large was in the phrase "the South Seas," and this, of course, referred not so much to a place on the map as to a state of mind—a dream of islands. As white men entered the Pacific and eventually began to take control of the islands, the *idea* of the South Seas was taking possession of them, or at least making its own special claim on them. The Pacific was literally the other side of the white man's world.

* See the front end-paper map.

In the South Seas, among islands and islanders, the white man was shown the other side of his own civilized humanity. A voyage to the South Seas was likely to turn out to be a journey into the self, and that is what this book is about.

The essential South Seas is to be found in Polynesia rather than in the other oceanic regions of Melanesia and Micronesia. Take a map of the Pacific; locate Hawaii, New Zealand, and Easter Island; draw lines connecting these places; and you have constructed a great triangle that encloses—among many other archipelagoes and solitary islands—Samoa, Tonga, the Cooks, Tahiti and the Societies, and the Marquesas. This is Polynesia,* and with some excursions to other parts of the ocean and a good deal of necessary to- and fro-ing between the islands and Europe and the United States, this is where the book is set.

It is unquestionably in Polynesia that the great oceanic pull is felt most strongly, away from continents, from civilization, toward ease, voluptuousness, warm beauty of place and people. Robert Louis Stevenson has caught as well as anyone the special quality of the white man's ideal encounter with the South Seas. Sailing the Pacific in 1888, the better part of a century too late to be any kind of real explorer, in fact a kind of tourist, Stevenson feels himself to be a discoverer just the same, and one of his discoveries is about himself. His first South Seas landfall is among high islands. His schooner drifts gently to rest outside a coral reef, in the lee of a wild green mountain. The scent of the land, of a hundred fruits and flowers, flows forth on the caressing air. The anchor plunges—a small sound, Stevenson writes, but to him "a great event; my soul went down with these moorings whence no windlass may extract nor any diver fish it up. . . ." The South Seas are revealing themselves to Stevenson for the first time, and the experience stirs something deep in him, touching what he calls a virginity of sense.

The five men I write about in this book—Stevenson, Herman Melville, Paul Gauguin, John Williams, Walter Murray Gibson—all respond to this deep experience. Two authors, an artist, a missionary, and a man who wants to rule an empire of brown-skinned islanders—all of them find their fate in Polynesia. Each of them is a notable man. Each feels great powers stirring within him. Life in the South Seas means a mobilization of these powers, self-expression, self-realization, self-justification, a feeling of being most powerfully and valuably alive.

In some of them there is an appetite for rule which they cannot indulge at home. They want to colonize their South Sea islands—put the clothes

* See the rear end-paper map.

of the West upon the brown bodies of islanders, so to speak, be a white king among brown subjects. In one or two of the others there is a driven, almost panicky flight from civilization. They are desperately searching for some island where they can decolonize themselves, shed the constrictions of civilized life, and experience the feeling of living like a savage. Whatever they want, whether it is domination over others or liberation from a civilized self, whether they surrender to the South Seas or impose civilized controls on themselves and their islands, it is here that they come into their kingdom.

The interesting thing is how persistently these white men who have known the South Seas—even those who claim they are renouncing the West—go on fighting the running battle of civilization and its discontents. On the far side of the world, living among savages, so-called, even the fugitives from civilization still labor at tasks that were set for every white man of their day. Just like those who never did leave home and run away to sea, who never laid eyes on a South Sea island, they have to decide who they will be, what kind of work they will take up, what kind of house they will build, what they will do concerning wife and family, who they will care for and care about besides themselves, what larger tribe of humanity they will attach themselves to, what faith they will keep, what they want their life to mean, what they want the world to think of them, what final monument they will try to erect to mark their existence.

This last is very important to them. They desperately want the world to know about them. They all want fame. And one way or another all of them achieve it, turning their struggles with themselves, with others, with their time and place, into accomplishments that the world will pay attention to. They stand on their South Sea islands, gesturing, signaling for recognition; and the world responds. The world is interested to hear about them, very much so, to the point where it might be said that in their lives among savages they are seen to be working out some of the basic human problems of the civilized white world in the nineteenth century.

Eminent Victorians of the South Seas, the five of them might be called. They are, as it happens, all men; though, of course, in their lives the power of women—mothers, wives, daughters, and the brown-skinned women of the islands—is palpable and, for more than one of them, overwhelming. For someone setting out now to write about these nineteenth-century lives in the Pacific, it is interesting to recollect the original biographer of eminent Victorians, Lytton Strachey, describing how an "explorer of the past" on paper should go about his work. He will, says Strachey, "row out over that great ocean of material, and lower down into it, here and there, a little bucket, which will bring up to the light of day some characteristic specimen, from those far depths, to be examined with a careful curiosity." These days, anyone who starts a book of short lives by quoting Strachey would be well advised to go on and issue some disclaimers. But here Strachey is doing no more than to give advice about fishing where the fishing is best, and I have found it best in these waters, among these men. The book opens with the dream of islands they shared with others who knew about the South Seas, and here there is no better starting place than Tahiti. Then the lives are looked at as they were lived, from the beginning to the end of the nineteenth century—first Williams, then Melville, Gibson, Stevenson, and finally Gauguin.

To be born is to be shipwrecked upon an island.
        —Araba Nightwing, in Paul Theroux's *The Family Arsenal*

It also struck him, poring over his rough map,
that viewed from a certain angle the island resembled
a female body, headless but nevertheless a woman,
seated with her legs drawn up beneath her in an
attitude wherein submission, fear and simple abandonment
were inextricably mingled.
        —Crusoe, in Michel Tournier's *Friday, or The Other Island*

A Dream of Islands

VOYAGES OF SELF-DISCOVERY
IN THE SOUTH SEAS

A Dream of Islands

IN APRIL, 1768, the French explorer Louis Antoine de Bougainville, sailing the South Pacific, sighted an island new to him, not down on any map that he carried. He was experiencing discovery. The land mass rose out of the sea before him like a superb work of art: amphitheatrical mountains, high and forest-covered, with one spectacular isolated peak like a pyramid in the middle distance, garlanded as if by the hand of some skillful decorator; open plains and groves of trees lower down; and a foreground along the shore of banana and coconut trees, with the huts of the islanders intermingled.

Here in the South Seas, Bougainville's ships were the bearers of civilization. He was a naval commander on serious business, extending the influence of the French Empire, broadening Europe's scientific knowledge of the world. For months his crewmen had been cooped up doing hard labor that was dangerous when it was not monotonous, living under harsh discipline, subsisting on appalling food. The ships were rat-ridden, cockroach-infested, stinking of sweat and bilge water and excrement. Now before the eyes of the crew a sweet green island shimmered in warm sunlight.

"As we approached the land," wrote Bougainville, "the natives surrounded the ships. The crush of canoes about the vessels was so heavy that we had great trouble mooring amid the crowd and the noise. They all came shouting *tayo*, which means *friend*, and giving us a thousand evidences of it. . . ." The canoes brought young women who "for charm of face yielded nothing to most Europeans, and who, for bodily beauty, could compete with any at advantage." Most were naked, "because the men and old women who accompanied them had taken off them the loincloth with which they usually covered themselves." The bare-skinned women offered themselves enticingly, and the men of the island made things even more clear: "they pressed us to choose a woman, to follow her ashore, and unequivocal gestures demonstrated the manner in which her acquaintance was to be made." "I ask," wrote Bougainville, "how to keep at work, in the midst of such a spectacle, four hundred Frenchmen, young sailors who have seen no women for six months?"

Somehow a girl got aboard and stood on the quarterdeck, on one of the hatchways, open for ventilation for the men working below. "Carelessly, the girl let her loincloth fall, and appeared to the eyes of all as Venus showed herself to the Phrygian shepherd: she had the divine form of the goddess. Soldiers and sailors rushed to the hatchway, and never was a capstan turned with such alacrity. . . ."

The anchor went down. And then, as another writer says, describing this eternal moment of Western access to the South Seas, white men stood upon the beaches of a dream world, embraced their nymphs, and walked into the golden age.

* * *

This was Tahiti, the Tahitian welcome was sexual, and it could be overpowering. Soon after Bougainville's ships anchored, one of the cooks slipped ashore against orders, located a willing girl, and then suddenly found himself surrounded by islanders who stripped him naked and examined every part of his body in a tumult of excitement. They meant him no harm, but they scared him out of his wits, and when their curiosity was satisfied and they urged him to go ahead with the girl, he could not manage it. He got his clothes back and went on board again "more dead than alive," telling Bougainville it would do no good to reprimand him—nothing could frighten him as much as what he had just been through.

Even when the Tahitians were quieter about their curiosity it was unnerving, at least to begin with. Some of Bougainville's men were welcomed to a grass hut with food and the music of a nose flute, and a girl was offered, very young, with the breasts of a Helen of Troy, as one of the delighted visitors said. She lay naked to receive her new lover; but, interested though he was, he could not put out of his mind the fifty Tahitians, also interested, who were watching in a circle. So a fine occasion came to nothing because of what one Frenchman, philosophically inclined, called "the corruption of our customs."

On the same day, though, several other Frenchmen were able to overcome the corruption of their civilized upbringing. One of Bougainville's passengers was a young aristocrat, Prince Charles Nicholas Othon of Nassau-Siegen. Caught in the rain, he took shelter in a "maisonette" where by chance there were six pretty girls. They welcomed him with great sweetness, took off their clothing, "that impediment to pleasure," displayed all their charms, and drew his attention in detail to the shapely grace of their perfect bodies. Then they undressed him. "The whiteness of a European body ravished them," Nassau-Siegen wrote in his journal.

"They hastened to see if I was formed like the inhabitants of their land." This time, despite the gathering of another crowd of interested Tahitian onlookers complete with flute player, there was no unhappy ending.

* * *

Bougainville and his men did not know it, but by a matter of months they had been beaten to the honor of discovering Tahiti for the West. The British explorer Samuel Wallis had already come and gone, in mid-1767, and was close to home again. Wallis took possession of the island "by right of conquest" and raised the British flag. And it was his men who first became—as Wallis's sailing master, George Robertson, put it—"madly fond of the shore." What Robertson called "the old trade" between sailors and Tahitian women began at once. There was trouble, but only over matters of style. "A dear Irish boy one of our Marins," wrote Robertson, "was the first that began the trade, for which he got a very sever cobing," a thrashing, "from the Liberty men for not beginning in a more decent manner, in some house or at the back of some bush or tree. . . ." "Padys excuse," so Robertson understood, "was the fear of losing the Honour of having the first." The Irishman, to be sure, was doing no more than planting his own explorer's flag. Bougainville in his turn "took possession" of the island for France, leaving an oak plaque with a carved inscription and a document buried in a bottle. In 1774 a Spanish exploring expedition raised a cross to signify the king of Spain's "indisputable right" to the island. So three times in less than a decade Tahiti was added to Western empires.

Wallis gave the island the name of his sovereign, King George III. The Spanish used the name Tahiti (which, incidentally, they had learned from one of Wallis's men in Europe). Bougainville, a cultivated man who knew his classics—nymphs, shepherds, gods and goddesses, and the golden age—called the island Nouvel-Cythère, New Cythera, after the Greek island where Aphrodite, goddess of love, had been born out of the sea.

Wallis reported his discovery in secret to his government, as he was instructed to do. Bougainville, also for political reasons, kept the location of Tahiti confidential, deliberately giving out wrong information about its latitude and longitude. But the London papers picked up stories about what Wallis's men had seen, and his ship's barber wrote a long poem about his voyage around the world and published it at his own expense. In the same way a scientific member of Bougainville's expedition, the naturalist Philibert Commerson, could not wait to tell what it was like where he had been. He wrote a letter to a friend and the letter found its way into print in Paris.

As Commerson described Tahiti, everything about the place and its people was perfect. Even before Bougainville decided on the name New Cythera, Commerson was privately calling the island a utopia. Tahitians, he wrote, were born under the most beautiful of skies. Wise in the ways of nature, they were nourished by the fruits of an earth fecund without cultivation. Their chiefs were family fathers rather than harsh kings, and the people lived free of dissension, need, prejudice, or vice. And they spoke a language of "noble simplicity," in which the "workings of the soul, the beatings of the heart" were one with the movement of the lips.

More remarkable still, the Tahitians knew "no other god but love; every day is consecrated to it, the whole island is its temple, all the women are its idols, all the men its worshippers." The mating of the sexes was an "act of religion," performed in public, watched and encouraged by well-wishers, its consummation applauded. Most delightful of all, the stranger too was admitted to these "happy mysteries." It was even a "hospitable duty" to invite him to take part. An austere censor, said Commerson, would find in this only moral excess, horrible prostitution, the height of shamelessness. But Commerson insisted that what Tahiti unveiled to the world was "the condition of natural man, born essentially good, free of all preconception, and following without diffidence or remorse the sweet impulses of an instinct always sound, because it has not yet degenerated into reason."

So in Europe Tahiti came to stand for the South Seas, and the South Seas came to stand for release from the constraints of civilized life, for the life of nature, for freedom and delight. Not every encounter between white men and South Sea islanders was like the first meeting that Bougainville and Commerson described, and indeed there was more to their encounter with the Tahitians than that. But it was the joyful parts of the Tahitian experience that struck a particular chord in Europe, as something worth considering among the rewards of the age of exploration, along with advances in scientific knowledge and extensions of European imperial power.

White men were never single-minded about what they expected to gain by exploring the world. They wanted to accumulate treasure, pile up knowledge, assert dominion—own the earth. But the kind of experience Bougainville wrote about offered something different—a chance for Europeans to ask themselves deep, self-critical questions about their own civilization, if they wanted to. At least some Europeans of Bougainville's day were receptive to the thought that the life of Polynesians might offer Westerners a lesson about the way they lived their own lives.

This was what Philibert Commerson was proposing when he called Tahiti a utopia. Commerson and Bougainville had read Jean-Jacques

Rousseau on the subject of the Noble Savage. Rousseau did not coin that phrase; the English poet John Dryden did. But Rousseau's name was most closely associated with the idea, at a time when a good many European thinkers were becoming preoccupied with questions about what was basic to human nature, and when the argument was being put forward that perhaps civilization of the Western kind was a crushing weight that produced deformities in humanity.

There were any number of notions about the perfect human being, the perfect society, the perfect natural environment, and what the connections between them might be. The phrase "Noble Savage" was new, but some of the ideas that clustered around the phrase were as old as ancient Greece. The Greeks themselves wrote of a time, lost and gone beyond recovery, when humanity lived a life of perfect happiness in a golden age. Christians had a Bible that began with the story of a man and a woman living in Eden, in freedom and delight, until the catastrophe of the Fall, which they brought on themselves; then they were driven from the garden, never to return. In these views, the long arc of human history was downward, a degeneration from perfect beginnings. An alternative view was that if only society could be arranged so as to bring out the best and not the worst qualities in human nature, then the perfect human being might appear on earth in the future. Then again, in the age of exploration it became possible to think that even if Europeans themselves had lost forever the perfect life of unspoiled man in an unspoiled state of nature, this happy condition might still exist somewhere on earth, waiting to be discovered by Westerners. It was an exciting thought. One of the earliest impulses for European exploring, especially by sea, was the search for some sort of earthly paradise.

When Columbus first sighted the Caribbean islands off the American continent, he was convinced that he was, if not in paradise, at least close to it. The "Indians" he found there seemed to him beautiful in their nakedness. And their physical beauty was the outward sign of a beautiful nature, peaceable, cordial, hospitable, frank, trusting, naturally good. They did not seem to be concerned about matters of rank and status, or about accumulating property for themselves, things which obsessed Westerners. So in every respect they were different from the white man, and superior to him. They were the first noble savages of the age of exploration.

As new places one after another were revealed to Westerners, new types of human beings were held up to inspection. Inevitably, as more and more of the world was mapped, the hope of finding perfect people in an earthly paradise diminished. But the vision persisted, and travelers' tales became the basis for general discussions about the nature of man and the prospects for improving European society. The perfect society was put down on paper in many forms, called utopias. Utopian writing was frequently satirical to the point of being scathing about existing European society. Invariably, Utopia was located far away from Europe, and there was something poignant about the whole concept. *Eu*-topia meant a good place; *ou*-topia meant no place, nowhere. Europeans were condemned to seek but not to find.

Columbus's Caribbean Indian turned out to be flawed, and so did the great cold-weather savage, the North American Indian. The black African in his turn failed to be perfect, and in the end was considered to be good only as a slave. Civilized nonwhites—Chinese, Persians, and others—disqualified themselves as possible noble savages by being too civilized.

The question, literally, was: Where in the world might the noble savage still be found? Far away, certainly. Goodness was likely to be distant from badness, and the more prolonged and difficult the voyage the more the traveler had the right to want to be rewarded for his effort. Overseas, then; and the voyage would wash away the grime of civilization. On an island, very likely; Western civilization was continental, and perfect societies of the kind described in utopian writing were by their nature small. And the island would be warm. Visions of the earthly paradise usually had tropical overtones, and for fairly obvious reasons. The noble savage would go naked, not hiding himself, displaying his body as the outward sign of inner spiritual beauty. Freedom of physical movement would be matched by social freedom. The noble savage would not be bound by restrictive clothes, or enslaved by restrictive custom. He would not be poor, and neither would he be graspingly rich. Nature would provide for him. He would be exempt from the grubbing work needed to stay alive and then prosper in a situation of scarcity. And there would be no grubbing meanness in his sexuality either, no repressive, constraining, monogamous Christian marital bonds, but instead the open realization of pleasure, freedom, and delight. And then Bougainville's ships put in at Tahiti, and the dream was made flesh.

The Tahitian body was seen, by those who knew about such things, as classically beautiful. Cultivated voyagers could not help seeing the islanders as Polynesian Greeks of some hazy golden age, living statues of a color between bronze and marble. Bougainville came across men who could have been models for Hercules and Mars. A later explorer measured a Polynesian chief and found his dimensions exactly the same as those of the Apollo Belvedere. The Englishman Joseph Banks, who sailed with James Cook on his first voyage to the South Seas, immediately gave Tahitian men Greek names: another Hercules, an Ajax, a Lycurgus, an Epicurus. As for the women, Banks was rhapsodic: "I have no where seen such Elegant women as those of Otaheite such the Greecians were from whose model the Venus de Medicis was copied undistorted by bandages nature has full liberty . . . and amply does she repay this indulgence in producing such forms as exist here (in Europe) only in marble or Canvas nay such as might even defy the imitation of the Chizzel of a Phidias or the pencil of an Apelles." And both the bodies and the souls of the women were made for love, the pleasure of the Tahitian garden, "modeld into the utmost perfection for that soft science. . . ."

How was it possible, one of Bougainville's men wondered to himself, for such a charming people, so fair to European eyes, to exist so far from Europe? Time and time again, Tahitians and other eastern Polynesians were described as resembling Europeans. The possibility does exist of a real affinity. Long before Wallis and Bougainville, some white men may have lived and died on shore in Polynesia—though not by choice. They were shipwrecked Spanish sailors from an expedition that followed Magellan's into the Pacific in the 1520s. They were never heard of again in the West, and had been forgotten by history. If they were cast away among eastern Polynesians, they could well have left descendants by island women, and their physical legacy, surviving visibly, could have contributed something essential to the mysterious shock of recognition so characteristic of first meetings between Polynesians and white explorers.

So the European voyagers of the late eighteenth century may indeed have been looking at versions of themselves embodied in islanders. This would have made it easier still for whites to be carried away by the beauties of the South Seas. They could imagine that they were seeing a human picture of themselves when young, before freedom and delight were civilized away from them, before guilt made them clothe their bodies. There was Eden before the Fall to think about, and the sexual universe of the Greek myths as well, in which gods and humans and animals could join in mating. So Tahiti came to stand for the power of the erotic; and dreams that were damped down by life in civilized society, forced to the underside of consciousness, surfaced again in all their seductiveness in the South Seas.

* * *

The Tahitians, of course, had more on their minds than just offering their women to white men. They wanted to get things from the ships. Here the women were useful. Their value came to be measured in iron.

Metal in all its forms was one of the great wonders of the white man's world. The Polynesians had none. A great deal of the interchange between ship and shore had to do with sex and technology, and this had been so since the earliest days of European exploration. On Ferdinand Magellan's voyage, off the coast of South America, so a member of the expedition wrote, "one day a pretty young woman came aboard the Captain General's vessel for no other reason than to find something to take. And glancing around the Master's cabin, she saw a nail somewhat longer than a finger, and at once she seized it and neatly thrust it into her vagina, and suddenly jumped overboard and left." At Tahiti, once the islanders found out about iron on board Wallis' ship, it became the prize trade item. It would buy drinking water, firewood, fruit, chickens, pigs, and women.

At first a woman cost a twenty-penny nail (meaning a nail that cost twenty pennies a hundred). The law of supply and demand pushed the price up. When Wallis's men went ashore on liberty, "young girls," as George Robertson wrote, very seldom "faild to carry off a nail from every man of the party." The ship's guards relieved each other regularly, and "got Value for their nail, and returnd back to their duety, some of the fellows was so Extravegant that . . . they spent two Nails. . . ." Within a couple of weeks the ship's carpenter was complaining that "every cleat in the Ship was drawen, and all the Nails carryed off," and the boatswain was reporting that two thirds of the men were "oblidged to lie on the Deck for want of nails to hang their Hammocks." Robertson stopped liberty and made inquiries, and was told that the "Young Girls . . . hade now rose their price . . . from a twenty or thirty penny nail, to a forty penny, and some was so Extravagant as to demand a Seven or nine Inch Spick, this was a plain proof of the way the large nails went." Bougainville in turn found the natives to be "fine traders," clamoring for iron. In one of the canoes that came out on the first day, there was "a young and pretty girl almost naked, who showed her sex for some little nails. . . ." The cycle had begun again.

The "old trade," to be sure, was not exclusively for nails. It was a way for Tahitians to make human discoveries, just as exciting to them as Philibert Commerson's were to him. An obvious puzzle for the islanders was why such big ships with so many white men aboard had no women. One Polynesian theory was that there were no women where the white men came from, and this was why they went exploring. At Tahiti the puzzle was quickly cleared up. Wallis's men showed a young chief a miniature of a "very handsome well drest young Lady." They made him understand, wrote Robertson, "that this was the picture of the women in our country

and if he went with us he should have one of them always to Sleep with."
In "raptures of Joy," the chief "hugd the picture in his breast and kist it
twenty times, and made several oyther odd motions, to show us how
happy he would be with so fine a woman. . . ."

The greatest sensation occurred during Bougainville's stay. A young
Tahitian man was aboard ship, being dressed in Western clothes and
shown himself in a mirror, learning how to eat food Western style, when
he caught sight of Commerson's servant and called out in his own language that it was a woman. And so it was, a woman dressed as a man. All
the way from France to Tahiti she had kept herself more or less successfully disguised among several hundred Frenchmen, only to be unerringly
identified by an islander as soon as he set eyes on her at close quarters.
Her name was Jeanne Baré, and her story was that she was an orphan in
desperate straits who had saved herself by deciding to live a man's life.
She went to sea out of curiosity, and she became the first woman known
to have circumnavigated the world.

Once her secret was out at Tahiti she had a difficult time. First the well-
dressed islander made "propositions" to her in front of the crew. Then
one day when she was ashore collecting seashells for Commerson, she was
set upon by the other servants, "who found on her the *conchu veneris*, a
precious shell they had been searching for." The Tahitians pursued her as
well, shouting and wanting "to do her the honors of the island." Baré did
not go ashore again. She stayed aboard with loaded pistols. But excitement spread among the Tahitians, until any French sailor who looked in
the least feminine was likely to be hunted down and seized, forced in his
own interest to produce "the certificate of his sex." What Commerson
with his scientist's eye had observed about the sex of his servant is not
known. Baré had been working for him for some years; surely he must
have had some notion. In any case, Baré was useful to him, and he remembered her in his will. He also named a plant after her, *Baretia*, for its
"uncertain sexual characteristics."

* * *

The Tahitian who saw through Baré's disguise was named Ahutoru.*
He wanted to take his discoveries further, in fact was eager to go with
Bougainville back to France. Should an islander be taken away from his
home with no certainty that he could ever be returned? It was a moral
problem. But Ahutoru was persistent, and Bougainville could see advan-
tages in bringing home a live exhibit from Tahiti. So it was agreed.

* Bougainville wrote this down as Aotourou.

Ahutoru did his best to take care of Bougainville's men. Finding a sailor temporarily unable to perform one of those daunting public acts of love, Ahutoru volunteered to show him how it was done. As Bougainville's ships were leaving Tahiti with Ahutoru aboard, he offered while he was still in familiar waters to steer them to another island where there were pretty girls. He hoped that he would be looked after in the same way where Bougainville lived, indeed was anxious about it. He said that if there were no white women for him where they were going, he would cut his throat.

He did not have to. He was the sensation of 1769 in France. As a Parisian remarked, for Bougainville to have sailed around the world and brought home a South Sea islander was like an "aeronaut" bringing back an inhabitant of one of the other planets. Ahutoru was presented to the king, and was inspected and interviewed by learned men. The wife of Bougainville's patron, the Duc de Choiseul, "adopted" him. Ahutoru learned his way about Paris, and developed a taste for the opera, especially the dancing. He liked to meet actresses, and "one night, he pretended to tattoo . . . a young German dancer in the Tahitian fashion." As he made clear from the beginning, his "grand passion" was women, and as a chronicler of the time wrote, he gave himself up to them "indiscriminately."

The British got their own islander. On James Cook's first voyage to the South Seas, following Wallis's discovery of Tahiti, the question came up of bringing home a Polynesian. Sailing with Cook was a well-born, wealthy, talented, and highly self-confident young man named Joseph Banks, a naturalist, interested in the idea of collecting specimens of all sorts. He liked the idea of a human one. There was a willing volunteer, an intelligent man named Tupaia, a priest in the Tahitian religion, who was knowledgeable about navigation. "I therefore have resolvd to take him," Banks wrote in his journal. "I do not know why I may not keep him as a curiosity, as well as some of my neighbours do lions and tygers at a larger expence than he will probably ever put me to; the amusement I shall have in his future conversation and the benefit he will be of to this ship, as well as what he may be if another should be sent into these seas, will I think fully repay me." But Tupaia and the young attendant who went with him fell ill and died along the way, and not till Cook's second expedition was an islander brought alive to England.

This was a young man named Mai.* He had no particular talents, but

* Cook and his men heard this as Omai.

he had been obliging to Cook's people. And when in 1774 he came to London—where Banks took him under his wing—he was a great success, just as Ahutoru had been in France. Mai learned an engagingly mangled brand of English, was presented to King George ("How do, King Tosh"), developed good taste in food and clothes, liked the theater, enjoyed the company of well-bred and less well-bred ladies who enjoyed him, and handled his dress sword gracefully. So well did he accommodate himself to the ways of the high-born that Dr. Samuel Johnson, a great eighteenth-century authority on everything and by no means a lover of the uncivilized ("one set of Savages is like another"), was led to remark that Mai at the dinner table with the light behind him was indistinguishable from an aristocrat.

Mai and Ahutoru had their moment of celebrity in Europe, then, and a Polynesian vogue persisted for some time. Travel literature was popular, and the idea of the South Sea islands was something new to play with. "Tahitian" items were manufactured for sale, toys and jewelry. "Tahitian" verandas were designed for country houses; "Polynesian" wallpaper was fashionable; artificial "South Seas" lakes were built into landscaped vistas. Cook's ethnographic collections were exhibited in London. The work of his expeditions' artists formed the basis for costume designs used in a spectacularly successful pantomime titled *Omai*. There was a French ballet about Cook, and a French play that had as a hero an islander who had lived for a long time in France, and as a villain another islander who had lived for a long time in England. Joseph Banks came back from Tahiti with a small tattoo, and common sailors had themselves decorated more extensively. *Tatau* was one of the great Polynesian arts, fascinating to white men seeing for the first time blue skin-breeches and intricate lace-work patterns applied directly to the flesh of men and women. The word entered the English and French languages from the Pacific, and the time would come when a white castaway or beachcomber returning to civilization with a complete cover of tattoo could exhibit himself for money.

The "old trade" of Tahiti interested Europeans even at a distance, and a French publication with illustrations showed the "amusements" of the "Otahitiens" and the "Anglais." In London, these amusements were staged live by a famous brothel keeper named Charlotte Hayes. Madam Hayes had evidently seen a popular published collection of British voyages to the islands, edited by a man of letters named John Hawkesworth. The story that caught her eye was from Cook's first expedition. One Sunday at Tahiti, after the British had held divine service, the Tahitians offered a variation on Vespers. A young man "above 6 feet high lay with a little Girl about 10 or 12 years of age publickly before several of our people and a number of the Natives." Cook observed that it seemed to be done "more from Custom than Lewdness," because there were several women present of "the better sort," and "these were so far from showing the least disaprobation that they instructed the girl how she should act her part, who young as she was, did not seem to want it." Very likely this was a performance by the Tahitian *arioi*, who were traveling virtuosi of sexual entertainment. They were much more than that, an exclusive and highly privileged sect with access to one of the most important of the Tahitian gods. But white men who were at Tahiti for a matter of days only, weeks at most, could hardly have been expected to understand this. Philibert Commerson had made a connection in his literary way between sex and religion in Tahiti. Cook in his plain way talked about custom. Hawkesworth added some remarks about whether shame was an instinct or a matter of convention. Charlotte Hayes, who ran a business regarded by her society as shameful, made a spectacle out of the episode, a cabaret of sex and technology.

She chose some young men and women, a dozen of each, rehearsed them in what she wanted, then issued invitations. "Madam Hayes presents her respectful compliments to Lord . . . and takes the liberty of informing him that tomorrow evening, at exactly seven o'clock, a dozen beautiful nymphs, spotlessly virginal . . . will perform the celebrated ceremonies of Venus, as they are practiced at Otahiti, under instruction and leadership of Queen Oberea, in which role Madam Hayes will appear." There were twenty-three acceptances of the invitation, from "the highest nobility, some baronets and five members of the House of Commons." The male performers, some of them artist's models from the Royal Academy, the others equally well made for this entertainment, presented to the females "a nail at least a foot long, in imitation of the presents received on similar occasions by the women of Tahiti," and "commenced their devotions," passing with "the greatest dexterity through all the different maneuvers on the command of saint Charlotte." As in Tahiti, the stranger was invited to take part in the happy mysteries, and some of the spectators joined in, to "lively applause."

* * *

So enthusiasm for the noble savage in his earthly paradise in the South Seas burned hot, at least for a time, and this enthusiasm tended to obscure the truth that on the subject of nonwhites in the age of exploration the mind of the white man had always been variable, even where Polynesians were concerned. Some of the earliest Polynesians seen by whites, for example, were inhabitants of the Marquesas Islands, which had been discovered for the West and named by the Spanish expedition of Álvaro de Mendaña at the end of the sixteenth century. The chief pilot, Pedro Fernández de Quirós, was struck by the physical beauty of the young Marquesan men, especially a boy with the face of an angel. Quiros was a good Catholic; and never in his life, so he said, had he felt such pain as when he thought that "so fair a creature should be left to go to perdition." But the Spanish ships carried soldiers with guns, and while the sign of the cross was being made and mass was being celebrated, and it was being proposed that white men should marry Marquesan women and colonize the islands, Marquesans were being shot and killed. It was one soldier's "diligence to kill, because he liked to kill," another's pride that he could shoot two with one shot and thus maintain his reputation as a skilled marksman. When the expedition sailed away, it left something like two hundred islanders dead.

In the late eighteenth century, the supreme moment of the Noble Savage, when the Polynesian was regarded as the noblest savage of them all, perhaps the embodiment of perfect humanity, white men still fired their guns at Polynesians. When Samuel Wallis declared that he was taking possession of Tahiti by "right of conquest," he did not mean that he literally laid waste the island. But in fact in his first days there he fired musket and cannon at the Tahitians, killing he did not know how many—probably dozens. He found this necessary in order to persuade the population to be obliging. Bougainville's men killed Tahitians. And when the greatest white explorer of the Pacific, James Cook, in the course of his three technically superb voyages between 1768 and 1779, added most of uncharted Polynesia to the eighteenth-century map of the world, along the way he destroyed property and several times took lives.

So what *was* the proper relation between whites and islanders to be? If nonwhites, anywhere in the world, were seen to be useless or a problem, they could be disregarded or disposed of. Again, if they were taken to be not fully human, then presumably they could be exploited in good conscience, as black Africans were. But if they were seen as fully human, however different from Europeans, then the question arose as to what white men might owe them as fellow human beings.

It was beginning to appear that any kind of contact might turn out to be hazardous to the islanders. This was true, from the beginning, even of enjoyable sexual contact. With the "old trade," no matter where it was practiced, went venereal disease, and this was a vexing problem. It was everywhere in Europe, in Charlotte Hayes's establishment, no doubt in the House of Commons too; and certainly Western ships carried it to the South Seas. But was it—or something like it—already present in the islands when the white man arrived? And if not, who brought it—the British, the French, or the Spanish? No one wanted to accept the honor of being the first in this regard. Yet with each ship that visited the South Pacific, an increase was noted in venereal diseases among Polynesians. And in other Western diseases. The age of exploration was the age of contamination.

Ahutoru and Mai knew about this. Ahutoru, going home to the islands in 1770, after eleven months in Paris, got only as far as Madagascar, off the east coast of Africa. There he had to wait for a ship to take him the rest of the way. Compared with Paris, the island was not exciting, and something he saw made him somber and thoughtful, as well it might: a black slave with an iron collar on his neck. Before another French expedition was formed for the Pacific, Ahutoru fell ill and died, possibly of venereal disease. As for Mai, he went home in 1776 with the third expedition of James Cook, outfitted with a horse, a suit of armor, guns, some toy soldiers, fireworks, a "Lectrifying Machine" given to him by Joseph Banks, a hand organ, a globe of the world, port wine, and on and on. Evidently Mai took venereal disease back with him too.

What did South Sea islanders gain by being discovered, then? Looking at what was becoming of them as early as the 1770s, James Cook was somber. "Such are the concequences of a commerce with Europeans and what is still more to our Shame civilized Christians," he wrote, "we debauch their Morals already too prone to vice and we interduce among them wants and perhaps diseases which they never before knew and which serves only to disturb that happy tranquillity they and their fore Fathers had injoy'd." The French thinker Denis Diderot read the book that Bougainville published about his voyage and wrote his own philosophical "supplement" to it, in which an old Tahitian cursed the French as they sailed away leaving disease behind them, their future return threatening invasion and enslavement, the sword and the cross of Europe's corrupt civilization poised to bring down ruin on a culture beautifully in tune with nature and its own gods.

In this view, then, it would be in the islanders' interest if white men went away forever. Another view was that the islanders were becoming so dependent on European goods that they could not do without them. They were, so to speak, addicted to the outside world now, and this made it a duty for the West to supply what had become indispensable. Then again, perhaps it was positively good for islanders to become part of the greater world. It would enlarge their ideas and heighten their aspirations, in general improve them.

There was, of course, no chance that the West would leave the South Seas alone. Europe was in its expansionist phase, had been ever since Columbus, and would be all through the eighteenth, the nineteenth, and on into the twentieth century. Polynesians were just one kind of people in a world full of different peoples encountered, inspected, evaluated, and made use of by white men.

And this meant that the question of the relative merits of life in the South Seas and life in civilization went on being ruminated by thoughtful white men. What was the particular quality of the islander's life? Surely it was that he did not seem to have to work hard. Joseph Banks was certain that Tahitians had so much time for love because they did not have to labor. By his calculations, a Tahitian who planted four breadfruit trees, "a work which can not last more than an hour," did as much for his generation as a European who with "yearly returning toil" had to plant, harvest, and store corn for his family. So the Tahitian had "Leisure," which was given up to "Love." Surely, release from grinding labor had something to do with happiness. The paradox was that civilization was built on work. Subsistence on the savage level might be pleasant because it was effortless. But civilized men had risen far beyond that, and it had taken toil of all sort. John Hawkesworth saw the quandary. Tahiti made nonsense out of any theory of human improvement, human progress. "If we admit that they are on the whole happier than we," he wrote, "we must admit that the child is happier than the man, and that we are losers by the perfection of our nature, the increase of our knowledge, and the enlargement of our views." Hawkesworth, a Londoner who never saw the South Seas, concluded that civilization was worth the trouble after all.

In the same way, one of the scientists who sailed with Cook thought that islanders who knew nothing of the world beyond their shores might indeed be happier than white men, but that it was simple-minded of white men to think of finding long-lasting happiness among islanders. Some sailors disagreed. Once they had sighted paradise in the South Seas they did not want to go home to civilization. Ship captains one after another had to deal with desertions, and it was Polynesia that gave the world its most famous naval mutiny. William Bligh, who became an involuntary expert on why sailors rebelled against civilized authority, was succinct about the reasons for the mutiny on the *Bounty*. Tahitian chiefs seemed to like Englishmen, even common sailors, and promised to provide for them if they would stay; and Tahitian women were beautiful. So the mutineers imagined it "in their power . . . to fix themselves in the midst of plenty in the finest Island in the World where they need not labour, and where the alurements of disipation are more than equal to anything that can be conceived." In their revolt against civilization the *Bounty* mutineers—nearly all of whom, incidentally, got themselves tattooed—chose the sweetest possible version of savagery.

The difficulty was that once the mutineers had got rid of Bligh, they themselves turned into Blighs and worse among the islanders. Their idea of happiness was to control others without setting controls on themselves. In these civilized men there was savagery. They kidnaped Tahitian men and women and took them to Pitcairn Island. They forced the men to do hard labor, and quarreled with them over the women. The human bill for all this excess inevitably came due for payment. Liquor was being distilled and drunk on Pitcairn, and a great rage brewed up over race and sex and dominance. It led to plots and ambushes and ax murders, a welter of blood and destruction.

Mutinous sailors with little education were not the only ones attracted by the idea of exercising control over islands and islanders. Joseph Banks, for one, thought of enjoyment and dominance in the same breath. At Tahiti he tried everything new. He sampled baked dog and liked it, got himself tattooed (within reason), took off his clothes and had himself smeared black so that he could take part in a funeral ceremony, and dallied with the beautiful island women. Voyager, Amoroso, Monster Hunter, a satirist called him. But Banks never had any intention of ceasing to be Banks the Englishman, and part of his project was to expand his dominion, to impose himself on the world. Banks had fun with this idea, but the drive was a powerful one. When he was considering sailing with Cook a second time, on a voyage to the Antarctic, he wrote: "O how glorious to set my heel upon the Pole! and turn myself around three hundred and sixty degrees in a second." At Tahiti, his first journal entry described the pleasant shade of breadfruit trees and coconut palms, and a Tahitian "creeping" almost on hands and knees with tokens of peace, and Banks summed up the scene as the truest picture the imagination could form of an "arcadia"—of which, he went on, "we were to be kings."

Bougainville, for his part, having sailed around the world and returned safely home, immediately put forward a plan to colonize Tahiti. He had had this sort of thing in mind for another set of islands he was involved with earlier in his career, the Falklands in the South Atlantic. Tahiti was more attractive in all ways. The islands of the Pacific in general were rich and interesting. European livestock would flourish, and so would certain kinds of European plants. Tahitians were intelligent, and they were agreeable to the idea of being colonized—witness Ahutoru, who had taken to calling himself Poutaveri, his way of saying Bougainville. And of course Bougainville considered himself just the man to govern Eden. This unquestioning assumption of the right to rule was strong in him. He was before his time in suggesting the colonization of Tahiti, but what he proposed was essence of Europe.

There were two great texts about white men and islanders composed long before the islands of the South Seas were charted. One was Shakespeare's play *The Tempest*, written with the Caribbean in mind. Prospero on his island had power through his magic, a technology that the natives lacked; and he dealt out rewards and punishments with absolute authority. The other was Daniel Defoe's *Robinson Crusoe*, in which the first word Crusoe taught Friday was "Master."

* * *

So if white men were pleased to have found noble savages in the South Seas and were even willing to learn something from them, they were ready for other sorts of experience as well. In fact they were ready for anything. Along with the theory of the Great Southern Continent as a physical counterweight to Europe went a corresponding notion, that of an ethnic counterpoise, the idea being that people discovered on the other side of the globe, standing with their feet toward Europe, might very well behave—so to speak—upside down. It was an interesting idea to play with. It included, for example, the possibility that explorers might discover not only perfect human beings but also monsters in human form— the possibility that savages might not be noble at all, but ignoble.

And in reality, not every savage the explorers saw on the way to the South Seas and back was attractive to European eyes. One people who lived at the extreme south of South America, on the very fringes of human existence, were given the name Big Foot, Patagonian. They were supposed to be giants, and travelers' tales multiplied about the strangeness of their cold, harsh, outlandish life. They could push arrows halfway down their throats. They ate rats without skinning them. (Bougainville noted that the men "pissed squatting," and wondered if this was "the natural way." Here he allowed himself an educated man's joke about Jean-Jacques Rousseau, the philosopher of the Noble Savage. Rousseau had a congenital urinary difficulty, and Bougainville concluded that the great apostle of noble savagism, "who pisses very badly our way, should adopt the other. He refers us so often to savage man!")

Bougainville, so he said, had no time for salon philosophers. He was a practical man, he had been around the world, and he placed his reliance on facts, not on airy systems of thought that had no basis in experience.

This was the same man who told Europe about the Tahitian Eden. But the fact was that after the magical first days at Tahiti, which left an indelible impression, Bougainville had months to talk to Ahutoru, and what he learned changed his views of Tahitians. The same thing happened to other white men who visited the islands, were enraptured, then learned more, and as often as not came home reporting distasteful things. So almost as soon as the Polynesian was announced to the world as the new and definitive Noble Savage, experience began to show that he was a fallible human being like all others, with some special flaws all his own.

Polynesians were thieves. If they did not steal among themselves, they were certainly ingenious about making off with European property. The beautiful burnish on the skin of the island women came from coconut oil, massaged into the body in a delightful way; but in the subtropical heat the oil sometimes went rancid, and the smell was bad. The islanders had lice in their hair, and they would groom each other, catching and eating the vermin. Healthy animal passion in women was something that sailors were grateful for; but they were staggered to see Polynesian women, including female chiefs, being physically affectionate with their pet dogs and pigs, beyond anything that would be called decent in Europe, to the point of literally suckling baby animals. William Bligh reported homosexuality at Tahiti, and the island turned out to have a bizarre specialty in men called *mahu*, who dressed as women and did women's work. Perhaps most disconcerting, the *arioi*, those performers of exciting sexual theater, also practiced infanticide. Denis Diderot, who was in favor of incest in principle, and applauded the Tahitians for practicing it, would have balked at some of these other practices, which in Europe were taken as evidence of Polynesian perversity. There was one late eighteenth-century Frenchman, though, who paid close attention to explorers' accounts of savage life as a guide to all the possible pleasures and pains of the human body. This was the Marquis de Sade.

Polynesian chiefs turned out not to be loving family fathers. They could be as arrogant and despotic as any European king who claimed to rule by divine right. At their command, islanders waged war and clubbed their captives to death. The chiefs and priests offered human sacrifices to their gods; Cook saw this ceremony on his third visit to Tahiti. Some Polynesians took heads, and some ate human flesh. Cannibalism caused a horrified shiver among Europeans at home, and of course even more among sailors in savage seas, especially after a boatload of Cook's men were killed and eaten at New Zealand. Polynesia was only one of many places in the world where flesh eating was known, and in the age of exploration a folklore grew up among sailors about cannibals who could tell the nationality of a white man by his taste. Among Polynesians, the Marquesans preferred Englishmen to Frenchmen, according to an Englishman; but the general verdict seemed to be that white men as a dish were too salty, and that tobacco smokers tasted particularly objectionable. If it was any comfort, at least the Polynesian appetite for flesh seemed to be more restrained than that of some Melanesians. There were stories about islands in the western Pacific where whole shipwrecked crews washed up on shore might be herded together, kept for killing and eating at festival times. (As for white women, in 1814, a little more than half a century after Jeanne Baré circumnavigated the globe by way of the islands, Ann Butcher, the "consort" of a trading captain, made melancholy history by becoming the first—and apparently the only—white woman to be eaten by Polynesians. She was eaten by Rarotongans, from an archipelago several hundred miles southwest of Tahiti. The crew she was sailing with got mixed up in local feuding, and were committing the customary visitors' depredations, stealing food, property, and women. Some of them were killed, Ann Butcher too, and she was baked in an oven.)

This was the white man and woman as victim for once. In many ways, of course, the white man was a deliberate victimizer. And in other ways his presence did encourage bad habits among islanders, even if in principle the islanders had the choice whether or not to indulge in the bad habit. The traffic in women's bodies with iron as the payment turned out to include a traffic in disease. White men traded in alcohol, which was new in the islands, and in guns—also new. In New Zealand, which was cool-weather, warlike Polynesia, a particularly gruesome trading arrangement was made. The Maori traditionally kept tattooed heads taken from enemies as trophies. Whites liked these as curios, and would trade guns for them. For many years the customs house at Sydney, the port of the British penal colony of New South Wales on the east coast of Australia, listed "baked heads" as a separate item of import; and even after the trade was prohibited by law in 1831, it went on illegally. Business was brisk, so if enemy heads taken in battle lacked markings, the Maoris would tattoo them *post mortem*, the more the markings the higher the price. Maori chiefs even took to tattooing their slaves, who ordinarily would not have the privilege of being decorated, and decapitated them to order.

* * *

For a brief moment in the eighteenth century the savage, and especially the Polynesian, had seemed to offer the white man a vision of what it might be like to go naked in the world once more. The idea of some sort of earthly paradise in the South Seas in fact lived on into the nineteenth century. It was by its nature inextinguishable, irrepressible. The nineteenth century repressed it. It returned, only to be repressed again, only to return once more. But it no longer represented—if it ever had—the dominant view of the great civilizations of the West. In fact, those who continued to believe that savages could teach civilized men how to live were more and more regarded as maladjusted—strange people such as writers and artists, who went wandering in the tabooed and subterranean regions of the mind. As early as the turn of the nineteenth century, and more and more as time went on, those Europeans who thought about such things concluded that there was very little to be said for savagery of any kind, and a great deal to be said for civilization. The workings of world history were teaching lessons about whose way of life was superior and whose was inferior, and the civilized way was winning. Obviously—look at the political map of the world.

The nineteenth century turned into the century of imperialism, in which the white man stood above all others. Increasingly it was thought that the best that could be done with the savage was to control him. This was part of a great exercise in control in the nineteenth century, control over self as much as control over the world. Decade by decade, Europeans more and more took charge of themselves and took charge of the world. The civilization that recoiled in horror from cannibalism was itself swallowing up place after place, the islands of the South Seas along with the rest. Polynesia was being incorporated in the body politic of the world.

The white man deserved to rule: this was the truth that made the West strong in the nineteenth century, and it was a truth that the West set out to teach all the peoples of the world. That truth came to the South Seas by way of the Bible. The nineteenth century was the great missionary era in the Pacific, as elsewhere.

In its way missionary work was a form of imperialism, and in Polynesia the empire of God in the making was British. The founders of this new empire had been seized by the grand vision revealed to them by the eighteenth-century explorers of the Pacific. The Englishman William Carey, a driving force in the setting up of overseas missions in his day, had read the published voyages of James Cook. Carey was a bootmaker, and over his workbench he kept a map of the world on which were shown the natural resources of the earth and the various religions of man, civilized and uncivilized. Carey's idea was that as the world was made to yield up all its treasures, so all its religions would become one, and that one would be evangelical Christianity.

In this view there was no such thing as a noble savage; he had never existed. The South Sea islander was in a state of sin, and the missionary
would have to voyage to the South Seas to redeem him, to save him from
himself.

*   *   *

John Williams

THE FOUNDERS of the London Missionary Society wanted to save the world. The question was where to start, and in the 1790s the most promising place appeared to them to be the South Seas. There was, as a matter of fact, a plan to send missionaries to Tahiti with William Bligh on his second expedition to the Pacific in 1791. This came to nothing, but when the first LMS ship sailed for the islands in 1796 the missionaries did have the benefit of a hundred-page vocabulary of the Tahitian language put together by one of the captured *Bounty* mutineers while he awaited trial for his life. Evangelical Christians were interested in Polynesians because the islanders were such degraded heathens. They copulated in public with every evidence of disgusting enjoyment and a total absence of shame. They strangled innocent babies at birth. They sacrificed human lives to their senseless idols. They clubbed each other to death in ferocious wars. Yet, paradoxically, there was a mildness of temper about them, an openness, suggesting that they could be reached by the good word. So there was work to be done in the South Seas, and every chance of success. The language there was simple—the *Bounty* mutineer's vocabulary showed that, and the LMS had been assured that a marine corporal had taken only three months to learn Tahitian on the spot. Certainly it would be easy and inexpensive for missionaries to keep themselves alive in an environment so benign and fruitful that serious work was unnecessary for subsistence. William Bligh thought that if any obstacle existed, it could only be "the fascination of beauty, and the seduction of appetite," and, of course, this was exactly what evangelical Christians knew how to resist.

Two LMS missionaries were landed at the Marquesas Islands. One was found asleep by some interested women, and they looked him over sexually. He panicked and left. The other stayed. He in turn was stripped of all his clothes and belongings. He was found months later by a sealing ship, wearing only a loincloth and burned almost black by the sun. With a new outfit of clothes he went ashore on another island in the group, but he was glad enough after several months to be taken off by a passing whaler. At Tonga in western Polynesia ten missionaries were put ashore. One went native; the others got caught up in local wars; three were killed and the rest did well to escape to New South Wales. At Tahiti the eighteen who started work together were scattered within a few years. There had been a visionary idea, put forward by a founder of the LMS but never officially adopted, that single missionaries might find wives among the "first converts of the natives," especially those "connected with the superior families; who would thus, receiving them into their bosom, be more engaged to protect them." What happened was a parody of this, a missionary's bad dream of islands. Some got entangled with Tahitian women. One went mad, crazy with infatuation for a female chief, refusing to be fed except by her. Another took a Tahitian woman for a wife—better to marry a heathen than to burn—and apparently got himself killed in some local argument.

As for the evangelists who remained in good moral standing, they made next to no impression on the Tahitians. The chiefs went their own way, and the commoners would not attend to the good word except when it was offered to them along with cloth or iron. After a year or so of this, and especially after several of the LMS people were stripped and beaten, most of the missionaries fled to New South Wales.

The handful who stayed, and some reinforcements who arrived in 1801, attached themselves to a chief named Pomare. For many years this seemed to have been a bad idea. Pomare's rivals for power among the chiefs forced him off Tahiti and into exile on the neighboring island of Moorea, and at that more of the missionaries left for New South Wales. What eventually brought about a change was Pomare's conclusion that since he was not doing well politically with his traditional gods, he should take up the Christian god. Having made this decision, he fought his way back to Tahiti and ultimately to power there.

In the course of all this the prospects of the LMS brightened. The missionaries who had been watching from New South Wales came back a few at a time to the islands. More had been recruited at home in England. One of the new men to come to the South Seas was John Williams, and his life and death were to make him a hero of religion.

*   *   *

Williams was born in 1796, in London, almost within the sound of Bow Bells, and he grew up among Cockneys. The fifth of six children and a second son, he was a good boy, a willing helper about the house, obliging, honest, punctual, an early riser, dutiful about his prayers, and sunny-tempered with it all. His father was in trade, his older brother went to work in a business house, and John's own "destination" in life was assumed to be "commercial." When he was thirteen he was apprenticed to a furnishing ironmonger named Enoch Tonkin, in the City Road. Behind the counter in Tonkin's shop Williams was brisk, orderly, and efficient, and he got on well with everyone. Tonkin gave him more and more responsibility, and Williams shouldered it all enthusiastically, until, still an apprentice and only in his middle teens, he was virtually managing the business.

At the same time he was watching Tonkin's tradesmen and laborers at their work, and in his spare hours he tried himself out with the hammer and the anvil. As a commercial apprentice he was not obliged to do this; it was not part of his indentures. He did manual work because he liked it, and he got very good at it. Other commercial apprentices might not have wanted to dirty their hands, but Williams saw nothing degrading in what he was doing. He would even volunteer for jobs out of doors, away from the shop; and Tonkin and his wife, watching him get ready for the day's labor, used to "smile to each other as they saw him adjust his working apron, and with a basket of tools slung across his shoulder, sally forth, with as light a step and as cheerful a countenance, as if he had been the happiest being in the world."

Williams's mother wanted him to be a good Christian. Her own husband was not seriously religious, and that was a worry to her. She had been brought up an Evangelical Anglican; her faith expressed itself in fervent devotion; and she wanted her children to have the same sort of closeness with Christ. So she prayed with them every day, morning and evening, and made sure that when John began his apprenticeship it was with someone she could trust, a pious master, living and working in what was called holy worldliness.

It was the understanding of people like Mrs. Williams that a life in trade, lived according to an intention to please God, became by definition a life of holiness, devotion, and piety. Enoch Tonkin lived this way, but not her husband, and as time went on it began to seem as if John was growing up to be his father's son. Four years into his apprenticeship he still came home to his family every Sunday, but if he went to church with his mother it was obviously to please her and not to please God. In his eighteenth year he took to hanging about taverns on the Sabbath with "several irreligious young men." To his mother's way of thinking this was dangerous moral drift, and she prayed hard for him.

Williams was not really going to the devil. He was just a good boy playing, in late adolescence, at being bad. One Sunday evening he went as usual to meet his friends for a drink at a tavern not far from where he worked. Even when he was setting out to waste time Williams was punctual, but the others turned out to be late. This annoyed him. He was walking about the streets in something of a bad temper when Mrs. Tonkin, on her way to chapel at the Tabernacle near the City Road, stopped to ask him what he was doing and urged him to go with her instead. Mostly out of irritation at his friends, Williams allowed himself to be persuaded.

As it happened, there was a powerful preacher at the Tabernacle that night, speaking to a text that might have been aimed at Williams: "What shall a man be profited if he gain the whole World and lose his own Soul or what shall a man give in exchange for his Soul." The idea that the soul was a negotiable item, that an individual could be called to account by God for his conduct, that there was a balance to be struck between worldliness and holiness—these notions of the economics of salvation were familiar to Williams. But somehow on this night he felt himself receptive and responsive as never before. He was transformed—converted. He did not collapse physically under the sudden awareness of his sinfulness, thrash around on the floor, and rise again saved, as Wesleyans used to do, and as the "enthusiastically mad," especially among the lower classes, were still likely to do. Williams's class of person, the respectable lower middle class, did not do that sort of thing. Even so, Williams had no doubt that the conversion experience was a genuine one, putting him in a right and proper relationship with God; and certainly it determined his future, his life from then on and the manner of his death. He set down the date, the evening of January 30, 1814, as the beginning of his new life, when God opened his "blind eyes."

For Williams in this new mood, religion was something to be "diligently attended to," the "solemn business of man," in other words a kind of work. He joined the Youths' Class at the Tabernacle, meeting every Monday night with about thirty other self-improvers to pray and discuss topics of mutual interest. He taught Sunday school, and went on to useful work outside the Tabernacle, distributing religious tracts, visiting the sick, instructing the inmates of a poorhouse and almshouse. What he was doing was apprenticing himself to the idea of missionary life.

By late 1815 he was ready to think about the real thing. At the Tabernacle there was a well-organized auxiliary of the London Missionary Society, devoted to the conversion of the heathen of Africa, India, and the South Seas. The members of the auxiliary put together their ideas about the proper use of time and money with the idea of an investment of effort in religious duty, and went in for pious competition in fund raising. No one in London was better at it. Williams went to the auxiliary's meetings, which were emotional, and found his heart "frequently with the heathen." He took his feelings to his pastor, who looked him over for good faith and good sense and encouraged him to go ahead and offer himself for missionary service.

As Williams described his "motive" in his "frank and plain" written application to the LMS, it was "a sense of the debt of love I owe to God" and "a sense of the value of an immortal soul." For Williams, the greater the number of souls involved, the more intensely the forces of spiritual economics operated, and he had taken to heart what his pastor said about "how many millions there was destitute of and daily perishing for lack of knowledge, and how much Missionaries were wanted, and it was a great duty incumbent upon every Christian to exert themselves to the Uttermost. . . ." The task he was proposing to take on was immense, and he was not sure he would measure up. The thought of insufficiency humbled him; but, as he said, if the LMS wanted him he was ready. He was in his twenty-first year.

He was accepted as a suitable candidate for missionary work in August, 1816. Enoch Tonkin released him from the remaining months of his indentures. In September he was ordained, and it was decided to send him to the South Seas in mid-November. Late in October he got married—on short notice, like many departing missionaries in need of a spouse to stand between them and the fascination of beauty in the South Seas. His bride was a young lady he had met at the Tabernacle, Mary Chawner, a businessman's daughter of "placid manner and apparent timidity."

* * *

A few days before the Williamses were due to sail they went aboard their ship, the merchantman *Harriet,* to look over their accommodations. They found them unsuitable. It was not that John and Mary Williams were looking for luxury; they were not showy people (except perhaps morally). But they knew what was proper and what was not. "As soon as we came aboard," Williams wrote to his sister, "we set to work at our cabins, put them in very nice order, made our beds, hung up our looking glasses, drove hooks and nails in various places for our hats and coats, fixed our cabin lamps, laid down our little bits of carpet, and now it looks very comfortable indeed." So much so that though it was a "boisterous night" Mary insisted on sleeping aboard, and they "slept as comfortable and undisturbed as possible"—just like home.

It took Williams and his wife a year to the day to get where they were going—nearly six months between England and Sydney, a delay of almost four months there waiting for a ship to take them on, then a last leg of several weeks by way of New Zealand to Tahiti. Williams enjoyed himself enormously at sea. He had fallen in love with ships the moment he stepped aboard the *Harriet,* and all the way out to the Pacific he took detailed mental notes on how a sailing vessel was built, rigged, and run. Mary Williams, though, hated the open ocean. For the rest of her life, as she learned by experience, she was condemned to be "well when in harbour, but very ill and helpless at sea." She could hardly have enjoyed the last part of the voyage any more than the beginning; she arrived at Sydney pregnant and was within two months of giving birth when she went ashore in the islands. She bore up well, as she always tried to do, and Williams gave her credit for making the effort, as well as for other good qualities that would be useful in a missionary's wife. "My dear Mary & I," he wrote in a long letter home that did not mention either his wife's pregnancy or her chronic seasickness, "are very happy & comfortable & are sincerely attached to each other, I have reason to be very thankful, for indeed, she is a help meet, she is ev'ry thing I can desire she should be, she is an excellent domestic, a good needle woman, an excellent disposition, & I hope a real Christian, desires to make me comfortable & happy, & I regard it as a striking answer to prayer. . . ."

Williams's first experience of a South Sea island was on Moorea, a few miles from Tahiti, certainly one of the most beautiful places in the world. Williams did not waste time admiring the landscape or the nobility of the savages who lived there. What interested him was nature improved by man and man improved by religion. So the chapel impressed him, hay-stack-shaped, tidily thatched, all done by the natives, the whole thing of a "neat and clean appearance." To go to services there was a moving experi-ence for Williams—seven or eight hundred islanders, their brown bodies swathed in white *tapa* (bark cloth), the women with their "little cocoa-nut leaf bonnets, and their heads decorated with red and white sweet-smelling flowers," all attentive to the preacher. Williams reflected that not five years before, these people would have been bowing down to idols, wallowing in the most dreadful wickedness. Now here they were, serious, decorous, praising God. Though there were still "hundreds in these islands who do not know our Lord and Saviour, they are as eager to learn as the miser is to get money."

Williams stayed on Moorea a year, learning the language he would need in the missionary work to come. When he arrived, the LMS people already there were building a schooner, and Williams did all the ironwork singlehanded. Not long after the ship was launched, the Williams's first child was born, a son. He was given his father's first name and his mother's family name—John Chawner. A dear little treasure, Williams wrote to his mother, but inevitably a source of "anxious cares" to his parents, who would have to bring him up in difficult circumstances.

Williams was sensitive to family responsibilities, to what was owed be-tween parents and children. His mother had made him so. She always wanted the best for him, and for her this meant essentially that John should do what she wanted, preferably not too far away from her. John as a little boy praying at her knee was perfection in a son. John as a wayward apprentice was cause for alarm. John safely converted was home again with his mother—she became a member of the Tabernacle society with him, and they went to services together and shared communion. But when John announced that he was going to live on the other side of the world as a married man, there were passionate objections; the LMS could not help becoming aware that "much had been done by his connexions to dissuade and terrify him from his purpose."

When some islanders asked Williams if his family had not cried at los-ing him, "I told them," he wrote home, "that you would not have let us come, had it not been out of compassion for them, and had we not come to teach them the word of God." This was a way for Williams and his mother to deal with their relationship: they offered it to heaven and put a high value on the offer. The mother prayed that the son who was lost to her might be preaching "the unsearchable riches of Christ" to the perishing heathen. Williams also talked as if personal emotion had a money value. He always assumed that feeling was in short supply, that a deposit in one place meant a withdrawal from another. To make a transfer of energies and affections from one home and family to another cost him a great deal, so he said. "I frequently think of you," he wrote to his family in England, "with feelings I am obliged to suppress." And he said that if he were not so fervent in his desire to win souls for the Lord, "not the gold of Ophir, or the luxuries of the East would keep me from those for whom I have so strong an affection." All in all, though, he considered he had made a notable gain for himself and the family he had left behind in England. And here again he used the language of self-improving commercial respectability to describe what he was doing as a missionary. "Grieve not at our absence, for we are employed in the best of employments—for a good master . . . & upon the best of terms . . . do not persons of the world consider it an honour to have any of their family in the employment of any great man . . . we are employed for the King of Kings. . . ."

Having learned the language of the islands in record time for an LMS worker—not the three months it took the marine corporal, but at least he was preaching within a year—Williams went with his wife and child to help found a mission settlement on Raiatea, a hundred miles northwest of Moorea. Williams based himself there for several years, working sometimes with colleagues, sometimes alone. Raiatea was the largest island in a group to the leeward of Tahiti, with mountains about two thousand feet high and something like fifty miles of shoreline enclosed by a reef. Perhaps fifteen hundred people lived in scattered villages of thatched huts, cultivating small vegetable patches and groves of fruit-bearing trees and taking fish from the lagoon. Raiatea had been a great center of pagan religion, and the missionaries were highly gratified when the ruling chief Tamatoa (the missionaries called him a "king"), the archetypal Polynesian aristocrat, six feet eleven inches tall, asked to be instructed in the new faith and all that went with it.

Williams came ashore in September, 1818, and was welcomed ceremoniously with a feast of pig, yams, *taro*, coconuts, mountain plantain, and bananas. He and his fellow worker, a former professional actor named Lancelot Threlkeld, found Tamatoa and his wife open to suggestions about how the new era should begin.

According to the instructions the LMS gave its workers, the great bane of the savage was his idleness. It would be a blessing to him to be taught how to work. The natural productions of the earth in the islands could be turned to good account, and this would give the saved heathens a chance to sell what they produced, and once they were making money they could donate some of it to support their missionaries and send the blessings of the Gospel to other islands. For this kind of missionary work an evangelist did not have to be particularly learned—"godly men who understand mechanic arts may be of signal use to this undertaking." (David Livingstone, the missionary explorer of Africa, remembered one of the founders of the LMS saying that a godly man who could read his Bible and build a wheelbarrow was sufficiently qualified.) Williams seemed cut out to be just this sort of civilizer-evangelizer, and his instructions as much as invited him to make Polynesians over into versions of himself.

Tamatoa had already started to build a chapel for Williams and Threlkeld, at a place called Opoa, but this was the stronghold of the old pagan religion, and so the missionaries did not want to use it. They wanted to build a new town entirely. Their reasoning was that evangelists should not have to waste time forever walking between villages. Instead the Raiateans should all live together and all learn religion at once. This system was already working on one of the other islands. Obviously it would cost a lot in energy during the resettlement, but after that it would be economical in religious effort. There were some disadvantages to the idea, but these did not become obvious until later, and so Williams, Threlkeld, and Tamatoa went ahead with the creation of a town on the leeward coast.

As a beginning the islanders could watch a missionary build a house for himself, and Williams intended this to be an improving experience for them. "It was my determination when I originally left England," Williams wrote, "to have as respectable a dwelling as I could erect; for the Missionary does not go to barbarise himself, but to civilise the heathen. He ought not therefore, to sink down to their standard, but to elevate them to his." Williams did not stint himself. He made his house sixty feet by thirty, seven rooms, three in front, four behind, wood-framed, walls wattled and plastered, whitewashed outside, orange and grey inside, all the plaster and paint worked up from coral lime. The floors were carpeted, and all the furniture—tables, chairs, sofas, bedsteads—had turned and polished legs and pillars. The fenced front garden was laid out in lawns, gravel walks and flower beds. Behind the house was a poultry run with chickens, turkeys, and ducks, and a big kitchen garden planted with English vegetables.

There had never been anything like it on Raiatea. Tamatoa was impressed, and he had himself a house built close by, a four-roomer. Month by month more and more of his people followed his example. Williams was proud to say that in less than two years there were dozens of houses along the beach, more than in any of the other islands. Granted that they were nothing more than neat little cottages, "low and small," still "upon the whole, they are very good, and do the natives great credit." In time most of the Raiateans, a thousand or more, came to live at the settlement.

The houses were only the beginning. Williams set out to turn Raiatea into a workshop, with himself the master. He found the natives to be good apprentices. They "learned to work very well indeed, and some of them can saw, and adze, and plane better than I can. . . ." Complicated or exact construction Williams still had to take care of himself, but it was worth it to be able to keep putting new things before the Raiateans, so as to give them "many new and important ideas." These "they readily receive and act upon, and it is with some delight I observe them engaged in the different branches of carpentering, some box-making, some bedstead-making some making very neat sofas (which we have lately taught them) with turned legs and looking very respectable indeed, some, again, lime-burning, some sawing, some boat-building, some working at the forge, and some sugar-boiling; while the women are equally busy in making gowns, plaiting bark, and working neat bonnets—all the effect of the Gospel."

Williams wanted to see the "moral wilderness" present the same "improved appearance." He and his colleagues used to make inspection tours of the households at the settlement, taking care to appear unannounced, "as we wish to catch them exactly as they are." They had encouraging words for the industrious and rebukes for the lazy, delivered on the spot and repeated at a special meeting, "which fails not to stir them up to activity."

Increasingly the islanders were expected, "exhorted," to do new things and behave in new ways, change their lives: sleep and wake up at regular hours, work regularly, go to school regularly, go to church regularly. One of Williams's projects was to install a large clock at the settlement. In a word, the islanders were being told to account for their time. And to obey the new moral and legal code. Christians did not follow the "pernicious custom of living several families together in one dwelling," cohabit with more than one wife at a time, lightly leave a spouse, do away with unwanted infants, tattoo themselves, bathe naked in the stream at the settlement, dance lewdly, wear their hair long, eat raw fish. Christians slept one to a bed, in separate rooms, put on clothing in the morning, contributed coconut oil and arrowroot to the mission auxiliary to help pay for evangelical work in the less fortunate parts of the world, sat on chairs, and drank tea.

What Williams was attempting was nothing less than a complete re-channeling of a people's energies and appetites and expressiveness. To get Polynesians to submit to these new controls was bound to be difficult, and Williams and his colleagues understood this. "To pluck and eat the ripe fruits of their generous clime, or to slumber in the deep shade of the luxuriant trees upon which they clustered; to fish or sport within the placid waters of their lagoon; to ride in triumph upon the crested wave; to race, wrestle, and recite their traditions; or at evening, to mingle in the wild frolic, or the favourite dance were among the chief occupations and enjoyments of their life, except, when inflamed by revenge or stimulated by fear, they girded themselves for the battle. What a task to induce them to exchange such a state, for the patient and continuous labour of acquiring knowledge, and forming habits. . . ."

For Williams and those who thought like him, this was the problem: Polynesians were self-indulgent; they were addicted to the gratifications of the body; they did not rein in their passions, either sensual or violent. Mostly it was that they valued ease. Williams himself did not come from a culture of ease, but a culture of profound unease. Most of the LMS workers were like him in that there was poverty in their family and class background, often poverty and deprivation recently escaped and clearly remembered. Hence the gospel of work. They would have said that their appetite for labor represented the powers bestowed on them by grace. In practice they were likely to give themselves over to laborious accumulation, self-denial in the interest of security, the piling up of substance, the reassurance of solid material goods that somehow embodied spiritual values. Williams's task—the task of any LMS missionary—was to make the islanders feel deprived of something valuable, make them feel guilty because of this deprivation, then make them see that their condition was the result of pagan self-indulgence, and finally offer them the gospel of work as the way to salvation.

Williams was very good at stage-managing little technological morality plays, and soon he had his people talking about industrial productivity in a way remarkably like his own. He showed some islanders how coral could be burned into lime, and they marveled at it: "The very stones in the sea, and the sand on the shore, become good property in the hands of those who worship the true God, and regard his good word." For the rest it was a matter of defining the culture of the Raiateans in general as sin, and encouraging them to work toward Christ's blessing and their own redemption by way of competitive bedstead making, bonnet weaving, and church building. Wherever the LMS workers went in the islands, their churches were the biggest buildings, and soon wood and thatch gave way to stone and coral blocks, chiseled into shape and hauled into place by islanders—in the South Seas there were no other beasts of burden. Williams kept count of his laborers and the way they piled up the products of their labor for the new faith. He called his converts living stones in the spiritual building he was erecting.

To impose self-denial on savages took extraordinary effort and extraordinary self-denial in the missionary himself. But the gratifications were great, none greater. In the islands the lower-middle-class servant of the King of Kings could become a master in his own right. Looking back over a year's work on Raiatea, Williams could write: "The natives generally are fond of us & are agreeable to any thing we propose." And he went on: "We are little kings among them."

This was heady stuff. Williams was heatedly enthused about what he was accomplishing, almost to the point of ecstasy. Describing his feelings in a letter to England, he used words that linked labor with wealth and with joy. "I am happy in my work & desire to spend and be spent in the work of the Lord."

* * *

It turned out that Williams weighed too heavily on some of the islanders. They experienced the new regime as repression, and they wanted their old life back. One Sunday some young men broke into a missionary's house and drank up all the spirits they could find (in Williams's day the LMS was not teetotal). Four of them came reeling into the chapel during service, looking for trouble, and while they were creating uproar there, another went to Williams's house. "He was dressed in a most fantastical manner," Williams wrote later, "having his head decorated with leaves, and wearing a pair of trousers as a jacket, his arms being passed through the legs; he also wore a red shirt instead of trousers, his legs being passed through the arms. . . ." The missionaries who made him put on clothes were turning his life upside down. "He came, brandishing a large carving-knife, and danced before the house, crying, 'Turn out the hog, let us kill him; turn out the pig, let us cut his throat.' Annoyed with his conduct, and not apprehending any danger, I arose from the table to desire him to desist. On opening the door, one of the deacons, almost breathless from running, met me, thrust me back, and exclaimed, 'Why do you go out? why do you expose your life? you are the pig he is calling for: you will be dead in a moment.' " At the chapel the Christian chiefs had had the drunken young bloods tied up and questioned, and from what they said it appeared that they wanted to get rid of the missionaries, kill them, and kill the missionaries' friend, the ruling chief Tamatoa, as well.

The Williamses were badly shaken. Mary, who was heavily pregnant—

she had conceived not long after Williams wrote his letter home about spending and being spent—went into premature labor. The new baby lived only one day, and for weeks afterward Mary was so ill that Williams thought she might die. When her crisis was safely past, Williams wrote to the LMS in London asking to be taken away from the islands. His letter was long, vehement, rambling, in places almost incoherent. He was obviously going through a difficult period—a baby dead, his wife nearly dying, his own life threatened, and all this in a place where he had thought he was the king of an affectionate society of islanders. He was having trouble keeping his life together, and loss of control was particularly unsettling to a man like him, someone used to being in charge of things, able to work things out. It stirred up deep fears in him.

He talked at length about his life as a family man and a missionary. He discussed the position of missionary wives and the likelihood that there would be missionary widows. And then he went on to talk about the children of missionaries. Here he made some extraordinary despairing statements. He claimed that it was impossible for mission children to grow up properly in the islands. Born, bred, living, and maturing among Polynesians, "what can be expected—they will naturally degenerate. . . ." A child had to learn to be a man, and Williams was saying that if a child learned from South Sea islanders he would grow up a wild man.

Now, if Williams meant what he said, all talk of missionaries "improving" islanders was a mockery. He was saying that the Polynesian, for all the busy making of bedsteads and sofas and bonnets that took up so much time and energy, was still a wild man, a savage. All it took to make this case was to look at Pomare, the chief who had turned Christian and opened the way for the LMS. Whatever Pomare might have done for the mission, he kept on drinking to excess, and he was an unregenerate sodomite; he always had some pretty brown boy or other with him in his sleeping-house. Worse still, Williams seemed to be saying that if the Polynesian wild man called, there was within the white man a wild man who would answer. Already the LMS had had to cope with that embarrassing history of the early workers who had been seduced by Tahitian women. And soon the missionaries' children, born in the islands, would be wanting to do what Polynesian children did—take off their clothes to swim, learn to dance from the hips, play games with their bodies, and sing loud happy songs about what they were doing. A few years more and they would be wanting to get themselves tattooed. The boys would have themselves circumcised Tahitian fashion;* the girls would run away from

* Actually supercised.

school and hide in the hills with their young brown-skinned lovers. All this happened in time. And worse—in one missionary family on Tahiti there was incest.

Williams had only one child, less than three years old, but already little John Chawner was speaking mostly in the island language (learned from the servants, of course; and to have a Polynesian woman around the house was hardly like having an ideal English nanny). Williams was likely to have more children, and he did not want to multiply his risks. "I see the evil—& desire as a 'prudent man' to hide myself."

Williams never said that he wanted to give up missionary work. What he wanted was to be able to think of himself as valuable, doing valuable work, and to be recognized for it. Send him, he said, to a place where there was real work to do, where his family could grow up in the tradition of missionary service. The LMS, he said, had led him to expect to find scores of thousands of heathens in the islands. But he found nothing of the kind—no more than ten or twelve thousand in the whole leeward group, and the number was falling all the time as disease, introduced disease, cut them down. He had been reading some global figures which showed that if thirty thousand missionaries were sent out into the world "it would only be one Missionary to 20,000 Pagans & here we are in these Islands—3 Missionaries to 1,000." A "comparatively lazy life" for an evangelist, and as Williams thought about the stupidity of the ratios, "my soul as it were leaves my body in idleness (or almost so) in Raiatea—& is flying among one tribe of 1000s, another tribe of millions, witnessing their awful state of ignorance—& telling them in imagination of a Saviours dying love—but after this imaginary range, my soul returns dejected—to her solitary once a week work in Raiatea. . . ." He knew that one soul was worth more than one body, or a thousand bodies, but—and this was pure Williams—"how does the merchant act, who goes in search of goodly pearls—supposing he knows where there is one pearl which would pay him for his trouble in searching & procuring it, and he knows where there are thousands of equal value—to which place would he direct his course—I should naturally suppose to the latter—then let us not act a more inconsiderate part, than those who seek earthly riches."

Then, providentially, a storm-blown canoeload of Polynesians from the Hervey Islands,* a little-known archipelago several hundred miles to the west, drifted ashore at Raiatea. They expressed amazement at the works of God, and asked for teachers. Talking about their own islands, they

---

* Now known as the Cook Islands.

mentioned a particularly big one called Rarotonga, far larger than Raiatea, and this was enough to set Williams to framing a modest proposal for the LMS. The South Seas mission needed a ship. A twenty- or twenty-five-ton schooner would do. It could be based at one island, and he suggested Raiatea—not, he hastened to add, because this happened to be his own island, but because it was central. Perhaps, he went on to suggest, he might even go to live in these new islands, "superior" as they seemed to be.

For a letter from the South Seas to get to London and for the answer to get back might take eighteen months. In the meantime providence—again—put Williams in a position to acquire a ship. His wife had been in poor health ever since the death of her second baby, and now Williams himself developed some distressing symptoms. It was nothing that a missionary would have chosen to talk about, and Williams was circumspect about what he put on paper, but it is clear enough that he had got *feefee*, as the islanders called it, filariasis, a mosquito-borne disease that led to swollen extremities, elephantiasis. It affected Williams's legs, and—embarrassingly—his scrotum as well. There was no cure. The only treatment was to tap the enlarged parts and draw off accumulated fluid. Williams's fellow worker on Raiatea, Lancelot Threlkeld, was an amateur doctor, and he had a try or two at helping Williams with his problem, but the fluid kept gathering. This was depressing for both the Williamses, and they even began thinking of giving up on the Pacific and going back to England. But then a ship called at Raiatea on its way to Sydney, and they decided on short notice to take a chance on the colonial doctors. A stay in New South Wales would also give Williams a chance to forward a scheme to bring the chiefs of the leeward islands into trade with Sydney. Pomare of Tahiti was already trading with the colony. It is not clear whether all the leeward chiefs relished the idea of going into competition with Pomare, but it is clear that Williams thought trade was a good idea, and that ships were a good idea.

Williams really had ships on his mind all the time. When he prayed for good health for his wife and himself he put his faith in Christian hope as an "anchor" for "Tempest-tossed souls." Not long before he and Mary sailed for Sydney he got a letter from his family in England to say that his mother had died. "You seem to me," he wrote home, "as a Ship tossed, a boat in a tempest without a pilot." He had brought a portrait of his mother with him to the islands. It hung in the bedroom of his house on Raiatea, "an inestimable treasure." Looking at it now, he said, he had to fight to overcome his feelings; he feared he might have to put the picture away altogether to keep control of himself. His mother left him a useful inheritance. Williams decided to put the money toward buying a ship.

The ship that took the Williamses to Sydney was going to touch at the Herveys, those "superior" islands Williams had been so excited about, so he brought with him two native teachers. At Aitutake canoes came out and surrounded the ship, filled with shouting, gesticulating natives, tattooed or smeared with colored clay. The ruling chief was more than willing to have the two teachers stay. He also wanted the Williams's four-year-old son John, the first white child he had ever seen. He would take good care of him, he said, and make him a king. The Williamses declined the honor. Talking with the chief, Williams heard of several more islands, some of them "numerously inhabited," including Rarotonga.

Williams had his *feefee* treated in Sydney, and set about looking for a ship for the leeward chiefs. The longer he looked the more his mind worked. Eventually he sat down and wrote the directors of the LMS another letter about the businesslike organization of missionary work. This time he suggested nothing less than a sort of evangelical joint-stock company for the South Seas, bigger than anything ever imagined and much more efficient. The three Protestant missionary societies that now had interests in the South Seas should co-operate in fitting out a ship to take their representatives on a floating investigation of the major island groups, "all large, important, and numerously inhabited," after which the work of conversion could be divided up: New Zealand and thereabouts for the Anglicans of the Church Missionary Society; Tongatapu and neighboring islands for the Wesleyans; and the central and eastern archipelagoes for the LMS.

Williams was so taken with his scheme that he was tempted to set out there and then and hand-carry it to London. But he came across a ship for sale, and that took precedence. The *Endeavour* was somewhere around seventy or eighty tons. Williams secured it by persuading the agent of the LMS in Sydney to advance part of the cost; the rest he put up himself, out of the inheritance from his mother. The leeward chiefs would pay back these advances from the profits of trade, which Williams would manage. And Williams would have a way of "branching out."

With his great new plan in the mail to London and a ship's deck under his feet, Williams could head back to Raiatea in the best of moods. The "palliative" treatment he had got for his *feefee* in Sydney was helping him somewhat; his wife was feeling better for the time being; anything seemed possible. He had given up all thoughts of leaving the islands. "Now our Sphere is extending to the right & the left so that nothing but health should induce me to remove."

He was taking with him a "decent young man" to instruct the Raiateans in boiling sugar and growing tobacco; these were the crops the *Endeavour* would carry to market in Sydney. He also had on board cows, calves, sheep, two chapel bells, and "decent clothes for the Women, Shoes, Stockings, &c Tea Kettles, Tea Cups & Tea, of which they are very fond & it will be a great stimulus to them in their Sugar concern, for when they have Tea they will want Sugar, Tea Cups—they will want a Table . . . then they will want seats to set on, Thus we hope that European customs in a very short time will be wholly introduced in the Leeward Stations."

Along the way Williams made a stop on the northeast coast of the north island of New Zealand, at Bay of Islands. Some warlike Maori chiefs were skirmishing nearby, and big canoes passed close to Williams's ship, decorated bow and stern with heads taken in battle. Ashore, Williams saw the head of a defeated chief, "a very fine and noble-looking man . . . hair, whiskers, eye-brows, beard &c . . . just as they were when he was alive," and the eyes stopped up with red and black sealing wax. Other heads were being kept as spoils of victory or "to *sell* to *Christians* for muskets and powder." Williams was appalled, but he was sure savagery would yield to the right kind of persuasion. "All that is wanted . . . is active exertion," he wrote, doing some more public-relations work for his comprehensive scheme. "Good enterprising missionaries might, with the blessing of God, turn the lion-like New Zealander into the humble and peaceful Christian."

At Raiatea Williams's illness came back again almost straight away. Palliatives obviously did not work, and a navy surgeon from a passing warship operated on him. He was still consulting his health when his wife, pregnant again since the voyage to Sydney, had another child, a girl, "the fairest, fattest, most beautiful little babe," but again stillborn; and once more Mary was sick to the edge of death for several weeks. It was all taking on the look of a pattern, persistent, upsetting, disheartening, and the Williamses were advised by their colleagues to go back to England for good.

Williams resisted. He wanted to get the sugar and tobacco plantations going, get the products to market in Sydney, get the *Endeavour* paying for itself. Besides—and this was really what was in his mind—there were all those other islands over the horizon to the west.

When he was well enough to go sailing again, Williams took his wife on a combined evangelizing and convalescing trip to the Herveys in the *Endeavour*. The native teachers he had left at Aitutake on his way to Sydney were doing well. They had persuaded the chiefs and heathen priests to burn their wooden gods and build a chapel. Buoyed up by this, Williams

took the teachers and their wives aboard again and set out to find
Rarotonga, the most superior of these superior islands. For a week the
Endeavour cast back and forth without sighting Rarotonga's high mountains, and then Williams steered instead for Mangaia, whose position was
known.

The Mangaians turned out to be skittish and hostile, and when finally
the two native teachers and their wives went ashore, with Williams
watching from the ship, they were mobbed. A box of bonnets intended as
presents for the chiefs was dragged into the sea and broken into pieces.
Bedsteads were instantly disassembled. The looters took the coconut oil
the teachers had brought and poured it all over each other; "it streamed
down their bodies till they glistened as they stood in the sunbeams." Two
pigs, which were animals new to Mangia, were shown every respect; they
were dressed up in chiefs' clothing and shown to the wooden gods of the
island. But the unfortunate teachers' wives were treated with "great brutality." "They dragged them through the water, pulled them about in the
most indecent manner in order to gratify their vile passions. They seized
them by their throats, threw them down on the ground . . . Some of the
ruffians were holding them down while others were holding their legs,
and others endeavouring to tear off their clothes, but their having European clothes, it was a great means of preserving them." The *Endeavour*
fired its cannon and the Mangaians ran away.

Williams did better at the tiny island of Atiu, where a chief told him he
was only a day and a half from Rarotonga and pointed him in the right direction. But the *Endeavour* ran into baffling winds, and after several long
days of getting nowhere provisions were low. It looked as if they would
have to turn back or starve. "This was an hour of great anxiety," Williams
wrote. "Hope and fear alternately agitated my mind. I had sent a native to
the top of the mast four times, and he was now ascending for the fifth; and
when we were within half an hour of relinquishing the object of our
search, the clouds which enveloped its towering heights having been
chased away by the heat of the ascending sun, he relieved us from our
anxiety by shouting '*Teie, teie, taua fenua, nei!*' Here, here is the land we
have been seeking!"

One of the chiefs of Rarotonga, Makea, came out to the ship, a commanding six-footer, his body "most beautifully tattooed, and slightly coloured with a preparation of turmeric and ginger, which gave it a light
orange tinge." Makea had heard of Christianity, and he more than will-
ingly took the teachers and their wives ashore. But next day another chief
took a fancy to one of the Christian women and wanted to add her to the

nineteen wives he already had. She resisted, there was a struggle, and the native evangelists fled back to the ship with a terrible story to tell, exhibiting their tattered garments "in confirmation of their tale of woe." Williams decided out of prudence to leave just one male teacher.

For the rest of his life Williams talked as if he had discovered Rarotonga. He had not, but he had discovered it for himself, and that was the important thing in his mind. He had big plans for the place. Heading back to Raiatea, Williams summed up the voyage, troubles and all, as a great success, and he signaled his triumph by entering the lagoon at Raiatea with wooden idols from Aitutake hoisted to the yardarm of the *Endeavour*, heathenism conquered and captured by the forces of God. (This was the missionary version of the heads on New Zealand war canoes, or perhaps a coda to the bad old days of Western contact with the islands where Williams now worked, when a ship captain had been known to have his way with women, then run a rope around their bodies, hoist them up to the yardarm, and sail around showing off to the people on shore.)

Williams wrote to the directors of the LMS in London from Raiatea, arguing that every island within a thousand miles ought to be *"Now"* under instruction. He did more of his arithmetic about souls and missionary energies, and calculated that the resources were there to do the job. And he went on to make an affirmation that became celebrated: "For my own part I cannot content myself within the narrow limits of a Single reef & if means is not afforded a continent to me would be infinitely preferable for there if you cannot ride you can walk but to these isolated Islands a Ship must carry you."

No less a man than James Cook, who had sailed the Pacific in a ship called *Endeavour*, once said he had "Ambition not only to go farther than any one had done before, but as far as it was possible for man to go." Now Williams was thinking on the same grand scale.

* * *

As soon as he could find time, Williams went off again in the *Endeavour*, to the Tubuai group, three hundred fifty miles to the south of Raiatea, and no sooner was he back than he began planning a very long voyage indeed, to the Navigators Islands, Samoa, fourteen hundred miles to the west. Then he got the worst possible news from Sydney. The governor of New South Wales had changed the colony's fiscal regulations, and the effect was to wipe out the possibility that the *Endeavour* would pay for itself as a trading vessel. That was a bad blow, and a worse one fell at the same time. The directors of the LMS in London, unknowingly committed to paying part of the cost of the *Endeavour*, finally learned that Williams had committed them to this business speculation. They wrote censuring him harshly. In the circumstances there was only one thing to do—get rid of the *Endeavour*, and Williams unhappily loaded her up with a last consignment of local goods and sent her off to Sydney to be sold.

Williams was willing to say he was sorry for giving his masters pain, but on the subject of a missionary ship he was aggressively unrepentant. He kept putting the case in terms of the most efficient allocation of scarce resources. With a trifling additional expense, he said, "our labours might be extended ten-fold." The Devil knew this. "Satan well knows that it [the ship] was the most fatal weapon that was ever formed [against] his interests in the great South Sea; and has wrested it out of our hands as soon as he felt the effects of its first blow."

Williams was ready to concede that a single island, measured against the whole of the heathen world, was not worth the sacrifice of life and property devoted to it, "but the whole of them collectively and relatively considered, are worthy of your utmost efforts, and demand as the first born of your strength a proportionate inheritance."

This matter of the first-born and his inheritance was a sensitive one. The LMS, after the disastrous failure of the original South Seas mission, had begun to put most of its manpower and its money into India and Africa, big continental missions, and the evangelists in the Pacific developed a grievance. Then, too, the LMS was open about sending what it considered to be its best people to the newer, more extensive fields, and that too was a source of bad feeling in the Pacific. Williams's colleague Lancelot Threlkeld had wanted an African station but had been assigned to Raiatea. It chafed him, and his disgruntlement showed up in the joint letters he wrote with Williams, the one about the "first-born" among them. It might even have been Threlkeld's voice Williams was using when he talked in his famous letter about the sweep of continents as against the confinement of narrow reefs, although of course Williams's own sense of blocked expansiveness and insufficiently used powers could hardly have been stronger. Indeed the maps in Williams's mind kept on getting bigger and bigger. He described himself to the directors of the LMS as a servant who had to urge his masters to their duty. "The Marquesas—Navigators—Hebrides—New Guinea, New Caledonia, &c"— now Williams was adding Melanesia to Polynesia—"could all be obtained by us. Why cramp us. . . ."

Confined for the time being to Raiatea, Williams kept on improving the place. That was one of his great skills. A visiting LMS deputation considered Williams's settlement to be the most impressive of all the South Seas mission stations, and so if Williams's directors disapproved of him from halfway around the world, at least the LMS people who actually came to the islands from London were placing a proper high value on his usefulness.

Williams's people put on a show for the visitors, something they loved to do. It was a great feast out in the open, with a thousand people eating together, all "seated on sofas, chairs, or stools, with convenient tables before them, on which their provisions were decently set out, and around which they enjoyed their social meal, in such a manner as had never been witnessed before in their own or their fathers' times." They had been up since before daybreak, getting the food ready, cutting fresh grass to strew over the ground and setting up awnings of tapa. From their table in the middle of proceedings the deputation members could count two hundred forty-one sofas for sitting on and more than a hundred tables for eating from, plus chairs and stools, all home-made except for fancy legs turned on a lathe by four specialist native tradesmen. Dress was mixed—an old chief with a white shirt on over a black coat, women "loaded with flowered and figured garments of native or English manufacture," hats and bonnets everywhere, of bark or woven leaves. The midday meal was served and eaten, there were spirited speeches by chiefs and others about the bad times of the past and the good times of the present, and then a shower of rain broke up the gathering.

In the evening everyone came back to drink tea, *pape mahanahana*, as the Raiateans called it, warm water. This was the period of tea mania in the English-speaking world, and evangelicals were especially keen on it. For them it had almost a sacramental value. At home in England it was drunk at the meetings where missionary money was raised; indeed sarcastic people said that evangelical philanthropy was a matter of old maids getting inflamed on tea and high-minded talk and impulsively offering their well-meant sixpences for good works to be done at great distances. Among missionaries in the field it was an article of faith that tea was good for the health. At the very least the drink and its ceremonies were a way to hold onto Englishness, and after a fashion this was a health matter, a matter of general well-being. Evangelicals of Williams's day, wherever they were, dressed and slept English, and they wanted to eat and drink English. There were any number of people in the South Seas mission who would never bring themselves to be happy with the islanders' diet, which was quite adequate. The lack of "bread, and tea, and sugar, and salt, induced great weakness" in them, so they said. They had to mix taro and sweet potato with their precious flour to make bread, and though they "tried hard to persuade each other that the new compound still retained the taste as well as the nutriment of English bread," their "diminished strength and failing health told another tale." Fish and pig and dog might give islanders protein, but they did not give English men and women satisfaction, and meat salted down and shipped in kegs from halfway round the world had its defects. They all retained the most vivid and piercing folk memory of English roast beef.

Williams on tea was particularly evangelical. He was sure the drink was a potion that would transform the islander. As he said, get a Polynesian into the habit of taking tea and he would go on to crave all the good things the West had to offer. The Raiateans were on the way, as the deputation observed, even if they still had some distance to travel. "The equipage for tea-drinking was quite as heterogeneous as the dinner-services had been. Some had kettles, and others had tea-pots; these could manage very well together, if, in addition, one could raise a cup, a second a saucer, and a third a porringer. A few—a few only—had got tea, many had no sugar; but everyone had something—whether an ingredient or a utensil— employed in preparing or partaking of this favourite refreshment. A spoonful of tea, for example, was put into a kettle full of water, and brewed into a beverage very passable for such accommodating palates as were waiting to taste it. One party heated water in a frying-pan, and were happy to exhibit so precious a sample of outlandish luxury to their less fortunate neighbours. But the principal supply was from a large vat, or sugar-boiler, which was brought down to the shore, and filled with water slightly sweetened, but without any infusion of the Chinese plant. The variety of drinking vessels was ludicrous—pots, plates, delf-ware, porringers, cans, glasses, and even bottles—but principally cocoa-nut shells, their own native and elegantly-sculptured cups. More enjoyment, with less indecorum, among so numerous a company of revellers, is rarely to be found in this world, where a feast and a fray are so often concomitants as to convert the words themselves into synonymes in certain regions even of civilized Europe."

When tea was over, the islanders went off home with their tables and sofas and chairs on their shoulders, or loaded them on canoes and rafts and paddled away down the coast. And at nightfall "nothing was to be seen but the flitting or fixed lights in the scattered dwellings, and nothing to be heard by the casual passenger but the song of praise, or the voice of prayer, in family circles at their evening devotions."

* * *

John Williams was an impressive evangelist, no question. He was the center of a busy little world of missionaries, chiefs, and commoners, all making and doing. By his example, and by the force of his energetic and outgoing character, he could get a thousand islanders to change the place where they lived and the way they lived. A man who visited Raiatea for a short time in 1826 characterized him as "the humble, and obliging, but deep imagining Williams," who "was then at his meridian—a King in benevolent power; and walking in as much success, as his limited sphere could furnish." Williams was thirty now. His health was good; the filariasis that had made his life so uncomfortable a few years back had subsided, and he never had to mention it again. If his wife was chronically in poor health, at least she managed to bring a pregnancy to successful term in 1826. The baby was a boy, and he was named Samuel Tamatoa. So Williams was more than ever a family man, and he had been on Raiatea for longer than ever before at a stretch. It was interesting, then, that his visitor observed that Williams "always appeared to me of an unsettled look; as if he was only on the way to his destination. . . ."

Williams always made a point of saying how happily married he was, how "comfortable" he was with his wife. And certainly no one could have piled up more evidences of good intent as a householder—the interior decoration of the sleeping space on the *Harriet*, the seven-room house on Raiatea (and later two more exemplary houses on other islands), and the repeated attempts to increase the number of his children. Everything in his background pushed him in the direction of being a comfortable family man. And yet something in him pushed him into getting away repeatedly from his family.

There was important work to be done, he knew; he was the man to do it; and it was always to be done somewhere else. He had to be *away*. This feeling grew increasingly strong in its demands for expression, until it took over his life. Ships were on his mind all the time. Year by year he got more and more ingenious in arranging long sea voyages for himself. This became the pattern—if he had to live in a house he had built for his wife and children for as much as twelve months at a stretch, he somehow managed in the following twelve months to be gone for weeks or months. The visitor to Raiatea who saw him as unsettled, looking as if he was only on his way to his destination, had got him exactly right. Williams was one of those nineteenth-century figures who kept turning up on the edges of the world's maps, compelled to go looking for themselves in one place after another.

In fact Williams was a mixture of a man. On the one hand he was solid, practical, commonsensical, sociable, helpful, outgoing, and on the other hand he had a solitary, driven, almost uncontrollable streak. His whole life in the islands was double. His plan for savages involved "taming their ferocious dispositions, reforming their savage habits, and rendering intercourse with them safe and beneficial." In a word, domestication. Yet he never stayed long enough in one place to see this accomplished. And his attitude to his own domestication was highly ambivalent. He got married and had a family and built a house for them to live in. But he also bought and later built ships as big as a house, and he kept sailing away from home, coming back only to sail away again.

When Williams was a little boy at his mother's knee, he had a morning and an evening prayer and a morning and evening hymn of his own. The morning hymn was about the God who made little birds with their nests on high, and little boys who sang their Maker's praise like little birds. The evening hymn was about the moon like a pearl among diamonds, and God being in everything. The words were childish, but the themes were powerful. God nourished and sustained the little boy and sent the blood pumping vigorously through his veins. The sun rose, the little boy jumped out of bed. The sun ran its course across glaring skies, the little bird left the nest and mounted on beating wings.

Williams had actually been leaving home all his life: the family home for the ironmonger's shop, the shop for outside work, work for the tavern, the tavern for the tabernacle, the tabernacle for the mission field, and now one group of islands for the next. His mother, whom he left behind at every step, came with him all the way. Her portrait watched over her son in his marriage bed, in the house that he built. It was a bed in which Williams impregnated his wife repeatedly, in which she miscarried and endured stillbirths, suffering almost literally a life sentence at hard labor. And it was a bed that Williams left repeatedly, a nest from which time and time again he took flight.

* * *

Williams had not forgotten Rarotonga. A new missionary, Charles Pitman, had been assigned there, and he and his wife took some time at Raiatea to get used to life in the islands before setting out for the Herveys. Williams decided he would go with them and help them settle in. He took his wife and little Samuel with him (his first boy, John, was now off on Moorea at the missionary children's school). He expected to stay at least a few months.

The missionaries were welcomed by two or three thousand natives, and nothing would do but that they must all shake hands like white men.

Williams's arm ached for hours afterward. The Rarotongans were eager to abandon their old religion. They brought fourteen or fifteen carved wooden statues of their gods and dropped them at the evangelists' feet. Williams sent one to England, some were broken up, others were used to decorate the rafters of a huge chapel that was built in the first flush of enthusiasm after Williams and Pitman arrived. The church was to be the centerpiece of a big new settlement, on Raiatean lines. The natives delightedly carried the missionaries' goods along a muddy track to the town site. "One took the tea-kettle, another the frying-pan; some obtained a box, others a bed-post." The high chief himself, Makea, "felt honoured in rendering assistance, and during the journey he ceased not to manifest his admiration of the devices printed upon the articles of earthenware with which he was intrusted, and to exhibit them to the crowd that surrounded him." Makea was carrying the missionary chamberpots.

Williams had been hankering after Rarotonga for years, and now here he was. But quite soon it turned out that the work there was nothing more than Raiatea all over again—the endless setting of example, painstaking discussion of the simplest Gospel questions, the making of a new moral and legal code, the turning of sofa legs on a lathe, the setting up of a sugar mill, the imposition of bonnets on the women, the inculcation of tea drinking all round. It was not enough for Williams. There were all those other islands yet to think about, in particular the Navigators, which were now to Rarotonga as Rarotonga had once been to Raiatea. Within a few months Williams was hankering after yet another long voyage.

But he had no ship. That was one obstacle. Another was his wife, and he used the very word about her. Before leaving Raiatea for Rarotonga he had raised the subject of a voyage to Samoa, and Mary got most upset. He would be gone six months, hundreds of miles away, among savages; and if anything happened to him she would be a widow with fatherless children, twenty thousand miles from home and friends. "Finding her so decidedly opposed to the undertaking," wrote Williams, "I did not mention it again." But, he added, his mind was "still fixed upon the object."

Rarotonga did not agree with Mary. She got sicker than she had ever been, with an illness that came on so rapidly and severely that within a few hours she was unconscious and Williams feared for her life. She recovered, and one day while she was convalescing Williams went into her bedroom to find that she had changed her mind about his going to Samoa. Williams's way of putting it was that she had "thought upon the evil of her ways I suppose." However it went, she had connected her illness with the thwarting of her husband's wishes, and after her brush with death she concluded that if she withheld her consent any longer "the Lord may remove me altogether. . . ."

Williams was delighted. He looked upon Mary's change of mind as "the first indication of Providence favourable to my design, and began immediately to devise the means by which I might carry it into execution. After some deliberation, I determined to attempt to build a vessel."

He had carried the memory of the *Harriet* and his first ocean voyage with him for ten years and more, he had done the ironwork on a schooner as soon as he arrived at Moorea in 1818, he had built small boats for himself, and he had sailed thousands of miles in the Pacific. Now a ship of his own design sprang full-blown from his brow. He worked virtually non-stop, often not going home for dinner, staying alive on breadfruit and water, anything so as not to lose momentum. In three months, from scratch, he built a schooner of between seventy and eighty tons, eighteen feet in the beam, sixty feet in length, as long as his house on Raiatea.

The story of Williams and his ship became famous later on; and as he told it, the tale was as good as anything out of the life of Robinson Crusoe. He had no bellows to heat his ironworking forge, so he cut some wooden boards to shape and then killed three of Rarotonga's four goats and skinned them for leather. But making "so common an article" as a bellows was not as simple as he thought. His home-made one blew out air but "drew in the fire." He consulted every useful modern book of reference he could find, which on Rarotonga could not have been many. They were filled with thorough descriptions of perfected industrial methods. But none told him how to make a bellows. This led him to a very sensible observation about appropriate technology: in situations such as his, what was needed was "plain and simple instructions for manufacturing the article without the expensive machinery in common use" in countries where the industrial revolution had occurred. "Let the circumstances of the Missionary, and the state of the people to whom he goes, be taken into the account, and it must be at once obvious, that the simplicity of the means used two or three hundred years ago would better suit both his conditions and theirs than the more complex improvements of modern times."

That was one problem about the bellows. Another was that the rats of Rarotonga, which were legion, ate his goatskins. Williams could hardly bring himself to kill the last goat on the island and nail its hide to a faulty design, only to lose it to hungry rats.

It struck him that if a pump pumped water, a pumplike machine could be made to pump wind. So he made a wooden box with a piston, a lever, and an outlet pipe, and tried again. This construction blew wind, but like the goatskin model it sucked in fire and burned itself up. Williams refined the valve arrangement so that it opened to let out the wind under pressure and closed when the machine was filling. To get over the problem of too much delay between blasts, he made another box and ran the two in alternation. It took eight or ten men to work the levers, but the Rarotongans loved to do it. Blacksmithing amazed them, especially welding, and Williams made converts at the forge. "Why," his Rarotongans asked themselves, "did we not think of heating the hard stuff also, instead of beating it with stones? What a reign of dark hearts Satan's is!" With his wooden-pump bellows Williams did all his ironwork, "using a perforated stone for a fire-iron, an anvil of the same material, and a pair of carpenter's pincers for our tongs. As a substitute for coals, we made charcoal, from the cocoa-nut, *tamanu,* and other trees."

On to the hull. "As we had no saw, we split the trees in half with wedges; and then the natives adzed them down with small hatchets, which they tied to a crooked piece of wood as a handle. . . . When we wanted a bent or twisted plank, having no apparatus for steaming it, we bent a piece of bamboo to the shape required, sent into the woods for a crooked tree, and by splitting this in half obtained two planks suited to our purposes. Having but little iron, we bored large auger-holes through the timbers, and also through the inner and outer plank of the vessel, and drove in wooden pins. . . ." For oakum Williams used coconut husks, banana stumps, the natives' bark cloth, whatever he could improvise. "For ropes we obtained the bark of the *hibiscus,* constructed a rope machine, and prepared excellent cordage from that article. For sails we used the mats on which the natives sleep, and quilted them that they might be strong enough to resist the wind. After making a turning-lathe, we found that the *aito,* or iron-wood, answered remarkably well for the sheaves of blocks." All in all a classic of self-help, finished off with a splendid piece of Crusoelike resourcefulness. "The hanging of the rudder occasioned me some difficulty; for, having no iron sufficiently large for pintles, we made them from a piece of a pickaxe, a cooper's adze, and a large hoe. They answered exceedingly well. . . ."

But after all that, would she sail? Williams's maiden voyage as captain of the ship he had built himself started badly. Only six miles offshore from Rarotonga, his native crew let go a sail at the wrong moment in a high wind and broke the foremast. Williams made his way back to harbor, replaced the mast, set sail again, and completed a successful trip to Aitutake and back, almost three hundred fifty miles altogether. For the

Rarotongans he brought back pigs, coconuts and cats—English pigs be-cause they were better than the local variety, coconuts because in some fighting before the Rarotongans were converted to Christianity all the food-bearing trees in one part of the island had been cut down, and cats to do away with the Rarotongan rats.

Williams had now been the better part of a year away from Raiatea. It was time to go back. The trip would be nearly six hundred miles. His ship stood up to it, but it was lucky the weather was good all the way: as it was, the calking fell away and trailed in long strips from the hull, and the mat sails would never have lasted in high winds. Mary Williams had her trou-bles too. She was pregnant again, sick all the way at sea, and not long after they landed at Raiatea she had yet another stillborn child.

* * *

Williams gave his creation—"my ship"—the name *Messenger of Peace.* His plan now was to do what he had been bursting to do for years, take the gospel everywhere the ship would sail: missionary enterprise at its boldest, and above all *his* enterprise. "My head—my hands, & I trust my heart is fuller than ever of missionary work," he wrote to the LMS. "I am not contented yet, I wish to do more, much more. . . ." He had never been just a meek compliant servant of the LMS; now he was the captain of his own ship, made with his own hands, and he was making it known that he was the captain of his soul as well.

More than anything Williams wanted to be off to Samoa, but the *Mes-senger of Peace* was not adequately rigged and fitted for a voyage of that range. Williams sent to England for good-quality ironmongery, and while he was waiting—that inevitable round-the-world wait which was so much a part of life in the South Seas—he worked on the ship as best he could and sent it off to the Marquesas to land some missionaries there. By the time everything was at last ready for Samoa it was well into 1830, and the *Messenger of Peace* was more than two years old.

Williams flew an LMS flag made up for him by some evangelical ladies in England: a dove with an olive branch. He took with him some native teachers with their wives and children, thirty in all. His idea was to seed the islands he encountered with these useful brown mission workers, all of whom he had educated in tradesmen's skills as well as Bible teachings.

On Mangaia, where several years earlier the first teachers he had tried to land were robbed and chased back to the ship, Williams found a big chapel and neat white cottages everywhere, and five hundred Christians waiting to shake his hand. There were still heathens on the island, and in some fighting not long before the Christians had hacked some of them to pieces. This was not Williams's own idea of the best way to spread the Gospel. But at least the Christians won. And they were serious enough about the new faith to have cut their hair and to be thinking hard about the way they lived. They had any number of questions for Williams: Was it sinful to eat rats, and was it Christian to make young girls and old women work in the *taro* patches?

At Savage Island,* which Williams was seeing for the first time, the *Messenger of Peace* was met by islanders with spears and slingstones. It took a long time to persuade even one man to come aboard. The man who took the chance was old, about sixty, with long gray hair and a beard twisted and plaited into rat's tails. He was naked except for a loincloth, and his body was smeared with charcoal. He was so excited he could hardly stand still, leaping about and shouting at everything he saw. He would not tolerate being dressed, not even in some bark cloth—he tore it off in a rage and stamped on it. And then he did a war dance, shaking his spear and running to and fro on deck, distorting his features "most horribly by extending his mouth, gnashing his teeth, and forcing his eyes almost out of their sockets. At length he concluded this exhibition by thrusting the whole of his long grey beard into his mouth, and gnawing it with the most savage vengeance. During the whole of the performance he kept up a loud and hideous howl." Williams did not like the look of Savage Island, and rather than put teachers ashore there he decided to take two islanders with him, teach them Christianity, and drop them off again later. Even then there were difficulties. The young men regretted going, howled for days, and were terrified when they first saw animal meat being cooked—they thought it was human, and that they would be next to be killed and chopped up.

Still on his roundabout way to Samoa, Williams put in at Tonga, in westernmost Polynesia, where he found Wesleyan missionaries at work. Williams had been intending to use Tonga as a jumping-off place into islands still farther to the west, but here he was on the very margin of Polynesia, on the borders of another great Pacific culture area, Melanesia, and the Wesleyans and some white traders at Tonga warned him off. The New Hebrides, where Williams wanted to go, was savage territory, and things were particularly unsettled there at the moment. The islanders had been having some nasty experiences with white sandalwood gatherers, their bad habits and their diseases. No white man was sure to be safe there, not

---

*Now called Niue.

even if he came with a dove and an olive branch and a Bible. The New Hebrideans were head-hunters.

When Williams arrived at last in Samoa he could not be altogether sure about his reception there, either, though of course the Samoans were Polynesians and thus had at least a family resemblance to Raiateans and Rarotongans. Some chiefs were at war, and Williams saw villages going up in smoke, plantations of fruit trees in flames, and he was told that bodies were being burned too. The great chief with whom Williams made contact, Malietoa, had a businesslike approach to Christianity. First he would finish his fighting, which he was duty-bound to do, and then he would be interested to pay attention to the teachers Williams wanted to leave under his protection.

Williams intended this voyage only as a reconnaissance. He was delighted with what he saw in Samoa. The islands were his biggest yet, he could see nothing serious in the way of obstacles to ultimate success, and there were all those other Melanesian islands, bigger still, to the west. He headed back to Raiatea in high spirits.

* * *

There was no one else like Williams among the missionaries in the South Seas, and there was no denying that he was putting the LMS on the map of the Pacific in a very broad-ranging way. But he was not universally admired for it. The directors of the LMS were irritated by him. They had slapped his wrist over the *Endeavour* business, and his response was just to go ahead and build the *Messenger of Peace*, a bigger ship, capable of sailing thousands of miles. It was clear that he was making these spectacular voyages pretty much to please himself. There were other ways to be a good Christian, and the feeling among his colleagues on the spot was that Williams might have paid more attention to these.

There was, for example, the matter of his wife. In twelve years in the islands she had been pregnant eight times, had saved two children and lost six, two by miscarriage and four by stillbirth. She was old before her time, perpetually exhausted, and somewhere along the way she had picked up *feefee*, filariasis. If after her first two unsuccessful pregnancies there had been a case for going back to England in the interest of her health, there was surely more of a case after six lost babies and now elephantiasis threatening. But Williams's own health was good, and he had big things in mind to accomplish. And then, of course, Mary Williams had promised, on pain of death at God's hands, so to speak, not to stand in the way of the Samoan voyage. When Williams came back from Samoa he was made aware that he was not popular for leaving his wife alone so much.

He had gotten her pregnant again before he left for Samoa, and when he came home he took her off to Rarotonga, where he had work to do, in the hope that a change of place would do something to help her fight the *feefee* which had taken hold of her. The trip turned out to be a disaster. Mary kept on being sick. And in the middle of it all, Rarotonga was struck by a hurricane.

As the wind rose, Williams went out to look after the *Messenger of Peace,* landed all the ship's stores and tied the vessel down as best he could. It was a dreadful night, and when he went to the harbor again next morning he found the entire settlement flattened, church, schoolhouse, everything, hardly a house standing, trees uprooted all over the place, the Rarotongans battling terribly heavy winds and lashing rain, and his ship washed inland on giant waves, stuck in a hole in a grove of trees hundreds of yards from the shore.

The only good thing about it all was that the *Messenger of Peace* was apparently unharmed, and once the hurricane abated and the Rarotongans picked themselves up again, Williams was able to refloat his ship. He was as ingenious in this as he had been in building her. "Long levers were passed under her keel, with the fulcrum so fixed as to give them an elevation of about forty-five degrees. The ends of these were then fastened together, with several cross-beams, upon which a quantity of stones were placed, the weight of which gradually elevated one end of the vessel until the levers reached the ground. Propping up the bow thus raised, we shifted our levers to the stern, which was in like manner elevated, and, by repeating this process three or four times, we lifted her in one day entirely out of the hole. The bog was then filled up with stones, logs of wood were laid across it, rollers were placed under the vessel, the chain cable passed round her, and, by the united strength of about two thousand people, she was compelled to take a short voyage upon the land, before she floated in her pride upon the sea."

Not for the first or last time in her life, Mary Williams did worse than her husband and his ship. On the night of the hurricane, the house where she was trying to sleep shook to pieces, and she got up and out of the bedroom just before the roof came down. She was out in the storm for hours after that, badly frightened, and a few days later she gave birth to a dead child, her seventh lost baby. There was a nineteenth-century English notion that it was often a woman's lot to suffer and be still.

As well as criticizing him for the way he treated his wife, Williams's colleagues criticized him for neglecting Raiatea, where he had started his missionary life and where he lived for some years before voyaging took hold of him. There was substance to the criticism. Williams's pride and joy on Raiatea was the settlement that gathered most of the islanders in one new township. But after a few years it became clear that the site had been badly chosen. It was windy, prone to flooding, and the shoreline was unstable—which, of course, was why the Raiateans had not lived there before Williams came. So it was decided to build a new and improved town to windward.

Williams used the shift to perfect his devices for promoting "aspiration" among the islanders, and while the new town was being built, he offered them prizes for the first this and the best that. The new chapel was far bigger than the old one. By good luck there was no stream at the new site, which meant no more naked bathing in public; water was piped in, and each home had a private bathhouse inside its garden fence. Williams was open about the value of the resettlement exercise as a way of drawing off surplus energy among his people. They had started to become restless, and it was necessary to occupy them properly or they would occupy themselves improperly. Williams prescribed work, and claimed that the project was a great success.

But the fact was that he left on the seagoing phase of his life before the resettlement scheme was complete. Even before he went off in the direction of Rarotonga, there had been disregard for the moral code of the missionaries on Raiatea, and this continued after he was gone. Then in 1831, while Williams was absorbed in his big plans for a return to Samoa, the old ruling chief Tamatoa died on Raiatea, and fighting followed between some rival claimants for power. At this point it became clear—if it had not been clear before—that by packing Raiateans together in one settlement, Williams had brought into close contact the rival factions who had always fought each other in traditional times. Christianity did not do away with faction fighting.

The situation was further complicated by the fact that in the islands where the South Seas mission had been established for years, native prophets were cropping up, preaching a religion of their own, a mixture of tradition and special interpretations of Christianity, talking about the end of the world, about shiploads of cargo that would arrive to enrich the islanders, generally creating unrest. They went by the name of Mamaia, and their "heresy" took hold particularly strongly on Raiatea.

Here, conspicuously, was a case in which the steadying presence of a strong, experienced missionary would have been useful. But Williams went back and forth about his responsibilities. He did involve himself in negotiations to get the chiefs to work things out without violence, but the attempts failed; and there were stories that Williams supplied arms to the chiefs who in his view represented legitimate rule. But then he was gone, off to Rarotonga, and when he came back there was disorder everywhere on Raiatea, and again he did not seem concerned to stay as long as it might take to straighten things out. Or perhaps it was really that he had a horror of entanglement, in whatever form it might take, and a perpetual need to break free. Whatever—Samoa was calling again.

* * *

On his second visit to Samoa, in 1832, Williams brought more native teachers. He stayed almost a month, visiting most of the islands in the group and firming up his ideas about what the LMS ought to be doing in the whole western Pacific.

He took with him the Rarotongan chief Makea, and Makea made a deep impression on the Samoans with his speeches about the blessings of peace, the sanctity of property, literacy, and his own salvation by the Gospel from the horrors of death as a heathen. Makea was obviously a Polynesian, obviously a chief, and he wore a splendid red coat. Samoans, like all Polynesians, were attracted to Christianity for what it might bring them in the way of new goods, and Williams was interested to feed that appetite. So it was not surprising, from the time of his earliest contact with Samoa, to hear the Samoan chiefs begin to talk like Makea—at least as Williams transcribed their words. "Can the religion of these wonderful *papalangis* * be anything but wise and good? . . . their heads are covered, while ours are exposed to the heat of the sun and the wet of the rain; their bodies are clothed all over with beautiful cloth, while we have nothing but a bandage of leaves around our waist; they have clothes upon their very feet, while ours are like the dogs';—and then look at their axes, their scissors, and their other property, how rich they are!"

For Williams, Samoa now became what Rarotonga had once been, and Raiatea before that, a place where he had gone and made his own mark, where he had seeded the Gospel at the expense of great effort, and—most important—a place from which he could see other places where the same thing might be done. He estimated the Samoan population at fifty thousand, multiples more than he had been used to on Raiatea or Rarotonga—but still not enough for him. He wrote home to a friend in England: "What an extensive field opens as we proceed Westward the Fijis—New Hebrides, New Caledonia, Solomons Archipelago—with many other isolated Islands scattered thickly over the Pacific ocean so that the Ocean is teeming with hundreds of thousands still who have never heard of the Gospel of Salvation—I should like very well to take a kind of Missionary

* White men.

Voyage of observation through the whole of these extensive & thickly
peopled Islands. . . ." And as always he talked in terms of business pro-
posals. What he had in mind was an undertaking beyond his own "narrow
resources," but he thought like an entrepreneur of religion. "If ever we
reach England I perhaps may propose a plan to the Society. . . ." Or, he
added, a "select number of religious friends for accomplishment of the object."

*   *   *

Williams was beginning to think more and more about going back to
England. There was his business proposal about the western Pacific.
There was his wife's health, as always, though here there was a consola-
tion of sorts; in 1833, Mary, pregnant again, managed to bear a living
child, a third son, christened William Aaron Barff. And there was something else—the way in which Williams was beginning to see himself. He
was in his late thirties now. He was concerned about what he had accomplished and about what remained for him to do. He felt himself to be
somehow unjustified and unvalidated in his life; and in every way, personal and professional, he was coming to want to re-establish connections
with his homeland.

"How long it is since last we saw each other!" he wrote to friends in England. "Parents dead, brothers and sisters married, a new race of relatives
growing up, some of them towards manhood, and we ourselves passing
the meridian of life. Ah! how soon will all be 'as a tale that is told;' . . . and
although, to ourselves, we may seem of so much importance, we shall slip
off the stage unmissed, and be as though to the world we had never
been."

Early in 1834 the chance came up of passage around Cape Horn to England on a whaling ship. Williams, his wife, and his three boys went
aboard, and in a few months they were home. It was almost eighteen
years since Williams had seen London.

Williams in the South Seas was not a favorite of the directors of the
LMS, who had often lectured him about his "highmindedness." But in
England he turned out to be their most valuable single asset. Like other
missionaries back from the field, Williams was duty-bound to speak to
religious groups about his experiences. It was years since he had used the
English language in public, and he was not in any case an educated man;
he worried that when he got up to speak he would lack polish. He need
not have worried. He quickly developed a characteristic businesslike
method of getting his message across: a plain style, nothing overdemon-
strative or overwrought, a strong, pious argument, a sprinkling of inter-

esting anecdotes, some of his arithmetic about souls, and for variety a set of big colored pictures. Within a matter of weeks he began to develop a reputation, and soon he was a celebrity, an evangelical phenomenon. The appetite to hear him grew and fed upon itself. His lecture bookings stretched for months ahead, then a year ahead, and when eighteen months had gone by the demand for his speeches was still growing. It was like a run on a bank, said Williams, but "happily" he found his "resources unfailing;" he could meet the demands made on him and still have "stock on hand."

Sometimes he might have to share the platform with a competing evangelical attraction—in Liverpool it was a Kaffir chief and a converted Hottentot—but no one ever outshone John Williams. The accolade came when he was invited to speak at the annual meeting of the LMS, and as well at the annual meetings of the "Bible, Wesleyan Missionary, Religious Tract, Christian Instruction, and other kindred societies." Perhaps he was not just "highminded;" perhaps he had been right all along, merely ahead of everyone else.

Williams did not miss the significance of his success for his own plans. By no accident the one story he infallibly included in his stage narrative, the story that time after time captivated his audiences, was the tale of how he had built his own ship. Williams was now converting Englishmen to his own schemes.

He had other things to do in England besides make speeches. He was seeing Polynesian Gospels and other books through the press for the LMS (one volume was a Rarotongan translation of *The Pilgrim's Progress*). And he was trying, with help, to work up his missionary experiences into a book. All this he had to fit into a speaking schedule that kept him on the move virtually nonstop for four years.

It was the South Seas all over again—his wife and his boys did not see much of him. He was away most of the time, and when he was at home at the house he had taken in Bedford Square in London, he was preoccupied with work.

Occasionally, though, there would be an evening free, and Williams would invite a few people to call. He liked such times to be both "instructive and pleasurable," which meant that he would talk about what he had done in the Pacific. "Very frequently on these occasions," so a friend of his recalled, "the curiosities which he had brought from the islands were drawn from their hiding places, and the various contents of several cases covered the table or the floor . . . a singular medley of idols, dresses, ornaments, domestic utensils, implements of industry, and weapons of war

. . . and not unfrequently, Mr. Williams arrayed his own portly person in the native tiputa and mat, fixed a spear by his side and adorned his head with the towering cap of many colours, worn on high days by the chiefs; and, as he marched up and down his parlour, he was as happy as any one of the guests whose cheerful mirth he had excited."

As for the book he was working on, Williams wanted it to have the same effect as his platform lectures and his evenings with friends, to be "generally interesting and instructive," useful as history and ethnography, in effect to "take his reader with him to each of the islands he had visited" and to "show him what a Missionary life is. . . ." And, of course, to accomplish through this the purposes of the author and the LMS. Williams's *Narrative of Missionary Enterprises in the South Seas* was an extended tract, meant to grip, persuade, touch the heart, and loosen the purse strings.

When Williams got the first copies from the printer, in April, 1837, he put another business suggestion to his directors. "I would beg to propose," he wrote, "that a number of noblemen be selected, say a hundred, and that I be allowed to send each a copy . . . with a respectful letter from myself, inviting their attention to the great work." The LMS thought fifty would be enough. Williams settled for that, beginning with the mother of Princess (soon to be Queen) Victoria.

In its way this was pious audacity on Williams's part. Evangelical Christians of his kind often lived under considerable social tension. They were lower-middle-class men and women pulled this way and that by the humble need to know their place and the eager drive to improve themselves and their station in life. Some of them, for example, continued to believe that the differences between pious mechanics and real gentlemen were inherited (and some repaired the deficiency by inventing high-born ancestors for themselves: English earls, French countesses, and so on). A missionary from their own social class might do noble work—they knew there was nothing nobler—but this was no guarantee that noblemen would become interested in the work. On both sides the feeling persisted that because common folk went into evangelical work, evangelical work was common.

Williams was not defensive about this. Far from it. He wanted to see the day when not only the poor and formerly poor but the rich and the noble would feel "honour in identifying themselves with Missionary operations, and in consecrating their influence, their wealth, and even their *sons* and their *daughters,* to this work."

The response to Williams's book with its respectful accompanying letter was pleasing. A good many of the "great folks" on his list wrote kind letters back and sent donations. Some even invited Williams to meet them in person and talk to them. And, most gratifying, on those social afternoons in stately homes, Williams was judged as being, apart from "false forms," a gentleman among gentlemen. So often he had been criticized by his superiors within the Society for pushing things too far. Now he was distinguishing himself not just as an evangelist but also—and this was remarkable—as an explorer of the class structure of his own country, opening up the social heights to his religion. This was a coup for the LMS.

Along with his fellow missionary William Ellis, Williams was invited to give testimony to a parliamentary committee on British settlements overseas, with special reference to "aborigines." Williams told the committee what his book was intended to tell the world, that missions were good for commerce, and that anyone interested in enriching himself or his nation could not fail to appreciate mission work. Among islanders, he said, Christianity was the prerequisite of civilization. "You cannot get a barbarous people to attend to anything of a civilizing process, or to aspire to any European principle, till you give them Christian principle." Once this was accomplished, though, there was no limit. "Think of hundreds and thousands of them wearing European clothing, and using European articles, such as tools. . . ."

What about commerce without Christianity? Baneful, said Williams. Merchantmen and whalers brought the islanders liquor, guns, disease, degradation. "I had ten times rather meet them in their savage state than after they have had intercourse with Europeans." So Western contact with the islands meant disease and depopulation. But Williams's assertion was that mission work halted depopulation, even restored population. If the committee had been able to interview Rarotongans, they would have heard things put rather differently. In the years when Williams was concerned with Rarotonga, when the *Messenger of Peace* was in and out of there more than any other ship, disease cut into the population dreadfully, and the hurricane of 1831 was followed by a famine that raised the death rate from disease to a critical point. A good many Rarotongans reacted by saying they had been evil and that God was punishing them, but a good many others gave up on Christianity altogether, saying that nothing but bad things had happened since the missionaries came.

Williams was closer to the truth when he said in his book that missions, successful ones anyway, made the islands safe for Western ships and their crews. In the bad old South Seas days there was a fair amount of calculated theft by islanders, cutting of anchor cables so that ships would run on the reef, and killing of sailors for bad deeds done ashore, or killing just

for the excitement of it. Christianity curbed all that. On this general subject Williams had a macabre tale to tell. While he was at Raiatea in 1823 a
ship put in, and one of its passengers, himself a ship captain with a history
of bad luck at sea, recounted what had happened to him a few years
before. He had been in command of a New England whaling ship, the
Essex, in the Pacific close to the equator. His harpooners had struck two
sperm whales and the boats' crews were out to secure them when a third
whale, huge, eighty or ninety feet long, swam straight at the ship and
smashed into it, bursting a hole in the hull. An hour later it came back and
struck again, and the incredible happened—the *Essex* was so badly dam-
aged that it had to be abandoned. The crew all got off safely, in three
boats, and they sat stunned as their ship sank. They were not all that far
from Tahiti, but, as the captain said, they were "so ignorant of the state
and temper of the inhabitants that we feared we should be devoured by
cannibals, if we cast ourselves on their mercy." So the whalermen set off
in their boats for the coast of South America, more than two thousand
miles to the east. They ran out of food, and finally from brute necessity
they turned cannibal themselves. They ate the emaciated bodies of their
shipmates who died of starvation, and at last drew lots to see who would
be shot and eaten. This was in 1819, and of course by then the LMS missionaries were well in place all through Tahiti and the neighboring islands.

*   *   *

Williams always intended to return to the islands. What he wanted to
do, of course, was to go back with a ship of his own. He began seeding his
talks with this idea. He even suggested to his directors that perhaps the
government could be persuaded to buy a ship for missionary work. The
directors would not support any such approach. Williams went ahead anyway and put the proposal to the government himself. He was refused.
Undaunted, he suggested a public campaign to raise funds for a ship. This
the LMS could agree to. The principal fund raiser—of course—was Williams himself, and once more he went boldly to stand where no missionary had ever stood, before the Court of Common Council of the Cor-
poration of the City of London. There he had another triumph. He talked
about what missions and commerce could do for each other, and what
both could do for the city. His peroration was applauded, and the alder-
men voted him £500.

This and the rest of the money Williams raised paid for the purchase
and outfitting of the ship *Camden*, commanded by a Christian captain
named Robert Morgan, to be used—and this was important—for Wil-

liams's purposes, at his discretion. By April, 1838, everything was ready for Williams's departure. All through his long-drawn-out leaving he was at center stage, and he made the most of it, drawing once again his huge missionary maps of the islands, bigger than ever before, including now much of Melanesia in detail. At some of the islands he proposed to open up the natives might be "particularly savage," he knew, but God had preserved him so far, and if he was to die, then he would die working.

On the day he sailed, a crowd lined the banks of the Thames to watch the great man go downriver. His wife was at his side, in tears. She was leaving one of her sons to be educated in England, and was going back herself to the appallingly difficult life she had endured for years, "with a constitution apparently broken, health but very imperfectly established, spirit naturally far from high."

God be thanked, said Williams's eulogist John Campbell at the public farewell, that for all his well-merited fame the great missionary had not fallen prey to the baneful influence of popularity. Not everyone would have agreed with Campbell. In London and in the Pacific there were LMS people who thought Williams had always been conceited and was now insufferably puffed up. He had especially been a target because of his mania for ships. Too much native labor went into building them, too much evangelizing time was used up tinkering with them and sailing about in them, and too much of Williams's perennially calculating, figuring mind was fixed on the profitable cargoes that could be carried back and forth in them. Now his passengers on the voyage out to the Pacific, a contingent of new young missionaries, complained that Williams had filled the *Camden* with his own goods and the commercial stock of his oldest son John, who had married in England and was planning to go into business as a merchant in Samoa.

Williams was not willing to let anyone tell him what the *Camden* should be used for, where she should sail, or when. "He says," one missionary reported, "the vessel is my own—to take where I please—or to burn if I please." And he went on to claim that not even the LMS directors could control him. Remarks like this, and behavior to back them up, worried even his supporters in the South Seas mission. "Do you consider Mr. & Mrs. Williams real friends to the cause, or to their own Interest only?" one wrote home anxiously to the LMS. "I fear England has spoiled them—they are now going to heaven with Dukes, Lords, &c." Here was the sensitive question of social class again. After he reached Samoa, Williams told a not altogether sympathetic Wesleyan missionary: "I could go home now, and I could form a society of many noblemen with the Queen at the Head, who would soon send out 100 missionaries." Then, said the Wesleyan, you can do what no one else can. And Williams replied: "I never yet undertook a thing which I could not accomplish."

"Mr. Williams the Explorist," as one of the Tahiti missionaries sarcastically labeled him, decided to base himself and the *Camden* close to the Melanesian field he was poised to enter. He chose to live in western Polynesia, on the Samoan island of Upolu, and there he set himself up well. Indeed, he had never been so completely a householder. With him lived his wife, his oldest son John and his new wife, and his youngest son William. The house, in typical Williams style, was spacious, and coral-lined for cleanliness. Young John had built it, and he built as well a thirty-ton schooner for the use of the Samoan mission (and for his own business). Clearly he was a chip off the old block, and Williams was delighted that his first-born, the son who bore his name, had turned out energetic and knowledgeable enough to build a house, not a ninny or "too great a gentleman to touch a tool."

Williams was also pleased with the way his women coped. His wife had "made shift" all her life and was doing so still. His daughter-in-law, blessedly, was turning out sensible too. Williams, so he said, liked women who could fend for themselves, not the fancy, foolish, finicking kind who would swoon at the sight of a cockroach.

Mary had been through her last pregnancy; there were no more children to be born living or dead. In the house on Upolu the portrait of Williams' dead mother, moved out of the bedroom now, hung in the parlor by a picture of his dead father. A third face adorned the walls, that of the new young queen of England, Victoria, looking upon Williams's works and finding them good. Outside the house was a productive garden, beyond that a strong fence, and beyond that again the Samoans, learning how to house and clothe themselves properly and praise Williams's God. This was where his voyaging had brought him.

The American explorer Charles Wilkes, whose ships were at Samoa late in 1839, visited Williams and was impressed. The situation of the missionary's cottage was pretty, the lawn "nicely-dressed," the supper good, the beds for the overnight stay comfortable. "Mr Williams," wrote Wilkes, "seemed to me exactly what a missionary ought to be, pious, cheerful, and meek, although resolute. . . . His views were pointed not only to the diffusion of the gospel, but also to the extension of the useful arts, and whatever could tend to elevate the condition and eradicate the vices of the natives." At least one of Wilkes's men was less taken by this person who amazed the Samoans with magic lantern shows and electric-shock machines. He heard Williams preach aboard ship and was scornful: "such a gross, absurd tissue of Nonsense, ignorance & fanaticism . . . I never listened to." The islands, so Wilkes's man remarked, seemed not to render the ignorant wiser or less fanatical, but to work an undesirable change even in those who came with the best intentions: "a little while, & they sink the Missionary, in the Merchant, the preacher in the Magistrate." He could have got some of Williams's critics within the LMS to agree with this. Williams was always trying to make a market for island products in England—arrowroot for one thing, fancy woods for another; he had loaded the *Camden* with goods for his son's business; and now Wilkes appointed young John acting United States consul at Samoa, and presented him to the chiefs in this capacity.

* * *

Wilkes and his ships could hardly have failed to impress Williams. The two men were about the same age, and they had the sea in common. Williams was a self-made navigator who had to build his first ship with his own hands, and later had to struggle to acquire the modest *Camden*. Wilkes had the resources of a nation behind him. He was in charge of an official United States exploring expedition, the biggest and most ambitious venture of its kind ever mounted in the Pacific, with five ships and far more specialist scientists than even James Cook had commanded. The ocean was at Wilkes's disposal. He had been in the islands around Tahiti, where Williams had begun his missionary life, and he was equipped to go anywhere.

Yet Williams was sure his own labors were the more valuable. He had never been able to see why the missionary should be less free-ranging than any scientific seagoer. His particular interest just now was in the large and populous islands of Melanesia, beginning with the New Hebrides. In the book Williams published in England as part of his endless campaign to get what he wanted, he wrote about how the labors of the LMS in the Pacific had been confined entirely to the "copper-colored natives" of Polynesia, and how farther west, in the direction of the sunset, were men of "immense stature, with black complexions." They lived on the dark islands of Melanesia, "large and extensive groups of which little is known," beautiful, "rich in all the productions of a tropical climate," and "inhabited by several millions of immortal beings, suffering all the terrific miseries of a barbarous state." There was darkness in Melanesia, and there was treasure. Williams was an explorer and a treasure hunter for God, just as Wilkes was for government.

Before all of Wilkes's ships left Samoa on the next stage of their expedition, Williams sailed on his first missionary voyage into Melanesia. Some of the explorer's boats helped to tow the *Camden* out of Apia harbor on Upolu into the open sea.

On the eve of his departure, Williams preached a farewell sermon that reduced his Samoan listeners to tears. He himself sobbed as he spoke. The text he chose was about the apostle Paul: "And they all wept sore, and fell upon Paul's neck and kissed him; sorrowing most of all for the words which he spoke, that they should see his face no more." Aboard ship, with the *Camden*'s captain, Robert Morgan, running things, Williams wrote letters to while away the time, and it was now, sailing away again from home, wife, and family, that he put on paper for friends in England the details of his Samoan domestic idyl. He wrote as well about what he was on his way to do, and about death. "We live in a dying world. . . . Ere long some friend will communicate to surviving relatives and connexions the information of our death. The grand concern should be to live in a constant state of preparation. This I find a difficult matter, from the demand incessantly made upon my energies both of body and mind; but I find great comfort from the consideration that very many of God's people pray for me, and also that *all* is spent in the *best* of *all* causes." When he penned these words, he was sixty miles from his first Melanesian landfall. "Oh! how much depends upon the efforts of tomorrow. *Will the savages receive us or not?* . . . I am all anxiety. . . . The approaching week is to me the most important of my life."

Williams's first New Hebridean island was Futuna. Offshore, the *Camden* picked up a man in a canoe. He was pleased to be given a red shirt, a mirror, a knife, some fishhooks and a small pig. When he was taken ashore in a ship's boat the crowd that came down to the water's edge was friendly and unarmed.

Two days later the *Camden* was off Tanna, a striking island, much bigger than Williams had expected, as big as Upolu, with high volcanic mountains, and obviously heavily populated. The inhabitants were boisterous about giving and receiving gifts, but nothing alarming happened, and Williams was able to leave three Polynesian teachers there in good heart. He went back to the *Camden* elated, sure that he was on his way to greater things than ever. "This is a memorable day," he wrote in his journal, "a day which will be transmitted to posterity, and the record of events which have this day transpired, will exist after those who have taken an active part in them have retired into the shades of oblivion, and the results of this day will be ——" And there he broke off.

To the north, another island was in sight: Eromanga. The *Camden* steered for it, then coasted the southern shore until sunset. Williams leaned on the rail, talking enthusiastically about his fine reception at Tanna. With Samoa already well taken care of, and the New Hebrides obviously so promising for mission work, he had almost decided, he said, to move his family there. He went to bed cheerful, but then began to worry about what he was committing himself to—years more of uncertain work before he could claim any sort of success for himself and for those in England who believed in him. He got no sleep.

At daylight the *Camden* moved in again to the southern coast of Eromanga. At a place named Dillon Bay, Williams saw three men in a canoe. A whaleboat was lowered so that he could go and talk to them. Captain Morgan went with him, and so did two of the *Camden*'s passengers: William Cunningham, who had been a lay worker for the LMS and was now British vice-consul at Samoa; and James Harris, a young man intending to take up mission work.

The Eromangans were short and dark. They were also wild-looking and shy, and they spoke a language unlike anything Williams had ever heard. He could not make himself understood. He had the whaleboat pull inshore, and threw gifts to the watchful natives. He and Morgan got them to bring fresh water, and the islanders also offered the whites some coconuts. There seemed no risk in actually going ashore. Harris got out of the boat and waded through the shallows. The natives ran away. Williams called to Harris to sit down on the beach. The natives came back with coconuts and opened them. Williams saw children playing, and remarked that he thought this was a good sign. Captain Morgan said he was not so sure. He could not see any women on the beach, and it was his experience that when islanders had their mind on mischief, women were sent out of the way. Williams decided to go ashore just the same. Cunningham went with him. The natives would not shake hands with Williams, so he got Morgan to pass him some cloth, and he sat down and divided it among them.

Harris went inland a little way. The other two walked along the beach, Cunningham picking up shells, Williams reciting the Samoan numerals to a crowd of boys. Suddenly there was a yell, and Harris came running out of some bushes, with Eromangans pursuing him. He stumbled and fell into a stream. The Eromangans leaped in after him and clubbed him and killed him. Cunningham ran for the whaleboat. He got safely aboard, but only just. Williams ran down the beach into the water with two natives after him. He floundered and was caught. The Eromangans clubbed him savagely, and before the whaleboat could get anywhere near him he was dead.

The islanders plunged arrows into him, dragged his body out of the water and flung it down. Boys picked up rocks and pulverized the corpse. No one in the whaleboat was armed, and the Eromangans were hailing stones at them. Morgan ordered the boat to pull for the *Camden*, and then he brought the ship around to try to frighten the killers away from the bodies with cannon. But the wind was against the white men, and they were still a mile off when they saw the corpses of Williams and Harris being stripped and carried off into the bush.

*   *   *

It was November 20, 1839. The *Camden* sailed for Sydney with the news of the tragedy, and a British warship was dispatched, with William Cunningham aboard, to recover the bodies and take them to Samoa for burial. The Eromangans reluctantly handed over some bones and two skulls.

Over the years different theories were advanced to account for the killings: that Williams and Harris paid the price for insults by earlier white men at Eromanga, sandalwooders who took women and food and left disease; or that they unknowingly blundered into preparations for a ceremonial feast and were killed when they did not respond to the Eromangans' signals to leave. One story was that Harris was cooked and eaten by the men who killed him, and that Williams's body was trussed to a pole and carried away to be exchanged for pigs to be eaten at the feast. Later, a New Testament with Harris's name and a handkerchief with his initials were recovered, and a club, supposed to have been the one that killed Williams, found its way to the LMS rooms in London.

The Eromangans were unregenerate. Indeed for decades the New Hebrides, and Melanesia at large, continued to be the savage frontier of evangelism in the Pacific. The missionary George Gordon and his wife, inspired by Williams's story, came to convert his killers and were themselves killed, dismembered with axes. Gordon's brother took up the work, and was hacked to death with hatchets.

But in Samoa, which Williams had opened up to the work of the LMS, the word of his death set off an immediate and widespread religious "awakening," resulting in a great many conversions. And in England, the missionary martyr became the center of a sort of Protestant cult. Color prints of Williams being clubbed to death were sold. When his book was brought out in a cheap edition, sales doubled. And the LMS, which for years had regarded Williams somewhat askance, coming to appreciate his quality only when he made his case in person during his sojourn in England, now paid him unreserved homage. It was said that he should have been knighted; that he ranked for perseverance and moral courage with Columbus, Isaac Newton, and the prison reformer John Howard; and that his accomplishment matched anything in the Acts of the Apostles.

To the outsider this was extravagant. But the evangelical Christians of England were sure that the future was theirs, that in "ages to come" the period they were living through would be remembered as "the era of modern missions." The LMS was on the way to converting the whole world. So to LMS people Williams now appeared as a great man showing the way to the promised land, who died before the promise could be fulfilled, but whose death made fulfillment all the more certain.

"Much reflection has convinced me," wrote John Campbell, who had spoken the eulogy of Williams at his farewell from London in 1834, "that for popular effect, for the reputation of Mr. Williams, and for the purposes of history, he died in the proper manner, at the proper place, and at the proper time." Without question, Williams's life and death had their uses for the LMS. What happened at Eromanga was also part of a complicated set of transactions in Williams's own interior evolution. In him there was a great deal of the frontiersman, the kind of man who withdrew his energies, his personal resources, from the domesticated routines of life with wife and family to go and do the dirty work of the world, battling with the savage elements of life, confronting them in some sort of personal test. Perhaps this had something to do with the manner and the occasion of Williams's death. He had worked in Polynesia from his early twenties to his late thirties. By the time he went back to England in 1834 he had made up his mind that Polynesia was sufficiently domesticated, which meant too domesticated for him. He needed Melanesia, islands that were bigger, blacker, wilder. Beyond that, even—and this had its ironies—he had come to see some strengths in the Polynesian culture he had originally vowed to reduce to nothing. He could see that Polynesians themselves were human beings, with some fine qualities. They were physically superb, the men "perfect in proportion and exquisite in symmetry," the women inferior yet often presenting "the most elegant models of the human figure." They had intelligence equal to that of whites, however differently they saw things. Williams had reached the conclusion that the best way for the LMS to proceed was by a gradual approach to conversion, by an accommodation to Polynesian culture, rather than a frontal attack on heathenism. But that was not how he personally wanted to proceed with his life and work. He was not made for the gradual. He thought of himself late in his life as able to accomplish anything, in voyages that were great sweeps of action. And so he came to Erromanga.

Missionaries were, in their own way, like the realist novelists of the nineteenth century, opening up the world of the unknown and despised, bringing this world to the attention of the well placed and comfortable in their safe English homes. The novelists charted the unknown wilds of the lower classes, the missionaries the savagery of oceans and islands and black continents. The more savage the better. When the popular color prints of Williams's violent death were being readied for the engraver, the instructions were to make the savages darker and Williams more "heavenly." Williams was being deliberately ennobled. And what happened to him at Eromanga was conceived of as ennobling the missionary enterprise. It helped—immeasurably—in making the missionary appear as a fine type of British manhood overseas. Notions of imperialism and colonialism had not yet appeared in the form they took later in the century, but certainly the British people of Williams's day could be led to take pride in what their countrymen were doing in distant places. Williams took his exploits in the South Seas and skillfully put them to use at home. Through his life, and then through his death, the missionary became a deserving and valued son of the great national family of Queen Victoria.

There was a generation or more of this to come. A contemporary of Williams named Robert Moffat was assigned to Africa when Williams was assigned to the South Seas. Moffat had what was denied to Williams, a continent to contemplate, and he coined a famous phrase in which he spoke about the powerful attraction of the smoke of a thousand villages signaling to him from heathen territory. Moffat became famous, very much as Williams did, though without martyrdom. Moffat's daughter married the LMS missionary David Livingstone. Livingstone in many ways was another version of Williams, if anything more driven, at once harsher and more mystical. He was hardly a selfless servant of the LMS, any more than Williams was. But like Williams he was presented to the British people as a symbolic hero. In Livingstone, the British were able to see a great evangelist, a great humanitarian, a superb explorer who used the African rivers like highways in the jungle, a harbinger of empire who talked in terms of a civilization to be built in black Africa by white men prepared to carry commerce and Christianity to the ends of the earth. Mrs. David Livingstone had an appalling life, more harrowing even than Mary Williams's suffering sojourn on earth. The great Dr. Livingstone was buried in Westminster Abbey. With this, the lowly missionary as a national type had at last come into his inheritance, come into his kingdom, arrived in the promised land of national acceptance; and it was John Williams who had shown the way.

* * *

Herman Melville

HERMAN MELVILLE had strong ideas about missionaries. He had lived among savages in the South Seas, and he could not see that they were any more sinful than white men. In fact, as Melville saw things, if the savage needed saving it was not from himself but from civilized man. Western civilization had descended on the South Seas like a headhunter, slaughtering and dismembering savage culture. That was the real sin, the real savagery, and missionaries were just as much involved in it as other whites. Between civilization and Christianization there was nothing to choose, according to Melville; and for Polynesians the result was disaster.

Melville was very young when he went ashore on his first South Sea island. It was a revelation. For the rest of his life he remembered the high islands of Polynesia as authentic Edens in a pagan sea, fresh as at the moment of creation. Tahiti, he wrote in late middle age, should have been the place for the coming of Christ. But in the South Seas Melville did not encounter Christ, only the Protestant missionary, and he was appalled: "No sooner are the images overturned, the temples demolished, and the idolaters converted into *nominal* Christians, than disease, vice, and premature death make their appearance. The depopulated land is then recruited from the rapacious hordes of enlightened individuals who settle themselves within its borders, and clamorously announce the progress of the Truth. Neat villas, trim gardens, shaven lawns, spires, and cupolas arise, while the poor savage soon finds himself an interloper in the country of his fathers."

Without the missionary, the trader, the consul, the soldier, and the sailor, the savage got along very well, Melville thought. He had passed some weeks in a valley on the island of Nukuhiva in the Marquesas, and he found the people there—the Typee, he called them—better looking, healthier, better natured, happier than whites. The young warriors led lives of easy sociability. The young women bathed leisurely and oiled their skin until it glistened and decked their hair with flowers and danced by moonlight. Old men and women were free to gossip and doze. The fruit was on the tree for the taking; work did not bring out sweat on the brow; the "penalty of the Fall" weighed lightly. "There were none of those thousand sources of irritation that the ingenuity of civilized man has created to mar his own felicity. There were no foreclosures of mortgages, no protested notes, no bills payable, no debts of honor in Typee; no unreasonable tailors and shoemakers, perversely bent on being paid; no duns of any description; no assault and battery attorneys, to foment discord, backing their clients up to a quarrel, and then knocking their heads together; no poor relations, everlastingly occupying the spare bedchamber, and diminishing the elbow room at the family table; no destitute widows with their children starving on the cold charities of the world; no beggars; no debtors' prisons; no proud and hard-hearted nabobs in Typee; or to sum up all in one word—no Money! That 'root of all evil' was not to be found in the valley." Melville's suggestion was that Polynesians should go as missionaries to civilized countries.

* * *

When Melville wrote about destitute widows and poor relations and duns and debtors' prison, he was talking about his own life. He came to the South Seas as an ordinary seaman, and if he had had more money he would never have gone to sea in the first place. John Williams's ship was his way up in life, something to command and control. Melville was part of a family on its way down. In his mind he deserved better than to be a common sailor, and when he wrote about life at sea his stories frequently had for their heroes elevated men brought low, uncomfortable, unsuited to the rough work of a deckhand, voyagers with mysterious backgrounds of blight and dispossession.

Melville's father, Allan Melvill (the "e" was added to the family name in Herman's time), was a businessman, an importer who traveled to Europe every so often on business and was on speaking terms with important men on both sides of the Atlantic. He was proud of his family background. His father Thomas had taken part in the Boston Tea Party, and his father-in-law, General Peter Gansevoort, was a Revolutionary military hero; Allan wore the old soldier's ring in respectful memory. On one of his trips to Europe, Allan found out things about the Melvill ancestry that delighted him. He was looking into a vague story about a big inheritance from some Scottish Melvills. Nothing came of this, but he did meet some distinguished family connections, including Alexander, Earl of Leven and Melvill, "our legitimate Chief," and from there he went on to discover a man with a title who fought and fell for Scotland on Flodden Field; further back still a thirteenth-century Sir Richard de Melvill, founder of the line; a collateral line descended from Hungarian royalty; and on his mother's side a line which sprang originally from kings of Norway. "So," he wrote home, pleased, "it appears we are of royal line in both sides of the House. . . ."

Allan Melvill had the business virtues. He did well enough in New York during Herman's childhood to be able to move his growing family from one house to another, a better address each time. Wanting to do better yet, he overstepped and ruined himself. He made a less-than-ethical business arrangement using ten thousand dollars borrowed from a brother-in-law, got good money out of it for three years, then found himself caught in a credit squeeze and was forced into bankruptcy. He moved his family to upstate New York and for two years struggled unsuccessfully to re-establish himself. Nervous, insomniac, physically exhausted, he came down with a fever that brought on encephalitis, and died at last insane, "fierce, even *maniacal*," shouting crazily in an upstairs bedroom.

This was in 1832. Herman was an unremarkable youth of thirteen, a second son, one among eight children, four boys and four girls. He had always lived in the shadow of his older brother Gansevoort, a first son named for the general, at sixteen exceptionally bright and energetic, the apple of his parents' eye. Great things were confidently predicted for Gansevoort. Now he turned himself into a boy businessman. For five years he kept the family afloat, but in 1837 a general financial panic sank him, and he in turn went bankrupt. Again the Melvilles were down to no money.

Herman had been taken out of school when his father died and set to

work clerking in a bank where one of his mother's relatives had some influence. After that he worked for a while with Gansevoort, and improved
his mind part-time at a "Classical School." At age seventeen he got himself qualified as a teacher and went off to a schoolhouse in rural Massachusetts, one room full of unteachable country children. It was gloomy
and difficult work, and after some months he abandoned it and came
home to study engineering and surveying, probably with the idea of getting a job on the Erie Canal. While he waited for something to turn up—
and nothing did—he tried his hand at writing, and had two pieces printed
in the local paper. But there was no money in that, in fact no money anywhere that he could see. In 1839 Gansevoort left for New York to see
what he could do about drumming up some business. He also had it in
mind to get Herman placed as a merchant seaman. Hard times after the
crash of 1837 were driving young men to sea, and Melville was one of
them.

Put down on the crew list of a trading vessel as a ship's "boy," nineteen
years old, five feet eight and a half inches tall, complexion light, hair
brown, Melville crossed the Atlantic in the summer of 1839, to Liverpool
and back, working hard and earning practically nothing. At home again he
found his mother worse off than ever, unable to pay the butcher and the
baker, the furniture advertised for sale by the sheriff. Herman taught
school again briefly, went looking for work on the western frontier in Illinois, came back to the East Coast, lived for a time in New York on two
dollars a week plus dinner with Gansevoort, and finally decided, for want
of anything better, to go to sea again. He made his way to New England—
Boston, New Bedford, Fairhaven—and in January, 1841, shipped aboard
the whaler *Acushnet*, bound for the South Atlantic, Cape Horn, and the
Pacific. He was twenty-one. Since his first sea voyage he had grown an
inch, to his full height of five feet nine and a half inches, and his complexion was now described not as light but dark.

His mother, Maria Gansevoort Melvill, had a low opinion of the sea.
When a young Gansevoort boy joined the crew of a merchant ship, Maria
gave it as her view that this was suitable work for the talentless. Certainly
it would never have been thought of for her own brightest son,
Gansevoort. Herman, at that, was only one of several Melvills and Gansevoorts who went to sea, before and after him, on Navy ships and merchantmen and whalers. The family record was a kind of shorthand sum-
ming-up of the sailor's life: years of uneventful work, any amount of
tedium, some unwanted excitement when a ship ran on the rocks, two
deaths at sea, a case of scurvy, a case of venereal disease, some scientific

exploring, heroism under fire, one court-martial that had no important consequences and another that did, and a notable desertion. A ship commanded by an uncle of Melville's collided with a whale in the Arctic, no harm done on either side. This same captain sailed the South Seas and put in at the Marquesas. And later—though still a good many years before Melville ever saw the South Seas—young Thomas Melvill, Herman's cousin, visited the Marquesas too, aboard a United States man-of-war; he went ashore on the island of Nukuhiva, and walked a few miles inland to a valley inhabited by people who called themselves Taipi. So when Melville shipped aboard a whaler bound for the Pacific hunting grounds, he had at least some idea of what he was doing and where he was going.

The American whaling industry was a big and important business, and would be for another twenty years, as late as the Civil War. Just now it was doing well, better than the rest of the economy. Useful technological advances were being made in the harpooning, cutting up and boiling down of whales. The *Acushnet* was a new ship, on her first voyage. Her superstructure was not black from the try-pot fires, she did not sail in a miasma of old cooked blubber, and belowdecks she was clean, with the smell of new wood. Melville was getting as good a start as a beginning whalerman could have expected, and the Pacific was the great ocean of whales.

* * *

The *Acushnet*'s cruise went well, at least as far as the equatorial Pacific, and there Melville had a curious experience, one that interested him greatly. It turned out that one of his shipmates had sailed with Owen Chase, first mate of the *Essex*, the ship that was attacked and sunk by a whale in 1819, leaving the crew to draw lots to see who would be eaten on the horrible boat voyage to the South American coast (and to provide John Williams with a moral tale). Now, not far from where the *Essex* lay in three thousand fathoms of water, the *Acushnet* came across another New England whaler. The crews passed some time together in what was called a "gam." One of the forecastle hands on the other ship was a son of Owen Chase. Melville talked to him about his father's gruesome experience, and the boy gave him a copy of the little book Chase had written. "The reading of this wondrous story," Melville wrote later, "upon the landless sea, & close to the very latitude of the shipwreck had a surprising effect upon me." And then some months later, when the *Acushnet* was gamming with yet another whaler, Melville was led to believe (wrongly, though he never knew it) that the captain of the other ship, a powerfully built and handsome man in middle age, was Owen Chase himself. With the aura of the *Essex* story about him, he seemed to Melville "the most prepossessing-looking whale-hunter I think I ever saw."

All this was exciting. But somehow the *Acushnet* stopped catching whales. As day after day went by without even a sighting, the prospect of a long, drawn-out voyage loomed, years at sea before all the barrels were filled and the *Acushnet* could head back to her home port for the division of proceeds that would pay off the crew. Melville had signed on for the duration of the cruise, but as an ordinary seaman his "lay," his cash percentage of the catch, would be insubstantial, so he did not have a great financial incentive to stay with the ship. What was more, the *Acushnet's* captain had turned out to be a tyrant. The law entitled ships' captains of all sorts to be despots; and especially on whaling ships working conditions were bad, as bad as anything in American industry. Melville was locked up indefinitely in a floating prison with a brutal jailer.

In mid-1842, eighteen months out from port, the *Acushnet* put in at the Marquesas Islands to refresh, and stayed two weeks at Nukuhiva. Melville was ready to desert, and he discovered that a shipmate, a young fellow named Richard Tobias Greene, was having the same thoughts. The two of them came to an agreement, made some quiet preparations, and finally slipped away from a shore party and headed for the hills.

For a captain to lose crew members like this was bad business—apart from anything else it might give others ideas. Rewards were regularly offered to Marquesans to bring back deserters (this was common practice in the South Seas). But Melville and Greene managed to stay hidden in the rugged uplands until the *Acushnet* ran out of waiting time and had to sail.

The two deserters made their way down a dangerously steep-sided valley to take their chances among the savages of Taipivai. These were people with a bad reputation as flesh eaters even among other Marquesans, themselves cannibals. But the inhabitants of the valley turned out to be friendly. Melville had hurt his leg and was in pain, and while he was suffering the Taipi looked after him well. The leg refused to heal, and Greene eventually left the valley to go back to the harbor and try to get some sort of medical help. He did not reappear. Time went by, and after a few weeks Melville decided he would have to make the effort to get out of the valley on his own. He managed it, and was picked up by a whaler out of Sydney, the *Lucy Ann*. He signed on and sailed away to Tahiti. Melville never saw Greene again in the South Seas.

A few weeks among the Taipi was as savage as South Seas life ever got for Melville. The *Lucy Ann*, though, was worse than the *Acushnet*. She had been losing crew members, and was recruiting by collecting the leavings of other ships—men who, like Melville, had dropped ashore for one reason or another and then wanted to get away again. Melville's new shipmates were a frowsy bunch. Five of them had venereal disease of some sort. The captain himself was seriously ill, incapable of command. At Tahiti a good part of the crew quietly mutinied, refusing duty. Melville did not join the revolt outright. He did not have to—he had a reason for not working, his bad leg, still not healed. But a doctor ruled that in a couple of weeks he would be fit to work, whereupon he cast his lot with the mutineers and was locked up with them in the makeshift jail at Papeete, a straw hut called the "calabooza." (This was one of the legacies of the United States exploring expedition: Queen Pomare IV of Tahiti had taken Charles Wilkes's advice about how to maintain law and order among white sailors ashore.)

The calabooza was not the worst place in the world. The Tahitian jailer was easygoing. He might put a lock on a sailor overnight; but even if Melville's address, recorded on doctor's prescriptions, was "the stocks," he was free to wander about most of the time—his leg was improving—and go back to the calabooza just to eat and sleep.

Melville was seeing Tahiti at an important moment. In 1842 the French were in the process of taking control of parts of Polynesia. There had been French warships at Nukuhiva when the *Acushnet* arrived, and they were at Tahiti too, securing the island as a French protectorate. (There had even been a suggestion that the mutineers off the *Lucy Ann* should be locked up aboard the French flagship.) One of the main issues in bringing the weight of the French to bear was the mistreatment of Catholic missionary priests by Pomare and her chiefs, under the guidance of the LMS missionaries. There had been visits from French naval commanders insisting on fair treatment for French interests of all sorts in the islands; and finally the French home government, which had come to regard a Pacific base of some sort as desirable, decided to move in on Tahiti.

The Catholic priests were secure there now, and Melville often took a stroll from the calabooza to their makeshift mission. To Melville, the French fathers were two of a kind, little dried-up men in black gowns and black three-cornered hats so big that the priests were almost extinguished beneath them, peeping out from under the brims "like a couple of snails." The man Melville liked to see was Father Columban Murphy, a jolly, red-faced Irishman in a big straw hat and what Melville called "a sort of yellow, flannel morning-gown"—the white soutane of the Congregation of the Sacred Hearts of Jesus and Mary. Murphy was always good for some food and a swig of brandy, and this attraction of Catholicism was enough to bring Melville and some of the other mutineers, among them an Irishman or two, to Mass each morning.

One of the men off the *Lucy Ann* had a certain style about him. This was the ship's steward, who signed himself John B. Troy. He had skipped ashore in the Marquesas, was brought back protesting, and refused duty with the others in Tahiti. One of his jobs aboard ship had been to look after the medical supplies, and he had taken them with him when he deserted in the Marquesas, which resulted in a further charge against him. In the calabooza Troy kept up his medical interests. He was able to get the Papeete consular doctor to prescribe a laudanum concoction, so that he and his friends could lie about in a pleasant state of drugged suspended animation between visits to Father Murphy and his brandy flask at the Catholic mission.

Troy was a familiar South Seas type, one of those drifters who for whatever reason needed the ocean to hide in, forever changing islands, jobs, names, selves.* Still, Melville was attracted to him. Troy's own story was that he was fallen from high places; he "threw out hints of a patrimonial estate, a nabob uncle, and an unfortunate affair which sent him a-roving." And Troy was something of a literary person, which Melville liked. The two of them were the aristocrats of the forecastle on the *Lucy Ann*.

They decided to escape from the calabooza. It did not take much effort. They simply rowed away in a small boat to the beautiful island of Moorea just a few miles from Tahiti (where John Williams had landed in 1817, and where the LMS' South Sea Academy for mission children still stood). There they stayed for a week or so with two white men who had given up the sea in favor of potato farming, and they looked in briefly on the makeshift court of Queen Pomare, who had withdrawn from Tahiti when the French came to take over.

Melville wanted to move on again. He saw a whaler, the *Charles and Henry*, provisioning in the harbor, made inquiries, and signed on for a hunting cruise as far as Hawaii. Troy was left behind, and as with Richard Tobias Greene it was years before he made contact with Melville again, after he heard he had been put in a book, under the name of Doctor Long Ghost.

The Hawaiian Islands were nothing like the Marquesas. The two biggest and busiest ports in all the Pacific islands were Honolulu, on the

---

* Troy turns up again under different names in different parts of the Pacific, on the Californian gold fields, and in South America. There are even hints, unverifiable, that Troy was actually a man named Cunningham, the same William Cunningham who sailed with John Williams on his last voyage and saw him killed.

island of Oahu, and Lahaina, on the neighboring island of Maui. Between them they attracted hundreds of whaling ships and scores of merchant-men each year. Whaling put millions of dollars into the economy of Hawaii and thousands of wild sailors on the streets each whaling season, spring and fall. Most of the business was in American hands; most of the whalermen were American; and to be United States consul at Honolulu or vice-consul at Lahaina was to be a busy man, looking after the problems of sailors discharged, beached, abandoned, ill, runaway, or just shiftless or otherwise in trouble.

It was at Lahaina that Melville came ashore off the *Charles and Henry*, not as a deserter or a minor mutineer, but for the first time in the Pacific properly discharged at the end of a cruise he had signed on for; he was not carried as an expense on the consular books, not a charge on his country. He moved from Lahaina to Honolulu, and after a short spell as a pin setter in a bowling alley, he contracted to work for a merchant in town, as a clerk and bookkeeper, for one hundred fifty dollars a year and his keep. Soon after he left Lahaina, his old ship, the *Acushnet*, turned up there and its captain swore to Melville's desertion in the Marquesas, but apparently no effort was made to track him down as a runaway.

Melville seemed to be following the great powers about. Three times in Polynesia he came ashore in the wake of European imperialists. In the Marquesas and Tahiti it was the French. In Hawaii it was the British, or at least one impetuous Britisher. In the early 1840s at Honolulu, some British residents had been complaining about the way they were treated by the law courts of the independent Hawaiian monarchy. They sent for a man-of-war to help them put their case, and its aristocratic commander took it upon himself to force King Kamehameha III, under the guns of the British Navy, to sign away the islands to Britain. This was gunboat diplomacy for which there was no authority from the Foreign Office. Indeed, official British policy was to support the independence of the Hawaiian monarchy. As soon as news of the forced cession reached London, another warship was sent to hand the islands back to their king. Melville was at Honolulu in mid-1843 for the last of the brief British period and the return of sovereignty to the Hawaiian crown: stirring days.

This was the scale of international politics in Polynesia, and increasingly its style: a warship in port and independence was at risk. Melville, not altogether justifiably, took the British commander's side in the affair, his own version of things being that anything would be an improvement on the New England Protestant missionary dominance he saw every-where—in the councils of the Hawaiian king, where missionary "advisers" told Kamehameha III what to say, and in the streets of Honolulu as well. Melville took away with him the indelible picture of a missionary wife, robust and red-faced, riding through town in a cart pulled by two Hawaiians, one young, one old, civilized into draught horses, evangelized into beasts of burden, tugging and hauling while the woman sat looking about her as magnificently as any queen driven in state to her coronation. On an uphill stretch of road the cart got stuck, but the lady would not climb down and take the weight off the wheels. Leaning forward in her seat, she rapped the old man on the head with her fan and bawled, "Hookee! Hookee!"—pull, pull. Times had changed, Melville remarked, since she used to drive the cows out to pasture in New England.

Evidently Melville expected to stay in Hawaii for a while, and he must have written back to the United States saying where he was, because letters for him arrived much later at Honolulu and were listed in *The Temperance Advocate and Seamen's Friend,* a paper that specialized in sailor news along with Protestant missionary exhortation. But for whatever reason, Melville decided after only a few weeks of steady employment to go home. An American man-of-war, U.S.S. *United States,* bound for Boston, was in Honolulu harbor signing on crew members. Melville shipped aboard her.

He went back across the Pacific the way he had come: the Marquesas again, fifteen months after his desertion from the *Acushnet* to the valley of the Taipi and his escape on the *Lucy Ann;* Tahiti again, where he sailed close to Moorea, his refuge from the calabooza. On the South American coast he took some shore leave in the Spanish-Peruvian colonial city of Lima, a strange place, old, corrupt, decayed, with the wreckage of earthquakes everywhere, yet fascinating, the whole town a strange and deathly white, but teeming with life in the streets.

The *United States* was a man-of-war, run according to the articles of war. Between Hawaii and home one hundred sixty-three men were flogged for breaches of naval discipline. Melville managed to stay out of trouble. He was assigned to the maintop, seventy feet above deck, where he waited for orders that would send him higher still, to the main royal yard almost two hundred feet up. Among his watchmates were a few unusual sailors who knew something about books, and one who privately wrote poetry. So there were things more interesting to talk about than what was happening aboard ship, and with one well-read sailor, a man who went by the name of Edward Norton, Melville passed a memorable night deep in conversation; they "scoured all the prairies of reading; dived into the bosoms of authors, and tore out their hearts." The captain of the maintop, John J. Chase—another Chase—was a remarkable man in Melville's life, someone to admire unreservedly. Chase knew Shakespeare and Homer and could recite the Portuguese sea epic, *The Lusiad* by Camoëns, in the original. He declaimed some homecoming verses, for the last sea miles of the voyage of the *United States*.

Melville went ashore at Boston in October, 1844. He had been away the better part of four years. He was twenty-five. He never went to sea again, except as a passenger. He never saw another South Sea island. Yet for the rest of his life—and he lived to be seventy-two—he was known as the man who lived among cannibals.

*   *   *

Some years later, when Melville was well known as a novelist, he had one of his characters, a lad named Wellingborough Redburn, of good family but down on his luck and making his first voyage as a common seaman, talk about his belief that he was destined to be a great voyager. What a fine thing it would be, said Redburn, to recount his adventures to an eager audience; he would talk about remote and barbarous countries, and people would regard him with reverence and wonder. Whether or not this was Melville literally speaking for himself, he did decide, soon after he got home, to write a book about the South Seas. He was ashore with nothing to look forward to in the way of a good job. He had time on his hands and a story to tell. When he had told it to his family for long enough he started to write it down.

Other young men had done the same sort of thing: Richard Henry Dana, Jr., for one, had made a book out of his two years at sea before the mast, and Melville admired Dana's work. But when he came to write his own first book he put it together in his own way, setting things down as he remembered them, embroidering incidents, bending actual events when that was needed to keep up pace and suspense, inventing when he felt like it. When he was not sure of himself or where he simply needed more substance in his descriptions, he borrowed outright and at length from other people's South Seas narratives; he was always a great incorporator.

He wrote quickly. Within a few months he had a pile of manuscript pages. The New York publishing house of Harper Brothers read what he had written, but decided against buying it on the ground that although it compared with *Robinson Crusoe* for interest, "it was impossible that it could be true and therefore was without real value." The manuscript did better in London. Melville's older brother Gansevoort, who had blossomed into a political orator, had got a minor patronage job as a reward for his work on behalf of the successful Democratic presidential candidate

James Polk, and went to London as secretary to the American Legation. Gansevoort showed the manuscript to the publisher John Murray, whose Colonial and Home Library specialized in the experiences of white men in exotic places, and Murray thought well enough of the prose and the subject to make Melville an offer. At the same time Murray was worried about authenticity. He asked Melville to add some more straightforward factual material, and he wanted some other alterations as well. Early in 1846 the book went into print in London. A New York imprint was found: Wiley and Putnam's Library of Choice Reading. *Typee* was launched on both sides of the Atlantic.

Melville was still learning to be an author, and as yet he had not begun to feel anything like his full powers, but he had a good idea of what people would like to hear about the South Seas: "The Marquesas! What strange visions of outlandish things does the very name spirit up! Naked houris—cannibal banquets—groves of cocoa-nut—coral reefs—tatooed chiefs—and bamboo temples; sunny valleys planted with bread-fruit trees—carved canoes dancing on the flashing blue waters—savage woodlands guarded by horrible idols—*heathenish rites and human sacrifices.*"

So in *Typee,* between discussions of wood carving, fire making by the rubbing together of sticks, burial practices, ways of fishing and dividing the catch, religious observances, marriage customs, and descriptions of flora, fauna, and insects, Melville dropped hints that the Typee were cannibals, and that the narrator of the book, Melville thinly disguised under the name of Tommo, was being kept prisoner in the valley, to be fattened and eaten. Sailors used to say that cannibals found the flesh of white men unpleasantly salty, but as the weeks passed and the Typee showed no signs of being willing to let him go, Tommo became more and more anxious about his situation, more and more fearfully interested in the details of food habits among savages. The Typee kept telling him that the biggest and juiciest item in their diet was pig, but he was not reassured, especially when he came upon some men inspecting three human heads, two brown and one white. Soon afterward, some warriors returned from a battle on the walls of the valley with the corpses of enemies killed in combat slung on poles like pigs (or deserters), and there was great excitement. Tommo was not allowed to watch where the bodies were taken or what happened to them, but he heard loud drumming all day. Drawn irresistibly to the mysterious Taboo Groves, he found warrior chiefs taking their ease, reclining on woven mats, and in a curiously carved wooden vessel "the disordered members of a human skeleton, the bones still fresh with moisture, and with particles of flesh clinging to them here and there!"

As against this lurking horror, the valley had its delights, and the greatest of these was the Typee girl, a sailor's delight—any young man's delight. They were friendly; they had next to no work to do and so were always available for the Typee equivalent of picnics and swimming parties. The water was their element. Tommo's ship was welcomed at Nukuhiva in the classic island way, by a bevy of "swimming nymphs" who climbed aboard "dripping with the brine and glowing from the bath," and stayed to dance voluptuously for the sailors. On swimming excursions with Tommo the girls frolicked in the water, "springing buoyantly into the air, and revealing their naked forms to the waist, with their long tresses dancing about their shoulders, their eyes sparkling like drops of dew in the sun, and their gay laughter pealing forth. . . ." They were good to Tommo. They offered him, among other relaxations, luxurious massage: all those soft brown hands on the body at once. "Every evening the girls of the house gathered about me on the mats, and . . . would anoint my whole body with a fragrant oil, squeezed from a yellow root. . . . And most refreshing and agreeable are the juices of the 'aka,' when applied to one's limbs by the soft palms of sweet nymphs, whose bright eyes are beaming upon you with kindness; and I used to hail with delight the daily recurrence of this luxurious operation. . . ."

The great thing about Typee girls was that they were beautiful, more so even than other Marquesans, who were generally agreed to be the most striking of Polynesians, who as a race were the handsomest of all humans. And among the Typee, to Tommo's eye, the most beautiful girl, the one who became his special friend, was Fayaway. Her loveliness was essentially indescribable: "The easy unstudied graces of a child of nature like this, breathing from infancy an atmosphere of perpetual summer, and nurtured by the simple fruits of the earth; enjoying a perfect freedom from care and anxiety, and removed effectually from all injurious tendencies, strike the eye in a manner which cannot be pourtrayed." Still, Melville tried a figure sketch in words: a free, pliant body, the very perfection of female grace and beauty, a complexion of rich and mantling olive, soft skin—all that anointing with oil—clad only in the "primitive and summer garb of Eden," with occasionally a becoming wraparound of *tapa*, the Polynesian bark cloth, and flowers for jewelry. Fayaway played a nose flute, to more pleasing effect than any white girl torturing a guitar. She smoked a pipe, and it was not at all incongruous; it only made her more engaging, "holding in her delicately formed olive hand the long yellow reed . . . with its quaintly carved bowl, and every few moments languishingly giving forth light wreaths of vapor. . . ." She ate shrimps raw and wriggling—but elegantly. And she was tattooed—but only lightly, not much more than a few beauty spots.

Fayaway had not much to say for herself, in fact her conversation was apparently nil, but her gestures were winning. Melville had her do one thing in particular which all by itself made her—and him—famous. In the middle of Typee valley was a "miniature lake," and Tommo was allowed to go canoeing there. To his amazement he found that canoes were forbidden to the girls—tabu. He expostulated, and the Typee priests relented enough to allow Fayaway an exemption. One day Tommo was adrift with her on this dreamlike stretch of water—glowing sky above, transparent lake depths below, and the pensive gaze of his beautiful savage girl upon him—when Fayaway suddenly stood up, "disengaged from her person the ample robe of tappa which was knotted over her shoulder (for the purpose of shielding her from the sun), and spreading it out like a sail, stood erect with upraised arms in the head of the canoe." American sailors, remarked Tommo jocosely, prided themselves on their straight, clean spars, "but a prettier little mast than Fayaway made was never shipped aboard of any craft." Nor, to be sure, a more unlikely one. But Fayaway naked in the canoe with her *tapa* sail was remembered for the rest of the century, looked for on the spot by well-read travelers, painted at a distance from imagination by artists who never saw the Marquesas. She was the stuff of the eternal South Seas dream, and she guaranteed the success of Melville's book.

Typee did so well that Melville was encouraged to try again. *Typee* had taken him into a savage valley and out once more; the sequel, which he called *Omoo*, meaning a rover, took him to Tahiti, into the calabooza, out again with Doctor Long Ghost and away to Moorea. He wrote it quickly, on the same principle as *Typee*, following his own experiences but embroidering at will, drawing heavily on other people's books for his descriptions of life in Tahiti.

In London John Murray published him again. In New York, with *Typee* a success, the Harpers showed an interest in *Omoo* and bought it for a reasonable price. Less than three years after coming home from the South Seas, Melville had two books on the market, selling well. He was making much more money out of the Pacific as a writer than he ever would have as a sailor.

And he and his creations were well known, all the way from England and the United States to the South Seas. An English trader who had been more or less accidentally incarcerated in the calabooza at the same time as the *Lucy Ann* mutineers published a book in which he claimed he had been assaulted there in dastardly fashion by a roughneck American sailor who could only have been Herman Melville. The British consulate doctor at Tahiti took offense at Melville's not too flattering description of his practice and threatened to sue, long-distance. While Melville was still revising *Typee* for reprinting, another young sailor, a United States Navy lieutenant, was going ashore on Nukuhiva. He made a point of inquiring about Melville's "former associates" in Taipi. He found, of all people, a "damsel named Fayaway from that valley—who was maid of all work to a French Commissary of the garrison—she was attired in a gaudy yellow gown, ironing the Crapeau's trowsers. . . . There was also a diminutive young 'oui oui' tumbling about the floor—so I judged she had become childish of late." He could not be sure it was the "genuine Fayaway"—she was evidently not an outstanding beauty, and islanders changed their names when they felt like it—and ironing trousers was a step down from standing as a naked mast to a *tapa* sail, but still . . . In the United States a tendency persisted for romantics gazing at lakes to be transported in imagination to Fayaway-land. And Melville, Mr. Typee, Mr. Omoo, was a literary celebrity. Suddenly people wanted to know him. "You remember someone who woke one morning and found himself famous," he wrote, referring to Byron's well-known remark. "And here am I, just come from hoeing in the garden, writing autographs."

* * *

The lake where Tommo floated in a dream with Fayaway was invented by Melville. No such lake existed in the real valley of the Taipi on Nukuhiva. *Typee* was full of such things—*Omoo* too. Melville tacked between fact and fiction all the time, excusing himself, as far as he made any effort to, by saying that he was writing some years after the events he described, and that his story was the kind of narrative, "spun as a yarn," that diverted his shipmates during the weariness of night watches at sea. One English reviewer thought he had gone further than that, and invited Melville to a dinner on April Fool's Day—just a small party, Messrs. Crusoe, Sinbad, Gulliver, Munchausen . . .

Part of this skepticism grew from a feeling that Melville was not what he seemed to be, that he wrote too well for someone alleged to be a beginning author, especially one who was also a deckhand. The first observation was praise of a backhanded sort, but the second chafed; Melville of all people had never wanted to be a common sailor. British reviewers ran this line about the link between social class and literary polish more strongly than Americans. Melville could do not much more than protest that he was what he said he was. "Bless my soul, Sir," he wrote to John

Murray, "will you Britons not credit that an American can be a gentleman, & have read the Waverly Novels, tho every digit may have been in
the tar-bucket?—You make miracles of what are common-places to us."

Murray kept on asking, belatedly, for documentary proof that Melville
had really been in the South Seas. Melville got half angry, not to say
defensive. How could he possibly subpoena a Marquesan savage to satisfy
some carping Englishmen? In any case, what he wrote, so he said, was "a
little touched up . . . but *true*." In the midst of this, a piece of living proof
materialized—Toby, the sailor who deserted with Melville, went with
him into the valley, left to get medical help, and then disappeared. Toby
ashore was Richard Tobias Greene, a house and sign painter of Buffalo,
New York. He had come across a bad review of *Typee* in a religious journal ("plenty of what pleases the vicious appetite of a sailor . . . slurs and
flings against missionaries and civilization . . . unblushing walks along the
edge of modesty . . ."), and had decided to write to the papers to say that
he was the "true and veritable Toby," and that he was happy to testify to
the "entire accuracy of the work, so long as I was with Melville. . . ."
Greene hoped Melville would see his letter and get in touch with him.
Melville did, and he made a trip to Buffalo to hear what had happened to
Toby on his own. He had been more or less pressed aboard a whaler and
carried off. Melville brought back a daguerrotype portrait and a lock of his
friend's hair, and wrote to John Murray about how Toby had come to life,
"tho' I had long supposed him to be dead"—as Toby had supposed Melville to be. "I send you by this steamer several papers . . . containing
allusions to him. Toby's appearance . . . produced quite a lively sensation
here—and 'Truth is stranger than fiction' is in every body's mouth."

Religious journals of the kind Toby had seen gave Melville a bad time
over his two books, which was understandable enough, since he was very
hard on missionaries, especially Protestants. In *Typee* he had begun by
saying that he had no animosity against missionaries as individuals, nor
against their "glorious cause." But then he went straight ahead to do his
devastating sketch of the red-faced missionary wife at Honolulu in her
kanaka-drawn carriage, and to talk about the fatal impact of the Truth in
Polynesia. Even without this, Melville would have been savaged by the
righteous because he talked about the charms of bare brown flesh, and
because he said he could see virtue in the sexual arrangements of the
Marquesans, who had good times with their bodies from an early age and
later took marriage partners loosely and very differently from Westerners—one woman to several men, polyandrously. Melville was an
enemy of the good, and the *Christian Parlor Magazine* of New York took

ten pages to destroy him for his attack on the "cause of MISSIONS," so steeped in hatred, so pertinacious in its misrepresentations, and for his love affair with the debauched Marquesans. "An apotheosis of barbarism! A panegyric of cannibal delights! An apostrophe to the spirit of savage felicity!"

As a matter of fact, at the urging of his publishers on both sides of the Atlantic, Melville had toned down *Typee* before it was first published, and as it went through its various reprintings he made more changes, taking out a good many of the passages that had given offense (and adding Toby's story for authenticity). In a sense Melville owed the missionaries something. Of all the books he used to reinforce his account of life in the South Seas, he drew most heavily on *Polynesian Researches* by William Ellis, an LMS missionary, a colleague of John Williams. Without Ellis, *Typee* would have been a thinner book, much less to John Murray's liking. And when Melville was writing *Omoo* he used Ellis again, whole pages at a time. But on the topic of evangelical religion Melville was unrepentant. *Omoo* was, if anything, harder on missionaries than *Typee* had been.

When Melville took a wife of his own, in 1847, just after *Omoo* was published, it was a respectable New England woman, Elizabeth Shaw, daughter of Lemuel Shaw, chief justice of Massachusetts. The Protestant press made something of this news. The story traveled as far as Hawaii, where *The Temperance Advocate and Seamen's Friend*, which had once listed in its columns letters waiting at Honolulu for Melville the wandering sailor, and which had reviewed *Typee* and *Omoo* as affronts to mission work, remarked that it was a perversity in Melville to live among the "fashionable circles" of American cities. He should go back to his beloved savage islands where the gifts of God were so lavishly strewn but where there was no evidence of Christianity. And take his bride: "it may be, the gentle Fayaway would stand upon the beach to extend a cordial welcome." There were other newspaper jokes about Fayaway filing a breach-of-promise suit, and some mock wonderment at Melville's desertion of his "delightful fairy" for a woman brought up in "odious" civilization.

And indeed this was a serious question. If Typee was such a dream world and life in civilization was so dire, why did Melville ever come out of the valley? It could not have been just that the real-life Taipi were cannibals. Tommo in Melville's book had a harder time with the flesh eaters than Melville himself did. Marquesan cannibalism, in any case, had to do with war and religious sacrifice, and beachcombers need not get involved in this. Some did, of course. Melville's narrator came across a real white

savage. A foundling who never knew his father, he passed his childhood
in the parish workhouse, went to sea, worked as a "dog before the mast"
for years, then deserted off a trading ship at the Marquesas, taking a
musket and ammunition with him. He chose a chief to fight for and did
extremely well for himself: military prowess, a "princess" for a wife, any
amount of property, hogs, fine *tapa*, woven mats, grass houses everywhere, and the protection of a tabu. But he was exceptional. In Melville's
time there were already white men ashore in the Marquesas who expected to live out their lives peaceably, and the same was beginning to be
true even in the cannibal Fiji Islands in the western Pacific (though Melanesia as a whole was a much riskier proposition than Polynesia—witness
John Williams—and would continue to be for decades). And if the Marquesas were still too savage, there was always Tahiti, where the warriors
had long ago laid down their spears. A good number of white men were
living undisturbed on the beach there. Yet Melville chose to leave the
Marquesas for Tahiti, Tahiti for Hawaii, Hawaii for home, leaving savagery farther and farther behind.

So was Melville at all serious in what he said about the superiority of
the primitive life, or was he just spinning yarns about it, playing with the
idea of savagery as so many civilized men had done before him? He knew
what Cook and Bougainville and Commerson had said, but, of course,
neither they nor any of the other well-placed men who wrote about the
noble savage had themselves given up civilization in favor of the primitive
life. They had something to go back to at home: career, reputation, reward. Westerners who jumped ship in the South Seas mostly did it from
the forecastle; and they were obviously getting out from under a civilization that to them was unbearably oppressive. Melville was a common
sailor who was uncommon; he tried the South Seas life and then went
home and wrote books about it.

Actually, though he deliberately set out to make his readers shiver,
Melville did not overwhelm them with savagery. He did not allow
Tommo in *Typee* to be eaten or even seriously threatened. Tommo caught
glimpses of a dismembered brown body and even a severed white head.
But he himself stayed intact. Bad things might loom, but nothing disastrous happened to him. When the Typee did lay hands on Tommo it
was—with one exception—either for healing (therapy for his bad leg) or
soothing (the splendid daily massage by the Typee girls). So much for the
savage as a threat.

As for the seductiveness of the savage, the Typee girls, so strangely
beautiful, so innocently carnal, were given a sort of civilized blessing by

Melville's observation (and not only Melville's) that Marquesans, the most beautiful of Polynesians, were at the same time the most European-looking. This was their distinguishing characteristic, and it made them superior to other Pacific peoples, even the "voluptuous" Tahitians, and certainly the "dark-hued" Hawaiians and the "woolly-headed" Fijians. So Melville's readers were given a kind of quiet permission to think about Marquesans as "safe" savages, as a version of themselves, strange but somehow kin, in fact what the white race might have been before some of its primitive freedoms were civilized away. And, at that, there might have been the blood of white castaways in the Marquesans Melville saw. In any case, along with everything else beautiful, Melville gave Fayaway—the ultimate brown-skinned girl—blue eyes.

Melville did have a real horror of the real savage, and it surfaced clearly not just in *Typee* but in his later works as well. He was willing to take a chance on the savage valley in the first place because it could never have been as bad as a whaling ship, and he was more than willing to enjoy primitive pleasures as they came his way. Tommo's everyday clothing in the valley was just a piece of *tapa*. He would dress up correctly, Typee style, for a ceremonial feast. But he would not go further. In a later book Melville gave his narrator a shiver of horror when he discovered that a Polynesian harpooner, fantastically tattooed, had one of those notorious New Zealand heads for sale. The chance came up to secretly try on the harpooner's cloak, woven and fringed, shaggy and thick. "I went up in it to a bit of glass stuck against the wall, and I never saw such a sight in my life. I tore myself out of it in such a hurry that I gave myself a kink in the neck." That was putting on savagery only for a few seconds. At the sight of the indelible mark of savagery, tattooing, Melville had Tommo react even more strongly. To Marquesans, tattooing was beautiful. The white warrior who had gone from workhouse foundling to tabu chief was tattooed: "A broad blue band stretched across his face from ear to ear, and on his forehead was the taper figure of a blue shark, nothing but fins from head to tail." He had volunteered for the tattooing, and Tommo was horrified. "What an impress! Far worse than Cain's." When a Typee tattooer saw Tommo he got wildly excited at the prospect of a white face to work on, and Tommo was instantly appalled "at the bare thought of being rendered hideous for life." The man persisted, would not give up, danced about gesturing with his tools of trade. Tommo tried to buy him off by offering him an arm to work on. No, it had to be the face, and as "his fore-finger swept across my features, in laying out the borders of those parallel bands which were to encircle my countenance, the flesh fairly crawled upon my bones." Tommo was utterly revolted at the thought of becoming a living tattooed head, disfigured and marked in such a manner (and this was the real point for Melville) "as never more to have the *face* to return to my countrymen. . . ."

After Tommo had played with savagery for some weeks, it became overwhelmingly urgent for him to be able to be seen again as a civilized man and not as a savage. Tommo very likely had a harder time getting free of the Typee than Melville himself did in reality—this for the sake of an exciting climax to the book. But Melville's attitude is clear. He had a howling mob pursue Tommo along a coral beach and into the water as his escape boat was rowed frantically away. A fierce one-eyed chief swam close, tattooed and with a hatchet between his teeth. Tommo seized the boat hook and struck him in the throat. It was life or death. Savagery was death, and escape to civilization was life.

* * *

D. H. Lawrence, who was fascinated by the primitive forces that exercised power over the lives of civilized people, said a very sensible thing about Melville. "The truth of the matter is," wrote Lawrence, "one cannot go back"—meaning back to savagery. "Some men can—renegade. But Melville couldn't go back: and Gauguin couldn't really go back: and I know now that I could never go back. Back toward the past. . . . We can't go back to the savages: not a stride. We can be in sympathy with them. We can take a great curve in their direction, onward. But we cannot turn the current of our life backward, back toward their soft warm twilight and uncreate mud. Not for a moment. If we do it for a moment, it makes us sick." This is a good diagnosis of Melville deciding between the South Seas and home. One world was frightening and alluring at the same time. It was distant and deep. It had savage children of nature and strange gods in it. It might have been mad. It was anyway a fantasy world. And in *Typee* it made Tommo sick. As long as he was in the valley, even when he was with Fayaway, bathing in tropical freedom and delight, his infected leg stayed poisoned. He did not start to recover until he gathered strength enough, and will power enough, to escape from the valley and go back to the real world of his own kind—even if this meant shipping aboard a whaler worse than the one he had deserted.

As soon as he was safe aboard ship, bad leg, *tapa* cloak, and all, Tommo went through a sort of desavaging ceremony. His leg was doctored from a Western medicine chest, someone took off his *tapa* and dressed him in a sailor's blue frock, and he was given a haircut. Now he was a "civilized mortal" again, on the first stage of a long return journey that took him back to where he was born. In no time at all he was looking back on life among the savages of the Marquesas as a dream.

The tragedy of Melville's life was that once he was settled again in the United States he began to find in his own world, his own society, his own inner life, manifestations that were just as strange as anything in the valley of the Taipi, alluring and frightening things, glimpses of savagery and even madness. He tried hard to make his peace with the conventional world around him. For a start, he had to have money to live. The only work he ever found that seemed proper to him was writing books. With the money he made as an author he took on the responsibility of providing for a wife and family. But in its own way the respectable, settled life of a family man, a householder, made Melville sick too.

Or rather did not make him well. There was a condition that Melville had suffered from since childhood, a wound that would never heal, that was incurable. Here again D. H. Lawrence was right about him: "Melville hated the world: was born hating it. But he was looking for heaven. That is, choosingly. Choosingly, he was looking for paradise. Unchoosingly, he was mad with hatred for the world." This was complicated, but it was so, and there were good reasons for it. And, tragically, it meant that no matter where Melville was, in savagery or in civilization, he could not be at rest.

The world, Melville once wrote, is a ship on its passage out, and not a voyage complete. In his own life he was never assured of a desired destination, or of a safe homecoming. Consider, he said, the sea and all its mystery and danger, and then turn to the "green, gentle, and most docile earth; consider them both, the sea and the land; and do you not find a strange analogy to something in yourself? For as this appalling ocean surrounds the verdant land, so in the soul of man there lies one insular Tahiti, full of peace and joy, but encompassed by all the horrors of the half known life. God keep thee! Push not off from that isle, thou canst never return!" For Melville the trouble was that he had pushed off, or rather, as he saw things, that he had been pushed off.

He was aware that it had happened to him young. In the novel that he wrote about the sensitive sailor boy Wellingborough Redburn, "confessions and reminiscences of the son-of-a-gentleman, in the merchant service," he had Redburn complain of the flinty-hearted world and the hard times that had blighted him and sent him off to sea hopeless: "Talk not of the bitterness of middle-age and after life; a boy can feel all that, and much more, when upon his young soul the mildew has fallen; and the fruit, which with others is only blasted after ripeness, with him is nipped in the first blossom and bud. And never again can such blights be made good; they strike in too deep, and leave such a scar that the air of Paradise might not erase it."

Melville went through life feeling dispossessed, disinherited, betrayed, bereft, and part of the reason was that his father had died bankrupt, leaving his widow and children to suffer in a cold world. So Melville could write with strong feelings about Typee as a safe, warm place where a father could provide for his family. In fact in Typee there were no fathers of a Western kind who betrayed their children by dying bankrupt, but instead "fathers" of another sort, tribal chiefs, natural aristocrats, born to rule, who made the valley safe for their "children." Beginning with Melville's first book, there was a sustained yearning for a situation in which a good, strong, noble man would look after his family, whether the family was a civilized American one or a savage tribe in a valley on a South Sea island. Or the crew of a ship—to a boy washed out to sea on the tides of life, a crew might be a family of friends, even brothers, and a good captain might be a good father.

Melville never did find a father to guarantee him a safe place in the islands, or a good captain at sea. And at home in the United States he never managed to make a safe place for himself out of domesticity. In the early years of his marriage he lived unusually close to his own family, he and a married brother and their four unmarried sisters sharing a house in New York with their widowed mother, a domineering woman. Less than two years after his wedding Melville was a father himself, and in the end he had four children, first two sons and then two daughters. Melville's wife was devoted to him after her fashion. But he could not make himself into an ideal husband and father. He was not a good provider, and he turned out not to be a good parent to his own children.

Although Melville gave every sign of wanting and needing a conventional middle-class safe place, there was something else in him, very powerful, paired with the idea of bourgeois respectability but ferociously hostile to it. He was sure that by fleeing from the Marquesas he had escaped a savage fate, but then by going home he condemned himself to the punishments of civilization. He was never a natural householder. Indeed his life as a family man turned out to offer him a safe place only in the sense that a prison is a safe place. Cannibalism might be hideous, but just as hideous to Melville was the civilized punishment of solitary confinement, "perpetual solitude in the very heart of our population." This jail Melville inhabited for the rest of his life. He never broke bodily out of prison, but his mind and soul were forever pacing the cell, rattling the bars. Melville wanted, as strongly as anyone who ever lived, serenity, surcease, a still center. But somehow, wherever he went looking he could never find what he wanted. And so he was condemned to be another of those eternal voyagers of the nineteenth century. He used his books, time after time, to set out to sea, forever making journeys into himself.

*   *   *

Melville the literary celebrity had published two spectacularly successful books about the South Seas in a period of not much more than a year. As a beginning author he had been ready to oblige his publishers by altering his work to fit their specifications. But having done this twice and been well rewarded for it, he refused to do it a third time. He was beginning to feel his powers as a writer, and even more as a thinker. Starting work on *Mardi*, the novel that was to follow *Omoo*, he talked about it as another South Seas narrative, "authentic," and then he crossed out this word and used instead a phrase about the book having the right stuff in it—he was angling for a bigger advance from his publisher. Soon, though, he was saying that he had changed direction and was writing a "romance" about Polynesia, and that a romance of his would be nothing like *Typee* or *Omoo*. Proceeding, he said, "in my narrative of *facts* I began to feel an incurible distaste for the same; & a longing to plume my pinions for a flight, & felt irked, cramped & fettered by plodding along with dull common places. . . ."

What had happened was that Melville had started to read seriously. Working up *Mardi*, he did what he had done before, and relied heavily on other writers for inspiration, but this time more in the way of ideas than facts. He borrowed Bougainville's voyage from a library. William Ellis turned up again. So did Charles Wilkes and his narrative of the United States exploring expedition, which Melville used for *Omoo* and then bought. But far more important were the deep thinkers Melville was trying himself out on, the classics of literature he was coming to know for the first time. He was a self-made intellectual. As he said, a whale ship was his Yale and Harvard. (His spelling was bad all his life.) Now everything he read by great authors seemed worth using. *Mardi* kept getting longer and longer and going more and more out of control. A chartless voyage, one of the characters in the book said, and that was so.

Mardi turned out to be a bizarre work. It had the Pacific Ocean in it, and high islands, and coral reefs, and brown-skinned natives, and it opened with a recognizable plot of sorts, but then it sailed right off the map of reality into hundreds of pages of tortured allegory and interminable philosophical discussion, much of it in dreadfully stilted dialogue, about the world and the way it worked, about the eternal dilemma of determinism versus free will, about what humans could believe in, about life and death and eternity. Melville was in deep intellectual water, but that was where he wanted to be. "Better," he wrote, "to sink in boundless depths, than float on vulgar shoals; and give me, ye gods, an utter wreck, if wreck I do."

Mardi was not quite an utter wreck, but it was a substantial one. Some critics saw genius in it, even if it was genius perversely or incomprehensibly deployed. Most people, reviewers and readers, found the enormous three-decker novel unwieldy, intractable, a hundred ninety-five chapters of bewilderment. It was clear within weeks of publication that *Mardi* was not going to sell well. Melville was deeply hurt by the bad notices. He talked about his book being "cut into" in one review, "burnt by the common hangman" in another. He tried to comfort himself with the thought that attacks of this sort were a matter of course in an author's life, essential to the building up of a permanent reputation. Perhaps the book would flower a hundred years later. In the meantime it could find asylum only on the library shelves of a friend—almost everywhere else it had been "driven forth like a wild, mystic Mormon into shelterless exile." His public wanted Mr. Typee back.

Yet even if it had been unwise to write *Mardi* when he could have been writing something to please the general public, Melville had done it—because he had to, so he said. "Some of us scribblers," he wrote to his publisher, "always have a certain something unmanageable in us, that bids us do this or that, and be done it must—hit or miss." The something unmanageable in Melville was his genius beginning to make itself felt. From the time of *Mardi* on, his life became more and more a matter of managing the unmanageable.

This put him in a difficult position. He was a married man, with a child now, a son, christened Malcolm, born not long after *Mardi* came out and did so badly. More than ever Melville had to be a good family man, a father, a provider. For his part, what he wanted to do was to stay totally immersed in great thoughts. Profundity was the thing. "I love all men who *dive*," he wrote. "Any fish can swim near the surface, but it takes a great whale to go down stairs five miles or more; & if he don't attain the bottom, why, all the lead in Galena can't fashion the plumet that will." And he talked of "the whole corps of thought-divers, that have been diving & coming up again with bloodshot eyes since the world began." But for the moment he had to have money, and all his diving in deep water was not bringing up treasure.

In a matter of months he wrote two new books: *Redburn*, based on his first voyage across the Atlantic on a merchantman, and *White-Jacket*, based on his tour of duty aboard the U.S.S. *United States* between Hawaii and Boston. He lumped the two together as jobs of work, no more and no less. They were meant to be money-makers, pure and simple. One was perhaps tolerably entertaining, though some might think it dull; the other was sure to be attacked because it attacked the Navy. With luck both would pay their way. "But," he wrote to his father-in-law, to whom he had dedicated his first book, and who all his life kept a benevolent eye on Melville's finances, "no reputation that is gratifying to me can possibly be achieved by either of these books. They are two *jobs*, which I have done for money—being forced to it, as other men are to sawing wood." His only desire for their success, so-called, "springs from my pocket, & not from my heart." And he added frankly (and to a father-in-law, however well disposed, this must have sounded ominous): "So far as I am individually concerned, & independent of my pocket, it is my earnest desire to write those sorts of books which are said to 'fail.' "

With his first two books, *Typee* and *Omoo*, Melville had succeeded in making money and a reputation. Now he was turning against them too, for the kind of success they represented. Offering *Mardi* to a publisher, he said: "Unless you should deem it *very* desirable do not put me down on the title page as 'the author of *Typee* & *Omoo*.' I wish to separate *Mardi* as much as possible from those books." And he took to calling "those books" names—"Peedee" and "Hullabaloo" (and, possibly because failure really grated him as much as cheap success, he gave *Mardi* a slighting name too: "Pog-dog").

He had a certain fame, and to begin with it had not been at all unwelcome. But with the weighty failure of his first effort at true seriousness and the wood sawing he had to do after that, he found himself caring much less about mere celebrity, and in time this became a fixed position with him. In his new seriousness he wanted to distinguish between real literary originality and mere circumstantial originality, and soon he would be writing of "inferior instances of an immediate literary success" among very young writers: "it will be almost invariably observable, that for that instant success they were chiefly indebted to some rich and peculiar experience in life, embodied in a book, which because, for that cause, containing original matter, the author himself, forsooth, is to be considered original." Melville's "originality" in this low sense lay in the fact that he was the only writer of great creative talent who had actually experienced the fantasy world of the South Seas that he put on paper. He had been ashore on a gorgeous tropical island. He had lived with tattooed warriors and had given his narrator a glimpse of their trophies, severed heads and dismembered bodies. He—or Tommo—had bathed with naked brown females. He had become famous for writing about it all. And this, as he was coming to see things, was to be his punishment.

On his way across the Atlantic in 1849 to arrange for the publication of *White-Jacket* in London, Melville had a little comic experience with an edge to it. He went back to his sailor ways, climbing the masthead for before-breakfast "gymnastics." This made him noticeable, and he remarked in the journal he kept on the voyage that he had seen a lady passenger with a copy of *Omoo*, and that "now & then she would look up at me, as if comparing notes."

It was ten years since Melville had been in England, "*then* a sailor, *now* H.M. author"—but only of Peedee, Hullabaloo and Pog-dog, and the piece of sawed wood he had with him. Already he was past all that, and it would not be long before he was writing about fame as the most transparent of vanities: "All Fame is patronage. Let me be infamous: there is no patronage in *that*. What 'reputation' H.M. has is horrible. Think of it! To go down to posterity is bad enough, any way; but to go down as a 'man who lived among the cannibals!' "

* * *

Melville made some quick money out of *Redburn* and *White-Jacket*, and on the strength of this and a loan from his father-in-law, in 1850 Herman and Elizabeth were able to leave the crowded, congested family house in New York and buy a property of one hundred sixty acres, mostly woodland, at Pittsfield, Massachusetts, in the Berkshires. Here Melville wrote *Moby-Dick*.

Melville was never a totally serious farmer and certainly not a skilled one—meditative small-scale gardening was more his agricultural style. More than once he wrote a letter with bruised or blistered hands, and said that because of it he could not sentimentalize his surroundings. But he took pleasure in the workaday routine of the farm. As a boy he had enjoyed laboring on a relative's farm at Pittsfield, and now he had his own property and was working to make it livable for his family. His wife became pregnant for the second time. Melville liked to get up and go to the barn, say good morning to his horse and give him his breakfast, then visit the cow, slice up a pumpkin or two and stand watching her eat it. There was wood to cut, apples to be pressed into cider, the harvest to bring in. The seasons turned. And the farm seemed to be turning into a safe place.

Melville himself was pregnant, with a new book, his sixth in seven years.

His royalties were supposed to guarantee his safe place, but of course there was no guarantee that a book would sell. Before the selling came the writing, and Melville himself had announced that he preferred to write the kind of book that "failed."

At least he was approaching the task of writing confidently. He was doing yet another sea story. The subject was the only part of his life as a sailor that he had not so far turned into a story he could sell: his experiences as a whalerman. By the summer of 1850 Melville was offering a publisher first chance at the new work, to be called *The Whale.* He described it as a "romance of adventure, founded upon certain wild legends in the Southern Sperm Whale Fisheries, and illustrated by the author's own personal experience, of two years & more, as a harpooneer." (This was stretching things for the sake of "authenticity"—if Melville was ever a harpooner, which is not likely, it could only have been for a few months on his third whaler, *Charles and Henry,* between Tahiti and Hawaii.) The manuscript would be ready by fall, he said.

* * *

Melville was a part-time farmer who was a full-time author, and his part of rural Massachusetts was literary country. It was in the Berkshires that Melville met Nathaniel Hawthorne, and no single event of his life was more momentous.

Hawthorne and his wife Sophia had come to live not far away from the Melville farm, and Hawthorne got to know Melville on a summer outing to Monument Mountain, where they did some high-spirited climbing and exploring together with some other New England and New York literary lights. One of the party later recalled Melville on the mountain climbing onto a projecting rock that looked like a bowsprit, where he "pulled and hauled imaginary ropes for our delectation." They all came down to drink champagne and eat a big meal, three hours from turkey and roast beef to ice cream.

When *Typee* was published, Hawthorne, without knowing anything about Melville, read the book, liked it, and wrote a favorable unsigned review of it. Now his wife was pleased to find that "Mr. Typee is interesting in his aspect—quite—I see Fayaway in his face." Decades later, the Hawthornes' son Julian remembered his mother telling of a night when Melville talked about "a fight which he had seen on an island in the Pacific, between some savages, and of the prodigies of valor one of them performed with a heavy club. The narrative was extremely graphic; and when Melville had gone, and Mr. and Mrs. Hawthorne were talking over his visit, the latter said, 'Where is that club with which Mr. Melville was laying about him so?' Mr. Hawthorne thought he must have taken it with him; Mrs. Hawthorne thought he had put it in the corner; but it was not to be found. The next time Melville came, they asked him about it; whereupon it appeared that the club was still in the Pacific island, if it were anywhere." Mr. Typee was evidently still a yarn spinner.

Having the author for a neighbor now, Sophia Hawthorne read *Typee* again and found it a *"true history,* yet how poetically told—the divine beauty of the scene, the lovely faces & forms—the peace & good will—& all this golden splendor & enchantment glowing before the dark refrain constantly brought as a background—the fear of being killed & eaten—the cannibalism in the olive tinted Apollos around him—the unfathomable mystery of their treatment of him." Melville interested her more and more, and she went to some trouble to capture his particular quality on paper. "He has very keen perceptive power; but what astonishes me is, that his eyes are not large and deep. He seems to see everything very accurately; and how he can do so with his small eyes, I cannot tell. They are not keen eyes, either, but quite undistinguished in any way. His nose is straight and rather handsome, his mouth expressive of sensibility and emotion. He is tall and erect, with an air free, brave, and manly. When conversing, he is full of gesture and force, and loses himself in his subject. There is no grace or polish. Once in a while, his animation gives place to a singularly quiet expression, out of those eyes to which I have objected; an indrawn, dim look, but which at the same time makes you feel that he is at that instant taking deepest note of what is before him. It is a strange, lazy glance, but with a power in it quite unique. It does not seem to penetrate through you, but to take you into himself." All in all, Mrs. Hawthorne was not quite sure that she did not think Melville "a very great man."

Admiration, in fact, was mutual. Melville took time to write an essay on a book of Hawthorne's in which he came close to calling Hawthorne the American Shakespeare. Hawthorne and his wife were delighted. The Shakespeare comparison aside, it was a good, perceptive appreciation of Hawthorne's special qualities, a measure of needed intellectual and moral support. The essay was signed with a pseudonym, and the Hawthornes were doubly pleased to discover in due course that the intelligent and sensitive unknown admirer of Nathaniel Hawthorne was their new Pittsfield friend Melville.

Melville, on his side, was delighted to have, essentially for the first time in his life, someone to talk to as eloquently and unreservedly as he wanted, needed, hungered to, about the great questions of life and literature. He himself, so he told Sophia Hawthorne, was "naturally a silent man," and was "complained of a great deal on this account; but . . . he found himself talking to Mr. Hawthorne to a great extent. He said Mr. Hawthorne's great but hospitable silence drew him out—that it was astonishing how *sociable* his silence was." Hawthorne was the senior, in accomplishment as in years; he was in his mid-forties, Melville in his early thirties. They were men of differing personal style, at different stages of life, yet they chimed together. The day Melville turned thirty-two he rode his horse over to see Hawthorne, and the two men stayed up most of the night smoking cigars in (as Hawthorne put it) the "sacred precincts" of the sitting room, and "had a talk about time and eternity, things of this world and of the next, and books, and publishers, and all possible and impossible matters."

Before he met Hawthorne, Melville had been at work for some months on his new book. Now he was about to be "unmanageable" again. He could feel it in himself, and the Hawthornes could hear it in his nonstop talking about cosmic matters. Melville's genius was surfacing out of the deep waters of his self, looking for a means of expression. Genius was being born in Melville, then. And in so many words he named Hawthorne the father.

What he said about it was extraordinary. Melville always had a powerful need for closeness with other men, and it was in his nature to want to give to a meeting of minds and hearts between males a warm, even extravagant physical expression—on paper, at least. When, in the New England summer of 1850, he read Hawthorne seriously for the first time—the book was *Mosses from an Old Manse*—and then wrote about the effect it had on him, he used the language of sexual ravishment. "A man of a deep and noble nature has seized me in this seclusion. . . . Stretched on that new mown clover, the hill-side breeze blowing over me through the wide barn door, and soothed by the hum of bees in the meadows around, how magically stole over me this Mossy Man! . . . Hawthorne has dropped germinous seeds into my soul. He expands and deepens down, the more I contemplate him; and further, and further, shoots his strong New-England roots into the hot soil of my . . . soul." Melville is recounting here, in almost so many words, a surprise first encounter with an ideal lover long awaited, unexpectedly revealed and instantly known, and a willing acceptance—indeed an urgent seeking—of surrender in seduction, a profoundly felt moment of conception, and joyful impregnation.

Melville was being born again in his mind, and his book about the whale was reborn, rethought, reworked. The reshaping took a year. What finally went to the publisher was *Moby-Dick*.

All through the fall of 1850 Melville wrote and rewrote, and on to the end of the year and into 1851. Outside the Massachusetts winter had descended, and he took it into himself, incorporating it, involving it in his work. "I have a sort of sea-feeling here in the country, now that the ground is all covered with snow. I look out of my window in the morning when I rise as I would out of a port-hole of a ship in the Atlantic. My room seems a ship's cabin; & at nights when I wake up & hear the wind shrieking, I almost fancy there is too much sail on the house, & I had better go on the roof & rig in the chimney." He immersed himself in his book. "My own breakfast over"—after the feeding of the animals—"I go to my workroom & light my fire—then spread my M.S.S. on the table—take one business squint at it, & fall to with a will." He worked nonstop till mid-afternoon, when there would come "a preconcerted knock at my door, which (by request) continues till I rise & go to the door, which serves to wean me effectively from my writing, however interested I may be." He did not write in the evening, and could not, with those uncertain eyes of his, even do any serious reading by lamplight, "only now & then skimming over some large-printed book." But his own book would not leave him, and he passed the dark hours in his room "in a sort of mesmeric state. . . ."

His mind was teeming. "Can you send me," he asked a literary friend, hyperbolically, "about fifty fast-writing youths, with an easy style & not averse to polishing their labors? If you can, I wish you would, because since I have been here I have planned about that number of future works & cant find enough time to think about them separately."

In the restless sea of Melville's imagination great submarine currents stirred and swirled, bringing material to the surface and releasing it to sink down again and then be borne up again to consciousness transformed. Outside his house, the New England countryside under snow had become Melville's Atlantic. Inside in his workroom, as the fire burned through the day and on into the mesmeric night, he merged himself with the Pacific, "this mysterious, divine Pacific" that "zones the whole world's bulk about; makes all coasts one bay to it; seems the tide-beating heart of earth."

Meditation and water, he wrote in his opening pages, are wedded forever. And now Melville, the great incorporator, was admitting the Pacific to himself as he had done Hawthorne. His words made the ocean and his mind one: "this sea, whose gently awful stirrings seem to speak of some hidden soul beneath. . . . And meet it is, that over these sea-pastures, wide-rolling watery prairies and Potters' Fields of all four continents, the waves should rise and fall, and ebb and flow unceasingly; for here, millions of mixed shades and shadows, drowned dreams, somnambulisms, reveries; all that we call lives and souls, lie dreaming, dreaming, still; tossing like slumberers in their beds; the ever-rolling waves but made so by their restlessness." And through the waters of Melville's meditations cruised the great whale Moby-Dick, breaching and sounding and breaching again.

* * *

In the early part of 1851 Melville's father-in-law brought him a copy of Owen Chase's narrative of the sinking of the *Essex* by a whale. Melville made notes in the little book, reminding himself of his own whaling cruise to the South Seas ten years before, recalling talk in the forecastle about the *Essex*, his meeting at sea with Chase's son, and the whaling captain he believed to be Chase himself. The story of the *Essex* stayed with him, and long after *Moby-Dick* was written he kept adding to his notes.

He had another famous sperm whale to think about as well. This one was known among whale hunters as Mocha Dick. The monster had been heard of as early as 1810, and he reappeared for decades more, reported in all the oceans of the world, especially the Pacific, sighted and chased, harpooned any number of times, but always escaping, apparently invulnerable—and, more than that, as murderous as the whalers. They wanted to kill him; he wanted to kill them. He would pulverize whaleboats, striking them head-on or coming up underneath them and overturning them, opening his huge jaws and chewing them and their crews to bits, or simply beating them out of existence with his giant tail. And he would attack not just whaleboats, but ships. In his time he charged and sank a lumber ship and two merchantmen, and he stove in three whaling vessels. He was as big as any sperm whale that ever existed. And he was instantly recognizable because he was an albino, a sport of nature, a white whale.

Out of the whale that sank the *Essex*, and the incrustation of sailor superstition that made up the legend of Mocha Dick, and every other whale story he heard at sea, Melville created Moby-Dick, a sperm whale huge in size, with a body streaked and spotted and marbled white, "a peculiar snow-white wrinkled forehead, and a high, pyramidical white hump," and a crooked lower jaw, a crunching instrument of destruction. Moby-Dick was unkillable; and at the heart of the terror he inspired lay an "unexampled, intelligent malignity." He was a frightful force of nature. He made nonsense out of any idea that nature was benevolent, that man mattered and should prevail.

To stand against this "grand, hooded phantom, like a snow hill in the air," Melville created Ahab, captain of the Nantucket whaling ship

Pequod. Ahab had lost a leg to Moby-Dick, reaped away by that awful jaw. Now he walked on an ivory leg made from the jawbone of another sperm whale, and he lived for only one thing—the death of Moby-Dick. Ahab was not simply someone who had suffered bodily disability and recovered. He was aging, gray-haired, still solid in build, durable as a statue. But there was an unearthly quality about his physical presence. He looked like "a man cut away from the stake, when the fire has over-runingly wasted all the limbs without consuming them, or taking away one particle from their compacted aged robustness." The visible mark of devastation was on him. No one knew whether it was a birthmark or the "scar left by some desperate wound," but it was some dreadful lightning burn of body and spirit, a "slender rod-like mark, lividly whitish," threading its way "out from among his grey hairs, and continuing right down one side of his tawny scorched face and neck, till it disappeared in his clothing"—where, according to one old sailor, it snaked the length of Ahab's frame, marking his whole body from crown to sole.

Melville is supposed to have got the idea for the lightning blast on Ahab's body from the trunk of an elm tree at Pittsfield, struck and laid open in an electrical storm. But there was another place from which he could have taken a mark to set on Ahab's face. Melville had bought in 1847 the huge six-volume *Narrative of the United States Exploring Expedition.* He used it when he was writing *Mardi,* and again for *Moby-Dick.* The frontispiece was a portrait of Charles Wilkes, and the print made him look as if he was marked from hairline to collar.

In his own way Wilkes was an Ahab, an overmastering, driven man who would drive others to the edge of exhaustion and destruction, chasing huge white apparitions on the rim of the unknown. At enormous risk, Wilkes committed himself and his expedition to go south beyond the safe latitudes of the Pacific and explore Antarctica. This was his snow hill. He sailed his ships and his men to the edge of disaster, and when the expedition's doctors petitioned him to turn back he went on, pursuing the snowy white unknown. There was something of Ahab's madness in Wilkes, grandeur and the fatal flaw of monomania. Melville was responsive to this sort of unmanageability. "All men tragically great," he wrote, "are made so through a certain morbidness. Be sure of this, O young Ambition, all mortal greatness is but disease."

There was a cluster of associations to interest Melville in Wilkes. A man who lived in the same small upstate New York town as the young Melville sailed with Wilkes. So did a relative of Richard Henry Dana; Melville met this man in Dana's company. And so did a relative of Melville himself,

Henry Gansevoort (who wound up being put ashore with venereal disease at Callao, on the Pacific coast of South America). One of the earliest strong advocates of a national exploring expedition was Jeremiah N. Reynolds; and in the year Melville first went to sea, Reynolds published a long account of Mocha Dick. And Melville's indispensable friend Hawthorne had once been an applicant for the post of historian to the exploring expedition.

To top everything off, wherever Melville had been in the Pacific, Wilkes had gone, and beyond. The *Narrative*, with all its navigational and scientific and ethnographic data and its fine illustrations, was like a twenty-five-hundred-page album of Melville's own Pacific experiences, and more, offering any number of descriptions to draw upon and ideas to ponder.

For one thing, Wilkes had been instructed to gather oceanographic information about the Pacific in the interests of the American whaling industry. The scientists of the expedition developed the idea that ocean currents carried the food of whales, and that whales migrated along the currents. Melville took hold of this notion and intensified it by having Ahab pore every night in his cabin over charts and logbooks, calculating—with all the concentrated rigor of single-minded madness—where in all the oceans of the world, among all the whales of the world, he might come to confront the one sperm whale he wanted, Moby-Dick.

Aside from parts of Ahab, Wilkes's *Narrative* gave Melville the outlines of another notable character in *Moby-Dick*, the Polynesian harpooner Queequeg. There was a picture of a New Zealand chief that would have served as a physical model for Queequeg even if Melville had never seen a Polynesian in the flesh. Queequeg was the savage who carried around a New Zealand head for sale; and Wilkes's men had been offered such a head by a steward on a missionary ship during their stay in New Zealand. Queequeg's tattoos came from the descriptions of Wilkes and the drawings of his expedition's artists, reworked in Melville's words. As Melville used the tattoos, they became a way of trying to resolve the tension between savagery and civilization that impelled him years before to shrink back from the tattooer of Typee and ultimately to flee from the valley itself. Queequeg began by terrifying the narrator of *Moby-Dick* just by his physical presence. Later, though, the two got on very well together, better and better all the time, in one of those male "marriages" that Melville returned to again and again; until ultimately the white man began to think of the majestic savage as offering him some sort of healing and self-completion, as if the two men were parts of the same human whole, the one part essential to the other. A tattooed skin did not necessarily mean an evil soul. Indeed, Queequeg came to stand for human dignity and honest impulse, and his tattoos, "hieroglyphic marks" made by a "departed prophet and seer of his island," amounted to a "complete theory of the heavens and the earth, and a mystical treatise on the art of attaining truth. . . ."

To find his book's narrator Melville looked, as always, into himself. This time he started his story with the words: "Call me Ishmael." Ishmael was the wanderer who turned up everywhere in Melville's work, the outcast, the man with a grievance, the man whose superior powers were not recognized and rewarded, the déclassé, the disinherited. Ishmael had nothing to keep him ashore. In fact the longer he lived in cities the less point he saw in living. He would find himself with little or no money in his purse, nothing to interest him, and a "damp, drizzly November" in his soul, depression that bordered on the suicidal. What rescued him from himself was the sea. It was his substitute for pistol and ball. Ishmael used to ship out as a common sailor, and he suffered sharp status pains in the forecastle. These he overcame by reflecting that if he was at home nowhere, he was least of all at home on the land; and so to that extent the sea was better. He was able to find faith in living, sustenance, and family—if at all—only as part of a ship's crew bound together in obedience to a captain for the time of a single voyage. Ishmael was the man for whom life was a ship on its voyage out, with nothing safe or certain behind or ahead.

For men like himself Ishmael had a word: "isolato." By this he meant a human being living in a condition of "not acknowledging the common continent of men, but each *Isolato* living on a separate continent of his own," the ultimate in loneliness. Ishmael needed Queequeg so as to be reassured of his own humanity. But in his alienation Ishmael felt as well a sort of harmonic vibration with Ahab. Both were orphans, foundling figures. The world was set against them from birth. Like Ahab, Ishmael was blasted by life; he talked about his own splintered heart and maddened hand set against a wolfish world. With nothing to gain or lose ashore, Ishmael was ready to chance anything at sea. "I am tormented," he said, "with an everlasting itch for things remote. I love to sail forbidden seas, and land on barbarous coasts." And in his own way Ishmael lusted after the whale, "the wild and distant seas where he rolled his island bulk; the undeliverable, nameless perils of the whale."

Only the experience of the sea released a power and depth of thought capable of contending with the idea of the whale. In the end, to go to sea, to contend with the whale and the idea of the whale, was to come head-on with the self and with the freedom of the self. And with death, perhaps self-destructive death. And to find that these two versions of the absolute, freedom and death, mingled and became one. "Glimpses do ye seem to see," Melville asked, "of that mortally intolerable truth; that all deep, earnest thinking is but the intrepid effort of the soul to keep the open independence of her sea; while the wildest winds of heaven and earth conspire to cast her up on the treacherous, slavish shore? But as in landlessness alone resides the highest truth, shoreless, indefinite as God—so, better is it to perish in that howling infinite, than to be ingloriously dashed upon the lee, even if that were safety!"

And so Melville sends Ishmael to sea, as one of a crew drawn from every odd part of the earth, uprooted, drifting men, mostly islanders, "isolatoes" like himself. With a monumental savage for his only friend and a cosmic madman for a captain, he goes in search of the great white whale.

Ahab swings the *Pequod* out of the Atlantic around the Cape of Good Hope and steers northeast across the Indian Ocean. Whales are sighted and pursued, and the savage life of chase, harpooning, flurry and blood spout, and devastating dismemberment of the huge carcasses goes on, with sharks snapping at whale flesh alongside the ship and whalermen slicing their way through stinking blubber aboard. The barrels fill, the sea miles go by, and the *Pequod* raises the strait of Sunda, Sumatra on one side, Java on the other, a pirate-infested gateway to the fabulously wealthy empires of island Asia—spices, silks, jewels, gold, ivory, everything in that eternal Western warehouse of fantasy about Oriental riches. Through the straits with the *Pequod* goes a grand armada of whales. They are following the great current of ocean life, and the *Pequod* sails with them into the Java Sea. From there Ahab will cruise northward and "sweep inshore by the Philippine Islands, and gain the far coast of Japan, in time for the great whaling season there . . . previous to descending upon the Line in the Pacific." His methodically mad charts have told him he will bring Moby-Dick to bay in the same equatorial latitudes where the *Essex* was sunk.

And that is where the final encounter takes place. Moby-Dick is sighted. For three days he and Ahab do battle, and on the third day the maddened whale rams the whale ship. From his boat Ahab harpoons Moby-Dick. The white whale lurches gigantically away, the harpoon line flicks and loops and catches Ahab around the neck and snaps him out of the boat in an instant, gone forever. The sinking *Pequod* creates a vortex, a whirlpool of death. The crew is sucked down with the ship, and "concentric circles seized the lone boat itself, and all its crew, and each floating oar, and every lance-pole, and spinning, animate and inanimate, all round and round . . . carried the smallest chip . . . out of sight." It is all over, and "now small fowls flew screaming over the yet yawning gulf; a sullen white surf beat against its steep sides; then all collapsed, and the great shroud of the sea rolled on as it rolled five thousand years ago."

Ishmael survives. Flung out of Ahab's boat by the last smashing blow of the whale, he is caught in the vortex and drawn down to its black center, until out of the dark oceanic end of the world there swims his salvation, a sealed but empty coffin, made during the voyage for his friend Queequeg the harpooner, decorated with carvings of his savage tattoos, bearing the secrets of the universe. For a day and a night Ishmael clings to his coffin-lifebuoy, floating on a "soft and dirge-like main," until on the second day "a sail drew near, nearer, and picked me up at last."

* * *

Melville dedicated *Moby-Dick* to Nathaniel Hawthorne. He depended very much on Hawthorne's understanding and approval. Melville felt eternally trapped by his society, constricted by the pressures it brought to bear on him. He had to resist. That is what he meant when he talked about the "unmanageability" in him. What attracted him so much to Hawthorne was that he detected in him the same powerful resistance: "NO! in thunder." For Melville the gap between those who said yes and those who said no was absolute: "For all men who say *yes*, lie; and all men who say *no*,—why, they are in the happy condition of judicious, unincumbered travellers in Europe; they cross the frontiers into Eternity with nothing but a carpet-bag,—that is to say, the Ego. Whereas those *yes*-gentry, they travel with heaps of baggage, and damn them! they will never get through the Custom House." So when *Moby-Dick* was published and Hawthorne sent a letter praising it, Melville wrote back immediately, celebrating the intimate communion he felt with Hawthorne, blood and body and soul: "Your heart beat in my ribs and mine in yours, and both in God's. . . ."

Melville went on to talk about *Moby-Dick* as if the book was celebrating a kind of Black Mass. He said there was a secret motto to the novel, and he revealed part of it to Hawthorne: "Ego non baptiso te in nomine—" and then he broke off, saying: "but make out the rest yourself." The rest was not hard to make out. Captain Ahab, dousing his harpoon in pagan blood, had howled an evil chant: "Ego non baptizo te in nomine patris, sed in nomine diaboli!"—I baptize you not in the name of the father, but in the name of the devil. "I have written a wicked book," said Melville, "and feel spotless as the lamb."

What Hawthorne had understood was that *Moby-Dick*, a novel about a white whale, was essentially a black book, a subversion of all that was comfortable, conventional, practical, and reassuring in mid-nineteenth-century American notions of the way the world worked, and of the situation of man in the universe. At the time Melville wrote *Typee* he was a young man just back from the South Seas, an amateur Rousseauist of a predictable kind, arguing along well-understood lines that savagery, the natural state, was better for man than civilization. (He kept up an interest in Rousseau; before he began writing *Moby-Dick* he bought and read the *Confessions*.) But the view of nature that Melville wrote about in his book on the whale was more savage by far. He had left the warm South Seas life far behind. The universe was not benevolent. Nature might crunch man up in mighty jaws or have him beaten into extinction with the sweep of a gigantic tail, and the universe would not even notice. There might not even be a God; there might not even be a devil.

This was an appalling vision of life. It had always been comforting to Westerners generally, and Americans in particular, to think of new lands (like the American continent) or new seas with islands (like the Pacific) as Edens, or at least as gardens that could be cultivated. In the extreme Puritan view, which used reward for effort as an organizing principle of life, new places might be wildernesses to be tamed. If Edens turned out not to exist, and if the wilderness was stubborn, then at least improvements in the human condition could be accomplished by purposeful work directed toward good ends. This was progress toward another kind of paradise.

In Melville's day, among Americans, this turned out more and more to involve setting men and machines to work on frontiers, on the land and on the sea. Canal systems and railroad networks were extended. Mine shafts were sunk into the earth to bring up metals to make more machines with. Scientific exploring expeditions charted the migrations of whales so that other ships carrying the newest technology of harpoons and lances and cutting spades and save-alls and try-pots could follow, to mine the seas for profit. So Captain Ahab and his crew could be seen as frontiersmen, embarking together on a business venture, for profit.

Of course, men might go to sea on business. But they might also go to sea out of a desperate unwillingness or plain inability to live according to the established rules of life ashore. A crew of misfits could be whipped into line and made to behave as though they were still in civilization. Shipboard routine, shipboard law would keep a vessel functioning, no matter what craziness was in a sailor's mind, and mutiny was a crime for which the civilized punishment was death. But on the frontier with all its freedom, who would control the captain? The same urge to dominate that produced captains of industry ashore in civilization might go out of control out of sight of civilization. It might even be that the workings of society produced madmen of a particular sort and then gave them the chance to become captains on the frontiers. So a captain like Ahab, with forty years of whaling behind him, could be a madman waiting his chance to sail a whale ship across the ocean, across the frontiers of sanity, into a world where nothing existed but his own monomania.

Ishmael saw all this. "Here, then, was this grey-headed, ungodly old man, chasing with curses a Job's whale round the world, at the head of a crew, too, chiefly made up of mongrel renegades, and castaways, and cannibals." Ahab could make the crew of the *Pequod* do anything he wanted. Some rousing words and the chance of a gold doubloon, and they would swear to hunt the white whale. And the ship's mates, men limited by ordinary good sense, good temper, or simple mediocrity, would never rise against their commander. "Such a crew, so officered, seemed specially picked and packed by some infernal fatality to help him to his monomaniac revenge."

Ahab would never be deflected. "Swerve me? Ye cannot swerve me," he says in soliloquy. "The path to my fixed purpose is laid with iron rails, whereon my soul is grooved to run. . . . Naught's an obstacle, naught's an angle to the iron way!" Ahab was comparing himself to a railroad engine. This was the new marvel of the United States, the straight-ahead, coal-consuming, smoke-belching, all-powerful continent tamer and frontier opener, whose surveyed tracks were like the maps of ocean currents, laid down to tap and mine riches. The locomotive was the black, huge, overpowering, panting, steam-spouting land whale of the prairie-oceans of America, and in Melville's lifetime it would do in fact what Melville wrote about the battering-ram head of the sperm whale doing in metaphor; it would smash the distance between coasts, reduce transcontinental travel to a mere isthmus of time, and bring about the mixing of the economic waters of the Atlantic and the Pacific. When Ahab exulted in his crazy dominance over his crew, he used the language of machine technology. Ahab could run mad along lines laid down for him by his society. He was a machine, a train, and the train was iron, and the iron flew as straight as a harpoon.

Ahab's harpooners were savages, Queequeg, Tashtego, and Daggoo, a tattooed brown man, a red man, and a black man. They were colonial people under the imperialism of a white captain, crewmen on a whaler very like the world, on a journey very like life in the nineteenth century, captained and officered by white men, doing the world's dirty work on a filthy frontier. They existed for the purposes of the voyage only as units of work, fillers of oil barrels, good property to the shipowner. They were seagoing versions of the brown-skinned converts of South Seas missionaries, who worked at diving for pearls or who brought bamboo tubes of pressed-out coconut oil to church as a contribution. Whaling was like Christianity; it turned the useless savage into something useful.

But at the same time, the hunting and catching of the whale transformed the white man, made him into a savage, and at last a savage who was mad. The crewmen of the *Pequod* lived in the vile stench of boiling blubber, doused themselves in blood, hacked their way through the monstrous carcasses and cathedral-tall skeletons of whales till they were grubbing with their hands "amongst the unspeakable foundations, ribs, and very pelvis of the world." And at last a sailor called the "mincer," who sliced the blubber for the try-pots—"bible leaves," the thin slices were called—would attack the giant penis of the whale, man-tall and black, skin it, stretch the skin to dry, and cut armholes in it, a barbaric cassock to wear as he worked, "invested in the full canonicals of his calling."

This was the true Western religion: death to the whale. Melville wondered about it. On the American continent there was a recognized difference between mining and gardening. Mining meant tearing up and disemboweling a new land and moving on, as against farming land in the expectation of a permanent human relationship with the earth. The frontier was classically the place where natural resources were ravished. The white man imposed his domination by killing and destroying. It was happening on the prairies, to red men along with animals, and the question was whether in the Pacific the whale would go the way of the islander.

The omens of apocalypse were there. At the wheel of the *Pequod* one night, Ishmael had a vision in which the workings of the forward-looking, government-encouraged American whaling industry turned savage before his eyes, and, having turned savage, turned mad. The try-works furnaces burned like funeral pyres. Flames licked up at the masts. The pagan harpooners fed the blubber fires and the pots with long pronged poles like so many devils, and the resting crewmen, smoke- and sweat-stained, lounged and swapped stories and looked into the red heat of the fires until their eyes scorched in their heads. "As they narrated to each other their unholy adventures, their tales of terror told in words of mirth; as their uncivilized laughter forked upwards out of them, like the flames from the furnace; as to and fro, in their front, the harpooneers wildly gesticulated with their huge pronged forks and dippers; as the wind howled on, and the sea leaped, and the ship groaned and dived, and yet steadfastly shot her red hell further and further into the blackness of the sea and the night, and scornfully champed the white bone in her mouth, and viciously spat round her on all sides; then the rushing Pequod, freighted with savages, and laden with fire, and burning a corpse, and plunging into the blackness of darkness, seemed the material counterpart of her monomaniac commander's soul."

A good captain was one thing, a father giving shape and purpose to the voyage of life. A strong captain could stand as well for the greatness and sweep of the individual, negotiating with the universe, commanding destiny. A mad captain with an imperial ego could incorporate the world, become the world, consume the world, and bring everything down to destruction.

* * *

Moby-Dick was published in New York in November, 1851. In the same month the whaler *Ann Alexander*, cruising the offshore grounds in the equatorial Pacific—where thirty years earlier the *Essex* had been destroyed—sighted, pursued, and got a harpoon into a whale, whereupon the whale turned and attacked and smashed and sank two boats and then hurled itself directly at the ship and rammed it, holing it so badly that it sank within minutes. The story reached the New York papers, and one of Melville's friends sent him the news. "Ye Gods!" Melville wrote back. "What a Commentator is this Ann Alexander whale. What he has to say is short & pithy & very much to the point." The whole thing, Melville said, "had a sort of stunning effect on me. For some days past being engaged in the woods with axe, wedge, & beetle, the Whale had almost completely slipped me for the time (& I was the merrier for it) when Crash! comes Moby Dick himself . . . & reminds me of what I have been about for part of the last year or two. It is really & truly a surprising coincidence—to say the least." And he went on, giving his created whale a historical reality of its own: "I make no doubt it IS Moby Dick himself, for there is no account of his capture after the sad fate of the Pequod about fourteen years ago." And he added: "I wonder if my evil art has raised this monster."

* * *

For Melville the strain of being an author was enormous. He wrote amazingly quickly, but never easily, in fact painfully and at great risk to himself, so he felt. Writing a novel, he said, was like performing a deep and delicate brain operation: "taking a book off the brain, is akin to the ticklish & dangerous business of taking an old painting off a panel—you have to scrape off the whole brain in order to get at it with due safety."

And after all that, "the painting may not be worth the trouble." He knew what it took to make a novel a success, but underlying this there was his "earnest desire" to write the kind of books that were said to "fail." Scraping away at his art, and with his brain being scraped away at the same time, he came to the conclusion that if he was to stay alive by his writing, he would have to stay in the safe top layers of the brain, restrain himself from going deep down to where the human truth lay hidden. His times would not allow true candor. "What a madness & anguish it is, that an author can never—under no conceivable circumstances—be at all frank with his readers." Try, he said, to get a living by the truth, "and go to the Soup Societies." If he were to write the Gospels in his own century, he would die in the gutter. Now, with six books finished in seven years, he was at an impasse—damned by dollars. "What I feel most moved to write, that is banned,—it will not pay. Yet, altogether, write the *other* way I cannot." And the upshot was that "the product is a final hash, and all my books are botches."

This was Melville at the end of an eighteen-month period in which he had conceived, reconceived, written, and rewritten *Moby-Dick*. It had been the most valuable time in his life as an author. Coming to know Nathaniel Hawthorne, Melville had been opened up to the depths in himself, had identified what it was he had been struggling to say, and had gone as far as he dared toward saying it. He had made a profound meditation on his life at sea in the Pacific, and out of this had come a novel as fine as anything ever written by an American. And yet after it was all over, he did not know if his book was worth anything as art—or if it would sell a single copy.

To Hawthorne he wrote about what *Moby-Dick* had cost him in personal resources, what the book meant to him as a piece of his life. "My development has been all within a few years past. . . . Until I was twenty-five, I had no development at all. From my twenty-fifth year I date my life." (He was talking about his birth as an author.) "Three weeks have scarcely passed, at any time between then and now, that I have not unfolded within myself." And, of course, the decisive unfolding had occurred when he came in contact with the fertilizing mind and heart of Hawthorne. Out of that came *Moby-Dick*. "But," Melville went on, "I feel that I am now come to the inmost leaf of the bulb, and that shortly the flower must fall to the mould." Melville was in his early thirties. He was saying that his creative power, in its infancy when he was twenty-five, was already close to being exhausted.

He had impregnated his wife again while he was rewriting *Moby-Dick*.

He owed his publishers, the Harpers, so much money that they would not give him an advance. To get himself and his family through the months before publication he borrowed $2,050. Then *Moby-Dick* got mixed reviews, and within weeks it was obvious that the book was not going to sell even as well as *Redburn* and *White-Jacket*, let alone as well as *Typee* and *Omoo*. Melville could see that he was in for some more wood sawing.

What he should do, he knew, was write some small nothing, composable in a month, for cash and appreciation. Having run through his years at sea, he decided on a domestic romance of the kind that would attract women readers. "My Dear Lady," he wrote to Sophia Hawthorne, who rather to his surprise had found things to like in *Moby-Dick*, "I shall not again send you a bowl of salt water. The next chalice I shall commend, will be a rural bowl of milk."

But he could not bring himself to do anything so simple. He was a voyager and a thought diver. His mind was more than ever an ocean. In the reach of his life and work, distance and depth were what fascinated him. In remote depths he found monsters. "Devouring profundities" had to be dealt with. "As long as we have anything more to do," he wrote to Nathaniel Hawthorne, "we have done nothing." So, he said, "let us add Moby Dick to our blessing, and step from that. Leviathan is not the biggest fish;—I have heard of Krakens."

His new hero, Pierre Glendinning, would be a youth who grew up in luxury on a country estate. Pierre had American military heroes in his background. His honorable father was dead; Pierre lived with his beautiful mother in a blissful relationship. All this sounded like Melville's own life with the black parts painted out for the benefit of the women's audience. So far so good, for a piece of wood sawing, but then Melville made Pierre pull his house down. Pierre was to marry an immaculate young fair-haired woman, a friend of the family. But he threw her over for a mysterious dark stranger, a beautiful poor young woman who claimed to be his half sister, a love child of his father's. By the end of the book Pierre had burned a portrait of his dead father, had shot and killed his much-admired cousin Glen, and had driven his mother to an insane death. His intended bride died of shock. The dark lady poisoned herself. And Pierre, condemned to death for murder, hanged himself in his cell.

While *Pierre* was forming in Melville's mind his second child was born, a second son, as he himself had been. The boy was christened Stanwix, a name from Melville's mother's side of the family, the Gansevoorts. Just then, as it happened, Nathaniel Hawthorne was getting ready to move house, away from Melville's district to another part of Massachusetts. The shift was an emotional withdrawal on Hawthorne's part, or at least Melville felt it to be so. In several ways Melville was under great stress at this critical point in his life as an author and a family man, and it showed up in an extraordinary form. On his new son's birth certificate, under "first name of father," Melville gave his name, Herman. Under "maiden name of mother" there appeared not the name Elizabeth Shaw, but Maria G. Melville, the married name of his own mother. Melville, a second son, was naming his own mother as the mother of his second son.

Writing his domestic novel, Melville dredged up the depths of himself. Deep down, where the brain was scraped away, Melville was involved with raging love and hate. *Pierre* was about incest; and at the same time it was Melville's revenge on family life. He was taking revenge on his beloved father for having died bankrupt. He was taking revenge on his older brother Gansevoort for having been more brilliant and more beloved when the two of them were children. And he was taking revenge on his beloved mother.

Here Melville was back with his sad, unsatisfiable hunger for a safe place, involving what D. H. Lawrence called his "choosing" search for paradise and his "unchoosing" mad hatred of the world. His father had made a good life for him and then had betrayed him by dying mad and bankrupt. But even before that Melville had been denied a safe place. In the complicated negotiations that go on between mother and child, something had happened between Maria Melville and her second son that convinced him he was not loved, he was being abandoned. Talking about his mother late in his life, Melville said simply: she always hated me. Where Melville's still center should have been there was a void. He wrote about this in *Pierre:* "Deep, deep and still deep and deeper must we go, if we would find out the heart of a man; descending into which is as descending a spiral stair in a shaft, without any end, and where that endlessness is only concealed by the spiralness of the stair, and the blackness of the shaft." Melville's heart had not been filled with love. It was empty and hostile. All his life he kept trying to bring things into himself to fill the void, ideas, feelings, people, to damp down the rage. In his novels he tried to fill himself up with words.

Pierre turned out to be a dreadful book. It was as absurd as any cheap gothic or romantic novel, and on top of that it was unreadable. Melville could not stop himself from loading the simple rubbishy novel he meant to write for money with tortured ideas, about truth and absolute good and how they might bring on absolute evil. And then he insisted on being "frank," and that was bound to lead to disaster.

Melville thought of publishing *Pierre* under a pseudonym, perhaps because he sensed he had made a spectacular botch of it. He decided to bring the book out under his own name. The critics savaged *Pierre* to death. They called it abominable trash, a literary mare's nest, a crazy rigamarole, a dead failure, disgusting, vicious, monstrously unnatural, written under an unlucky star, one long, brain-muddling, soul-bewildering ambiguity, an Irish bog, the dream of a distempered stomach, "the late miserable abortion of Melville." And on and on. In more than one place it was suggested in print that the author of this insanity had in fact gone mad. "HERMAN MELVILLE CRAZY" one headline announced, and the story was that his friends were taking measures to put him under treatment.

Melville did not deny the possibility of madness for himself—or for anyone with more than a "mouthful of brains." A literary acquaintance of his had gone mad, and Melville's comment was personal: "in all of us lodges the same fuel to light the same fire." The subject drew him. "What sort of sensation permanent madness is may be very well imagined—just as we imagine how we felt when we were infants, tho' we can not recall it. In both conditions we are irresponsible & riot like gods without fear of fate." This was Melville's intuition of what lay below the safe and sane adult bourgeois life of his day. He called the madman in question "just the man to go mad," and gave him many points of similarity with himself: "imaginative, voluptuously inclined, poor, unemployed, in the race of life distancᵈ by his inferiors . . . without a port or haven in the universe to make." In other words a man with the world against him, an artist in the nineteenth century, an Ishmael of literature, another Melville.

The madman was a bachelor, and Melville, a married man, spoke about this as if it were something that predisposed a man to madness. Yet it would have been hard to say that he found his own marriage altogether reassuring and stabilizing. Elizabeth was a conventional woman. She offered him sustenance as best she could and tried to draw sustenance from him. But Melville was a difficult husband. At the time they were married, he was writing *Mardi*; it was, so to speak, his wedding book. Elizabeth was a flower lover, and Melville wove any amount of flower symbolism into the novel. He even described a wedding between islanders, in which the bride was bound with a cord bedecked with flowers, and the groom was weighted down with a huge stone, also flower-bedecked. And, describing another character who was considering marriage, Melville said that the man "meditated suicide—I would have said, wedlock." In Melville's novels there were few women, and the only one who was important without being at the same time a great complication was Fayaway—and she was a fantasy of the flesh who never spoke a word. Melville did have marriages of his own to celebrate, but they were all symbolic, all uncon-summated, and all with men: Hawthorne in life, and on the pages of his books the shipmates he communed with in the long night watches, Queequeg the great savage, and the crew of the *Pequod,* all together squeezing spermaceti, the oil from the head of the sperm whale, for hours on end. "Come," said Ishmael, "let us squeeze hands all round; nay, let us squeeze ourselves into each other; let us squeeze ourselves universally into the very milk and sperm of kindness."

With *Pierre,* Melville had taken his latest, boldest step toward "frank-ness," and the critics had picked up clubs and beaten him back. What happened with the reviews of *Pierre* was particularly maddening. Melville had written a book of himself, becoming in the process, as has been said, discoverer of the darkest Africa of the mind—or the deepest Pacific. Since his first days as an author he had gone so far in his unfolding that he seemed to himself an entirely different person. Now he was told to go back to what he had been. In the South Seas he had lived with cannibals and beautiful brown naked women. The Americans who bought *Typee* and *Omoo* were delighted to read about South Sea savages in a book, un-derstanding that the South Seas were far away and a book was something that they could pick up and put down. Melville had become aware of the savage within himself, and this was what he wanted to write about. In the United States of his day a writer of that kind was as out of place as a white man in the valley of the Typee. Melville was being called a sick man, a madman.

The critics remembered him—just a few years ago—as a jovial and hearty narrator of traveler's tales full of incident and adventure, and now he was a specter. Why, they asked, did he not return to his native ele-ment, the ocean, and his original business of harpooning whales? His fun-damental error had been to fancy himself a genius, and the result was *Pierre.* Better by far to forget this and go back to what he did properly. Was Polynesia used up? Why ever did Melville not write more *Typees* and *Omoos?* "Let him continue, then, if he must write, his pleasant sea and island tales. We will always be happy to hear Mr. Melville discourse about savages. . . ."

It was as if Melville had tattooed his first books on people's minds, ac-ceptably, like the tattooed beauty spots on the skin of Fayaway. Or, rather, it was as if he himself was tattooed by his own early work. He was a marked man. He was that detestable figure from his own remote past, "Mr. Typee," the man who lived among cannibals and came home and made money out of exhibiting himself.

*   *   *

Along with the critics, Melville's close relatives were coming to see his writing as a sign of madness, or even as the thing that actually drove him mad. After seven novels, ending with *Pierre*, they looked at the onset of a book as an ominous recurrence of a dire illness: a feverish inflation of consciousness, an ugly mental swelling, a "condition." And it did not pay. There were days while Melville was writing *Pierre* when there was nothing on the family supper table but bread and tea. The common-sense view was that everyone would eat better if the author's sickness could be made to go away, and the proposal was to apply a poultice in the form of a steady job that did not require too much of the mind.

Perhaps Melville could get a post as a United States consul somewhere. Nathaniel Hawthorne had managed this, at Liverpool in England. Hawthorne was more willing than Melville to saw wood. He had written a campaign biography for the Democratic presidential candidate in the 1852 elections, Franklin Pierce. Pierce won, and Hawthorne was rewarded. For Melville, the Honolulu consulate was seen as the logical post; he could be put forward as someone who knew the whaling industry in the Pacific. His family recruited people to write supporting letters. But Melville was a political nobody, and the Honolulu consulship was a plum. The whaling industry was at its peak, and with all those thousands of whalermen ashore in the Hawaiian Islands, a clever consul could find ways to cook the official books and make himself a lot of money. Best reserve the job as a reward for one of the party faithful.

Melville's heart was not in being a consul. He took next to no part in this attempt to get him safely placed. The next thought was that he might get a paying job in the United States customs service. His heart was not in this either. In *Redburn* he had written about a luckless customs officer killing time reading a newspaper, idly rapping his knuckles on a transom out of sheer boredom: "He seemed to be a man of fine feelings, altogether above his situation; a most inglorious one, indeed; worse than driving geese to water."

Melville kept on writing. After *Pierre* he took the critics' advice, more or less, and went back to the Pacific for subject matter. He promised the Harpers a book about tortoise hunting in the Galápagos Islands, and evidently did some work on it, but never wrote it. He started a book-length account, based on fact, of a revolt by black slaves aboard a Spanish ship in the Pacific, off the South American coast. The writing generated a hallucinatory power, particularly in the descriptions of the ringleader, who was at last hanged, his body burned, his head stuck up on a pole in a city square in Lima. But for one reason or another Melville let the story trail away, and it was published incomplete. For some years he wrote magazine pieces for money, many of them excellent: honest wood sawing. The striking thing was that almost all of his stories now were about failures, victims, monsters of destruction, or stoical survivors who had been forced to settle for less in their lives.

And he wrote two more novels. In his last book, a confidence man aboard a ship fools passengers one after the other, time after time, using disguise after disguise. Melville's final statement was that the universe was only a bad joke. His ship of fools was a riverboat on the Mississippi. This was not Melville's kind of ship and not his stretch of water. The book could have gone on forever, and when it stopped it did so because Melville had decided it was time to quit novel writing. It would be twenty years before the man who was the true imaginative owner of the Mississippi—Mark Twain—took literary possession of it, just as Melville had done with the Pacific.

This last book was a failure—inevitably. Once again Melville's family began talking about a change for him, a sea cruise across the Atlantic, followed by some touring in Europe and the Holy Land. In Liverpool Melville visited Consul Hawthorne, and Hawthorne found him "much overshadowed since I saw him last," complaining of neuralgia, not doing well with his writing, which indeed, Hawthorne thought, had for a long while been indicative of "a morbid state of mind." Melville said he already felt much better than in America, "but observed that he did not anticipate much pleasure in his rambles, for that the spirit of adventure is gone out of him."

In the Mediterranean and the Near East Melville saw the great sources of civilization. He visited Jerusalem. He climbed a pyramid. Often he was moved, but rarely was he uplifted. He tasted the salt water of the Dead Sea, and reflected that it was bitter to be poor, bitter to be reviled. And often he simply could not respond to what was before him. Sailing among the Greek islands, he wrote: "Was here again afflicted with the great curse of modern travel—skepticism. Could no more realize that St: John had ever had revelations here, than when off Juan Fernandez, could believe in Robinson Crusoe according to De Foe. When my eye rested on arid height, spirit partook of the barrenness." Later he wrote a poem about the islands of the Greek seas as being like Polynesia bereft of palms. So much for Cythera.

Back from his travels, he had to get back to making money. There might have been a book in what he had just seen and done, but he was not up to writing books any more. Instead he went out as a lecturer. Under the right circumstances this could be lucrative, even if Melville's literary friend and occasional family doctor, Oliver Wendell Holmes, was outrageous about how the money was earned. A lecturer, so Holmes said over dinner with Melville, was "a literary strumpet for a greater than whore's fee to prostitute himself." As a beginning lecturer Melville had to solicit whatever engagements he could, which rather put him in Holmes's category, except that his fees were modest.

For his first lecture tour Melville chose the topic of "Statuary in Rome." The newspapers that announced his talks identified him as Mr. Typee, or as the author of *Moby-Dick*, and one reporter claimed to be able to see a spirit of adventure in his face and a Polynesian tan on his skin. This was nonsense, but obviously Melville would be able to make money by exhibiting himself as Mr. Typee. His shipmate Toby, Richard Tobias Greene, was lecturing in the Midwest, where he now lived, and even touring the East with a talk entitled "Typee; or Life in the South Pacific." (When he heard that Melville was going to be in Cleveland with his Roman statuary lecture, Toby invited him to pay a visit to the Greene home at Sandusky, Ohio.) If Melville had struck while the iron was hot, when his first book had just come out and was such a popular success, he could have made excellent money. Now, in Holmes's terms, he could only be an aging whore, past his prime as far as the paying public was concerned. Of course, he did not want to be a whore at any price. But for his second season he chose to speak on "The South Seas."

Irresistibly, he went back to his old theme of the dreadful effects of civilization in Polynesia. White men, he said, had a bad reputation there, as "the most blood-thirsty, atrocious and diabolical race in the world." They were not welcomed in the islands. He recalled being visited, not long after *Typee* was published, by a "poetical young man" who wanted his opinion on the prospects of, say, five score Fourierists—utopian socialists—forming a settlement in Typee valley. Melville did not encourage him. Quite apart from the fact that the utopians might be taken for invaders and eaten, Melville had too much regard for his friends the Polynesians to wish any such invasion on them. He argued that until civilization could do better for itself than prisons, almshouses and so on, civilization should leave the savage alone.

Oddly, for someone who was such a fine storyteller in private, Melville did not do well as a public lecturer. He had his good nights; a young Gansevoort relative heard him in New York before a half-full house and was delighted. Rare birds, luxuriant vegetation, uncouth monsters and peculiar fishes, the habits of the islanders, their religion, their tattooing—

an hour of fine talk, unpretentious, original, successful in its simplicity, all done in such "glowing and gentle colors that every mind seemed to quit its local habitation the while. . . ." It was in "Cousin Herman's true vein," bringing to mind his vivid and colloquial sketches "told under the inspiration of madeira after dinner. . . ." Once in a while Melville would even play with his audiences, telling them, for instance, that he would "direct the gas to be turned down, and repeat to his audience in a whisper the mysterious rites of the 'Taboo,' " but that since it would be more horrible than anything in gothic novels, he would spare them. There were other nights, though, when his listeners, or at least the reporters who spoke for them, found him too serious, withdrawn, lacking altogether in oratorical skill, without "depth, earnestness, consecutiveness, and finish." Melville started out on a third season of lectures but gave it up. Mr. Typee did not want to exhibit himself any more.

In 1860 he took another sea cruise, this one to the Pacific. His younger brother Tom, who had gone to sea as a boy after reading *Typee*, was now a ship captain, off around Cape Horn to California, and perhaps then to China and on around the world. Melville could go with him.

There was a small publishing matter to attend to first. Melville had been writing poetry. He had a small book's worth, and he decided to have his family look for a publisher while he was gone, in the full consciousness that "of all human events, perhaps, the publication of a first volume of verses is the most insignificant." He did not care about money, or "clap-trap announcements and 'sensation' puffs." And he added: "For God's sake don't have *By the author of 'Typee' 'Piddledee' &c* on the title-page."

His cruise did nothing much for him. Rounding the Horn again was exciting, and the Pacific leg of the trip took him into the latitudes where the whale sank the *Essex*. But by California seagoing had gone stale, and Melville left his brother's ship there and headed east again across the Panama isthmus. He got home to learn that no one had been interested in publishing his poems.

* * *

Melville was in his forties now, and his world was drawing in. One or two echoes from his days at sea were cheerful enough. While he was at work on *Moby-Dick*, his old disreputable companion from Tahiti, John B. Troy, with whom he had escaped from the calabooza, apparently came across one of his books somewhere and wrote to him from the California gold fields (and then disappeared into his various selves, permanently, as far as Melville was concerned). And, a great surprise, out of the blue the maintopman of U.S.S. *United States* with whom Melville had talked literature, Edward Norton, as he had called himself, wrote to Melville after fifteen years to say that he had gone to sea under an assumed name, that he was really Oliver Russ, that he was married and a father, and that without knowing anything of Melville's literary fame yet to come, he had named his son Herman Melville Russ. Richard Tobias Greene had named one of his sons Herman Melville too, and there was a Greene nephew called Richard Melville Hair, two boys for Melville to send small presents to. Toby stayed in touch with Melville as late as the 1860s, writing from time to time of his hope that they would see each other again, or to ask for a copy or two of *Typee*.

What happened to his other shipmates was less cheerful. While he was writing *Moby-Dick*, Melville had a visit from a man who sailed with him on the *Acushnet*, and he listed what happened to them all. This one had a fight with the captain and went ashore. That one was put ashore with a disreputable disease, another went on the beach half dead, spitting blood. Another ran away or was killed at the Marquesas. Another one still went ashore and committed suicide. Later the *Acushnet* lost a boat to a whale, and in the end the ship was wrecked in the arctic ice. But it did not take whales or pack ice to wreck the men who made up ships' crews. Life did it.

Melville survived two men who in the days of *Moby-Dick* had meant a great deal to him, each in his own way. Nathaniel Hawthorne died, and though Melville had not seen him for a number of years, since his cruise to Europe, he remembered him poignantly and wrote a poem about the death of their fine relationship. The other man was himself a survivor, Captain George Pollard of the *Essex*. After losing one ship to a whale, he lost another to an uncharted reef in the Pacific (and it was after this that John Williams heard his story at Raiatea). No shipowner would trust Pollard with a command any more, and he had to retire from the sea. Melville met him on a trip to Nantucket not long after *Moby-Dick* was published. Melville thought him admirable, and felt a sort of affinity with him. In his own way Melville had hunted the whale, had met shocks and reverses, had been told that he was an insupportable risk, and been forced to give up the career that gave meaning to his life. Pollard was working as a nightwatchman when Melville met him, and that was how he ended his days. Melville thought about him, jotted down notes about him, marked his death, and wrote about him years later in a long poem.

Melville's special whales were gone too. The *Ann Alexander* whale, the one that made such a devastating comment on *Moby-Dick*, was reported killed in 1854, identified by bits of ship's timbers still stuck in its head and harpoons from the *Ann Alexander* in its back. And five years later, off the

Brazilian banks, a Swedish whaler took Mocha Dick. He was one hundred ten feet long, fifty-seven feet in the girth, and his jaw measured twenty-five and a half feet. Eight of his teeth were broken off, and all the others were badly worn down. His big head was a mass of scars, and one eye was blind. He had had nineteen harpoons put into him and had survived, and if he gave no trouble when he was finally taken it was because he was dying of old age.

* * *

When Melville was younger, in fact up to the time he wrote *Moby-Dick*, he was physically vigorous, even boisterous. He might not have been a consistently hard-working farmer, but at least he was an energetic wood chopper, fire lighter, and cooker of outdoor meals. Picnicking, he would recite poetry in a loud voice, scale a tree on a mountain to call in straying hikers, climb a rock like a bowsprit and pull on imaginary ropes for everyone's amusement. He had an appetite for high places: the main-top of U.S.S. *United States*, the masthead of a passenger ship before breakfast, the top of a pyramid. But paired with this was a fear of falling, and in his books there were some dreadful falls, especially the one suffered by the narrator of *White-Jacket*, out of the rigging of a man-of-war into the ocean and down almost to drowning. Now a much less spectacular fall brought a whole phase of Melville's life to an end. He had been a daredevil wagon driver on mountain roads in the Berkshires, bringing his companions home from their picnics in equal parts hilarity and fright but always delivering them safely. Then in 1862, driving his wagon leisurely between Pittsfield and his farm, he was jolted out. He fell hard, did some serious damage to ribs and a shoulder blade, and was in bad pain for a number of weeks. After that he gave up wagon driving, and for some time would not even ride in a carriage.

Bedridden, then convalescent, with his arm in a sling and afflicted by twinges of neuralgia, he came to an important conclusion. He used to cherish, so he said, a loose notion that he did not care to live long. But now that he had looked death in the face, he decided he had no serious, insuperable objection to respectable longevity.

In fact he lived almost three decades. But the fall and his reaction to it brought to a crisis a condition that had been developing in him for a good many years. He was no longer the young man who had written so flamboyantly about the grand terror of life's voyage toward an unknown destination at sea that might be liberation, revelation, ruin, or all three at once. He used to be scathing about the ignominious security of life on land. Now he was drawing back from his endless reaching for distance and depth, back from spiritual risk. He was adjusting himself to a limited space in which he could go on living a life of sorts. This space would not be an insular Tahiti of the soul or a place at journey's end where treasure repaid the difficulties of the voyage. This kind of thing was denied him. Not wanting to end a total wreck, he would settle for what he could find, a place to beach his ship out of the storm, a lee shore.

In order to go on living a partial, diminished life, Melville let part of himself die. What perished was his professional authorship. He never again lived fully, as he did when he could bring all his powers to bear on what he was writing, wrestling with himself and his art, trying to compel some sort of hearing for the Truth. As an author, Melville had been something of a strange case all along, an isolato with an audience. Now he and his audience had parted company, and he would survive on his own.

Lemuel Shaw had died in 1861, leaving Elizabeth a substantial sum, enough to do away with the Melvilles' most serious money worries. Melville gave up his farm and moved his family back to New York. He continued to write poetry, and brought out a volume of reflections on the Civil War, mostly at his own expense, and scarcely noticed. The family did not consider this to be serious writing of the old alarming sort. Still, to keep Melville away from the morbid writing desk, get him out of the house, it was again proposed that he should take a regular job. He went to see someone he knew who might help, and was put on the payroll of the customs service. This was satisfactory. "Herman's health," wrote his mother, "is much better since he has been compelled to go out daily to attend to his business."

He began as a deputy inspector of customs, making four dollars a day. He was responsible and diligent. There is no shred of evidence that he took the slightest interest in the work for its own sake. After ten years on the job he wrote to a cousin: "They talk of the *dignity of work*. Bosh. True Work is the necessity of poor humanity's earthly condition. The dignity is in leisure. Besides, 99 hundredths of all the *work* done in the world is either foolish or unnecessary, or harmful and wicked." He worked where the life of the sea met the life of the land. His customhouse was not the kind he talked about to Nathaniel Hawthorne, where cosmic liars, optimists, were barred from access to eternity. It was the customhouse that his narrator in *Redburn* (Melville himself when young) described as no place for a man with any sense of his own worth, where the work was inglorious, worse than herding geese to water.

Melville never gave up the thought that he was worth something, if not in the coinage of his own day. He kept reading and he kept thinking. He read Matthew Arnold, who had things to say about the relation between talent, temperament, and malady. Arnold quoted Wordsworth, some lines about a mind forever voyaging through strange seas of thought, alone; and Melville marked the lines. He could feel an affinity as well with Camoëns, the great Portuguese sea poet, who had had the experience of being considered peculiar because he valued solitude. Melville wrote some poems in which he identified himself with Camoëns, a man in whom the ocean had liberated genius, and who ended his life in obscurity, his worth unappreciated. Melville would rather be Customs Inspector No. 75 than a publicly misunderstood genius—or Mr. Typee. He chose to disappear from view.

* * *

Melville survived the better part of twenty years in the customhouse. At home as well he was a stoic survivor. He and Elizabeth stayed together into middle age and old age. One of their daughters got married. The other lived and died single, the victim of painful and disfiguring arthritis and rheumatism. Melville's two sons were also singletons. He outlived them both. The death of the first son came just a few months after Melville started work in the customhouse; the death of the second just a few months after he retired.

At the age of eighteen the older boy, Malcolm, shot and killed himself in his bedroom. He was found with a bullet in the temple and a pistol in his hand. The verdict of the coroner's jury was suicide while temporarily insane. As a kindness, this was changed to death by his own hand but without premeditation. The second son, Stanwix, was a sad boy, hard of hearing and with eyes that gave him trouble. He grew up a drifter. He went to sea and came back, went out to the Midwest and came back, like his father. Looking for work, he took a trip down the Mississippi, drifted on into the Caribbean and Central America, and finished up walking the beach from Costa Rica to Nicaragua, sick with fever and ague, having to bury a companion who died along the way. His next berth was on a ship that got itself wrecked. Back in the United States, he drifted out to California, then up into the Dakotas, did some sheepherding, tried this and that, made a pass at learning dentistry, and somehow always found himself, as he said, "still stationary, and sailing in about the same boat" as when he left home. He drifted out of his twenties and into his thirties, and never found anything to stop him drifting but death. Eventually news came east to New York from California that Stanwix had died of tuberculosis, alone in a San Francisco hospital. So of Melville's two sons, one had gone to sea and come back unable to shake the damp November from his soul, unable to do what his father had done and make literature out of the pains of life. And the other had found no substitute for pistol and ball. Melville's sons lived and died like aspects of Ishmael.

* * *

Melville had kept writing privately. Only once more in his life did authorship take on that menacing look which so distressed and threatened his family. For some years in the 1870s he mulled over the experience of his trip to the Holy Land twenty years before, and eventually he wrote a long poem about it. He called it *Clarel*. It was immense, eighteen thousand lines. Hawthorne was in it, under another name, and Captain Pollard of the *Essex*, and the South Sea Islands of Melville's young days. And, of course, Melville himself, still trying to come to terms with a world that seemed to show nothing but contempt for efforts to reach the truth. The tone was ruminative, level, and above all elegiac, as if Melville were saying another good-bye to the fury and tumult that used to well up in him over talk of the universe. Knowing that two volumes of philosophizing verse, three hundred pages each, would not interest the public, Melville still agreed to have *Clarel* published. As much as anything the reviews regretted that Melville had become such a difficult author since the days long ago when he wrote so well about such interesting things, books like *Typee* and *Omoo*, even *Moby-Dick*.

After *Clarel*, Melville wrote on a small scale again. Especially after he retired, his family encouraged it: now some gentle writing would keep him occupied, since he no longer had a job to go to. One story he worked on took him back to sea. It was never published during his lifetime. In fact it remained unknown until well into the twentieth century. It represented a final statement on problems that had preoccupied him for most of his life. While Melville was sneaking away from the calabooza in Tahiti and arranging to ship out on his last Pacific whaling cruise as far as Hawaii, his cousin Guert Gansevoort was at sea in the Atlantic, a lieutenant aboard a United States Navy ship. There was a mutiny, or an alleged mutiny, and the court-martial, in which Gansevoort took a leading part, condemned three men to hang, one of them a midshipman, just a boy, the son of the secretary of war in the United States cabinet, another an extremely popular seaman, who became something of a legendary figure for his gallant death. The whole affair was an awful one for many reasons, and it marked Guert Gansevoort for life. Melville meditated the story, and made a story of his own out of it. Without necessarily wishing to tell the world, he was telling himself that he was willing to have things come to an end, that the universe was as incomprehensible as ever, and that he had made his peace with that fact. His hero is Billy Budd, a handsome young sailor, a fatherless foundling, the by-blow of an aristocrat, all natural beauty and goodness. Billy is goaded by an evil master-at-arms, and without meaning to, he strikes the man dead. The ship's captain is a fine officer, none better, a father to his crew, perhaps even Billy's real father, in any case his life's captain. But under the law of naval justice—the rule of life as it is lived on a voyage out with no destination—the captain must condemn Billy to death. Billy accepts the rope with beautiful resignation, forgives his captain freely, and dies with a blessing on his lips. So Melville in his last years was going back to his sailor days, shipping out one final time on life's voyage, and bringing the journey to an end in the one way he thought inescapably fitting.

*   *   *

Nothing is clearer than that Melville regarded his South Seas books as merely landfalls on his voyage as an author, or as outer leaves in his working and thinking life, to be shed with later, deeper unfoldings. And nothing is clearer than that he wanted to shed the shallow kind of reputation that went with them. He could not. The world never cared much about what he most deeply thought or most deeply felt. All the world ever wanted from him was to hear his tales of naked brown girls and frightening savages (which, to be sure, was as much as the world ever wanted to hear from those who had seen the islands and had come back).

Yet it is just as clear that Melville's actual experience of the islands, his voyaging in the South Seas, opened him up to the human possibilities that lay within him, as perhaps no other experience could have done. It let him see the distances and depths that were in him. He was given something to set over and against the life of his time and his society— something valuable, indispensable, indelible.

Polynesia kept surfacing in his late poems, always as a touchstone for a glimpsed, lost, but somehow firmly held vision to set against the sordid or grim or baffling realities of the life that the Americans of his day and age led around him—the life they expected him, the isolato, to lead among them. And however much of himself he managed to repress for the purpose of attaining a respectable longevity, the islands remained alive within him. The only time in the last three decades of his life when he was noted down on paper as being unreservedly alive, full of himself, dramatically communicative, was when at a social gathering he "spun the tale of his eighteen months cruise to the sperm fisheries in the Pacific, and held his hearers' close attention while he related the coarse brutality of his captain, who had forced him to desert at the Marquesas Islands. Then he traced his wanderings with his one companion through the trackless forest of Nukahiva and his capture by the Typee cannibals. . . . It was a thrilling tale to listen to" and it was told "far better than he had ever written anything. . . ."

Melville had a little granddaughter, and there were things about him that frightened her. He had had a portrait of himself done—he had come around to thinking his face was worth a private memorializing—and it hung in half light in the back parlor of the New York house. The portrait used to look at the little girl, and she would run past the open door to escape its following gaze. Melville's workroom was even more to be avoided, with its bookcase topped by strange plaster heads that peered sightlessly, a motto on the wall—"Keep true to the dreams of thy youth"—a great mahogany desk piled with books, an iron grate, and a narrow black iron bed. But her grandmother's room was sunny, comfortable, familiar, with a wide bed, like other people's, and in the corner a big armchair where Melville sat when he emerged from his dark privacies. The little girl would climb up on his knee and put her hands in his thick beard and squeeze it hard. "It was no soft silken beard, but tight curled like the horse hair breaking out of old upholstered chairs, firm and wiry to the grasp, and squarely chopped." She remembered these times as glorious fun, "mixed with a childish awe, as of someone who knew far and strange things." He used to tell her stories, "wild tales of cannibals and tropic isles."

* * *

In the world outside something of Melville's reputation survived. If his books among them no longer sold more than a hundred or two copies a year, at least they were kept in print, a few of them anyway, with the emphasis on his sea stories. From time to time publishers tried to get him to do magazine pieces. He would not, not any more. Occasionally a request for an autograph would come in the mail, or a letter of appreciation from some distant discriminating reader. An invitation would be offered by the Travelers' Club or the Authors' Club, and Melville would accept or decline as his mood dictated. A professor would write asking for information on his literary methods and his life, the better to set his works before the public. Melville would be polite but by preference noncommittal. In most of his moods he would not even talk about his own work, what he had written, or how he had written it. He preferred not to.

Very late in his life Melville was encouraged to think about a new edition of some of his books, and the titles chosen were *Typee, Omoo, White-Jacket,* and *Moby-Dick:* two pieces of amiable exoticism, as they were seen (Fayaway and her *tapa* sail again, and Doctor Long Ghost), one piece of wood sawing, and a masterpiece of thought diving that could also be read as a story about whaling. (The story goes that the New York Public Library catalogued *Moby-Dick* under Cetology.) Melville died before the edition was published.

Not much notice was taken of his death. It was 1891, more than four decades since he had published successfully, almost thirty-five years since his last novel of any kind. Some reference was made to his early fame, some surprise expressed that he had in fact still been alive all those years, and the *New York Times* got his name wrong.

* * *

Walter Murray Gibson

W HEN HERMAN MELVILLE made his trip to the Holy Land in 1856 he
visited his old friend Nathaniel Hawthorne along the way, at the
United States consulate in Liverpool. Hawthorne observed that as a
tourist Melville was still very much a sailor. Melville left a cabin trunk
with Hawthorne and set off for Europe with nothing but a carpet bag.
"This is the next best thing to going naked," Hawthorne wrote, "and as he
wears his beard and moustache, and so needs no dressing-case—nothing
but a tooth-brush—I do not know a more independent personage. He
learned his travelling habits by drifting about, all over the South Sea, with
no other clothes or equipage than a red flannel shirt and a pair of duck
trowsers."

As United States consul, Hawthorne saw a good many red-flannel-
shirted sailors, most of them in distress. He was used to making his way
upstairs to his offices of a morning through a jetsam of "sea-monsters"

beached at Liverpool as Melville had been at Lahaina in his day, "shipwrecked crews in quest of bed, board, and clothing, invalids asking permits for the hospital, bruised and bloody wretches complaining of ill-treatment by their officers, drunkards, desperadoes, vagabonds, and cheats, perplexingly intermingled with an uncertain proportion of reasonably honest men."

The sea monsters were dealt with in the outer office by the vice-consul or a clerk. Any "respectable visitor" could command Hawthorne's personal attention in the inner office. One kind of visitor was especially interesting to Hawthorne, and he became a connoisseur of their stories, which amounted to episodes in a continuing saga of his country's relationship with Britain. Up the consulate stairs came Americans, one after another, to lay claim to huge inheritances in the mother country. Hawthorne thought they all had a kind of madness about them, a "peculiar insanity." There was never any substance in their stories. No great estates were waiting for them. They were simply possessed by a "blind, pathetic tendency" to wander back along the old colonial-imperial road of history in search of a place that offered nourishment for their fantasies of distinguished parentage and elegant living.

It did not take much to set them off, these workaday Americans who needed desperately to think of themselves as dispossessed aristocrats, the forsaken children of kings. "A mere coincidence of names . . . a supposititious pedigree, a silver mug on which an anciently engraved coat-of-arms has been half scrubbed out, a seal with an uncertain crest, an old yellow letter or document, in faded ink, the more scantily legible the better—rubbish of this kind, found in a neglected drawer, has been potent enough to turn the brain of many an honest Republican, especially if assisted by an advertisement for lost heirs, cut out of a British newspaper. There is no estimating or believing, till we come into a position to know it, what foolery lurks latent in the breasts of very sensible people."

Hawthorne got great entertainment out of these claimants, and especially out of Walter Murray Gibson. When Gibson came to Liverpool in 1854 he was in his early thirties, good-looking, "slender, with a prominent nose and, handsome, intelligent, moderately-bearded face, of a light complexion." He seemed a man of some taste, well read, and once his "dignified reserve" was overcome he talked superbly. His great skill was in storytelling. He narrated his tales with wonderful eloquence, "working up his descriptive sketches with such intuitive perception of the picturesque points that the whole was thrown forward with a positively illusive effect, like matters of your own visual experience." Gibson had any number of stories to tell about voyages of adventure, treasure hunting, and political derring-do. Hawthorne listened to him at his office and invited him home to dinner to hear more.

Gibson was pursuing a claim in England, and this had a story attached to it—long and circumstantial, as most of Gibson's stories were. He told Hawthorne he had been born at sea, on a Spanish ship off Gibraltar. "Owing to some circumstances, he has been in doubt whether he was really the child of his reputed parents; they have not seemed to love him, and though both are still living, it is many years since he has seen or lived with them. Since he has been in England, he has been led to inquire into the subject, and finds that there were *two* births on board the Spanish vessel, nearly simultaneous; and the supposition is, that he himself was assigned to the wrong mother." Gibson had been searching for his true family, and had found in the picture gallery of an English nobleman a portrait "bearing a striking resemblance to himself."

Hawthorne had heard that one before. He put the story down as just another instance of the incurable American fancy for connections with aristocratic British lineage and great estates. As for the traveler's tales Gibson told, the trouble was—as Hawthorne saw it—that the very skill of the telling told against them: "In fact, they were so admirably done that I could never more than half believe them, because the genuine affairs of life are not apt to transact themselves so artistically." Hawthorne was willing to allow Gibson to touch up his tales with color, embroidery on the dull neutral tints of truth. Defoe, perhaps; or, on the subject of some hairy subhumans Gibson had come across in the Dutch East Indies, Swift and the Yahoos. But at Gibson's story of buried treasure Hawthorne balked altogether. "I did not suppose there was a man living who could talk, as a matter of fact, of so much wild and strange adventure." After a first installment of Gibson's stories Hawthorne concluded that the vicissitudes of life must have inclined the man to look upon himself as marked out for something strange. And the more Hawthorne heard, the more unlikely it all sounded. "One looks into his eyes, to see whether he is sane or no."

Gibson was a classic claimant, short of money to prosecute his claims. Because he had sung for his supper, so to speak, Hawthorne made him an advance. Gibson never paid it back. All his life he was better at making claims on his own behalf than at honoring the claims of others.

Gibson stayed in Hawthorne's mind for years, the "adventurer with the visionary coronet above his brow," and Hawthorne put him in a book as a particularly gaudy specimen of the American claimant. A wide-ranging one too. England was only one among many places where Gibson saw cloud castles. He was another of those people convinced that as a child he had been dispossessed and disinherited, and so must wander the earth in search of his lost kingdom. It took him the rest of his life—three decades after he borrowed money from Hawthorne—to come into his inheritance.

Even then he found only a kind of fool's gold. Gibson set himself to achieve great things, but reality was always too much for him. He dreamed perpetual dreams of glory, but time and time again he managed to accomplish only his own humiliation. He was a man of considerable talent imperfectly harnessed—in fact, out of control. His story was always heavily embroidered and always changing. There was always something insubstantial about him, spurious, imposturous. Now he is a political claimant with the backing of a powerful national government; now he is a treasure hunter; now he is the long-lost son of a lord; now he is a charismatic religious leader, the founder of an ideal community. He is never any single one of these figures for long, or else he is several at once and none truly.

Gibson was attracted to islands. He sailed most of the oceans of the earth, and finally in middle age he found himself a kingdom in the South Seas, in Hawaii. As a man in his sixties he became premier of the Hawaiian kingdom. His ambition as a statesman was to make the tiny island state into an imperial power in the Pacific. He challenged the great powers—Britain, the United States, and Bismarck's Germany—for leadership in Polynesia. This was Gibson's greatest moment. It did not last. His regime in Hawaii was overthrown by revolution, and he died in exile.

*   *   *

For most of what Gibson told people about himself there were no other witnesses, and since he changed his story as often as he felt like it the facts of his life were hard to come by. He never talked in any detail about his parents (or rather, in his version of things, the man and woman who brought him up). But certainly the story of the two births aboard ship and the exchange of the babies, Gibson as an infant of noble blood condemned to neglect and lack of understanding by unloving false parents—all this was fairytale stuff.

To come to the facts: Gibson was born in 1822, a third son among the eight children of a small farmer in the English country of Northumberland. When he was still a young boy the family migrated to Canada, where the father did well enough to be able to send his sons to a good Catholic school (probably at the mother's insistence—at one time Gibson described her as being a Catholic). Three of the children died in Canada, two of them in a cholera epidemic, and the rest of the family moved to the United States, to New York. When Gibson was about fourteen he left home.

He wound up in South Carolina. For the rest of his life he identified himself as a Southerner, and he had Southern ideas about the proper relationships between whites and those with darker skins.

Without a father, real or false, Gibson attached himself to some other grown men, or so he said in the book he wrote about his early life and later adventures: a wealthy and well-informed planter who knew about the great world across the oceans, an old man who had been a missionary among the American Indians of the Northwest Pacific territory, and an uncle who had run away to sea as a lad and who came back from time to time with gifts for Walter and stories about distant places. "He talked of Arabia, and of the islands of the far East: and more than all of Sumatra: of the perfumes that wafted from her shores; of the many dainty fruits, and myriad bright-feathered birds of her flowery groves: of the Malay princes, and of the mighty wars with Portuguese, Spanish, Dutch and English. And then he spoke of a great city in the centre of the island, a city once of mighty extent and population, whose Sultans had given laws to all the rest of the Malay nations. But this great city had decayed; and its empire had been divided into many small, and feeble portions. Now the Malays looked for the restoration of the sacred city; and their traditions had pointed to fair-skinned men from the West; who should come with wisdom and great power; and who should destroy the robbers of Islam, the evil genii of the woods, and a great plunderer called Jan Company." Gibson's uncle had made a fortune in the Orient, and he wanted Walter to join him there, take over the business, be his heir. This was potent stuff, and young Gibson would walk the South Carolina beaches and look at the ocean stretched out before him, a shining path "leading to fortune and to honorable renown." The sun's glistening rays were "dancing amid the mirage of its own making; there I beheld the sacred city of the Malay isle, with its shining walls and temple roofs; and then I wondered who should help, who should teach, and who should do good to the people of the Indian seas."

There was no doubt about who it would turn out to be, but even so it took Gibson until he was almost thirty to get as far as the Indies. For the time being he was just a boy wandering the backwoods of the South. He had no real job. He had not yet found his "calling." One day in his wanderings he came across some interesting ore-bearing rocks in a watercourse, and had them identified as silver deposits. It was his plan to mine the precious metal and use the money to pay his way to the East Indies, but he could not afford to buy the land.

In his mid-teens—and this is verifiable—he married a girl a few years older than himself (the daughter of a state governor, he said later, though this was not so). He fathered three children: two sons, and a daughter he named Talula, after a "leaping liquid silver" stream he knew well. His wife died after the birth of Talula, and this was what cut him loose from the South. He was perhaps twenty or twenty-one, a father of three, and desolate. But after a time, as he wrote later, his "young widowed heart felt free to range again; and I wanted to fly on the wings of the wind towards the rising of the sun." The East Indies were looming in his imagination again. But still he did not go there. At one time or another in the next several years, having left his children behind, he worked on a steamship sailing between Georgia and Florida, was in business in New York, traveled to the California gold fields, and then went on into Mexico where there were fabulously wealthy silver mines. And on the road to Acapulco he looked in the direction of the Pacific and "thought of early plans of fortune and renown."

During his travels he got to know some military men involved in the volatile state building then going on in Central America. Back in the United States he became consul general for Costa Rica, San Salvador, and Guatemala. Then in 1851 a Guatemalan general of his acquaintance arranged for him to purchase a small ship, fit it out and arm it, and sail it south, where it would become the Guatemalan Navy. Gibson located a surplus United States government revenue schooner for sale and went to New York to take possession and buy guns. But he ran into difficulties, what he called "trouble and loss." What he was up to was in violation of the neutrality laws of the United States—gun running, in fact—and he was forced to sail for Guatemala without guns and with an unglamorous cargo of ice, which at least would be salable in hot latitudes. All the way south in the Atlantic his troubles multiplied. His captain was incompetent, his crew unreliable, surly to the point of mutinousness. The ice melted. The Guatemalan connection evaporated. Gibson reached the stage where he hardly knew what he was doing or where he was going. He made a landfall at Brazil, came under the suspicious eye of the authorities there, narrowly escaped imprisonment, and decided that the time was right—never better—to strike out for the East Indies.

Along the way he visited the remote island of Tristan da Cunha in the South Atlantic, where he found a small community "living under the patriarchal rule of an old English sergeant," in pure and happy simplicity, much like the descendants of the *Bounty* mutineers on Pitcairn. According to Nathaniel Hawthorne, Gibson "seemed quite capable of appreciating the beauty and poetry of the affair; but he has done his best to spoil it, I fear, by representing to our government the expediency of taking possession of the island, and forming a naval station there."

The story Gibson told Hawthorne about treasure hunting was that somewhere in the East Indies two or three million pounds sterling worth of booty was buried, supposed to have been left by a Spanish ship, and that this was what he was looking for in the islands. To other Americans with an official interest in what happened to him in the Indies, he said that he was on his way to Singapore "to make inquiry after the estate of a collateral relative who had died there some eighteen years before which had descended to him." This, no doubt, was the fabulous uncle of his boyhood. In the book he wrote about his adventures he did not mention either of these fortunes waiting for him, but said simply that he was headed for Singapore as the central point and trading port of the region. There he hoped to hear "tidings" of his uncle, and he would in any case refit for a short cruise to the northern part of Sumatra and northeast Borneo. When he went ashore at Sumatra and the Dutch colonial authorities asked what he was doing in their waters—trading, perhaps, for tin, coffee, or spices?—Gibson said he was just there to see what was to be seen, to gaze upon the human and natural wonders of the island: a gentleman traveler with a taste for the exotic, nothing more. Certainly he collected exotic stories and told them to Hawthorne, tales of Malay pirates, men of primitive innocence and integrity, gentle-natured except that they would cut every Christian throat among their prisoners; accounts of incest between royal brothers and sisters; descriptions of a strange race of subhumans, "hairy, with spots of fur, filthy, shameless, weaponless, tool-less, house-less," hunted and caught in traps by the Malays, who used them as beasts of burden. They could be cross-bred with humans, to improve the stock.

Other things Gibson said in his book indicated a powerful and deep-running attraction to the Indies, having to do with his quest for a kingdom of his own. Gibson's Sumatra was "the chief seat of a great race, who without war, or proselyting zeal, had scattered their language, and customs, and traditions among numberless nations around. . . ." From Madagascar to Polynesia, from Malacca to Papua, "the teeming millions of the many thousand isles within the Indian Ocean, all bear some marks of the intellectual sway of the Malays of Sumatra." And Borneo was "an island continent; full of hidden wonders . . . where the human form with hairy skin lodged in the trees; where man sought the head of his fellow man, as the best of gifts to lay at the feet of his bride; and where an adventurous gentleman had become the prince and civilizer of a barbaric race, and filled the world with the fame of Brooke. . . ." Gibson was talking here about James Brooke, the White Rajah of Sarawak, another boy who had left home to seek his fortune in distant places. Brooke had finished by being offered the rule of an island realm. He had become the loving father of a grateful brown-skinned people, and Queen Victoria had knighted him. If ever there was a man who had come into his kingdom, it was Brooke. He was flourishing when Gibson turned up in the Indies in 1851. Brooke sounded, in fact, remarkably like a real-life version of Gibson's unfindable uncle.

Going ashore on Sumatra, Gibson, the gentleman traveler with nothing political in mind, got in touch with the sultan of Jambi. Dutch political control of Sumatra was by no means secure—there had been a recent revolt among the Malays in the interior, serious and not yet subdued—and the Dutch would not have welcomed any outsider coming to prospect on the fringes of their jurisdiction. They had a treaty with Jambi, so they kept a close eye on Gibson, and as soon as he made a move toward the sultan they descended and took possession of a letter with his signature on it, intended for the sultan, arrested him, and charged him with stirring up rebellion.

Gibson was aggrieved. He said his arrest amounted to entrapment. He had been spied on, maneuvered into a bad position, and railroaded into jail on charges completely without foundation.

Several translations of his letter to the sultan were made for legal purposes, from Malay into Dutch and English, and not surprisingly there were variations in what emerged. But undeniably Dutch rule was talked about as evil, and the power of United States arms was discussed, as well as the ability and willingness of Gibson to be of use to the sultan. In at least one translation the killing of Dutchmen was advocated, and Gibson was described as a man with ambition to take charge of Jambi. The Dutch could produce witnesses to say that Gibson had been heard talking enthusiastically about Rajah Brooke, and about his own membership in a secret organization in the United States able to call upon a dozen armed steam frigates. Gibson's ship was searched and a set of military epaulettes was found. Gibson maintained that these were nothing more than the insignia of a lodge he belonged to, the Oddfellows, but the Dutch were sure they knew better. They put Gibson on trial and looked forward confidently toward a conviction.

Strangely, they could not get one. They brought the case to court several times, and each time their own judges acquitted Gibson. While all this was going on, he was being held in the military prison of Weltevreden outside Batavia on the island of Java. He was incarcerated for more than a year. At last his case reached the supreme court of the Netherlands Indies, and there the prosecutors got what they wanted. Gibson was convicted of high treason, condemned to stand half an hour under the gallows, then to be imprisoned for twelve years, and after that to be perpetually banished.

Before sentence could be officially invoked, Gibson was gone. He had made some friends in Weltevreden, and one of them smuggled in a coat, "an officer's uniform cap, some false hair, a wig and moustaches, a dye for the face, a dirk, and some money." Gibson dressed up and at dusk simply walked past his guards, out of the prison grounds, through the outskirts of Batavia to the water's edge, where a boat from an American merchantman picked him up and carried him off to safety.

Back in the United States, Gibson was able to interest the Pierce administration in his case. The view was taken that American honor and interests had been injured. Gibson thought that what he had suffered was worth $100,000 from the Dutch. He went to Europe to pursue his claim (it was on this trip that he met Hawthorne), and he kept urging stern measures on his home government. Late in 1854 the official terms of discussion became angry, then angrier, until—amazingly—the possibility of war over Gibson began to be talked about publicly between the Netherlands and the United States.

Parts of the extensive file on Gibson had been printed so that American congressmen could study it. The Dutch ambassador to the United States got hold of a copy of the published document and noticed a curious gap in the record. A letter written by Gibson to the Dutch governor general at Batavia was not printed. From the Dutch point of view this was a crucial paper, because it could be read as a confession of sorts. And it turned out that Gibson had had access to the document file before it went to the printer. The inference was inescapable: Gibson had lifted the compromising piece of paper.

In the original, written after his arrest, in English, in his own handwriting and over his own signature, Gibson had thrown himself on the mercy of the governor general, admitting abjectly that he was a man "too often, led away in life, by some high coloured romantic idea." In this instance he had "indulged in bravadoes" that he would become "a potentate in the East." He could not imagine, however, that anyone could have taken this as more than "vainglorious boast." And he must "ever add in extenuation" that this was "after a plentiful indulgement in wine."

So Gibson was nothing but a man who drank too much and fantasized in his cups about being another Rajah Brooke. The Dutch made sure the Americans saw the text of this letter, and of course this was the beginning of the end of Gibson in Washington.

* * *

Nothing more came of Gibson's claim against the Dutch. And nothing more was ever heard of his golden uncle in Singapore—or his aristocratic father in England. So Gibson had circumnavigated the globe, crossed oceans and traveled continents, gone ashore on strange islands, kept appointments in the chancelries of ambassadors and paced prison cells, aspired to the sun, and been condemned to stand in the shadow of the noose, and the only place of all these where he had managed to extract any return on this staggering investment of self was the American consulate at Liverpool, where he succeeded in telling Nathaniel Hawthorne one hundred fifty dollars' worth of good stories, enough to take him back where he started from.

By now Gibson was in his late thirties, unable as always to find satisfactory expression for his sense of himself. He had not come into his kingdom. He was a man of powers who had never managed for any length of time to exercise influence in the world in a constructive or rewarding way, a man who drew nourishment from the thought of vast untapped riches in the earth beneath his feet but who had no piece of ground to call his own, a man of great immediate charm and persuasiveness who ultimately rang hollow, a man who dreamed of fortune and renown but whose life—to be blunt about it—was that of a confidence man.

* * *

Still Gibson thought of himself as a man who was bound to accomplish great things. He could not afford to think otherwise. Casting about for a new stage on which he could act out his destiny, he turned to the Mormon community of Utah, the Kingdom of the Latter-Day Saints on the Great Salt Lake. For Gibson this was attractive territory. The prophet and founder of the Mormon faith, Joseph Smith, was a self-made, self-invented man like Gibson. Smith had been a treasure hunter in his youth, poking about in the huge, mysterious Indian burial mounds of rural New York that were supposed to be the tombs of a lost race. Smith never dug up a conventional fortune, but he did unearth some miraculous inscribed golden plates that no one else was ever allowed to see, and from these he read out the gospel of a new religion. Smith was charismatic. He could get people to pay attention to him and follow him. In his day any number of experimental communities were being founded in the United States. Most of them fell to pieces quickly. Smith founded a cult that outlived him and drew strength from his death at the hands of his enemies. Smith was a remarkable man. By the last year of his life he was commander in chief of his own army, a candidate for the presidency of the United States, secret husband of perhaps as many as fifty wives, and self-crowned king of the Kingdom of God which would one day transform the earth. After Smith was killed, Brigham Young led the Mormons west to Utah, planted a community at Salt Lake, proclaimed a religious kingdom that stretched from the Rockies to the Sierra Nevada and from the Oregon territory to the Colorado River, continued the practice of polygamy, and set out to evangelize the whole world. In Joseph Smith and Brigham Young combined, Gibson could obviously see himself as he desperately wanted to be, as he believed he truly was: dreamer of splendid dreams, charismatic leader, envisioner of kingdoms, father of an as yet unspecified people, and at the same time great statesman and hard-headed man of practical affairs.

When Gibson came across the Mormons they were in trouble with the law, as he himself had been in Sumatra, and he proposed a way out for them that had worked for him, escape by sea. In 1857, President James Buchanan sent an armed force to Utah to subdue the Mormons to the authority of the federal government. The following year Gibson, at last giving up his claim against the Dutch, wrote to John M. Bernhisel, Utah's first delegate to Congress, and made a sweeping suggestion. "I hope," said Gibson, "to accomplish a long cherished purpose of establishing a colony upon an island of Central Oceanica"; and he proposed that the Mormons should abandon Utah and emigrate to New Guinea. Gibson had never been anywhere near New Guinea, but in his geography the thousands of islands of the ocean were pretty much interchangeable. Gibson had wanted Franklin Pierce to declare war on the Dutch for him. Now he wanted James Buchanan to pay for the resettlement of the Mormons. Buchanan did not take Gibson's proposition seriously. It would cost millions of dollars, and that alone was enough to stop him considering it any further—though in the end, of course, it cost millions more to maintain the federal troops who were supposed to turn the Saints into good Americans.

Undaunted, Gibson wrote to Brigham Young, breaking the good news of his enthusiasm for Mormonism. He gave it all the freshness and force of revelation. "While I lay in a dungeon in the island of Java, a voice said to me: 'You shall show the way to a people, who shall build up a kingdom in these isles, whose lines of power shall run around the earth.'" From that hour, said Gibson, his purpose in life was changed. He had sought "throughout the world" for his chosen people, and now he believed that he had found them in the Mormons.

He went out to Utah, met Young and impressed him, and gave some spellbinding lectures about the Malay islands; speaking in the social hall at Salt Lake, he drew such crowds that the series had to be moved to the Tabernacle. After several weeks' exposure to Mormonism and the obvious opportunities it offered him, he had himself and his daughter Talula baptized in the faith.

The upshot of all this was that Young offered Gibson broad powers to do missionary work in the Pacific and beyond. It was a minor curiosity that Young should have given Gibson so much credence (Gibson, for example, was claiming personal acquaintanceship with the king of Siam, and he had never been anywhere near Siam). Perhaps the reason is that there was in Gibson an echo of Joseph Smith, and Young had been willing thirty years before to change his whole life to follow Smith. Now, in any case, Young authorized Gibson to negotiate with all the nations of the world who would obey the gospel of Christ, and in particular Gibson was to carry letters from Young to the "Illustrious, Imperial Majesty and Tycoon of Japan," and to the "wise, powerful, and gracious potentates, even the illustrious Sultans, Rajas, Panjoranges and Kapallas of the renowned Malay People." There was nothing Gibson liked better than a grand flow of words. His commission amounted to an incantation, a kind of speaking in tongues over his collection of "rare and valuable maps and charts of islands and ports in the Pacific and Indian Oceans," a magic spell to give him power in the real world.

Late in 1860 Gibson left Salt Lake with Talula, on his way to San Francisco, carrying his elaborate commissions and an engraved gold watch from Brigham Young. He was headed for Japan, and from there Mormonism would roll on to the Philippines, Malaysia, Madagascar, and Polynesia, and those thousands of islands of the sea. But as he had done so many times before, Gibson took his time getting to where he so burningly wanted to be. Writing to Young, he talked about how "ardently" he desired to be on his "mission ground," how he was "foreordained for a special work." Yet he stayed in California almost four months, addressing the legislature, lecturing on "Malasia," debating with himself whether to go to the islands via Australia, weighing the pros and cons of buying or building a ship, and trying to add some political commissions to the documents Brigham Young had given him. Perhaps it was just that he was short of money, but just as likely it was the usual Gibson situation: he had large plans, things always looked best to him in prospect, and he wanted to hold back as long as possible before he had to subject himself to the harsh tests of reality.

When Gibson finally set out on his great voyage to the potentates of the East, he got only as far as Honolulu. There had been a Mormon mission in the Hawaiian Islands as early as 1850, but the elders had been called back to Salt Lake at the time of the difficulties with the United States government, and now Brigham Young asked Gibson to pause on his way to bigger things and look into the state of the faith among the Hawaiians. Gibson was pleased to help. "I shall rejoice," he wrote to Young, "to meet the simple hearted brethren of the islands, with words of instruction, encouragement and consultation." On board ship he recruited two young men, Haven B. Eddy and Charles O. Cummings, and when he arrived at Honolulu he baptized them Mormons and sent them to the outer islands as missionaries. Eddy and Cummings had been headed for Hawaii in business for themselves, to sell *Dr. Warren's Household Physician*, a home-cure book put out by a San Francisco patent-medicine firm. Eddy took to writing the Hawaiians money-raising letters, signing himself Chief President of Oahu and Kauai and Bishop of Lahaina and President of the Quorum (presumably meaning himself and Cummings).

Gibson kept quieter than Eddy. At Honolulu, he said nothing to begin with about being a Mormon. He was the same sort of interested visitor he had been at Sumatra, "an American gentleman travelling for scientific purposes connected with the ethnology of the Malaysian and Polynesian races." He gave some of his celebrated lectures and was well received, and if he had gone off with any promptness to the other islands of the sea he would have been cordially remembered. But he stayed, and because he would not be candid about his intentions, they were taken to be bad. It was the fall of 1861. The Civil War had just broken out. The American community at Honolulu was Northern almost to a man. Gibson was a Southerner. One theory was that he was a Confederate agent up to no good among the Hawaiians. He was not, but when it turned out that he was a Mormon he was discredited anyway. Hardly a white man in Hawaii had a good word for the Latter-Day Saints.

Typically, Gibson said more than one thing about his relation to the Mormon faith: that he had nothing to do with the Saints; that he had no creed of any kind, only a sympathy for island peoples, born as he himself had been at sea; that he knew nothing about Mormon doctrine; and that he thought Mormon social organization was the best in the world. All this time he was making contact with Hawaiian Mormons, and presently he turned up at a Mormon conference with a new scheme of organization for the church, a long string of titles for himself, and a specially designed Latter-Day Saints flag.

Gibson had already more than half-decided to stay in Hawaii. The impulse came over him when he first went to visit the local Mormon Zion, the "City of Joseph" in the Valley of Ephriam, otherwise known as Palawai, an extinct volcanic crater on the island of Lanai. The first Mormon missionaries to Hawaii had encouraged their converts to gather there in the 1850s. By the time Gibson came to the islands, the settlement at Palawai was run down and disorganized. Gibson fell in love with the place at first sight. (It had been part of the attraction of the Malay city in his uncle's story that it was decayed and needed a rebuilder.) He put the experience of Palawai on paper in his diary. "Rode up a rough stony hill, came to a ridge, and looked down into a lovely round valley, tears came into my eyes." Gibson was responding to a vision of the promised land, like the Mormon migrants coming through the Wasatch Mountain canyon and seeing their new home in Utah spread out below them, "this land," as even a nonbeliever of Gibson's time saw it, "fresh as it were from the hands of God." Gibson seeing Palawai was sure he was looking "with virgin eyes upon a new world." He rode on, down into the valley, and was given a warm welcome by the native Saints. They offered him food, a simple meal of boiled chicken and goat's milk. He was completely won over. "I said to myself, I will plant my stakes here and make a home for the rest of my days." He and Talula made arrangements to come and live among the Saints, and in a matter of weeks Gibson was talking of Palawai as his refuge and sweet home, where he had been born again, a place that could be made fit for the second coming of Christ.

One of the things Gibson liked best about the Hawaiian Saints was that they were, in his words, pliable people. There were never more than a couple of hundred Mormons at Palawai. As human beings they had a great deal wrong with them, so Gibson considered. In fact they were "terribly debased." But this did not affect his good feeling for them. As he put it, he was a South Carolinian and he believed "somewhat in the subordination of races," and yet he found himself strongly drawn to "black and brown people." So he was ready to take trouble over the Hawaiian as "an interesting yet feeble younger brother," or as a child. "They want to be led and to have a father and teacher to love." They might be "brown ragamuffins," "indolent and improvident," but they would "receive reproof with a cheerful spirit, and hasten to amend their shortcomings." It made no sense to compare them with the white Saints of Utah, and it would be disastrous to have them emigrate there, but in their own "tropic and fruity latitudes" they had the elements of a "delightsome people." They were simple, honest, and there was no cant in them. And here was Gibson, for want of better, as he said, "their Prince and their Father."

Gibson added some seals and colored ribbons to his commissions from Brigham Young and showed the documents around. He issued long statements to the Hawaiian Saints, half instruction, half prophecy, signing himself Chief President of the Islands of the Sea and of the Hawaiian Islands. It was his opinion that the natives needed to see "the King on his throne, the high priest in the robes of the temple, and the general with his trumpet and banner." He wrote to Brigham Young asking for something associated with the prophet Joseph Smith, a piece of his clothing, some handwriting, "a staff from the wood that enclosed his martyred body," to sustain him in his work among the peoples of the isles. And about half a mile from his house at Palawai he cut a chamber in a large rock to hold a Book of Mormon, telling the Hawaiians that this was a sacred spot, the cornerstone of a great temple to come, and that to defile it meant death.

For Gibson, Palawai was beautiful because it was remote. As in Melville's Typee valley, civilization was largely absent. "There is no vice and riot of cities here," Gibson wrote in his diary, "there is no pride and noisy pomp of courts, no hypocritic pretentions of stately churches, no plunder of enemies, no ambition of kings, no covetings for the miser, no stimulus for the whorehouse or civilized hell of any kind, no respectability, no quality, no cliques, no coteries, no mutual admiration society, no fashions, no newspapers, no long sermons read from manuscript, no soulless jobbing politics, no office seekers. . . ." And, Gibson added, in the middle of another long list of Palawai's attractions, no judge, no jury. Perhaps he was remembering the prison of Weltevreden. Or perhaps it was that Gibson's relationship with respectable, regularly constituted society was chronically uneasy, unsound, and he needed a place where he could be a law unto himself.

Gibson in effect emptied the outside world out of the bowl of Palawai, and then, feeling born again there, proposed to fill the new world with himself. His past was of no consequence now. He had a present and a future of his own dreaming. A family and a posterity surrounded him—his daughter Talula, his two sons brought from the American mainland, and the Hawaiian Saints, his other children. Somewhere along the way during his years on the island of Lanai he sired part-Hawaiian offspring, children of a people he regarded as his children, and interestingly enough there was talk that his relationship with Talula was incestuous. (This was put about by his enemies and the assertion was never tested, much less proved; but certainly the bond was a close and strong one.) And in his diary Gibson spoke literally of having taken Palawai for a lover. "I want to lay an arm around those . . . blue mountain tops, delicately curtained with cloud gauze." He was a lover who meant to be a parent and a dynast. "I would fill this lovely crater with corn and wine and oil and babies and love and health and brotherly rejoicing and sisters kisses and the memory of me for evermore."

There was another strain in Gibson's thinking that surfaced repeatedly, having to do with power, omnipotence, the idea of an island as the embryo of an empire. It had come up in his version of Malay history. He had repeated it in his first letter to Brigham Young about a people building up a kingdom in the Indies "whose lines of power shall run around the earth." He talked in this way about Palawai. What he had there, he said, was nothing more than a doubtful footing upon a poor bare island, "small material" after "all the hope and grasp" of his heart. But he had tremendous faith, and in that there was "domain and dominion." And he went on to say that Palawai was only the "baby," the "infant hope" of his "glorious kingdom," a nucleus of development, the "seed of Oceanican organization." "Lines of power"—that image again—"shall radiate from this shining crater. I set up my standard here and it goes hence to the islands of the sea. Lanai shall be famous in Malaysia, in Oceanica."

How much of this power would be used on behalf of Mormonism and how much on behalf of Gibson was not clear. After less than a year at Palawai, Gibson was writing to Brigham Young that he had organized a corps of Polynesian elders, "zealous and efficient, and eager to go forth with me, when the proper time comes, to preach the gospel to other Polynesians, to Malaysians, to Japanese; and throughout Oceanica;" and a little later he specified "five thousand island saints" who would "embark with me today, and sail to any part of the earth. . . ." He did in fact send missionaries to Samoa, two of them. In his letters to Young he was all enthusiasm for the Mormon Zion, and at Palawai he had his Book of Mormon in the sacred rock. But in his diary he said that if Moses or Elisha had things revealed to them by the Governor of the Universe, he himself had the same right to revelations. When he put on his white robes to preach, he was very much Walter Murray Gibson. After all, he was the one who said the sacred rock at Palawai was sacred.

At the same time as Gibson was writing to Brigham Young about the forces he could command for Mormonism in the Pacific, he was writing to the Hawaiian government, delicately suggesting that attention might well be paid to him as a force in local politics. He had, he said, a certain influence among the natives of the group. And elsewhere: there were about seven thousand natives of Tahiti and neighboring groups expecting a visit from him. Many of them wished to migrate to Lanai, and within a year he could have a thousand on the ground. Of course, he hastened to add, he would never take any such action without consulting the government. Again, close to the time of the 1862 elections in Hawaii, he wrote asking advice from the government about where he might best direct the twenty-five hundred votes he had at his disposal. (This was about the total number of votes cast in the kingdom in a normal election year, and bore about the same relation to reality as the twelve armed steam frigates Gibson once said he could summon to the East Indies.)

Gibson was all mysterious lines of influence, so it seemed. The Hawaiian government was curious enough about him to have his mail monitored and to quietly appropriate fifty dollars to buy information about him. All sorts of stories came out of Palawai. Gibson was or was not a genuine Mormon. He was or was not drilling a Hawaiian army to conquer the Pacific. He did or did not require Hawaiians to approach him crawling on their hands and knees, as the old high chiefs used to do. He was or was not anything and everything.

As a matter of fact, Gibson was collecting information for his own purposes. In his Palawai years he set himself to find out as much as he could about Kamehameha, the great unifying chief of Hawaii, and at the same time he decided he would write the life of Walter Murray Gibson. These two men seemed to him the most interesting personages in the history of Hawaii.

In Sumatra, Gibson had lasted no time at all before he ran into trouble. In Hawaii, where he had found a refuge and a sweet home out of the way of storms, trouble took less than three years to appear, and then it came from the Mormons. From the beginning Gibson had encouraged Hawaiian Saints on all islands to give whatever they could to the cause of building up the City of Joseph on Lanai. And he kept negotiating to buy or lease land on the island, more all the time. The name on all legal documents was his. This was worth some attention. Gibson eventually took to calling himself the Shepherd of Lanai; the question was whether he was shearing his Hawaiian sheep. At that time it was general Mormon policy, Brigham Young's idea, to keep the wealth of the church liquid for as long as the faith was not securely established (indeed under United States law the Mormon church was not permitted to hold large assets). There was, however, nothing against Mormons as individuals building up wealth. Brigham Young himself was doing it, spectacularly. So on the face of things, Gibson's control of all the Palawai land and the other leases he accumulated on Lanai was nothing reprehensible. He was a trustee, a steward. But this, of course, left open the question of what the Hawaiian Saints had actually bought with their contributions, and when they might come into their own kingdom. And then there was another thing still: Gibson was ordaining elders and making appointments in the church hierarchy in Hawaii, and he was charging money for doing it.

Some of the Hawaiian Saints were not sure Gibson was the same kind of Mormon as the earlier missionaries from Utah. They became uneasy and wrote to Salt Lake about their misgivings. Gibson's own view was always that things were going well at Palawai. Everyone was content, except for "a lot of pestersome old sore heads." But in the early months of 1864, a deputation of elders was sent from Utah to Palawai to make a firsthand investigation.

They were severe on Gibson, hauling him over the coals in front of his people, demanding that he transfer his land titles to the church. Gibson refused. When the deputation moved a motion of censure against him, he appealed to the Palawai Saints to consider what he had done for them and to compare it with what the earlier Mormon missionaries had failed to do. The censure vote was taken with Gibson in the room. He was a formidable presence. Only one Hawaiian Saint put up a hand in favor of the motion. So the deputation retreated from Palawai to the nearby island of Maui, and decided there to excommunicate Gibson. They named a new leader for the Hawaiian mission, and let the Palawai Saints know that they should break up the City of Joseph, go back to their homes on the other islands, and wait for word about a new gathering place. Gibson's excommunication was confirmed in Utah. Brigham Young was for it, not on the grounds that Gibson was wrong to accumulate property in his own name, but that he persistently refused to be directed by the Mormon priesthood.

When the news got back to Hawaii the Palawai Saints voted again, this time with their feet. In a matter of weeks the City of Joseph was deserted, and Gibson was left virtually alone.

It was all over now between Gibson and the Mormons. The men from Utah took away with them his temple robes, five hundred or so unbound copies of the Book of Mormon, and the engraved gold watch Brigham Young had given him. But Gibson kept Palawai. He stayed on Lanai, adding to his lands whenever he could, and when in 1867 he briefly considered leaving Hawaii and going back to South Carolina he offered to dispose of his estates to the Mormons for the right price—29,000 acres in fee simple, 12,000 on a six-year lease, 12,000 more under negotiation, more than five thousand sheep, and control over the only harbor on the island. The Mormons did not make an offer.

*   *   *

Gibson never gave up his idea of himself as a community builder. Not long after he was excommunicated and almost all his Hawaiian Saints walked out on him, he was telling a Honolulu newspaper that he had Hawaiian girls and boys working for him on a systematic plan, the boys doing farming work and learning reading, writing, arithmetic, and military drill in uniform, the girls going to school under Talula, doing domestic work and living closely supervised in a fenced-off area. "If I were King, and Parliament to boot," said Gibson, "I would, I think now, remove every

Hawaiian daughter from every Hawaiian mother and put them into industrial establishments." Hawaiian parents were not keen on this idea, and
Gibson's arrangements did not last long.

* * *

In 1866 Gibson became a Hawaiian citizen. From then on he began to
take an interest in the affairs of the kingdom at large. Hawaii, like other
places in Polynesia, was losing population to introduced diseases, and
here there were serious implications for white businessmen in the islands. Sugar planting was potentially extremely profitable, but only if
cheap labor could be found. Hawaiians did not like the work, and in any
case they were not available in the numbers needed. The planters had
tried Chinese, and were considering Japanese and Pacific islanders. Gibson suggested Malays, what he called the "cognate race" of Polynesians.
He negotiated a commission from the Hawaiian government as the kingdom's commercial agent to Singapore, with the idea that he would encourage Malay immigrants to settle in Hawaii as plantation laborers. Gibson liked nothing better than an imposing document entitling him to do
ill-defined official business in distant places.

Predictably, he never got as far as Singapore. Traveling via the United
States mainland, he reached the East Coast and went to Washington,
D.C., where he did some unauthorized lobbying for a treaty between the
United States and the Hawaiian kingdom that would let island sugar into
the mainland market free of duty in return for reciprocal trade privileges.
And here and there he did some lecturing on the subject of the Malays: he
was still a spellbinder on the platform.

On the side Gibson was pushing an immigration scheme of his own,
recruiting workers for his property on Lanai. He looked at farmers in New
England and thought they would be better off in sunny Hawaii; considered free black labor from the Southern states and decided against it; and
finally, on his way back to Hawaii (without having got any closer to Singapore than Washington), picked up some hopefuls from around the labor
exchanges of San Francisco.

They were to go shares with him on five-year contracts, growing sugar,
corn, and whatever else would grow at Palawai, and running sheep. None
of them saw the time out. They traveled in wretched steerage accommodations from the West Coast to Honolulu, then got becalmed on an inter-
island ship and had to row for hours to make Lanai. Tackling the hot,
dusty trek up to Palawai—rain was short, as it so often was there—they
came over the crater rim to see Gibson's promised land lying before them
"scorched to a cinder, and nothing green, and no sign of any stream or
water, as we had been led to suppose." Members of the expedition had

been dropping off at every stage along the way. More gave up then. Of the few who remained, some got dysentery from drinking Gibson's dubious barrel water. And so it went. It was a fiasco. A visitor who saw the remnant huddled in their little shacks up on the crater rim called them the most disillusioned, disgruntled, unhappy people in the world, and he described their situation in terms that identified it unmistakably with Gibson: "they had been undone for the actual by the glory of the imaginary."

Gibson himself was put out, but not mortally. Lack of rain had beaten him for the moment, he conceded, but he would not mind trying something of the kind again, perhaps with migrants from Scandinavia, where people were used to working hard for a small return. In the meantime he went on to get a number of Honolulu businessmen interested in the idea of forming a large-scale immigration society to serve the kingdom's needs.

By now, ten years and more after he first set eyes on Palawai, Gibson the Mormon was long gone, laid to rest in favor of Gibson the concerned citizen of Hawaii. At Honolulu in 1873 he started a little bilingual newspaper, Hawaiian-English, called *Nuhou*, and in it he took an early opportunity to explain what he had really been up to on Lanai. His connection with the Mormons, he said, was a temporary one. He had intended to form an industrial organization, a joint stock farm, a "combination of labor and skill without one dollar of capital" (which actually sounded very Mormon), and also to carry out an emigration scheme, though where from and where to he did not specify. So in this telling of his story there was nothing of the true Mormon about him.

At roughly the same time, in a long conversation with a Honolulu man, Gibson discussed the question of his religious faith. In religion he had been, so he said, "a Jesuit Catholic, after that an ardent Baptist, then a true Mohammedan, then a Buddhist, and last a Mormon. . . ." The stages of Gibson's life can be read off on this embroidered list: his education at a Catholic school in Canada, his adolescent years in the American South, his Sumatran adventure, his commission from Brigham Young to go to the court of the emperor of Japan, and his Palawai days. Then Gibson said that "could he have succeeded in starting his co-operative community on Lanai, he intended to have set up for them a *new* religion, one of his own make, a sort of cross of his philosophy with superstition." This was the Gibson who preached in white robes and wrote in his diary that he had as much right to revelations as Moses.

In the same conversation Gibson said something about what he still wanted for himself in life. He was doing well financially on Lanai, "but what he now desires is to make for himself a name, and it seems from his

*Noble savage and white man meet—Tahiti at the time of
Cook's second voyage. "Matavai Bay" by William Hodges.*

"A View Taken in the Bay of Oaitepeha, Otaheite" by William Hodges.

Missionaries and heathens meet in Tahiti. "The Cession of Matavai" by Robert Smirke.

*"The Reception of the Rev. J. Williams, at Tanna, in the South
Seas, the Day Before he was Massacred" by George Baxter.*

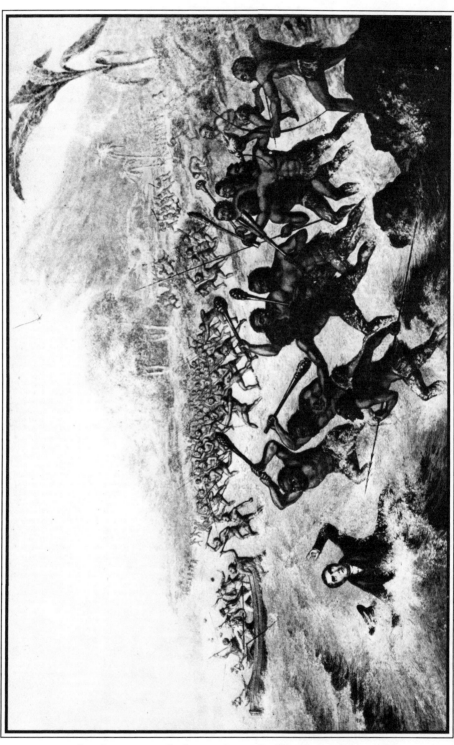

Make the natives darker and Mr. Williams more heavenly.
"Massacre of the Lamented Missionary, the Rev. John Williams . . ." by George Baxter.

*Tommo and Toby take ship for the South Seas. The crew list of
the* Acushnet.

The Acushnet's *boats among whales. Drawing by boat steerer Henry M. Johnson.*

"Fayaway Sails Her Boat . . ." by John La Farge, Henry Adams's traveling companion in the South Seas.

For a man who wanted to be visible down the ages, Walter Murray Gibson was remarkably shy of the camera. Here he is with Mother Marrianne's Sisters of St. Francis at Honolulu.

RLS and Fanny taking their ease in the islands.

Literary ectomorph and royal endomorph—RLS and King Kalakaua flanked by Fanny and Margaret Stevenson, at Honolulu.

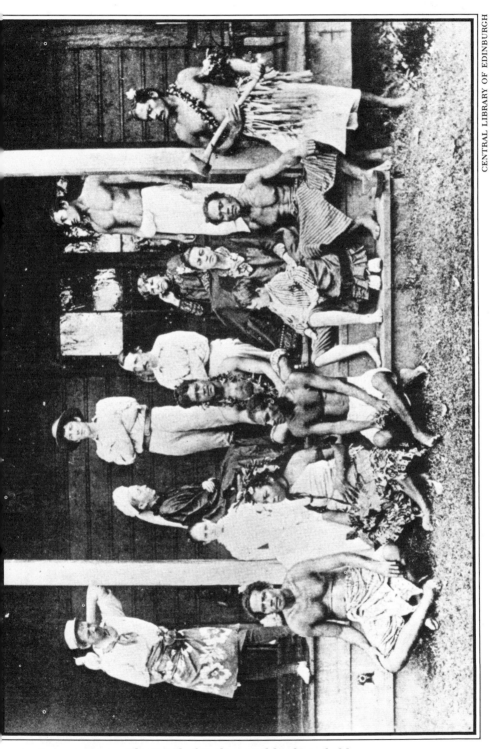

The Laird of Vailima and his household.

"D'où venons-nous? Que sommes-nous? Où allons-nous?"
Painted before Gauguin's suicide attempt.

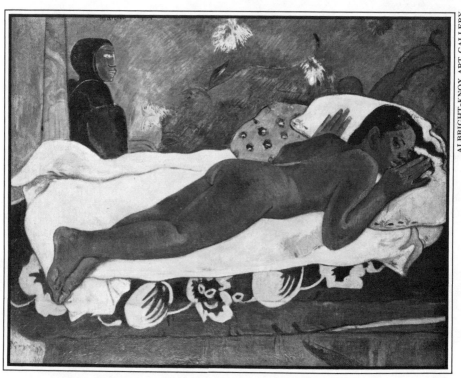

Gauguin's "Manao Tupapau."

*The savage returned from the south seas. Gauguin in Paris
between his two voyages to Tahiti.*

46

de leurs trompettes et à battre de leurs tambours, ce qui était le signal de la retraite et de la fin de la fête. Le roi retournait alors à sa demeure, accompagné de sa suite.

The dream made flesh—drawing from Gauguin's "Ancien culte mahorie."

own acknowledgements that he thinks if he could only get the office of Minister of Foreign Affairs he would be on the high road to success." So really the pages Gibson wrote for his newspaper *Nuhou*, and all the other noises he made publicly from then on, were so many announcements that he was on his way into Hawaiian politics. Again it took him a long time to arrive at where he burningly wanted to be, in fact the rest of his life. He was already in his fifties when he began to talk politics. But ten years later there he was, premier of the kingdom of Hawaii.

Politics in Hawaii was a volatile game, and certainly that was part of the attraction for Gibson. The old ruling house, the Kamehameha dynasty, had finally failed to produce an heir, and in the early 1870s the legislature had to elect a king. There were rumors around Honolulu that some whites were going to mount a filibuster and overthrow the Hawaiian government. Stories of this kind had surfaced in the islands on and off for the better part of a generation, without ever amounting to much. In the present case, one of the names mentioned in connection with the plot was that of Gibson. Given his history, it was not impossible. When he first turned up in Hawaii in 1861 one of the theories about him was that he might have been looking Hawaii over with a filibuster in mind. And that particular uneasiness about him stemmed in turn from what became known of his doings in Sumatra and before that again in Central America, with the Guatemalan Navy and his attempt to run guns for ambitious generals. A filibuster was a shorthand version of empire building in islands, and Gibson was interested in that notion as moths are interested in flame.

If a filibuster was really being thought about, nothing came of it. Publicly, Gibson made the suggestion that the new elected king of Hawaii, a bachelor, should take a Malay princess for a bride, linking the "cognate races" dynastically. The bachelor king died after a year on the throne, still unmarried. His successor, elected in 1874, was David Kalakaua. He and Gibson had a great deal in common. They shared a genuine interest in resisting the rise of white American influence in the islands, and in reinvigorating the disease-ridden and dispirited Hawaiian population. At the same time they would have been delighted to see the influence of the kingdom extend across the Pacific. In 1876 Gibson published an *Address to the Hawaiian People*, composed in his best platform lecturer's style and loaded with his lifelong preoccupations. "We can enliven once more the now silent shores of Hawaii with a thronging and busy people. And then when an electric cable unites us to our neighboring continent and to the rest of the world"—lines of power running round the earth, literally this time—"and the trafficking and traveling nations fill our marts with wealth gathered from all quarters of the globe,—then may little Hawaii the least, be one of the most blest of the family of nations; and being strong in her Christian, moral and enlightened attitude, sit royally as the Queen of the great ocean, and shine forth as a proud and redeemed state before an admiring world!" This could have been King Kalakaua himself speaking.

In 1878 Gibson took the predictable step of going into elective politics. He won a seat in the legislature, held it in 1880, and by 1882 had become—against not very severe competition—one of the leading white politicians in the islands. He and King Kalakaua were getting on very well together, and this was important. Under the Hawaiian constitution the king could make and unmake cabinets, and Gibson for almost ten years now had had his eye on a cabinet post.

For a good many white men in Hawaii, the thought of Gibson in a position to make national policy was too much. A great mover of no-confidence motions in the legislature, he inspired among the whites a perpetual lack of confidence. To the solid, well-established, respectably moneyed, mostly Protestant, mostly American planters and businessmen who made the dollars that the legislature taxed for public spending, Gibson looked like a suspicious character, and had looked like one ever since they first laid eyes on him in 1861. The programs he proposed on the floor of the legislature sounded windy and vague, the negation of good money management, fiscally ruinous. There was worse. Gibson talked about Hawaiians being allowed to run their own affairs, and to white men this sounded like dangerous demagoguery. By now Gibson owned two newspapers, one published in Hawaiian, one in English, and his editorial policy was highly distasteful to businessmen. They caught him saying one thing in one tone of voice in English, then altering style and substance for the Hawaiians, whose antiwhite feelings he obviously wanted to whip up. No white businessman would advertise in his columns. This did not seem to affect him, so when the 1882 elections came round, his enemies got together a series of articles about his past and his present, published them in a newspaper they controlled, and then put them all in a fifty-page pamphlet, which they called *The Shepherd Saint of Lanai.*

They got hold of Nathaniel Hawthorne's story of Gibson's visit to Liverpool and quoted the choicer passages at length. They got hold of the American congressional report on Gibson's one-hundred-thousand-dollar claim against the Dutch, and they reprinted his boastful letter to the sultan of Jambi and his abject appeal to the Dutch governor general of the Indies. They got hold of the account books of Palawai in the days when Gibson was running the City of Joseph, and they printed page after page to show that Gibson had systematically taken advantage of the Hawaiian Saints. And now here he was, they said, posing as the friend of the Hawaiians. What he was really doing, as they saw things, was stirring up race hatred as no one had ever done in Hawaii. "That some of the natives should feel restless at the natural domination of the whites in energy, skill, and education, is not surprising. That a white should aggravate this feeling and seek to disturb the harmony which has hitherto existed between the races, is a matter to be regretted." If Gibson got what he wanted, which was to see Hawaiians running their own affairs (under his guidance), the white man would have his back to the wall: "the natives may vote away the money of the foreigner, and may, indeed, ruin him; . . . an antagonism of the races may put his life in danger." Foreigners were beginning to ask, what next? Perhaps they should be looking to the protection of a foreign power.

And here the word *annexation* was mentioned, meaning annexation of Hawaii by the United States. This was the looming presence in all Pacific politics, more obvious with every year that passed in the late nineteenth century: island governments unable to control events, foreigners with economic interests to push and notions of racial superiority to insist upon, and always the great powers in the background, playing the world game, each watching the other, waiting for the right moment to descend.

Gibson was not to be stopped by pamphleteers, whom he regarded as a new edition of the pestersome soreheads he had had to contend with on Lanai. Then, too, however pestersome white men might be, they were still a small minority in the Hawaiian Islands, and many of Gibson's loudest critics had not had the grace to take out citizenship in the country where they were making so much money, and thus were ineligible to vote against Gibson. If Gibson did not have the white vote, he had the Hawaiian vote. He was one of the few whites to make a real study of the Hawaiian language, and he said things that Hawaiians wanted to hear. He courted them, and in his own way he cared for them and cared about them. In the election of 1882 he was returned by his biggest majority ever. During the legislative session that followed, the ministry got into trouble, as ministries under Kalakaua always seemed to do. Gibson was waiting. He was offered a minor post in a reorganized cabinet and turned it down. Then the king invited him to take the premiership and the foreign-affairs portfolio. He accepted, and went on to appoint himself to position after position in the government. His moment had come. He was running a kingdom. A visitor to Honolulu about this time looked him over and concluded that he had an evident "proclivity for primacy, a faculty for public affairs." At sixty, Gibson was a "tall, thin old gentleman," with "white hair and beard, a mild, cold blue eye, a fine patrician nose, and a tolerably port-wine complexion, which probably once was fair. The gen-

eral effect is that of a portrait of the Duke of Wellington in later life in parliamentary attire. The Premier's voice is soft and low, and confidential to
a rare extent. He is an unquestionably eminent-looking veteran, of
smooth address, silky manners, and a somewhat fascinating mode of
speech, in the estimation of the susceptible and sympathetic—a fine old
fellow, I should say; wise as a serpent, but hardly as harmless as a
dove. . . ."

* * *

Kalakaua was a man who wanted to reign in style, and Gibson encouraged him. The Hawaiian king had the curious distinction of being the
first reigning monarch in the history of the world to make a circumnavigation of the globe. He was received by the emperor of Japan, the king of
Siam (Gibson's old alleged acquaintance), the khedive of Egypt, the
queen of England, the president of the United States, and any number of
lesser potentates along the way.

Kalakaua came back to a new and expensive palace under construction
at Honolulu which ultimately sported everything from a seven-foot marble bath to the latest interesting inventions, the telephone and electric
light. After almost ten years on the throne the king decided, on the basis
of his world tour and on Gibson's advice, that he should have a coronation
ceremony. This was in 1883, and by then Gibson was his premier and his
public stage manager. Gibson put everything into the coronation: a coronation ball, horse races, a regatta, the unveiling of a huge gilt and bronze
statue of Kamehameha the Great, first king of Hawaii, hula dancing with
traditional chanting in praise of Kalakaua's physical and procreative powers, anthem singing by massed choirs (to words written by Gibson), pro-
cessions, and an investiture ceremony using symbols of ancient Hawaii
along with a sword of state and a jeweled crown which Kalakaua placed on
his own head.

Kalakaua went in for gathering the physical remains of great Hawaiian
chiefs, their bones and their famous feather cloaks. He had the creation
chant of ancient Hawaii, the *Kumulipo*, recorded in writing for the first
time, and he put a great deal of effort into the reconstruction of the
genealogies of chiefs, back to the Polynesian gods. Kalakaua also went
treasure hunting. Kamehameha the Great was supposed to have buried
an enormous accumulation of silver on one of the outer islands, the profits
from his trade with merchantmen in the early years of the nineteenth century, and this was good for a number of expeditions to explore caves and
volcanic lava tubes. Kalakaua hoped as well to find the old chief's sacred
and well-hidden bones. (He failed, as everyone has failed.) The king went
on to found a secret society for Hawaiian men of aristocratic blood, called
Hale Naua, for "the revival of Ancient Science of Hawaii in combination

with the promotion and advancement of Modern Sciences, Art, Literature and Philanthropy."

All this disinterring of tradition struck the forward-looking white businessmen as part ridiculous, part sinister, especially *Hale Naua*, which was nothing more than pagan rites mingled with a travesty of Masonry for political purposes—or so one critic said. But to Gibson it was all very congenial. He had come a long way from his home-made sacred rock at Palawai, his white robes, and his raggle-taggle following of Hawaiian Saints, but it was always the same road he traveled, the road of his life, stretching back to his identification with Joseph Smith the treasure hunter, the Indian-mound digger, the recoverer of the history of a lost race, the adapter of Masonic rituals for Mormon purposes. And further back still in Gibson's life there was the story his rich uncle told him about the treasure-laden Malay city, once full of pomp and power, decayed now but to be revived by the special white man of strength and wisdom. *Hale Naua* gave Gibson the chance to be associated with a ruler who performed incantations and at the same time commanded political power, real power.

Equally with the idea of Joseph Smith, Gibson liked the idea of Brigham Young. Smith was the dreamer of power, Young the wielder of power. Through Kalakaua, Gibson had access to the dream, the ceremonial aspects of power, and through another white man who attached himself to the king he had access to the realization. Claus Spreckels was a classic robber baron of the great days of developing industrial capitalism in the United States, a treasure hunter whose hunts paid off in the millions of dollars. Spreckels made his pile as a sugar refiner on the American West Coast, and when the Hawaiian plantation business grew big enough to interest him, he moved in on the islands. He got control of huge acreages, brought them into efficient production by bold and expensive irrigation schemes, and set up a steamship line to carry his product to his refineries on the West Coast (monopolizing in the process the transportation of his competitors' crops). In a remarkably short time Spreckels talked and bought his way into a position that made him the real controller of Hawaii's economy and the politics of the kingdom. Kalakaua, Gibson, and Spreckels ran Hawaii in the early 1880s, and really Spreckels ran the other two. He held the mortgages on Gibson's Lanai properties, and he held the notes on the king's gambling debts. And he was the principal creditor of the kingdom. The other planters and businessmen were alarmed and enraged by Spreckels because he was better than they at what they all did. Spreckels fascinated Gibson. Palawai on Lanai was nothing compared with Spreckelsville on Maui. And Spreckels himself was a human source from which lines of real power radiated.

It was inevitable that sooner or later the subject of imperial power radiating from Hawaii would come under consideration by Gibson and Kalakaua. They both wanted it. And it had been in the air in Hawaii for a surprisingly long time. Beginning in the late 1840s, a sort of Australasian Gibson named Charles St. Julian took it on himself to forward Hawaii's interests in Polynesia, looking toward a time when Hawaii would be recognized as the protector of other island groups which would be organized into a confederation. St. Julian lived in Sydney, never visited Hawaii, and did all his thinking and writing and planning on Hawaii's behalf for nothing, in return for the title of Hawaiian chargé d'affaires and consul general "to the Kings and Ruling Chiefs of the Independent States and Tribes in Polynesia South of the Equator." He worked up a diplomatic uniform for himself, "plain but 'spicy,' " and created an order of merit which he bestowed upon himself. For almost a generation St. Julian kept on dreaming his dreams of Polynesian primacy for Hawaii. Then at last he got the chance to realize some of his own dreams in another part of the ocean. He was appointed chief justice of Fiji, and took the bench there in scarlet robes and full-bottomed wig.

This happened at about the time when Gibson was beginning to interest himself seriously in Hawaiian politics. Later, just when Gibson was about to make his run at real political power, another Gibsonlike figure appeared at Honolulu, full of ideas of Polynesian primacy for Hawaii and lines of power radiating from the islands. Celso Caesar Moreno was Italian by birth, a naturalized American, imposing, a convincing talker, a spellbinder. Like Gibson he arrived in Hawaii by way of the East Indies. He had sailed a ship to Sumatra, where he had apparently married the daughter of a sultan. Again like Gibson, he appeared in Hawaii carrying impressive-looking documents with seals on them—a franchise to lay a cable between the United States and China. He also had interests in steamship lines and in the supplying of Chinese coolies to work on Hawaiian sugar plantations. The likeness to Gibson was amazing, and in fact Moreno was minister of foreign affairs in the Hawaiian cabinet before Gibson was. Moreno's term in office, in 1880, lasted only five days, beginning on the day he received his naturalization papers as a Hawaiian citizen and ending when the white businessmen forced the king to remove him. Moreno departed with his cable franchise (which was also a Gibsonian document—it had expired and was in fact worthless), leaving behind, among other memories, a renewed interest on the part of Kalakaua and Gibson in the idea of Hawaiian pre-eminence in Polynesia.

In the early 1880s, Polynesian primacy consisted of correspondence with some chiefs in the remote and tiny equatorial Gilbert Islands (not part of Polynesia) who wanted the benefits of a Hawaiian connection, and the annexation of even smaller Ocean Island, northwest of Hawaii, which Kalakaua's genealogists revealed as having been part of the ancient Hawaiian realm. Gibson, as foreign minister, kept up a paper campaign aimed at convincing the imperial powers with interests in the Pacific that Hawaii was worth listening to when policy was being decided, and that the policy of the great powers ought not to include annexation of islands. This approach was regarded by the powers—as far as it was attended to at all—as a minor irritation.

Then in 1886 Gibson got ready to make a big, bold move into the Pacific. Strategically and tactically it was all his own work, and it was made at the worst possible time in the worst possible place. It was so much like what he had done in Sumatra, except on a larger scale, that it raises the question of whether Gibson, in playing with lines of power, somehow always managed to arrange things in such a way that he got burned. Along with other things he was organizing at the same time, Polynesian primacy put him, for the second time in his life, under the hangman's noose.

Late in December, 1886, Kalakaua, at Gibson's instance, named a part-Hawaiian politician, John E. Bush, as his Envoy Extraordinary and Minister Plenipotentiary near His Majesty the King of Samoa and His Majesty the King of Tonga, and High Commissioner to the Sovereign Chiefs and Peoples of Polynesia. Bush was to go to Samoa and interest the Samoan king in an alliance with Hawaii, the idea being to reinforce the independence of the Hawaiian kingdom against the threat of annexation by one or other of the powers. If that worked, Bush was to do the same thing in Tonga, then in the Hervey Islands, the Cooks. As for the Gilberts, since they were sure to be annexed sooner or later by one power or another, it might as well be Hawaii. So Bush was instructed to look favorably upon any Gilbertese request to be put under Hawaiian control.

Samoa in the mid-1880s was being picked over by Germany, with Great Britain and the United States looking on not at all pleased. There was no such thing as a real "king" in Samoa. One high chief, Malietoa, seemed to have the support of a good many Samoans, but another, Tamasese, was being pushed forward by the Germans in their own interest. War between Samoan chiefs was always a possibility, and at the time of Bush's Hawaiian embassy it was a live possibility. So Gibson had put Hawaii in the middle of a complicated situation.

As if this was not enough, Bush was a man who found it difficult to stay sober for any length of time. He began his negotiations in Samoa with a gin-soaked entertainment for Malietoa, and when after some weeks Malietoa was persuaded to sign the articles of confederation with Hawaii there was a repeat performance which lasted all night and left the scene, as a later reporter said, "carpeted with slumbering grandees, who must be roused, doctored with coffee, and sent home." Bush's own despatches to Gibson were sufficiently coherent, but what was said about him privately and officially was acutely embarrassing, and eventually Gibson had to order his recall.

While Bush was working his diplomatic wiles, Gibson was putting into action the second stage of Polynesian primacy. He talked the Hawaiian legislature into buying a navy. It was, if anything, less fearsome than the Guatemalan Navy which Gibson had sailed as a young man: one ship, a secondhand guano boat, to be converted at considerable expense for the purpose of sailing Samoan waters and showing the Hawaiian flag. The *Kaimiloa* was a strange, strong-smelling idea from the start, and nothing it did ever gave the appearance of good sense. The captain was yet another nonstop drinker, a man named George E. Gresley Jackson, cashiered from the British Navy a long time before, now supervisor of a boys' reformatory at Honolulu, a place which supplied a couple of dozen crew members. The ship took along a Hawaiian band, and it was supposed to carry a knocked-down church and schoolhouse, a parson, and a teacher (none of these was ever loaded). It also sported saluting cannons and Gatling guns. The *Kaimiloa* was to exercise a "moral" influence. The night before sailing, there was a drunken brawl on board that turned into something like mutiny. Getting out of Honolulu harbor, Jackson almost rammed another ship and had to drop anchor in a hurry to avoid a collision. "Sick" for days on end heading southwest, Jackson finally became aware that his chronometers were not working properly. He could not be sure where he was headed. Wherever he was going, he was going slowly. The *Kaimiloa* burned an enormous amount of coal and put out billows of black smoke without making much headway: five knots on several tons of fuel a day. After a month at sea Jackson sighted Samoa, only one major island off course from where he had been pointing when he left Honolulu.

Once the *Kaimiloa* anchored at the principal Samoan port of Apia, Jackson got sick again, this time with dysentery, and while he was out of commission the crew went ashore and got drunk night after night. One night a gunner came back on board and got into an argument, and in the escalation that followed he came close to blowing up the powder magazine. At happier times, Ambassador Bush had the ship sail here and there among the islands, dispensing music and gin. The Samoans liked the ship's band, but not much else could be said in favor of the *Kaimiloa*'s outings.

Germany found the Hawaiian embassy and the *Kaimiloa*'s cruise offensive as well as absurd (the German warship *Adler* followed the *Kaimiloa* around the islands). Gibson, by getting Malietoa to sign an agreement with Hawaii, was coming down squarely against the German-backed chief Tamasese, and that was insulting. What Gibson meant by following this up with an armed vessel was unclear, but it was provocative. Gibson was given to understand this through diplomatic channels, and once he realized what he had done, which was to put Kalakaua's kingdom in the way of war with Bismarck's Germany, he recalled everybody from Samoa.

Gibson had made himself look ridiculous at home as well as overseas. The *Kaimiloa* in particular gave his enemies something to laugh about. And in the years during which he had been dreaming about Polynesian primacy, he had also been—to hear his enemies—running the Hawaiian kingdom into the ground financially, he and the spendthrift king and the money monster Claus Spreckels. By the time the *Kaimiloa* got pointed in the direction of Samoa, there was a well-organized and implacable opposition building up against Gibson in Hawaii, and by the time the *Kaimiloa* steamed back into port at Honolulu, Gibson was gone, out of power, deposed by revolution, threatened with lynching, and finally exiled.

Certainly Gibson gave his enemies every chance to do away with him. The situation was complicated, as all things in Hawaiian politics were, but essentially Gibson had come to be regarded as intolerable by powerful whites with a concern for economical government and a belief that the destiny of the Hawaiian islands was linked with that of the United States. Gibson was good at giving government contracts to his son-in-law (an Englishman named Fred Hayselden who had married Talula) and bad at accounting for public money. The national debt soared under the Gibson regime, and Claus Spreckels held the notes in large part. For years Spreckels had been able to get anything he wanted from the king and from the premier and thus from the country, and when finally he became too demanding and Gibson and Kalakaua with a mighty effort cut free of him, it was only to land the kingdom heavily in debt in another direction, to a London financial syndicate which made Hawaii a loan on criminally expensive terms.

The white reformers, being in a small minority, had nothing like the numbers to cleanse the kingdom electorally. Hawaiians would always be able to outvote them. So early in 1887 they banded together in a secret organization called the Hawaiian League, quietly and then not so quietly armed some volunteer militia companies, and waited for the right moment to strike. It came in June, when a particularly scandalous story broke over the king in his palace.

Kalakaua had accepted a bribe amounting to scores of thousands of dollars to award an opium-selling license to a Chinese merchant, and had then reneged, giving the license to another man and keeping the bribe money to pay off private debts. There was not much to be said in Kalakaua's defense: the story was essentially true.

The Hawaiian League called some public meetings, and the militia companies turned out with their rifles. The upshot was that the king was told to dismiss his cabinet—meaning, get rid of Gibson—and to submit to the framing of a new constitution which would reduce the Hawaiian monarch essentially to the status of a figurehead. Kalakaua had no way to stand up against the League. He had no reliable armed forces of his own. He was ready in any case to let Gibson go. He did.

For a day or two it looked as if Gibson might be lynched. He passed a tense night in his house with a mob outside, the only thing between him and them a detachment of the same militia which had taken up arms against him, commanded by a colonel who said that if he went outside he would be shot. The next morning, Gibson and Fred Hayselden were ordered out of the house and down to the waterfront. The militia colonel had decided to hang them, and it took a long, sweaty time in a dockside warehouse for other cooler heads among the revolutionaries to get the colonel to put away the rope. Gibson and Hayselden were taken back home under guard. Later the same day they were marched to the police station and charged with embezzlement. Then they were taken home again and kept under guard. The embezzlement case went to court a few days later and failed for lack of evidence. Next morning Gibson boarded a ship for San Francisco, alone, and sailed away from Hawaii forever.

He was in his mid-sixties. His life was in ruins, and he was ill, rake thin, consumptive, aging rapidly, under great stress, at the end of his tether. In August he went into hospital in San Francisco, and though from time to time he found himself well enough to go out and about, it was clear that he would not live long.

* * *

Gibson had one last indignity to suffer before he died. He was sued for breach of promise. For more than forty years he had been a widower, single, and if he had slept with Hawaiian women on Lanai he had evidently never thought of marrying one. In the midst of his appalling political difficulties in 1887, he began seeing a white woman socially at Honolulu. Her name was Flora Howard St. Clair, and she was the widow of a gambler, making her way through the world as a traveling bookseller. She was not unattractive, not unspirited, and she came to think that Gibson was interested in her to the point of proposing marriage. Gibson's daughter Talula was fiercely against the idea, and Gibson would not admit to having proposed. Mrs. St. Clair had circumstantial testimony to give—that Gibson had called himself white of hair but green of heart, and so on.

Gibson, for his part, said that the woman had forced herself on him, showing him pictures of naked ladies in the books she had for sale, comparing her own charms with those of the French art Venuses she was offering. Whatever he might have said to her in the parlor at her boarding house, in his diary Gibson took to calling Mrs. St. Clair "*that* woman," "a miserable schemer," "intriguing woman," and finally "devilish woman." She went to law, and Gibson was summonsed to answer the charge of breach of promise.

The case was not heard until after Gibson had gone into exile. It was a political trial, a relaxed substitute for the hanging of Gibson, good fun for the victorious reformers. Mrs. St. Clair retained as her attorneys a firm whose members were all reformers, and the jury was stacked with members of the Hawaiian League. Gibson duly sent sworn statements from San Francisco, but the verdict went against him and he had to pay eight thousand dollars damages. Someone made up a humorous minstrel song about the case, "Pa Gibby's Wooin' and de Breach ob Promise Soot!" and it was sung to great hilarity.

* * *

Gibson's enemies laughed him off the stage of life as something between a knave and a fool, a bad man and a figure of fun. His own view of himself was that he was a great man battling the fates. One of his heroes was the Portuguese poet Camoëns, about whom he wrote a series of long articles for a Honolulu newspaper. As usual, no matter what Gibson talked about, he was talking about himself. In Gibson's reading, Camoëns wanted nothing more than to be of service to his country, imperial Portugal, a nation "happy in cherishing the sanctities of domestic love" and at the same time leading "her lines of power around the world." Camoëns— generous, chivalrous, proud, refusing to crawl and fawn before the powerful—was cast adrift on the sea to lead a life of privation in the East, returning from exile only to die in poverty and obscurity, without a sheet to cover his body. Good Catholic sisters took care of his corpse. He was buried in a pit. Not till later was there a fitting reburial with praise for his poetic genius and his human greatness, and of course by then, as Gibson put it, the sun of Camoëns's love for his fellow man had set and could never be reillumined.

Gibson wanted his talents to yield him fortune and renown. This life-long project had two aspects. In one, Gibson would withdraw from the great world to a smaller world and make it his own. Here, islands were important to him, literal islands and islands of humanity, small communities: islands in the Caribbean, the small states of Central America, Tristan da Cunha, Sumatra, the Mormon community of Utah (to be relocated in

New Guinea), the City of Joseph at Palawai on Lanai, the Hawaiian kingdom itself. The idea of an island as a safe place, almost openly a comforting and nourishing breast, was strong in Gibson. He wanted as well to be a generative force, to create life out of himself, to be a father to his people. Then he wanted control, and to him control had its magical aspects, and so he appeared as a white Prospero among brown Calibans—the white leader, instructor, educator, healer, savior, a type of colonial. Then he wanted power. He would seek to attach his own enterprises to sources of power greater than his magic alone could generate. On his recommendation the United States was to take Tristan da Cunha. On his behalf the United States was to go to war against the Dutch. At his suggestion Brigham Young was to resettle the Mormons and President Buchanan was to foot the bill. In the Hawaiian kingdom, Kalakaua and Claus Spreckels were to give his magician's gestures validity and reality. And when all this was done, Gibson would appear in his other aspect, as the focus of lines of power that would radiate around the earth, binding the globe to him.

In all this, Gibson kept harking back to an image that had powerful value for him—the sun. It was a benign nourisher and warmer, a generative force, a source of power, a focus of attention. Gibson talked about the sun of Camoëns's love for his fellow man. The emblem of King Kalakaua was the sun at noon. In the dazzle of the sun on the water, Gibson saw the mirage of the Sumatran city that waited for him to bring it back to life. And he wanted powerfully to make his way to the source of power; he spoke of wanting to fly on the wings of the wind toward the rising of the sun.

In the Greek myth, Phaeton was the unacknowledged son of the sun god. His mother allowed him to discover his true paternity. He sought out his father among the gods, took the reins of the chariot of the sun, drove it wildly across the sky, lost control, brought disaster on himself and others by this attempt to go beyond his limited powers, and was finally struck down by a thunderbolt from Zeus. Gibson was a Phaeton. Well into his adult life he insisted on maintaining the fantasy of special privilege and disadvantage mingled in his story of his birth. Three times in his life—in Central America, in Sumatra, and in Samoa—Gibson directed ships into tropical areas of concentrated power, lost control, and was brought crashing down, twice to the brink of death by hanging. He tried to drive the sun and failed.

In his last year of life, when power was taken away from him, he retreated to a need for sustenance. At the same time as he was courting the widow St. Clair he was presenting himself as a suitor for another kind of love. Having been by his own account an ardent Baptist, true Mohammedan, a Buddhist, a Mormon, then an ex-Mormon, he was going back to his childhood faith, the Catholicism of his mother.

As a sick old man, politically beleaguered, he became infatuated with Mother Marianne Kopp, the mother superior of an order of Catholic sisters who worked in Honolulu among Hawaiian victims of leprosy. The health of the nation had always preoccupied Gibson as a politician interested in the increase of his people. Now he was both politically and personally ill. He threw himself at the feet of Mother Marianne. In what he wanted from her he was not uncomplicated. Sometimes he appeared to want to be her father, calling her "my little girl," "my own precious child." He spoke in his diary of needing her close, loving companionship. He wrote her tender notes and sent her presents. Once he compared her to a white rose with one drop of blood, striking imagery from a tubercular man half in love with a chaste nun who served the sick. And he decided that when he died, Mother Marianne should have the disposal of his body. In the meantime, he proposed to build a chapel at Honolulu. It was to be dedicated to St. Lucy. Lucy was his mother's name. The chapel was to be attached to a general hospital, where Mother Marianne would work. He would live close by.

The revolution of 1887 put an end to this plan, and Gibson, going into exile, had to give up Mother Marianne along with everything else. But he died in San Francisco in the care of Catholic nursing sisters, nursing mothers. Two of his last visitors were Claus Spreckels and Captain George E. Gresley Jackson of the *Kaimiloa*.

* * *

Robert Louis Stevenson

W HEN ROBERT LOUIS STEVENSON visited Hawaii in 1889 Kalakaua
was still king, and the two notables met at Honolulu. They made
an odd pair, a thin man and a fat man of ill-assorted bulk and background.
But they liked each other, passed a good deal of time together, and discovered some interests in common along the way. Literature, for one.
Stevenson was newly rich and famous, his *Dr. Jekyll and Mr. Hyde*
the sensation of the English-speaking world. So he was pleased to learn
that the king was a great admirer of his work, and it was easy for him in
turn to pronounce Kalakaua "a very fine, intelligent fellow." Polynesian
tradition was a growing fascination of Stevenson's, and it was the king's
particular passion. (He had recently published a collection of legends.)
Kalakaua brought books on Hawaiian subjects from his personal library
for Stevenson to study, had the royal *hula* dancers perform for him, and
invited him to a meeting of Hale Naua, the lodge dating from Walter

Murray Gibson's day, devoted to the secret lore of the ancient Hawaiian world. The two men entertained back and forth, breakfasting at Iolani Palace, whiling away some pleasant hours aboard the chartered yacht that had carried Stevenson to Hawaii; and at Waikiki, where Stevenson took a house on the beach, they sat down, literary ectomorph and royal endomorph, to a fine *luau*, a Hawaiian feast of chicken, crab, seaweed, pig, raw fish and *poi*, and baked dog with all the trimmings.

Kalakaua's appetites matched his size. In his early fifties, he had arrived at the classic settled bulk of the mature Hawaiian chief, wearing well-cut white tropical suits and filling them expansively. He was a metabolic wonder, able during an ordinary warm Hawaiian afternoon of relaxed visiting and casual conversation to put away bottle after bottle of champagne and brandy, then rise apparently unaffected—if, in Stevenson's phrase, more "dignified"—and go on effortlessly to a long, drawn-out evening of more of the same.

Stevenson, who was younger, not yet forty, watched this kind of performance in awe. He was by no means against a glass of wine himself, but he lacked Kalakaua's cubic capacity. A lifetime of wretchedly bad health had left Stevenson a stick insect of a man, a fleshless frame. Just under five feet nine inches tall, he weighed at his heaviest perhaps one hundred fifteen pounds. Kalakaua would have made two of him. But then Stevenson burned enough nervous energy for two, and talked enough for two. He used words as his means of grasping and keeping hold of life, and his whole body was at the service of his voice. He loved to hold the floor, pacing endlessly, conducting his storytelling like music with pale, long-fingered, "Frenchman's hands." People found Stevenson the most irresistible of conversational companions. And he was a good audience for himself, too, studying his effects with eyes of deepest brown, wide-set, flashing, compulsively self-aware. Part of the fascination, of course, was that at any moment Stevenson's bright flickering flame might gutter and burn out. The lungs cramped within his humiliatingly frail and skinny rib cage were treacherous, and he lived unremittingly under the threat of pulmonary hemorrhage—"Bluidy Jack," as he called his chronic affliction.

All his life Stevenson had been vainly chasing good health, first in Europe, more recently in the United States, and now in the Pacific, where he and his entourage made up an unlikely party for voyaging among strange, out-of-the-way South Sea islands. There was the invalid himself, who was paying for the charter but who might not survive the cruise. Then there was his American-born wife Fanny, older by ten years, definitely middle-aged, recently operated on for some kind of growth in her throat. With them traveled Lloyd Osbourne, Fanny's son by a previous marriage, just out of his teens, tall and strongly built but with eyes so bad he had to wear the thickest of glasses, and Stevenson's mother Margaret, a fine Scottish lady whom everyone liked, but who was nearly sixty, who wore white widow's caps and lace mittens, and whose previous experience of the sea was limited to a single Atlantic crossing by passenger steamer. No matter. With cameras, playing cards, musical instruments, a typewriter, a French maid named Valentine, and a captain who took some convincing that the enterprise was a going one, they had set out from San Francisco in the ninety-four-foot schooner *Casco*, heading south into eastern Polynesia—first the Marquesas (Stevenson had been reading Melville with the greatest admiration), then the atolls of the Tuamotu archipelago, then Tahiti, and at last, after seven months, Hawaii.

At Honolulu, as well as the meeting with Kalakaua, there was a reunion with the rest of the family Stevenson acquired when he married. Fanny's daughter Isobel and her husband, the artist Joseph Strong, born the son of a Protestant minister at Honolulu, had been living in the islands for several years with their little boy Austin. Belle, a bright young woman with a taste for pleasure, had taken Kalakaua's eye and become part of the court circle, helpful and useful to the king in small ways, someone he could trust. During the tense revolutionary days of 1887 she had acted as a go-between, carrying messages from the beleaguered Kalakaua to the imprisoned Walter Murray Gibson. Kalakaua rewarded her by making her a lady companion of the royal order.

Because the king enjoyed Belle's company, he looked out for her husband's interests. As a favor of sorts, Joe had been appointed official artist-photographer with the Hawaiian mission to Samoa in 1887. Joe, charming and not untalented, was an errant butterfly of a man, a philanderer, a self-indulgent—even self-destructive—drinker and opium smoker, with a record of ingenious evasion of work and a desk drawer stuffed with unpaid bills. But even if he drank in Samoa as he did in Hawaii, he still managed to bring back good photographs, and after Stevenson arrived at Honolulu the two men talked about working up a pictorial essay on the Samoan political situation.

For Stevenson this was a strange enough choice of subject. He could hardly have been described as a political person, and he had never been within fifteen hundred miles of Samoa. But Joe knew the place, after his fashion, and so did Henry Poor, who had been secretary of the Hawaiian mission; and it was Poor's house that Stevenson used during part of his stay at Waikiki. Just then, too, an American journalist came back from Samoa with stories of bloodshed between islanders and German marines.

The Germans had been marching about at night and the Samoan warriors had ambushed them and taken some heads. Stevenson felt caught up enough in the event, however vicariously, to write a long letter to the *Times*. It was not one of his best inspirations. In what he said about the Germans he was injudicious, and his attempt at defending the Hawaiian embassy was, objectively viewed, fairly silly. He really did not know what was happening in Samoa.

The odd thing was that quite soon Stevenson would find himself settling in Samoa, and there he lived the rest of his life. Yet when he wrote to the *Times* he was not planning anything of the sort. He did not even have it seriously in mind to visit the place. But he did want to stay in the Pacific, at least for a while longer.

From the first, Stevenson had been ecstatic about the warm latitudes of the ocean. He loved sunshine and soaked it up wherever and whenever he could. All his life, the color brown called up deep yearnings and satisfactions in Stevenson; for him, to be brown rather than white was to be more satisfactorily alive. Aboard the *Casco,* and ashore in the islands, he took off his shirt and shoes, padded about bare-shouldered, bare-footed, bare-headed, and wrote in amused delight: "as for colour, hands, arms, feet, legs, and face, I am browner than the berry: only my trunk and the aristocratic spot on which I sit retain the vile whiteness of the north." It was a real sea change, something more than skin-deep. Later he had a character in one of his South Seas stories speak about the transforming effect of the Pacific: "Day after day the sun flamed; night after night the moon beaconed, or the stars paraded their lustrous regiment. I was aware of a spiritual change, or perhaps rather a molecular reconstitution. My bones were sweeter to me. I had come home to my own climate, and looked back with pity on those damp and wintry zones, miscalled the temperate."

Stevenson was feeling the pull of oceans and islands. He had braced himself at the rail of the *Casco* as she heeled exhilaratingly in high seas, and he loved it, so he wrote to his literary friend Sidney Colvin. The ocean was dangerous, ocean sailing was a gamble, but this only put a sharper edge on living. "Fine, clean emotions; a world all and always beautiful; air better than wine; interest unflagging; there is upon the whole no better life." He had prospected for shells on the coral sands of remote atolls, recovered from a serious cold on a diet of chunks of raw mullet in a marinade of lime juice, coconut milk, and red pepper, hobnobbed with brown-skinned aristocrats dressed in white suits, and conversed with cannibals covered mostly in tattoos. The Pacific was taking him out of his literary world into a state of life where the nineteenth century existed only in spots, "a no-man's land of the ages, a stir-about of epochs and races, barbarisms and civilisations, virtues and crimes." Fascinating. He wanted more. To another literary friend, Henry James, he wrote about his love affair with the Pacific, "this precious deep," and went on: "to draw near to a new island, I cannot say how much I like."

All in all, he had never felt better. He decided he would not return to England for another year, and, having dismissed the *Casco*, he lay about at Honolulu "in a fine state of haze," as he put it, ruminating his next move.

* * *

Stevenson was not sure what direction he should take after Hawaii— west to Asia, or south toward Fiji and Tonga, where he could pick up the unglamorous steamer *Richmond* for Tahiti and from there return eventually to Europe. The availability of ships for charter at Honolulu decided him. He was informed that the Protestant vessel *Morning Star* of the Micronesian mission might take him and his family on its regular run from Hawaii into the western Pacific—if they engaged not to drink, smoke, or swear. Stevenson could have managed decorum, but he was relieved when something less determinedly respectable turned up: the small copra trader *Equator*, new and therefore not too smelly, captained by a twenty-three-year-old Scot named Dennis Reid, headed for the Gilbert Islands in the low latitudes southwest of Hawaii.

The *Equator* was a comedown from the luxurious *Casco*. It would take some remodeling to squeeze the party in, even though they were to be one fewer in number. They were adding Joe Strong but losing Mrs. Stevenson senior for the time being and Valentine the maid permanently, leaving Fanny the only woman aboard; Belle and young Austin would be joining them later. Stevenson had been writing travel letters from the Pacific to be syndicated in American newspapers (for excellent money). Now he was looking ahead to a lecture tour in the United States for himself and perhaps for Lloyd too. He wanted to use lantern slides and a diorama. Lloyd and Joe were bringing cameras, an eight-by-ten, a "detective five-by-four" and a hundred dozen plates, and Joe packed a water-color kit. A Protestant missionary Stevenson had gotten to know in Honolulu let him have a magic lantern and some Biblical slides to project for the Gilbert-ese, and Stevenson liked this; he could put on shows ashore and amuse the islanders without having them all over the ship. The day the *Equator* sailed, King Kalakaua came down to the waterfront, bringing some musicians from the Royal Hawaiian Band for departing serenades and champagne for copious farewell toasts.

On the way to the Gilberts, Stevenson, in better and better health, cooked up a scheme intended as a business proposition, serious and enjoyable both, that would give him a base of sorts in the Pacific. He and Lloyd would put their minds seriously to writing together, buy a ship with their earnings, and go into the island trade. Dennis Reid, an excellent seaman and a likable young fellow, so fervent about his Scottishness that he wore the bonnet of his homeland at the wheel, would actually captain the ship and run the business; Stevenson and Lloyd would sail with him when they felt like it. As a name for their ship, Stevenson favored *Northern Lights*, a remembrance of his lighthouse-building Scottish forebears. He and Lloyd did some costing and some animated planning for rifle racks, patent davits, a steam launch, and a ship's library. And they talked about a name for the firm; Jekyll & Hyde appealed to them.

But all this was before Stevenson reached the Gilberts and got a close look at what the island trade might actually mean. "The rotten pestilential civilization of the traders," another visitor to the Gilberts called it, and Stevenson agreed once he saw it in action. He was put off, and he concluded for the time being to take his profit from the Pacific in health and enjoyment and material for stories, letting the rest go by. (As if to point up the good sense of Stevenson's decision, Dennis Reid later got into trouble with the law. He sold a ship that was not his to sell and wound up in jail in Fiji.)

In the equatorial Gilberts, Stevenson was among coral atolls, on the Micronesian frontier of the open Pacific. This part of the ocean had not come up against the white man nearly as much as Hawaii, Tahiti, or even the remote Marquesas. Gilbertese women used to go naked before marriage and wore practically nothing after, just a fringe of grass around the hips—the "perilous hairbreadth" *riri*, Stevenson called it—and the men were warriors with mat armor and helmets and shark-tooth spears. But times were changing. The missionary was here, and white traders came and went, buying copra from the islanders and unloading whatever they could in exchange. Now at Butaritari, the *Equator*'s first major stop, there were two trading posts for San Francisco firms, two drinking houses, a missionary church, and a chief's "palace" of wood with a corrugated iron roof, a bell that would not ring, and two cannons that would not fire. The royal guards wore uncomfortable shoes, and the women were going in for cheap trade dresses instead of the *riri*.

The best of the white traders were like businessmen everywhere, distinctly in business for themselves. The worst—and Stevenson saw them at work—were masters of fast talk, short weight, vague accounting, outright fraud, and they dealt in guns and alcohol. When the Stevensons waded ashore at Butaritari lagoon in mid-July, 1889, everyone there was roaring drunk and had been since the Fourth, which was celebrated by the American traders and had caught on among the islanders. Stevenson saw a man lose an earlobe in a barroom brawl, watched a "tipsy deputation" wheeling along a case of brandy in a barrow, and came across the chief of the island and his guard with their Winchester rifles, drunk, tottering between the two drinking houses in search of the royal tipple—Kümmel, of all things, as Stevenson observed.

Butaritari just then was a nasty place. Stevenson made it known to the chief that he was an intimate personal friend of Queen Victoria—indeed her son—and that if he and his party were molested a man-of-war would be sent to take reprisals. The Stevensons kept their own guns loaded, though not exactly out of fear; in fact, as Stevenson said, they bubbled with delight, sitting "deep into the night like a pack of schoolboys, preparing the revolvers and arranging plans against the morrow." By day they held showy target practice, firing at empty bottles "to the admiration of the natives." Stevenson did some politicking among the whites at the drinking houses with the idea of having the selling of liquor stopped. Whether or not this carried any weight, the chief eventually put a tabu on drinking, swore off alcohol himself, and went to church, and Butaritari sobered up. Stevenson later made a great hit by showing the Biblical lantern slides he had brought from Honolulu.

Before the *Equator* left Butaritari, the Stevensons had the good luck to see some marvelous dancing and singing. It was better than anything they had come across in Polynesia. Marquesan dancing had not impressed Stevenson much; it was like a badly done cancan, he said, and all it brought out in him was a Scotsman's impulse to compare some of the steps with those of Highland reels. The Hawaiian *hula* he found deadly: "surely the most dull of man's inventions, and the spectator yawns under its length as at a college lecture or a parliamentary debate." But Gilbertese dancing and the singing of massed accompanying choruses was electrifying—no less than operatic, with a great rehearsed understanding among the performers, a wide range of emotions, a fierce expressiveness, fine stories stirringly told by voice and body together. It carried him away, his wife too. "The leading man," wrote Fanny, "in an impassioned ecstasy which possessed him from head to foot, seemed transfigured; once it was as though a strong wind had swept the stage—their arms, their feathered fingers thrilling with an emotion that shook my nerves as well; heads and bodies followed like a field of grain before a gust. My blood came hot and cold, tears pricked my eyes, my head whirled, I felt an almost irresistible impulse to join the dancers."

At the *Equator*'s next major stop, Abemama, Stevenson met the great personage of the Gilberts, Tem Binoka, who figured in the islands' war songs "like Napoleon in those of our grandfathers." He was a man far bigger than Kalakaua, down in middle age from the staggering overweight of his earlier years to something under three hundred pounds, with an extraordinary face, "a beaked profile like Dante's in the mask, a mane of long black hair, the eye brilliant, imperious, and inquiring." An absolutist of absolutists, Binoka did not like anyone else to talk, just himself, in a voice shrill, powerful, uncanny. His numerous wives and innumerable retainers carried out his bidding without question, in a sort of tropical slow-motion total acquiescence. If anyone did a displeasing thing, Binoka might reach for his Winchester. He was a crack shot whose warnings were deliberate near-misses, and in his time he had despatched with a single bullet disagreeables, disobedients, and unwanted wives. Binoka took a strong line with white men as well. The story was that his father had once put to death every white in his islands, and during Stevenson's stay only one white man lived on Abemama, in fear and at the chief's pleasure. "I got power," Binoka told Stevenson, and this was true.

Binoka's policy was to keep the outside world at arm's length, taking what looked good, rejecting the rest. He was not a mindless despot; he was intelligent, and he had traded (though not too successfully) with his own ships in places as far away as New Zealand. It was no good Stevenson representing himself here as a son of Queen Victoria. And Fanny's claim, supportable in principle, to be descended from a close relative of Captain Cook, turned out to count for nothing, because Binoka could not find Cook in his only reference work on the outside world, the Gilbertese version of the Gospels. So Stevenson had himself announced as "one of the Old Men of England," a "person of deep knowledge, come expressly to visit Tembinok's dominion," and eager to report on it to the no less eager British ruler. After lengthy consideration, Binoka approved the Stevensons and went on to supervise personally the arrangements for their stay. At a signal from his Winchester, laborers assembled and hoisted thatch huts onto their backs and walked them to the chosen site, big leafy carapaces moving beetle-legged among the coconut palms.

The Stevensons called their place "Equator Town" after the ship that brought them there, and after their location, only a half degree of latitude from the line. They liked the airy Gilbertese hut—the best in the South Seas, Stevenson thought—and were happy sketching, writing, photographing, making music (Stevenson was a great tootler on the flageolet, the others played guitars and banjos), encouraging a vegetable garden, going after birds with revolvers and a fowling piece lent by Binoka, and observing the islanders.

The great study was Binoka himself. In the matter of clothes he was whimsical, now wearing a woman's frock, now a naval uniform, now trousers and shirt of his own design in green velvet or red silk. He kept the equatorial sun off his head with a pith helmet, and the coral glare out of his eyes with blue spectacles. He was an insatiable acquirer of trade goods. His wives concentrated mostly on tobacco, but Binoka was eclectic, and his palace precinct was jammed, room after room, with "clocks, musical boxes, blue spectacles, umbrellas, knitted waistcoats, bolts of stuff, tools, rifles, fowling-pieces, medicines, European foods, sewing-machines, and, what is more extraordinary, stoves." If he saw something he liked, he wanted it, even if he had no use for it. (The sewing machines sometimes ended up as anchors.) He did not want others to accumulate wealth. One of his inventions was a card game with the special feature that he was dealt two hands to the other players' one each, and if he was amiable enough to let his wives buy their own tobacco from trading ships he took everything back from them in long lamplit evening sessions over the cards. He knew he would win. "Mo' betta," he said.

Binoka was also a writer and poet, Stevenson was interested to find. He had learned from missionaries how to put his own language on paper, and he had a surprising English vocabulary picked up from traders. He composed lyric poetry: "Sweethearts and trees and the sea. Not all the same true, all the same lie." And he was engaged in recording the history of his reign (which included a visit from an emissary of King Kalakaua, a part of the Polynesian confederacy scheme; Binoka tried to convert it into an alliance for expanding his own territories). Stevenson would come across Binoka, lying pensive on his belly, earthenware spittoon and leaden ink-pot beside him and a commercial ledger open to his remembered accomplishments. Writerlike, Binoka did not enjoy being interrupted, but once he paused to read aloud in translation a chapter of his annals for Stevenson, who found it as dull as the Hawaiian *hula*.

Binoka had a great appetite for Western cooking, perhaps because the traditional Gilbertese atoll diet was so restricted. He sent a cook to learn from the Stevensons. Fanny, a noted green thumb, labored over her garden at Equator Town, but the soil was unrewarding and the Stevensons found themselves eating mostly out of cans. Everyone's health suffered somewhat, and Stevenson came down with one of his colds, which could have been serious, even disastrous. There was no doctor even remotely accessible. Out of equal parts lack of choice and ethnographic curiosity Stevenson submitted himself to Gilbertese medicine, which consisted of sorcerers' incantations and a "suffumingation" with the smoke of burned leaves. This was general practitioners' treatment, and it did no good. But then the patient was referred to a specialist, a mesmerist who put him under successfully—something a dozen Western hypnotists had failed to do at one time or another in his life—after which he stumbled back to Equator Town "somnambulous," fell into a dreamless stupor, and woke to find his cold gone.

Stevenson was able to do Binoka a medical favor in return, curing a hangover for him with bicarbonate of soda (Binoka had a taste for something pink and terrible sold to him in Hennessy brandy bottles). Stevenson was constructing a pleasing relationship with another great Pacific chief. He drafted a letter "To the Officer commanding any Man of War calling at Apemama," giving Binoka the highest of marks for intelligence and competence as a ruler who exercised control severe but salutary. Fanny designed him a new flag, red, green, and yellow, featuring a shark. All in all Binoka found the Stevensons fine guests, well worth the time and trouble of a powerful chief. He had learned a lot from them. When they got ready to leave, Binoka wept. He made a moving little speech, presented Stevenson with some warrior's armor that had belonged to his forebears, and then, dressed in naval uniform, accompanied his departing friends out to the *Equator* in his own gig.

* * *

The *Equator*'s last stop with the Stevensons aboard was the port of Apia on the island of Upolu in the Samoan group, in tropical waters well south of the line. Coming ashore and making their way along the "beach," the straggling sandy track dotted with saloons and stores that constituted the Samoan commercial capital, Fanny, Lloyd, and Stevenson attracted the attention of the Protestant clergyman William E. Clarke of the London Missionary Society. Clarke had no idea who he was looking at. The *Equator* was an unremarkable trading schooner, and the Stevensons were down a peg or two in appearance since the cruise of the *Casco*. Fanny was wearing "a print gown, large gold crescent earrings, a Gilbert-island hat of plaited straw, encircled with a wreath of small shells, a scarlet silk scarf round her neck, and a brilliant plaid shawl across her shoulders; her bare feet were encased in white canvas shoes, and across her back was slung a guitar. The younger of her two companions was dressed in a striped pyjama suit—the undress costume of most European traders in these seas—a slouch straw hat of native make, dark blue sun-spectacles, and over his shoulders a banjo. The other man was dressed in a shabby suit of white flannels that had seen many better days, a white drill yachting cap with prominent peak, a cigarette in his mouth, and a photographic camera in his hand. Both the men were barefooted. . . ." Clarke's first thought was that probably "they were wandering players en route to New

Zealand, compelled by their poverty to take the cheap conveyance of a trading vessel."

The plan was to stay several weeks while Stevenson reduced the backlog of travel letters he owed the American newspaper syndicate. Then the family would catch the mail steamer to Sydney and from there book passage back to Europe. Where Stevenson would ultimately take up residence was still vague. One thought was that, having at last found the kind of climate that agreed with his lungs—warm rather than cold, oceanic rather than land-bound—he could base himself somewhere in the mild reaches of the Atlantic, for example on Madeira, wintering there and occasionally risking a summer in Edinburgh or London for the sake of seeing his treasured old friends. So it is a considerable surprise to find that within a few weeks of his Samoan landfall Stevenson was making plans to settle on Upolu.

It was a momentous decision, apparently rather hectically arrived at. Actually, though, Stevenson had had less civilized islands than Madeira on his mind most of his life, and there had been one or two signposts pointing directly to Samoa. As a boy he had met the author of the famous children's book *The Coral Island,* R. M. Ballantyne, and had been so impressed he decided to become a writer. He wrote his own boyish "Adventures in the South Seas," about a shipwreck that left two midshipmen stranded among savages who were going to burn them alive. In his early twenties a New Zealander talked at length to him about South Sea islands and the Samoan group in particular, "beautiful places, green for ever; perfect climate"—good for the lungs—and "perfect shapes of men and women, with red flowers in their hair; and nothing to do but to study oratory and etiquette, sit in the sun, and pick up the fruits as they fall." Later, Stevenson met an Australian painter, John Peter Russell, who had sailed the South Seas and had stories to tell. In San Francisco, Stevenson talked to the American author Charles Warren Stoddard—a friend of Joe and Belle Strong—who told old-Pacific-hand tales from his cruises among the islands and introduced Stevenson to the books of the almost-forgotten (though still living) Herman Melville. And not long before the *Casco* sailed, Stevenson had some conversation with a man who had been United States consul in Samoa, about a particular spot above Apia on Mt. Vaea, a most delightful place to live.

Considered in logistical terms, Samoa was not an impossible base for Stevenson. Mail connections with Europe were reasonable, and there was even a telegraph link, through Auckland, only a week away by steamer; he would not be altogether out of touch with the world. There was no overriding reason to think his earning power as an author would suffer. All the way across the Pacific he had been producing steadily. And in Samoa perhaps he could be a planter as well as a writer. At first he did not regard Samoans as highly as some other islanders he had met, but that was not a great consideration. He was most interested in land underfoot and a roof overhead in a climate that would allow him to live a halfway healthy life.

As it happened, the American trader Harry J. Moors, a prominent figure on the beach at Apia, knew of an estate that might suit. By wild coincidence, this turned out to be the very place so attractively described to Stevenson in San Francisco. And the owner, a blind Scottish blacksmith (a Stevensonian character indeed), was ready to sell. A deal was struck: 314½ acres, at ten Chile dollars an acre, half the money down, the other half in six months.

For Stevenson to have bought this place was as much as to say that he was abandoning plans to go back to Europe to live. He began to speak more and more of just a last trip, to see friends and settle his affairs. So, leaving Harry Moors to clear a few acres on Mt. Vaea and put up a small house, Stevenson took the mail steamer south. He went ashore at Sydney and immediately fell seriously ill; and with that he gave up irrevocably on Europe. If he went back there, he said, it would be to die. It was left to Lloyd eventually to make the voyage and sell the house where Stevenson and Fanny had lived for a time in the mid-1880s, at Bournemouth on the south coast of England. Ever since Stevenson entered the Pacific, eighteen months ago now, his body had been telling him unmistakably that here he could be well, that he could measure health in degrees of latitude, no more than twenty on either side of the equator. So after a restorative sea cruise he returned to Samoa. And for the rest of his days he traveled very little, leaving the tropics rarely and going beyond the Pacific never.

Stevenson's commitment to the acreage above Apia ushered in a new stage of his life. He became a householder. Once when he was young, he had humorously but more or less accurately told his parents they had a tramp for a son. He was a compulsive leaver of places, a mover-on; at the age of thirty-six he could count two hundred ten towns in Britain and Europe where he had spent a night or more. Now, in his fortieth year, with the question of his health apparently decided in his favor for the first time in his life, he was proposing to plant himself permanently and preparing to gather his family around him. Soon he was referring to his purchase, only half-jokingly, as his "ancestral acres," his "empire."

He christened his new home, Vailima—five streams. There were really only four, but Stevenson inflated the number because he liked the sound

of the word. "We range from 600 to 1500 feet," he wrote to his old friend
Charles Baxter, "have 5 streams, waterfalls, precipices, profound ravines,
rich tablelands, 50 head of cattle on the ground (if anyone could catch
them), a great view of forest, sea, mountains . . . really a noble place."
    Life as a beginning planter agreed with him marvelously. To his delight
he found that, given low latitudes and highish altitudes, he could work
hard in the open for hours at a stretch. For a man who not so many years
ago in England had passed most of his days huddled indoors "like a weevil
in a biscuit," this was liberation. He "went crazy" over the fierce unfamil-
iar exhilaration of bush clearing, and as usual he was able to make a great
adventure out of the everyday. At times Stevenson's relationship with nature was oddly queasy; now he was seized by the thought that to become a
planter he first had to be a murderer. "The life of the plants comes
through my finger-tips, their struggles go to my heart like supplications. I
feel myself blood-boltered. . . ." But he liked to look back on what he had
cleared, and he trained himself to ruthlessness about the "sensitive
plant," the especially recalcitrant weed that was his great enemy. "*Nothing,*" he wrote to Sidney Colvin, "is so interesting as weeding, clearing,
and pathmaking; the oversight of labourers becomes a disease; it is quite
an effort not to drop into the farmer; and it does make you feel so well. To
come down covered with mud and drenched with sweat and rain after
some hours in the bush, change, rub down, and take a chair in the veran-
dah, is to taste a quiet conscience."
    He and Fanny lived rough in the cottage Moors had put up for them:
endless hard labor and an erratic food supply, a single avocado shared for
lunch one day, a can of sardines another, for dinner a lone breadfruit. This
is how, late in 1890, they were discovered by visitors, moneyed tourists
cruising the Pacific as Stevenson himself had done, for health and diversion, seeking out interesting experience and appropriate company. The
distinguished American historian Henry Adams and his traveling companion the artist John La Farge rode up from Apia especially to meet the
celebrated author in his picturesque exile. They came unannounced and
evidently unadvised about what they might find. Adams, a New England
patrician of patricians, with a self-admitted "Bostonianism, and finikin
clinging to what I think the best," was flabbergasted by the encounter. In
a clearing dotted with burned tree stumps stood a shanty as squalid as a
railroad navvy's hut, and the man who appeared on the steps to greet
them was so emaciated that he looked, so Adams wrote, like a bundle of
sticks in a sack, wearing dirty striped cotton pyjamas, the baggy legs
tucked into coarse knit woolen stockings, one bright brown, the other—
purplish. So this was the literary lion of the world. And as for its mate—

Fanny, covered by a "missionary nightgown," was as grubby, dark, and wild as a Mexican halfbreed or an Apache squaw.

Stevenson, Adams, and La Farge met again several times before the tourists departed for Tahiti. Generally Louis and Fanny were cleaner, though never, by Adams's standards, entirely presentable. About his initial messy, foodless reception at Vailima Adams remained severe, and it led him to rank Stevenson below the Samoans themselves. "Our visit was as full of queerities as any social experiment I can recall, and in contrast to our visits to the natives, with their ease and grace of manner, their cleanliness and generosity of housekeeping, and their physical beauty, it gave me," he remarked ironically, "an illuminating sense of the superiority of our civilisation." Considered as a white man among white men, Stevenson came out no better. The "squalor" in which he lived "must be somehow due to his education. All through him, the education shows. His early associates were all second-rate; he never seems by any chance to have come in contact with first-rate people, either men, women or artists." This was a superb Adamsism. Henry James, for one, was Stevenson's devoted friend, with whom he often discussed the theory and practice of fiction.

Why Stevenson should have graveled Adams so badly is not altogether clear. Perhaps Adams was displacing some bad temper. Henry James had his own amused puzzlement about Stevenson's two visitors (themselves friends of James) and their enforced closeness on a prolonged tour. How "Adams and La Farge could, either of them, have failed to murder the other" James did not know. His conclusion was that "each lives to prove the other's self-control." Whatever the case, very likely the first few moments of Adams's acquaintance with Stevenson were decisive, when it became obvious that Stevenson had never heard of him. La Farge yes; he and Stevenson had friends in common, and could talk art together easily and congenially. Adams no, neither as an Adams of Boston descended from two United States presidents, nor as Adams the great historian and prose stylist. Stevenson's letters confirmed it. "I saw La Farge here," he wrote to his American publisher, "and another gentleman who knew you: name forgotten." And when the name did occur to him he got it partly wrong. "We have had enlightened society," he wrote to Henry James, "La Farge, the painter, and your friend Charles Adams."

By contrast, the whole world knew who Stevenson was, and Adams considered such celebrity sordid in itself. Before setting out for the South Seas, Adams had stipulated that "in thus imitating Robert Louis Stevenson," he was "inspired by no wish for fame or future literary or political notoriety." Adams was self-admittedly first-rate and perversely proud to be known nowhere, except for a precious fame among his select handful of friends, all of whom were also first-rate. Adams, who did not have to keep himself alive with his pen, never cared for the average reader, or for the average man of his day. If he could choose the right five hundred people to read what he wrote, he once said, he would affect five hundred thousand others. Or else posterity would provide him with a vast and appreciative audience. Stevenson, on the other hand, had done the common thing, writing for the here and now, selling in the thousands and tens of thousands. He was second-rate and known everywhere. Thus Adams.

Another thing, more private, was almost certainly present in what went on, unstated, between the two men. Adams had not had an easy time in recent years. Death had taken his father and mother, together with several other relatives. And his wife had killed herself. Adams's way of dealing with this closest of personal tragedies was to speak of himself as dead to the world. He was a man who needed a nourishing relationship with a strong woman, and it was denied him, and this was one reason why in late middle age he was willing to go drifting indefinitely about the Pacific. The best time in his life had been when, with his great American history underway, he and his wife planned, raised, and enjoyed a fine home in Washington. Now, widowed and dead to the world, Adams had concluded as well after his major work was finished to "retire" from authorship. Stevenson, by contrast, was flourishing as an author, writing on and on. A dreadfully sick man, he still displayed an energy and an appetite for life and labor that overwhelmed his intricately hypochondriac and consummately worldweary visitor. Adams described himself as running down like an unwound clock, barely able to summon up physical motion as a substitute for emotional vivacity. No wonder, then, that he wrote with such a mixture of fascination and horror about Stevenson, this dirty cotton bag with its sense of skeleton within, shirt-sleeves rolled up over the thinnest white arms Adams had ever seen, which Stevenson brandished as if he meant to throw them away. The man could not stop talking, and was incapable of stillness: "He seems never to rest, but perches like a parrot on every available projection, jumping from one to another. . . ." Stevenson was just too much for Adams.

By chance the two men shared a memorialist in the United States, of good times for Stevenson, bad times for Adams. The sculptor Auguste Saint-Gaudens's bronze portrait medallion of Stevenson, done from the life, was struck at the height of the author's fame, not long before he set out for the Pacific. And while Adams was in Samoa, privately railing at Stevenson and recoiling from Fanny, Saint-Gaudens was at work on a bronze statue to stand over the grave of Adams's wife in Washington.

Adams might understandably have been upset at seeing the author Stevenson, about the same age as himself when he had been happy, working indefatigably alongside his wife—in Adams's eyes a caricature married couple ferociously content, absurdly playing house in the jungle squalor of Vailima.

*   *   *

All the time Stevenson was dredging around in his sordid mountain mud heap in the way that Adams found so repellent, he was planning a great house. It was bigger in his head than it could ever be on the ground, and when he saw the cost estimates for his first grandiose conception, he had to do a lot of scaling down. Even so, once his home at Vailima was completed, a two-story structure put up in 1891 and a second building added "en echelon" in 1892–1893, there was nothing like it in Samoa, and it was famous as far away as Fiji.

From the outside it was barnlike, merely bulky rather than imposing, with wood siding and a corrugated iron roof. But inside there were five upstairs bedrooms, a big library, the only fireplace in Samoa (several hundred feet up from sea level the night temperature might drop to 56 degrees, at which point Lloyd Osbourne's "thermometer," coconut oil in a bottle, would solidify), and a great hall lined and ceiled in Californian redwood, with a superbly polished floor big enough for a hundred dancers and a piano standing at one end in a sort of giant tea cosy to protect it from the humid air.

All the materials for the house were imported, either from the Australian colonies or the West Coast of the United States—effect impressive, cost staggering. Seventy-two tons of Stevenson family furniture and household goods were assembled in England and Scotland, crated and shipped to Apia, and hauled up Mt. Vaea on bullock drays. "The big dining room," wrote Belle Strong to Charles Warren Stoddard, an appreciator of elaborate Pacific décor, "with its view of the sea over the treetops is papered with tapa of a yellowish colour—it looks like tapestry . . . the leather-buttoned chairs, the mahogany table, the Chippendale sideboard, the arabian curtains (of silver striped stuff over gold silk), the paintings, the display of arms, Japanese, Indian & South Sea," two gilt Burmese Buddhas and a Rodin nude in plaster, a gift from the sculptor, and "last but not least the wide doors opening onto the most beautiful view in the world, make up an ensemble that it is a pleasure to gaze upon. . . ."

The Stevenson table silver and linen bore a family crest (Lloyd told the Samoan servants it was a kind of totem, to discourage pilfering). Mrs. Stevenson senior brought out a damask tablecloth, the gift of Queen Victoria to her husband, with lighthouses worked into the stitching, and tea was taken from a silver service with a sugar bowl that Robert Burns and Walter Scott had used. The Stevensons had their own version of dressing for dinner—perhaps bare feet, usual all day indoors, but elegant *holoku* (a word they imported from Hawaii, meaning missionary long dresses) for the women, old Mrs. Stevenson, Fanny, and Belle, and white shirts and trousers with a cummerbund for the men, Stevenson, Lloyd, Joe, and Stevenson's young cousin Graham Balfour while he was there on an extended visit. For company Stevenson would sometimes put on the local white man's evening costume of drill jacket, silk sash, black evening trousers, and patent leather shoes. Stevenson spruced himself up in his established Vailima days. "Slovenly youth, all right," he wrote to Sidney Colvin, "not slovenly age." So now he was "very dandy"—"O a great sight!" Lloyd remembered him as looking well when he dressed up, and never better than at the head of his own big table at Vailima.

There was fine food and drink. Oysters were shipped in on ice. Stevenson imported bordeaux by the cask, and bottled it in festival fashion on the Vailima grounds. He even had some 1840 Madeira for special occasions. The everyday cuisine of their Samoan cook, a young man named Talolo, was excellent. Talolo had a gift for the kitchen and an appetite for household gadgets: an egg beater, a coffee machine, an ice maker. He worked his way up from plain beginner's dishes to roasts that came to the table "garnished with flowers made up of beets, carrots and turnips," and elegant pigeon pies, objects of art with the crusts "elaborately filled, fluted and beautifully glazed." Once in a while an apprentice servant might uncork a wine bottle with his teeth, but generally service at table was correct. And colorful: on banquet nights the houseboys were turned out in *lavalava* with the Royal Stuart tartan and flowers in their limed and combed-straight-up hair.

Stevenson decreed what would be discussed at table. In this, as in all sorts of other ways, he was the head of the house; he and he alone, for instance, could open a mailbag and dispense letters. He had strong notions altogether about how to run Vailima. One of his fixed ideas was that the best way to understand Polynesians was to think of Highland Scots. The missionary William Clarke had introduced him to the virtues of a household system on the "clan" principle, with the missionary as "chief" and a serving "family" of a dozen or so Samoan "children," some of them perhaps sons and daughters of village chiefs, formally adopted. This appealed to Stevenson. He had been a kind of householder once before, at Bournemouth (where he had named his home "Skerryvore," after a Stevenson lighthouse). His experience there taught him never again to be a middle-class master. "The Nemesis of the bourgeois who has chosen to shut out his servants—his 'family' in the old Scotch sense—from all intimacy and share in the pleasures of the house, attends us at every turn," he wrote in those days. "An impossible relation is created, and brings confusion to all." So at Vailima, as Graham Balfour put it, Stevenson's ideal was to "maintain the relation of a Highland chief to his clan, such as it existed before the '45, since this seemed to approach most nearly to the actual state of things in Samoa at the time, and best met the difficulties which beset the relations of master and servant in his own day."

William Clarke thought Stevenson let himself in for a great deal of unnecessary expense and effort when he opted to play the highland laird of Mt. Vaea. (Missionaries were presumably better *ex officio* than expatriate authors at running clans.) But Stevenson, having at first had trouble enough and to spare with white servants at Vailima, turned permanently and delightedly to Samoans and never regretted it. He loved being lord and master, and with Samoans it was easy. "Unquestioning and absolute obedience was insisted upon," Belle Strong recalled. "Every man had his work outlined for him in advance, and several even possessed typewritten lists of their various duties. Little proclamations and notices were often posted up in order to correct petty irregularities." Early on Stevenson had to fire a worker or two, but in time a fine or a lecture was enough to maintain discipline. Stevenson made the most of these domestic courts-martial—"beds of justice," he called them, after the way in which the divine-right monarchs of prerevolutionary France lolled in state while handing down the law. (Often he held sessions literally in his bedroom, from his bed, preferring, as he said, a little physical and therefore psychological elevation.) A disagreement among servants, a petty misdemeanor, and the whole case would be elaborately sifted and sorted, with everyone listening in breathless silence to Stevenson's summing up and judgment. A pig missing, and there would be supplications in the great hall and swearings to innocence on a Samoan Bible.

The Stevensons leaned to the opinion that Catholics (Mr. Clarke of the London Missionary Society notwithstanding) were better workers than Protestants. Their valuable cook Talolo was a *popé,* and they hired more and more of them. But there were Protestants at Vailima too (when a fine was levied at the beds of justice, the money would go to the missionary society of the offender's faith), and one of the great triumphs of the Stevenson clan system was registered on the day the household marched down to a Protestant missionary celebration dressed in white shirts, tartan *lavalava,* and striped blazers especially imported, to be accepted there as *Sa Tusitala,* the storyteller's clan, *Tama-Ona,* Children of the Owner—the MacRichies, in Stevenson's witty rendering.

Stevenson even held full-scale religious services at Vailima for the whole household—fine Samoan hymn singing led by the laundress, and prayers that he himself wrote. As a young man, the wayward son of strict Presbyterian parents, Stevenson had been a deliberate mocker of God, and though those outrageous days were long gone he was never a conventional Christian. More than anything strictly spiritual about the religious occasions at Vailima, Lloyd Osbourne thought—and Stevenson verified this, saying that one service a week was as much as he could manage—the laird liked the gathering of the big hushed household, the feeling of unity and fellowship, the "beautiful and touchingly patriarchal aspect."

The deliberate lordliness of the laird rubbed off on his senior servants, or perhaps just put a gloss on their own version of dignity. Most of them were well born, and one of them, Simele, was quite clear that he wanted to do things like a white lord. He would stand on a tree stump to direct work parties, and the most devastating thing that could be said to him was that something or other he had done was "not *alii* [chief] England." Scottishness rubbed off too, in its way. Stevenson one day was negotiating a contract with twenty-five laborers. "The second boss (an old man) wore a kilt (as usual) and a Balmoral bonnet with a little tartan edging and the tails pulled off. I told him that hat belong to my country—Sekotia; and he said, yes, that was the place he belonged to right enough." And the workers "laughed till the woods rang; he was slashing away with a cutlass as he spoke."

Over the women servants at Vailima Stevenson exercised only a benevolently interested literary type of *droit de seigneur*. He had never found women easy to handle, either in life or in literature. (When he was young he professed not to be really sure that they were people like men.) Brown women were possibly less complicated than white; he did not make extensive investigations to find out. He did love the look of Samoan women and wrote extremely well about them. There was the ravishing Faauma, beautiful as a bronze candlestick, "so fine, clean and dainty in every limb; her arms and her little hips in particular masterpieces." Bare-breasted in her *lavalava*, Faauma was a creature of minimum household efficiency and maximum carnal attractiveness, and she dispensed her sexual favors generously. Over her several affairs, episodes in a continuing serial, Stevenson had to hold beds of justice—"literally." Then there was Java, who cleaned Stevenson's bedroom-study with elaborately maintained silence as he worked, "a creature I adore for her wholesome bread-and-butter beauty. An honest, almost ugly, bright, good-natured face; the rest (to my sense) very exquisite; the inside of Java's knees, when she kilts her lavalava high, is a thing I never saw equalled in a statue. . . . If I look up from my work, she is ready with an explaining smile. I generally don't, and wait to look at her as she stoops for the pillows, and trips tiptoe off again, a miracle of successful womanhood in every line." The worst of civilization, Stevenson said, was that "you never see a woman." Seeing one "unde-formed, you recognize the rights of mankind. Sometimes when I look at Java, I am glad I am elderly and sick and overworked."

The two young men of Stevenson's house did not suffer from any of these disabilities. Lloyd took a Samoan mistress. Stevenson wanted him to marry the girl, but Fanny had the affair broken up. Many years later Lloyd published a collection of South Seas stories, most of them dealing—inevitably, he said—"with the loves of white men and brown women." Lloyd's opinion was that often the white man was the victim, bearing an unhealed wound, while the brown girl, having loved lightly and for the moment, could go on and marry a native missionary and live happily ever after. When Lloyd eventually got married, it was to a physically larger version of his mother.

Joe Strong was a constant problem, a real incorrigible. If it was not one thing with him it was another, frequently several at once. Eventually he was discovered raiding Vailima's locked liquor cabinet with a set of dupli-cate keys, and in the storm that blew up it turned out as well that he had been keeping a Samoan mistress in Apia. Worse still, he had been fouling the nest at Vailima, sleeping with the irresistible and readily available Faauma. Stevenson was enraged at Joe. His natural impulse was to be for-giving, perhaps because he himself as a young man with health problems and artistic leanings had been a drinker and a wencher who looked as if he would never amount to anything. But he had grown out of all this, and Joe was just going on and on, disgusting and dishonorable. Belle started divorce proceedings. Fanny suffered a nervous breakdown and some angina pectoris to go with it. Stevenson, as a gentleman and head of the house, had only one recourse, so he said—to kill Joe. That being unrealis-tic, he talked about "deportation" for the "traitor." Joe left, and in the end Stevenson contented himself with eliminating him on paper. He cut Joe out of a group photograph taken at Vailima, then matched up the remain-ing parts of the print and rephotographed his household as if Joe had never been part of it.

This was a bad business, but generally times were good at Vailima, and Stevenson was greatly pleased with his life. He wrote endlessly to his friends about his doings as laird, and was sorry they could not see him as "patriarch and planter." To hear him tell it, Vailima and its Samoans—*Sa Tusitala*—were a great success on all counts. In his version of things, he paid his help less and got more work out of them than any white man in the islands. It was widely said—so he said—that the only place you ever saw a Samoan run was at Vailima. Stevenson and Fanny had plans for putting in vanilla, coffee, and cacao, and for wholesaling bananas. Fanny considered the plantation an example to other whites to make investments and improvements, raising the overall value of the Apia community.

All this sounds so businesslike that it comes as a surprise to learn that of the 314½ acres of Vailima only fifteen were ever cleared, and eight or ten acres of this work was done by Harry Moors before the Stevensons moved in. Moors was sarcastic about Vailima as a plantation, and he put the problem squarely on the shoulders of the younger members of the household. Belle, of course, did not count for anything as a producer. Joe, before his disgrace, kept promising to apply himself, and he would in fact head off into the bush showing every evidence of actually intending to do some work, wearing a pith helmet, lavalava, and leggings, with a pet Australian cockatoo on his shoulder. But he was an eternal waster of time, too "aesthetic" for the planting life, in Moors's words. It would take, said Fanny, a philosopher to love Joe and a millionaire to support him, and there was neither at Vailima. Lloyd at least took an interest in the running of Vailima, even made something of a sacrifice to stay there and look after things. He was to have gone to Cambridge, but seeing his stepfather saddled, as Stevenson once put it, "with this mule-load of struggling cormorants," Lloyd gave up that idea. Stevenson himself had always been a hopeless manager of money, and so Lloyd took over the account books, complaining, for example, at the cost of feeding more Samoans than were on the payroll (every time he went into Talolo's kitchen there seemed to be relatives of servants and visiting unknowns enjoying a leisurely meal). But as for the actual work of planting, Moors said, Lloyd just liked to "sit down and watch things grow." And all this put the real burden back on Stevenson the author, still essentially a sick man, condemned to be, in Moors's words, "the work horse, supporting with difficulty, and in a trembling way, the whole expense of a large household of idling adults— Human Sponges."

So in Moors's opinion—and he considered himself Stevenson's friend— what went on up at Vailima was not real work, just an elaborate game; the people up there were only playing at planting. This was a harsh businessman's judgment, fair enough in its own terms, but not taking into account all the various purposes that were served by Stevenson's purchase of 314½ acres on Mt. Vaea. Stevenson's splendid letters made up the annual reports of Vailima. They were never balanced sets of books; they were chapters of life.

* * *

If the young men of Vailima did not earn their keep as planters, and if Stevenson after the first year or so of bush clearing retreated for the most part to his writing desk, Fanny worked as hard outdoors as she did inside the big house, on and on, as hard as a peasant, clearing land, planting crops, tending a fine vegetable patch, experimenting with a perfumery, setting up a botanical garden, doing any number of useful things. Vailima was valuable to Fanny, as something she helped to 'create, a place she inhabited with possessive pride. More than anything it was the home of Stevenson the world-famous, and this was indispensable to Fanny. Fulfillment was what she wanted. It was hard for a woman of her day to achieve this publicly in her own right. For Fanny it was a matter of keeping her husband alive and herself together, and at Vailima these projects were intimately, inextricably connected.

Stevenson was evidently faithful to Fanny all through their married life, and Fanny was tenaciously devoted to him. Theirs was not an easy relationship, but it was a close one, and a good case could be made for saying it was essential to Stevenson, that without Fanny he would have been long dead. She was a devoted, untiring, even domineering nurse, ten years older than her patient-husband, and she ran him like a hospital matron. It chafed him at times, and annoyed his literary friends in the English days; they did not appreciate having their after-dinner conversations cut short or even stopped before they were begun—Fanny would turn a guest away from the door if he had a cold. She took the British medical magazine, *The Lancet*, read it assiduously, and always had the latest drugs handy. In her care, Stevenson went from quinine to codeine to laudanum to a "pretty little flask of chloral and hashisch" to cocaine. (It was on cocaine, very possibly, that he wrote *Dr. Jekyll and Mr. Hyde*. He continued to recommend it enthusiastically for years as a great mood changer which he used for warding off colds, writing admiringly that it "at once produces a glow, stops rigour." Cocaine, of course, had many admirers in the 1880s, including Sigmund Freud.) A little medical knowledge might be a dangerous thing, but Fanny had confidence in her powers as a diagnoser and a healer, and in fact she was right about the communicability of colds before the medical profession recognized it as a fact. She was sure she knew what was best.

The important thing about Fanny's nursing impulses is that she was prepared to marry Stevenson at a dreadfully low point in his health, his finances, and his general prospects. When in 1880 she became Mrs. Robert

Louis Stevenson she was taking the name of a nobody who might die at any moment, but she never minded that she had to live rough, shabby, even squalid with him. She had her own toughness and unconventionality. She cut her hair short, preferred to go barefoot and uncorseted, rolled her own cigarettes (and would teach the genteel how), and was not afraid of pistols. She was willing to go anywhere with Stevenson, even— and this was often necessary—to places she did not like at all. The mountain heights that were supposed to do Stevenson's lungs good left Fanny depleted and dizzy, and she always hated life at sea. While Stevenson thrived she suffered. And said so. "Dear friend," she wrote to literary Sidney Colvin, who privately considered her no friend but at best a necessary evil, "because I make my sacrifices with flowers on my head and point out the fine views on the way do not think that it is no sacrifice, and only for my own pleasure." It was all part of nursing Stevenson. Fanny was sure she was nurturing genius, and this sustained her. Genius widely recognized would be her own validation, her triumph too.

Stevenson's attraction to Fanny went very deep. He loved the color brown, brown skin, dark and beautiful women. Fanny was dark and was a great unusual beauty in her day. So was the earlier Fanny in Stevenson's life, Fanny Sitwell, the first and formative older woman of his young days (after his mother, of course). In an amazing number of ways Fanny Osbourne was a continuation and elaboration of Fanny Sitwell, as has been remarked: "The same given name and nickname; the same age, same dark complexion, same famous pretty feet," even the same "bluestocking leanings, same history of disastrous marriage and one small son dying." When Stevenson came to write a poem out of his yearnings toward darkness in the body of women, he pluralized, generalized, and then particularized.

> I must not cease from singing
> And leave their praise unsung,
> The praise of the swarthy women
> I have loved since I was young.
> The hue of heather honey,
> The hue of honey bees,
> Shall tinge her golden shoulder,
> Shall tinge her tawny knees.
>
> Dark as a wayside gypsy,
> Lithe as a hedgewood hare,
> She moves a glowing shadow
> Through the sunshine of the fair;

And golden hue and orange,
Bosom and hand and head
She blooms, a tiger lily,
In the snowdrift of the bed.

Fanny Osbourne was more of a gypsy than Fanny Sitwell. She was the
one Stevenson took to bed. He was writing here out of a long relationship,
in which his wife had frequently had to assert herself, defend herself and
hers, attack life, make it yield—be a man. So Stevenson openly gave her
masculine qualities to go along with her blooming womanliness:

Tiger and tiger lily,
She plays a double part,
All woman in the body,
And all the man at heart.
She shall be brave and tender,
She shall be soft and high,
She to lie in my bosom
And *he* to fight and die.

And again, in another poem, he turned his wife not into a bronze candlestick, which would do for a decorative piece such as Faauma, but into a
sword: "Steel-true and blade-straight, The great artificer made my mate."
    Fanny and Stevenson were childless. Stevenson had started adult life
firmly against fatherhood, mock-solemnly advising his close friend
Charles Baxter that if he ever felt the parental impulse coming over him,
he should castrate himself. Four years into marriage Fanny thought she
was pregnant, and Stevenson panicked. A baby, especially a sickly one,
which was likely enough given its paternity, would ruin him financially.
But then, probably at the time Fanny's announcement turned out to be a
false alarm, he wrote a wistful poem to an unborn child. Later, in the
middle of their Pacific cruising, Fanny again thought she had conceived—
unlikely, since by then she was fiftyish—but again nothing came of it. Her
last biological chance to help create a major work of Stevenson's had
passed, and after that, for the Stevensons as a couple, the acquired family
was everything.
    The Vailima household was really a strange assemblage, and the tangle
of apron strings and other attachments around Stevenson made for perpetual pulling and tugging rather than any easy equilibrium. Here was
Stevenson's widowed mother living with her only child in the same house
as his wife. Margaret Stevenson was a mere ten years older than Fanny,

who was ten years older than Robert Louis. Fanny's daughter Belle was less than ten years younger than Stevenson, and attractive along her mother's lines. (Indeed when the Osbourne women, mother and daughter, first came into Stevenson's life in 1875 it might have seemed likely that the twenty-five-year-old man would make a match with the blossoming girl in her teens rather than with the thirty-five-year-old.) Belle and Joe Strong were married sooner than Stevenson and Fanny (and Belle lost a son early as her mother had done); and in time Joe, a bad copy of the young Stevenson, was to be treated by the middle-aged head of the house at Vailima as Stevenson's own father had treated the errant adolescent of Edinburgh. To Fanny's son Lloyd, Stevenson in his thirties had been first a sort of father and then an older brother. In his forties Stevenson became father-playmate to Belle's little son Austin, whose own father was delinquent, banished from Vailima.

Married to Stevenson, Fanny went from age forty into her fifties. The beauty departed, the fierce individuality and unconventionality remained and at Vailima took over even more. When Stevenson characterized his wife—vividly—for his Scottish literary acquaintance J. M. Barrie, it was out of profound knowledge and acceptance both: "Infinitely little, extraordinary wig of grey curls, handsome waxen face like Napoleon's, insane black eyes, boy's hands, tiny bare feet, a cigarette, wild blue native dress usually spotted with garden mould. In company manners presents the appearance of a little timid and precise old maid of the days of prunes and prisms—you look for the reticule. Hellish energy, relieved by fortnights of entire hibernation. Can make anything from a house to a row, all fine and large of their kind. . . . A violent friend, a brimstone enemy. . . . Is always either loathed or slavishly adored; indifference impossible. The natives think her uncanny and that devils serve her. Dreams dreams, and sees visions."

This was unmistakably Fanny, and unmistakably a middle-aged woman, evidently with a potential for considerable strangeness. Certainly Fanny's emotional life had its knots and tangles. She was by no means a frail nineteenth-century swooner, but three times she had what would have been called nervous breakdowns. The first struck when she was making up her mind to divorce her charming, feckless husband to marry a charming, mercurial, badly unhealthy, penniless writer. The second, at Vailima in 1892, occurred when her daughter divorced her charming, feckless, improvident artist husband (a combination of the worst features of Fanny's own two husbands). The third, worst, and most complicated came in 1893, and again it concerned what might go on between husband and wife. Stevenson's health in Samoa was as good as it was ever going to be, good enough to allow him to live a more or less normal life most of the time. Fanny's own health and emotional stability were increasingly uncertain. She was aging, and she seemed more than the calendar's ten years older than her husband. Now she began experiencing wild swings of mood that became frightening and approached madness. At one point she wanted to run away; at times her family had to hold her down on the bed for fear she would do something crazy. A doctor eventually diagnosed Bright's disease and was able to treat her with good results. But it had been a dangerous, unsettling time for her and her relationship with her husband-patient, who now had to do his own version of devoted nursing for his nurse of many years.

Henry Adams saw the Stevensons only briefly, but along with the fierce caricature of their life in the navvy's hut in the ugly clearing at Vailima he dashed off a quick uncanny sketch of what seemed to be going on between them. He was struck by the energy of Stevenson and the exhaustion of Fanny (which would have surprised anyone who had known the couple in England). Adams and his companion La Farge built up a fantasy that Stevenson was really an *aiku*, a Samoan ghost, and that he kept up his strength, as *aiku* did, by feeding off others. "He has done in these seas ten times what would have done me for life," wrote Adams; "he enjoys hardships that none but an aiku could face, and he is killing his poor wife, who, though another aiku of great promise, is yet unable to keep him from sucking her blood." Leaving aside the blood-sucking aspect of Stevenson's need to be the center of attention in anything he did, a quorum of Stevenson's old friends could have been assembled to agree that there was in Fanny something of the emotional vampire, a succubus attachment to Stevenson. She fed off him, without doubt, and certainly throughout their relationship life blood—literally—was at issue. Stevenson had to be well enough to stay alive, yet sick enough to need Fanny. Now, if what Adams sensed was true, these old mutual dependencies between Fanny and her husband were being altered by Stevenson's rising good health and his impulses toward serious maturity. The more he wanted to—and could—fend for himself, the less dependent he was on Fanny, and the less she could draw on his need of her for her own self-esteem. Husband and wife were finding themselves in unconscious competition for control of the limited resources of nourishing individual self-satisfaction available within their marriage. In any number of ways the Vailima period was the making of Stevenson. It was almost the breaking of Fanny.

* * *

The only way Stevenson ever made money was by writing, and even that was a recent achievement. Indeed for much of his life he was a kind of subsidized bohemian. When he was young, sick, unsettled in himself, and erratic in his work habits, making practically nothing with his pen, his solid bourgeois father Thomas supplied him with an allowance, and in fact this arrangement continued until Stevenson was past thirty-five. By the time Stevenson came to Samoa, he was as well rewarded for his work as any literary man could dream of being. But he still drew on family money; his mother contributed out of her widow's estate to the building and running of Vailima. There were times when Stevenson questioned his own good sense in saddling himself with such a burdensome overhead, especially when the second wing of the big house was being added. He began referring to his home as Abbotsford, after the folly of his famous countryman Sir Walter Scott, who made a great deal of money from writing, then went into bookselling and publishing on his own account, built a veritable castle to live in, and bankrupted himself. Vailima might not have been on the order of Abbotsford, but it was at least, as Stevenson reclassified it, a "Subpriorsford."

To Samoans, Vailima was a wonder. Stevenson had no way of making money that they could see. In general, the white man's access to wealth had its magical aspects for islanders. Most whites seemed just to sit on verandas doing nothing much between the regular arrivals of ships bearing amazing goods. Stevenson, for his part, lived spectacularly well, better than Harry Moors or the German traders at Apia, better than the consuls and other officials who decorated the beach and could summon up warships. Stevenson's fabulous home with its seventy-two tons of superb shipped-in effects amounted to a permanent dazzling three-dimensional magic-lantern show. While the big house at Vailima was going up, Stevenson was working on a Samoan translation of a story of his called "The Bottle Imp," about a genie who could grant wishes. It ran in serial form in an Apia newspaper, and it was the first piece of fiction Samoans ever read in their own language. Samoans, new to the printed page and believing that newspapers printed facts, were not clear about the nature of fiction, but they did know Stevenson was the author of the story. In the great hall at Vailima was a locked iron safe, and it was thought that the bottle imp was kept inside.

If there was a bottle imp at Vailima, it was Stevenson's talent. And if he wanted to keep Vailima, he would have to keep working at his trade. Throughout his Samoan patriarch-planter days he wrote and wrote. His productivity was amazing: about seven hundred thousand words for publication between the beginning of 1890 and the end of 1894. And more and more he came to link authorship with householding. He had a charge of souls, he said; he kept many eating and drinking.

When he was younger, married but not settled, rising in reputation but not risen, he had talked about art as more than family. It was a household in itself, an entire world which inhabited him, a life force: "An art is a fine fortune, a palace in a park, a band of music, health, and physical beauty; all but love—to any worthy practiser. I sleep upon my art for a pillow; I waken in my art; I am unready for death, because I hate to leave it. I love my wife, I do not know how much, nor can, nor shall, unless I lost her; but while I can conceive my being widowed, I refuse the offering of life without my art. I *am* not but in my art; it is me; I am the body of it merely." Later, a bit daringly for his day, he compared the artist's life with prostitution. The French had a lovely phrase for the whore, "fille de joie," daughter of joy; Stevenson thought of the artist as being of the same family, the son of joy, who chose his trade to please himself, "gains his livelihood by pleasing others, and has parted with something of the sterner dignity of man." That was Stevenson the bohemian. Now at Vailima he could say that "the first duty is to try to feed my family; it is only the second to publish chefs d'oeuvres."

Writing with his family in mind, Stevenson also involved them directly in his work. Lloyd, once he was grown up, generally had a story underway in collaboration with his stepfather, and at Vailima Stevenson revised his will and made Lloyd his literary executor. Stevenson liked to dictate, but Lloyd, a gadgeteer of great devotion, was wedded to the typewriter, and the noise distracted Stevenson, so he co-opted first his mother and then Belle as amanuenses.

With his wife Stevenson did not collaborate at Vailima. He had worked with Fanny in the past, in the Bournemouth days, on the story "The Dynamiter" and other tales. When the book was published, Fanny was piqued to find that reviewers treated her as if her name were invisible on the title page: "I thought in the beginning that I shouldn't mind being Louis's scapegoat, but it is rather hard to be treated like a comma, and a superfluous one at that." Certain aspects of the literary life, in fact, became a sore point between Fanny and her husband. A story she wrote and published not long before the Pacific cruise of 1888–1889 was, for complicated reasons, the cause of the breakup of Stevenson's long and valuable friendship with another collaborator of his earlier years, W. E. Henley. Then, in Samoa, Stevenson developed what was to Fanny "a most vexing theory," that "I"—Fanny—"have the true peasant nature, and lack the artistic temperament; thereupon my advice on artistic matters . . . must be received with extreme caution. He says I do not take the broad view of the artist, but hold the cheap opinions of the general public that a book must be interesting. How do I long for a little wholesome monumental

correction to be applied to the Scotch side of Louis's artistic temperament." It did no good for Stevenson to go on to assure Fanny that the
peasant class was a most interesting one, and that he admired it "hugely."
She felt depressed, so she told her diary; her vanity, like a newly felled
tree, lay prone and bleeding. Stevenson tried to make her feel better. No
one, he said, should mind being told he was not an artist unless he was
supporting his family by his art, in which case he could justifiably feel in-
sulted. Fanny was not mollified. Stevenson was stitching together art for
art's sake and his emerging conception of the artist as householder, and
Fanny felt it was all at her expense.

What brought on this argument was a question of literary authority. As
he aged, Stevenson grew more and more interested in authority—as distinct from mere celebrity. In the year when Jekyll and Hyde made him
world-famous, he wrote to his cousin Bob: "I know a little about fame
now; it is no good compared to a yacht. . . ." That was before Vailima. Afterward, on a trip to Australia, he became aware that people were pointing him out in the Sydney streets. He did not want that, he said. It was
better in Samoa, where to other whites he was merely a friend or an
enemy on matters of local politics, and to Samoans just a white chief in a
great house.

As for a chef d'oeuvre, Stevenson, almost from the time he encountered a South Sea island, had set his sights upon a big book about the Pacific. The travel letters that financed his Pacific cruises were one thing,
just journalism; the book was to be another thing entirely. He kept talking
about it, thinking about it, collecting material all the way through the
islands. By the time he got to Samoa he had an outline. "My book is now
practically modelled," he wrote to Sidney Colvin then. He intended to
call it The South Seas; "it is rather a large title, but not many people have
seen more of them than I, perhaps no one—certainly no one capable of
using the material." And no one had ever had such material, "such wild
stories, such beautiful scenes, such singular intimacies, such manners and
traditions, so incredible a mixture of the beautiful and horrible, the savage and civilized." He thought there was a book in it as good as anything but the greatest masterpieces of world literature.

So Stevenson was aiming very high indeed. But from the start Fanny
and Lloyd thought he had his sights set altogether wrongly. With all the
delirious color of the South Seas laid on, Stevenson perversely wanted the
book to have "serious interest," and to this they objected. Lloyd had no
doubt that the diary Stevenson started keeping aboard the Casco was in
the class of Melville or Kinglake as travel literature; Lloyd did not want to
see such fine raw material unsuitably worked up. And on this subject

Fanny was impassioned to the point of unstoppability. "I am afraid he is going to spoil it all," she wrote to Sidney Colvin. "He has taken into his Scotch Stevenson head, that a stern duty lies before him, and that his book must be a sort of scientific and historical impersonal thing, comparing the different languages (of which he knows nothing, really) and the different peoples, the object being to settle the question as to whether they are of common Malay origin or not. Also to compare the Protestant and Catholic missions, etc., and the whole thing to be impersonal, leaving out all he knows of the people themselves. And I believe there is no one living who has got so near to them, or who understands them as he does. Think of a small treatise on the Polynesian races being óffered to people who are dying to hear about . . . the making of brothers with cannibals, the strange stories they told, and the extraordinary adventures that befell us:—suppose Herman Melville had given us theories as to the Polynesian languages and the probable good or evil of the missionary influence instead of *Omoo* and *Typee*. . . . Louis says it is a stern sense of duty that is at the bottom of it, which is more alarming than anything else. . . . What a thing it is to have a 'man of genius' to deal with. It is like managing an overbred horse. Why with my own feeble hand I could write a book that the whole world would jump at. . . ."

Fanny, of course, never did write her own book. But she was adamant about what she wanted from her husband, which was that he should go on being the entertaining Robert Louis Stevenson he had always been. This running dispute had its comic aspects, but at the same time it was serious, the domestic side of the argument that Stevenson had with his critics and general readers over the next year or two. They wanted him to go on being—in his own unhappy, self-dissatisfied words—light, pungent, witty. He wanted to become an authority, dispensing wisdom.

Stevenson did have theories on broad Pacific issues, and these were generally sensible if not inspired or wholly original. He thought about cannibalism and decided it was environmentally determined. Take an island with a small resource base, a rising population, and think of an obvious response to food shortage . . . Looking back into Polynesian history for instances of islanders' efforts to do something about overpopulation other than kill and eat each other, he came up with the *arioi* of Tahiti, who made life-enhancing sexual theater out of childlessness. In the late nineteenth century, throughout the Pacific, it was either too many islanders or too few, never the right number in a given place; and Stevenson saw, reasonably enough, the white man's presence as the disturbing agent. Too much change too soon was bad, even if it was meant for the good. For an obvious example, successful missionary doctoring might lower a death rate and raise a birth rate to a dangerous degree. On the other side of the population ledger there were whole districts, even islands, empty where introduced disease had struck, and other places raided by the blackbirders, the labor traders, who carried young men off to work on plantations. This traffic in human life Stevenson deplored on principle, but if he pushed his thinking a little beyond simple right-mindedness he could see a grim mutual attraction between an over-populated atoll, which he compared with a wrecked ship running low on food, and the blackbirder's ships, which might then look like rescue vessels. And yet, and yet—there was no comfortable way to think about the labor trade, and Vailima usually harbored an escaped Melanesian "black boy" or two, refugees from cruel treatment on German-owned plantations.

As far as missionary work was concerned, Stevenson had come to the South Seas a skeptic. He himself had been under heavy Calvinist duress as a child, from both of his parents and from a devoted Presbyterian nanny who loved him overwhelmingly and terrified him with hellfire talk and regular graveyard visits. As a young man he made a determined point of being antireligious. After some observation of what happened in the mission field of the Pacific, he held onto his reservations about the missionary enterprise in general, and his advice to evangelists was to start with the culture they found and try to keep it alive: "Remember that *you cannot change ancestral feelings of right and wrong without what is practically soul-murder.*" He was pleased that William Clarke of the LMS showed signs of agreeing that if Samoans were to stay emotionally healthy, they needed their amusements, short of war. They should be allowed their tribal dances and their monumental cricket matches. Stevenson formulated a little amateur law of human energetics in places where the basic necessities of life—breadfruit from the trees, fish from the lagoon—were more or less readily available. Where hard work was not necessary, he reasoned, absorbing amusements were.

If Stevenson halfway changed his mind on missionaries, as distinct from missionary societies, it was because of individuals he came across. Catholic fathers, brothers, and sisters he got on well with, and he went ferociously into print in 1890 when a Protestant clergyman in Hawaii maligned Father Joseph Damien De Veuster, a Sacred Hearts priest who spent a quarter century among leprosy sufferers on the island of Molokai in the Hawaiian chain, caught the disease, and died of it.

Two Protestant missionaries in particular impressed him. George Brown, a Wesleyan, was a carroty-haired man who had been a sailor before he turned evangelist. He was an Old Testament Christian: in 1879, in Melanesia, he had led a punitive party against islanders who killed some native evangelists, and he and his men had killed some of the killers. Brown and Stevenson used to exchange ideas on Samoan politics, and at one point Stevenson was thinking of writing Brown's life. The other notable Protestant was James Chalmers of the LMS, a Melanesian version of John Williams. Chalmers, a Scot, wanted Livingstone's savage Africa for a mission field, but was assigned instead to Rarotonga, four decades after Williams. It was too safe for him there. After ten years he escaped, so to speak, to the dangerous frontier territory of New Guinea, and when Stevenson met him he was planning to go off up the Fly River, a "desperate venture," as Stevenson said. Chalmers knew what he was letting himself in for, and he also knew why he liked working on the very edge of empire: "I know well in England I am nobody—lost, unknown—here I am . . . a King with great power—far more than any other." Chalmers struck Stevenson as quite simply heroic. A "big, stout, wildish looking man . . . with big bold, black eyes, and a deep furrow down each cheek," he generated great personal force, and part of his attraction for Stevenson was that he was an unconventional missionary. He drank when he wanted to, gave expression to his moods, and had an appetite for mixing with the unsaved of the Pacific, white as well as brown and black. He was, as Stevenson put it, "as big as a house and far bigger than any church," someone to be admired for his virtues and loved for his faults—a very Stevensonian formulation. If he had met Chalmers when he was a boy and a bachelor, Stevenson once said, his own life would have been different. It was too late for that, but he wanted to outlive Chalmers so as to write his life. Stevenson died first, and Chalmers went on in old age to be killed in headhunter country, a death he seems to have half-invited.

Missionaries, cannibals, blackbirders, coral atolls, and *arioi*—certainly Stevenson was never short of material for his great work, and he looked forward to the writing of it with appetite. A few things to get out of the way first, then "hey! for the big South Sea Book: a devil of a big one, and full of the finest sport." This book and the making of Vailima were the two most substantial long-term projects he ever attempted. Attacking them together, he took to using planting and building metaphors for his writing. While he was still hopeful of doing well with the book, he categorized it as an "architectural" problem—to get it "jointed," "well-engineered, the masses right." But the laying of foundations, the spadework, proved more formidable than he had thought. Largely this concerned the travel letters he was contracted to write. He had a moral obligation to keep doing them, and they brought in money that was poured into Vailima. They were also to serve as a "quarry," a "laying-in" of material for the big book. Oddly, though, the published letters did not seem to be going well. They were not overenthusiastically received, and they got harder and harder to write. Absorbed in the clearing and building of Vailima, and at the same time becoming more and more involved in local politics, Stevenson came to think of himself as on a treadmill of travel letters. He began to talk of them too in householding terms: "days and days of unprofitable stubbing and digging." He worked away on the big book when he could, but that was not often, and he began to feel daunted.

In the end he was worn out by what he had attempted in combination. Something had to give. Vailima must go forward, the travel letters brought in money, politics pressed on him. So the big South Seas book, conceived in high endeavor as the piece of work that would at last establish Stevenson as a *serious* figure in life and letters, took last place. Capitulating, settling for less than second-best, Stevenson decided he would simply take the travel letters when they were all written and make a book of them "by the pruning-knife. I cannot fight longer; I am sensible of having done worse than I hoped, worse than I feared; all I can do now is to do the best I can for the future, and clear the book, like a piece of bush, with axe and cutlass. Even to produce the MS. of this will occupy me at the most favourable opinion, till the middle of next year; really five years were wanting, when I could have made a book. . . ." He was not given five years, and even the pruning-knifed, axed, and cutlassed letters were not published in book form until after he died. So Stevenson never appeared to the world as the great literary authority on the South Seas, just as resident celebrity.

* * *

There was another kind of authority that came to interest Stevenson in Samoa, and this was political. Samoan chiefs liked to visit Vailima, and Stevenson liked to receive them, man to man, dignitary to dignitary. So he passed a great deal of ceremonious time around the *kava* bowl. With his sensitive ear for language and his appetite for ritual, he learned the libations and salutations of the chiefs, when to drink, when to clap hands, when to be silent, when and how to speak, how to give and receive gifts. Eventually at an enormous feast he was given a *kava* name, a great privilege. He prided himself on this intimacy with Samoan society at its highest, and came to think it gave him a privileged insight into the politics of the islands.

The Samoan situation was tangled. Stevenson had picked up some of the threads in Honolulu in the aftermath of the Hawaiian embassy in 1887 and the strange voyage of the *Kaimiloa*. Walter Murray Gibson and King Kalakaua had been serious in their own peculiar way about the idea of a

Polynesian confederation. At least they did not get anyone killed in Samoa, and their diplomatic fiasco stopped them from going on to Tonga and other places as they had planned. The big powers with interests in Samoa—Germany, Great Britain, and the United States—were also serious, in a more threatening way, and among them they brought on so much death and destruction that they looked madder by far than the Hawaiian government.

When the *Equator* dropped anchor at Apia with Stevenson aboard in December, 1889, the harbor's outstanding sight—the biggest man-made structure for a thousand miles, by Stevenson's estimate—was the wreck of the German warship *Adler*, beam end and broken-backed on the reef. Five other wrecked men-of-war were strewn about an anchorage hardly big enough to contain them afloat. On the bottom below the reef was the German *Eber*. The American *Trenton*, flagship of a vice-admiral, lay half sunk on top of another American, the *Vandalia*. A third American, the *Nipsic*, was beached along with a third German, the *Olga*. Picking over the rusting, rotting carcasses were wreckers, salvaging what they could, dynamiting the rest.

The six men-of-war had been trapped in the harbor by a hurricane in March, 1889. A seventh, the British *Calliope*, had managed to make the open sea and survive. Why so many warships of so many nations should have been in Apia harbor at one time took some explaining. Germany had a substantial interest in Samoan plantations and trade stores, as well as a general interest in the power politics of the southwest Pacific, in competition with Great Britain and the British colonies of Australia and New Zealand. The United States had no firm policy for that part of the ocean, but along with Great Britain did not want to see Germany monopolizing affairs. Consuls on the spot in Samoa were always ready to use rivalries among the Samoan great chiefs for imperial purposes; and the chiefs, understanding this game well enough, played it in their own way for their own ends. Late in 1888—and this was the story Stevenson heard in Honolulu—a chief named Mataafa, regarded by the dominant Germans as a rebel, was raiding German-owned plantations, and German marines came ashore to chastise him. But they ran into an ambush, German lives were lost, and heads were taken. The arms and ammunition for the ambush had been supplied by British and American traders (Harry Moors was one). Mataafa's warriors went on to make menacing moves toward Apia early in 1889. The German consul declared martial law. The other consuls disputed his right to do this. The United States in particular got upset. Things went from bad to worse, and warships were called for.

March was the worst month for weather in Samoa. Hurricanes always announced themselves in advance, and of course all ships carried barometers. But even with the glass falling ominously low, no commander wanted to be the first to leave Apia harbor, despite the fact that its funnel-shaped entrance was ideal for building up massive waves. National interest, national honor kept the warships at Apia, steaming to their anchors as the waves rose and rose. "That any modern war-ship, furnished with the power of steam, should have been lost in Apia," wrote Stevenson, "belongs not so much to nautical as to political history." Trapped first by the excesses of empire and then, fatally, by the monstrous seas that roared in through the single narrow break in the barrier reef, the ships all through a day and a night rolled and bucked and smashed into each other and at last struck on the reef or foundered or were beached.

It was a comprehensive disaster, with scores dead and half a dozen ships lost. As an example of imperialism in practice it was a tragic absurdity. In Stevenson's curt Eurocentric phrase, "not the whole Samoan Archipelago was worth the loss."

The powers met at Berlin to see what they could salvage in the way of sensible policy on Samoa. They did not do very well. They agreed to run Samoan affairs jointly rather than allow any one nation to set up a protectorate. But this cobbled-together arrangement had not much chance of working smoothly. No matter what the treaty powers said or did, whites on the spot would go on bickering among themselves, like dogs over a bone, as Stevenson said; and chiefs would continue to maneuver against each other in the old way. In imperial terms Samoa was only teapot-sized, but it was a teapot that brewed tempests.

Stevenson became convinced that the officials appointed to supervise affairs under the Berlin agreements would run Samoa on the rocks. He could see it coming, and he hated to be just a watcher. "The sense of my helplessness here has been rather bitter," he wrote. "I feel it wretched to see this dance of folly and injustice and unconscious rapacity go forward from day to day, and to be impotent."

The cure for feelings of impotence was action, and so Stevenson went into politics. He hated to have to take the step, he said, but he would have hated himself more if he had done nothing. On and off for a couple of years he wrote long letters to the London press, principally the *Times;* and he urged his views on the Foreign Office and the Colonial Office. In Apia he talked to anyone who would listen; drafted policy documents, attended meetings (chairing one, successfully and to his own great pleasure); and tried to reconcile the principal rival chiefs Mataafa and Malietoa so that their differences would not lead to war.

Pushed and pulled by events and feelings, Stevenson set aside some of his planned writing so that he could get a short book on the Samoan situation into print in time to do some good among the treaty powers. He had been preparing a section on Samoa for his big South Seas book, but as he accumulated material he found it turning into a volume in its own right, and as he got more and more involved in local happenings the book became more and more political. It would be a history of recent events, "extending to the present week, at least." And in all ways it would be different from anything he had attempted before. It required scores of interviews to verify facts, hours—days—with a dictionary getting translations straight (his German was rusty), in short a sober seriousness of approach new to him.

The writer of children's books and romances for adults was painfully aware that Robert Louis Stevenson was not supposed to tackle *issues*. In fact he doubted that anyone lacking a direct connection with Samoa would want to read what he proposed to write, "matter so extraneous and outlandish." Still, he could not see why it should be dull. "Here is, for the first time," he wrote to his American publisher, sounding like his own hopeful publicity copy writer, "a tale of Greeks—Homeric Greeks—mingled with moderns, and all true; Odysseus alongside of Rajah Brooke, *proportion gardée.* . . ." Yet sales as such were not what he was after. The book was not a business proposition. He had "a purpose." In other words he was involved, committed. For his own part, he made an association between age ("I become heavy and owlish; years sit upon me") and growing seriousness of purpose. Whatever—"It begins to seem to me to be a man's business to leave off his damnable faces and say his say."

The title Stevenson gave his book was the dullest of the dull—*A Footnote to History: Eight Years of Trouble in Samoa.* He was pleased enough with what he had got on paper, and it was meant to be useful, but once the manuscript was actually on its way to the publisher he developed a revulsion against the whole project. This had happened to him before, but now author's postpartum depression was mixed with a loathing for politics. A disagreeable, abhorred task was accomplished, and he hoped he was "done with this cursed chapter of my career." He was not a stayer, physically or in other ways. He of course knew this about himself, and if he ever forgot it his body would remind him. Prolonged strain, overwork, and he was likely to collapse, coughing blood. This he generalized into a horror of the long-drawn-out in life, literature, and now in politics. "My imagination," he wrote to Sidney Colvin just as he was embarking on his Samoan campaign, "which is not in the least damped by the idea of having my head cut off in the bush, recoils aghast from the idea of a life like Gladstone's."

Heads being lopped off in the bush were what had originally interested Stevenson in Samoa. As well, there was a man very important to Stevenson's interior life who had recently been famous on another frontier of imperial Britain and who had had his head lopped off because of William Ewart Gladstone, prime minister of Great Britain. The man in question was General Sir Charles Gordon, who in 1885 had been besieged and finally overwhelmed by Moslems at Khartoum in the Sudan, decapitated, his severed head stuck on a pole to be shown to the crowds. One school of thought in England was that Gladstone could have saved Gordon. If Stevenson had to choose between a political survivor like Gladstone, however distinguished, and a military martyr like Gordon, he would always identify himself with the man who made the grand gesture.

Indeed, in the most roundabout way, what happened to Gordon was responsible for Stevenson's involvement in the politics of Samoa. Stevenson had followed the news from Khartoum closely at the time, brooding over what he considered the Gladstone government's base betrayal of a great man, blaming himself for sitting still while it happened: "I might not have been able to save Gordon"—this was surely true—"but at least I should feel I had done something." The memory of Gordon stayed with him the rest of his life. He told the Gordon story to a chief in the Marquesas. When he came to Samoa he found that the British consul at Apia, Colonel H. de Coëtlogon, had been with Gordon in the Sudan. Writing about the hurricane of 1889, he compared the American admiral drowned on the *Trenton* with Gordon. Somewhere Stevenson had acquired a tiny piece of paper on which Gordon had written a message he managed to have smuggled out of Khartoum, and this had a talismanic value for Stevenson when he was putting on paper his own dispatches from Samoa.

Stevenson himself was condemned to be a survivor rather than a soldier, his own grand gestures limited to writing about violent death and committing murder on the sensitive plant at Vailima. His continuing struggle for health humiliated him, and he often said he would prefer an exciting end to a tediously prolonged invalid's life. "I was made for a contest, and the Powers"—not the imperial powers but the fates—"have so willed that my battlefield should be this dingy, inglorious one of the bed and the physic bottle. At least I have not failed, but I would have preferred a place of trumpetings and the open air over my head." For him, to "secure a violent death" would be a "fine success." "I wish to die in my boots; no more Land of Counterpane for me. To be drowned, to be shot, to be thrown from a horse—ay, to be hanged, rather than pass again through that slow dissolution." Gordon had achieved the personal victory-in-violent-death that Stevenson said he longed for. Indeed there was only one man he said he would rather be than himself (besides James Chalmers), and that was Gordon.

When Stevenson came to think about alternative political futures for Samoa, he considered one-man rule—but only by a man like Gordon. And Stevenson even had moments when he thought of himself as the "one man" for Samoa. He let it be known at the Foreign Office that on the subject of Samoan native politics he was as knowledgeable as any white man. And he played with the prospect of the British consulship for himself (though this appointment was never seriously considered in official circles). He wanted the job, he said once, because he could not stand to see others do it badly. But then he concluded that he himself would do it badly because he would have to take orders from idiots. Divided in his serious thoughts, he made a kind of fun of the idea. Giving Sidney Colvin three reasons for being interested in the appointment, he wrote that first, there was the possibility of doing good: "2nd, larks for the family: 3rd, and perhaps not altogether least, a house in town and a boat and a boat's crew." Obviously the consulship would not have suited him—too much Gladstone, not enough Gordon—and he contented himself with occasional compliments from great men about the usefulness of what he was doing as a public-spirited resident. Stevenson was very keen on the good opinion of the great, whether they were chiefs of islands or captains of empire, and anything from a *kava* name to an approving letter from the Foreign Office or some encouraging words from the distinguished colonial governor Sir George Grey went a long way with him.

Unwilling to be Gladstone, ineligible to be Gordon, Stevenson in local politics was just Stevenson, feeling strongly that he must have his say and yet associating what he was doing with a loss of self, or at least an unwelcome shift in self. In general he found politicking among the whites of Apia a dirtier game even than the island trade. It was, he said variously, dirty, wretched, farcical, boring, revolting, vile, a low bungling business of going about intriguing, ratting, bearing tales, flattering, playing the rancid game of popularity—the organization of failure enlivened by the defamation of character. He felt himself above it, as he felt himself above most whites he had to deal with. But that was just the point. "Idiots" were in charge, and their idiocies were what drove him to act. Above all he wanted to see Samoans treated fairly, and they never would be as long as the treaty officials were running the islands.

As Stevenson said, politics made him feel heavy and owlish—old—and he was sure he was not suited to getting old, particularly if this meant getting dull. And in fact he never did take off every last one of the "damned faces" that were the masks of his perennial youthful self-dramatizings. As a young man he had played at being a criminal, dressing sinisterly, trying to get a London policeman to arrest him, purely for the experience. He failed, and was most indignant when on another occasion, not looking for trouble, indeed hiking innocently in France, he was jailed overnight as a suspicious vagrant. In Samoa he was privately delighted that politics gave him the chance to trail his coat in the old amusing way.

Certainly his letters to the *Times* and his campaign to get rid of the incompetent treaty officials were irritations in official quarters in Apia. Stevenson expanded on this, convincing himself that the powers had it in for him and would like to see him removed from the islands. One or two things he did might have been described, by stretching matters a long, long way, as courting deportation. As much as any attempt at playing the statesman, Stevenson enjoyed minor intrigue, quietly cocking a snook at authority. This was the corrective to the aging, deadening effect serious politics had on him, the equivalent of the dangerous edge on life at sea that livened him up so much.

Nothing ever came of his attempts to get himself in trouble. If the Foreign Office and the Colonial Office took Stevenson at all seriously, it was because he was RLS, the famous author. And being RLS meant that he was not taken seriously as a politico by others. His literary friend Colvin, disconsolate to begin with at Stevenson's decision to stay in Samoa, was plainly and permanently irritated when Stevenson took up the politics of "your beloved blacks—or chocolates—confound them; beloved no doubt to you; to us detested, as shutting out your thoughts, or so it often seems, from the main currents of human affairs. . . . Please let us have a letter or two with something besides native politics, prisons, kava feasts, and such things. . . ." Oscar Wilde, not a personal friend, remarked in passing on a minor perversity of Stevenson's life. Living in romantic places, said Wilde, evidently did not mean that a man would write romances. Quite the reverse. If Stevenson had been living in Gower Street in London he would have written a new *Three Musketeers;* living in Samoa, he wrote letters to the *Times.* When Wilde made this observation he was in jail, for a major perversity, his own career in ruins. On the literary grounds suggested by Wilde, jail for Stevenson was recommended facetiously in a Scottish newspaper. Imprisonment "would be a consummation almost to be wished, if it would turn Mr. Stevenson's thoughts from politics to letters, and cause him to give us, instead of 'Footnotes to History' more volumes to rank with his incomparable 'Master of Ballantrae.' "

Stevenson was being told almost in so many words to go on being what he always was, not to change, not to turn serious, not to grow up. There

was romance in what he wrote about so well, and a special romance about
his literary exile. "Since Byron was in Greece," remarked the poet and
critic Edmund Gosse, "nothing has appealed to the ordinary literary man
so much as that you should be living in the South Seas." There was even a
certain romance about South Seas politics, for example the story of the
great hurricane. But why push further? Herman Melville had gone
through the experience of being tied up in a youthful reputation, and had
come to hate being branded for life as the man who lived among cannibals. Now Stevenson was being urged to go on being an entertainer, a
romancer. At least a part of him needed not much urging. He was the one
who was against heavy owlishness, and so he found himself making romance out of politics.

Early on in Samoa he had chosen a political hero, Mataafa, a chief in
middle age, of such style and command that he satisfied even Henry
Adams as to his quality. For a time Stevenson hoped he might reconcile
Mataafa with his great rival Malietoa, but neither chief was really interested in reconciliation. Malietoa was the favorite of the Germans and the
treaty powers' recognized king of Samoa. Mataafa was officially a rebel,
but he called himself king of the Samoans, and he was prepared to lead his
followers into battle.

So, seeing war coming, Stevenson refurbished his household armory of
eight revolvers, one shotgun, swords galore, added several rifles (over the
objections of the treaty officials), and drew up orders for the defense of
Vailima—who would stand where and shoot what. He regretted not having taken war more seriously into consideration when he planned his estate. This of course was Stevenson the romantic. Samoans would not think
of attacking Vailima. They would kill each other, German marines too,
but never agreeable civilian whites like Stevenson. But as Stevenson's
cousin Graham Balfour said, observing him at Vailima, Stevenson always
had the capacity for making things exciting. A simple job like driving stray
horses to the Apia pound became a "Border foray." Once he found on his
property the skeleton of a long-dead Samoan, and among the bones a second skull—obviously a head taken in combat—and he held a funeral service with military salutes. Now, with rival chiefs contending and war
looming, he surpassed himself.

He and his family took to drinking toasts to Mataafa the rebel chief as
"the king over the water," a fanciful historical reference to the exiled
Stuart pretender to the British throne. And in this willfully romantic
frame of mind, Stevenson did a very silly political thing. In mid-1892,
with his book on Samoan politics just published and his standing among

treaty officials and consuls dubious, he took a house guest to visit Mataafa's camp. At the best of times, Stevenson's jaunts to rebel territory were not amusing to officialdom. This one was far worse than usual, because the guest who went with him under the incognito of a Stevenson cousin was Margaret, Lady Jersey, wife of the governor of the Australian colony of New South Wales. The whole thing was dressed up as a piece of Scottish romance, "an episode somewhat after the style of the '45." Everyone was to rendezvous on horseback at the Gasigasi River, so Stevenson instructed "Miss Amelia Balfour" in a letter dated August 14, 1745—the year of Bonnie Prince Charlie's last attempt to recover his throne. The "King over the Water," Stevenson said, would be pleased "to see the clan of Balfour mustering so thick around his standard." And political "to the bitter end," he smudged his signature against recognition.

The visit went off splendidly. Stevenson had some satisfactorily confidential talk with Mataafa, and there was a royal *kava* ceremony, showing that the Samoans knew they had aristocracy visiting. All in all, a huge "lark" for Stevenson. He wrote it up in "a bit of a supposed epic," and made "a little book of caricatures and verses about incidents on the visit."

Now, what he had done was irresponsible in the extreme. Mataafa was contemplating war on Malietoa, the chief backed by the treaty government, and Great Britain was a signatory to the treaty, and here was Stevenson smuggling the titled wife of a governor of a British colony into the rebel camp, for a lark. Stevenson knew he was being provocative. In fact he went so far as to wonder if he might not be bringing on war. But, he wrote with astonishing blitheness, "with this I have no concern, and the thing wholly suits my book and fits my predilections for Samoa." This was the same Stevenson who wrote long letters to the *Times* about the folly of whites in power in Samoa.

Clearly, one of the masks he never took off was that of the boy who liked to play soldiers. In his childhood he and his cousin Bob would dress up and draw maps and make inventions and fight and rule whole countries. Stevenson often told Lloyd Osbourne that if he had had his health he would have gone into the army, and when he first acquired Lloyd as a stepson he invented for the little boy, and obviously for himself too, "a mimic war-game that required hundreds of tin soldiers, the whole attic floor to play it on, and weeks of time." These games were passed on to another generation. Belle Strong's son Austin, growing up at Vailima among Samoan warriors, passed his days immersed in Scottish chivalry, learning *Young Lochinvar* by heart, building forts, and going about in a helmet made from a straw hat and a cotton coat of mail, with a wooden lance and a pasteboard shield. His instructors in the martial arts were Lloyd, then in his twenties, and Stevenson, in his forties, and Vailima had a "Soldier Room" full of toy musketeers and miniature cannons.

Real fighting was coming closer and closer. By mid-1893 it was in the air. There were rumors everywhere in Apia; the Samoan children were all playing with spears. Stevenson wrote to Colvin about waiting "with a kind of sighing impatience, for war to be declared, or to blow finally off, living in the meanwhile in a kind of children's hour of firelight and shadow and preposterous tales; the king [Malietoa] seen at night galloping up our road upon unknown errands and covering his face as he passes our cook; Mataafa daily surrounded (when he wakes) with fresh 'white man's boxes' (query ammunition?) and professing to be quite ignorant of where they come from; marches of bodies of men across the island; concealment of ditto in the bush; the coming on and off of different chiefs; and such a mass of ravelment and rag-tag as the devil himself could not unwind."

On impulse Stevenson rode out one night with Graham Balfour to Apia and beyond, into Mataafa territory. They passed parties of marching men and pickets with Winchesters, and heard a village orator in full cry; and a man ran out in front of them "with his face blackened, and the back of his lava-lava girded up so as to show his tattooed hips naked; he leaped before us, cut a wonderful caper, and flung his knife high in the air, and caught it. It was strangely savage and fantastic and high-spirited." For the first time in a life of make-believe war, Stevenson was seeing men actually under arms. He was enraptured. He and Balfour came home "like schoolboys, with such a lightness of spirits, and I am sure such a brightness of eye, as you could have lit a candle at!"

Stevenson could not regard Mataafa's men getting ready for battle as grimly efficient Western warmakers. He saw them, rather, as high-spirited capering savages like the man with the knife. All the better: he could think of the coming battle as a children's game fought in the children's hour by toy soldiers come to life for his delight. Still he felt the savage, the animal, stir in him; the "old aboriginal" awoke and "nickered like a stallion." He could hardly rein himself in. "Do you appreciate the height and depth of my temptation?" he wrote to staid Colvin, "that I have about nine miles to ride, and I can become a general officer?" War, he summed up delightedly, "is a huge *entraînement;* there is no other temptation to be compared to it, not one."

Stevenson did not ride the nine miles to become a general. But he did make himself into a war correspondent, and his war letters to London had all the old Stevenson color. "Women," he reported, "march with the troops—even the Taupo-sa, or sacred maid of the village, accompanies her father in the field to carry cartridges, and bring him water to drink,—and their bright eyes are ready to 'rain influence' and reward valour. To what grim deeds this practice may conduct I shall have to say later on. In the rally of their arms, it is at least wholly pretty; and I have one pleasant picture of a war-party marching out; the men armed and boastful, their heads bound with the red handkerchief, their faces blacked—and two girls marching in their midst under European parasols."

Samoan warriors took heads. Missionaries and consuls reasoned with them against this barbarism; Stevenson got up a petition against it. But it was the Samoan's way of proving himself. It had been done before the white man came. Mataafa's men had done it to white men, when they ambushed the German marines in 1888. (A Samoan once remarked interestedly of a big cabbage cut from the Vailima garden that it was like a German's head.) This time, five years later, Mataafa forbade his men to take trophies. But Malietoa did not. After no more than a day or two of fighting, it was clear that Malietoa was the winner. Mataafa was in flight, and the victor sat in triumph as fifteen heads were brought to him. Stevenson reported this with mournful relish, along with the horrible fact that tradition had been breached and women's heads taken, one of them that of a *taupo.*

However much Stevenson the child looked forward to war, Stevenson the adult was depressed and disgusted by it. He managed to put distance between himself and what was happening, characteristically turning it into a performance. Visiting the Apia hospital, he found it "wonderful generally how little one cares about the wounded; hospital sights, etc.; things that used to murder me. I was far more struck with the excellent way in which things were managed; as if it had been a peep-show; I held some of the things at an operation, and did not care a dump." He reserved his sorrow and anger for the "mismanagement of all the white officials" who had allowed fighting to break out in the first place (and to recur, as it did in 1894). Stevenson kept on with his private efforts to find a peaceful solution to Samoa's problems, but without much hope, "at heart very conscious of the inevitable flat failure" that awaited every attempt.

The romantic in Stevenson revived. He felt pity for Mataafa, so quickly routed and ignominiously bundled off to confinement on Jaluit in the German-controlled Marshall Islands in Micronesia. Now he had a king literally over the water to yearn after, and when Graham Balfour took a cruise in Mataafa's direction, Stevenson loaded him down with gifts for the exile—shirts, *lavalava*, trade cloth, *kava*. Going further, crossing into fantasy again, Stevenson talked several times with a visiting globe-trotter, the Hungarian Count Rodolphe Festetics de Tolna, married to an American millionairess and navigating a luxury yacht around the world, about descending on Jaluit and carrying Mataafa off.

Closer to home Stevenson continued to be attentive to Mataafa's interests. A number of Mataafa's chiefs were in jail at Apia. Stevenson made a point of visiting them, and when they laid on a huge feast for him and showered him with gifts to take home, he paraded with all this lavish display past the residence of Malietoa. This was another piece of conspicuous presumption. But at the same time Stevenson worked seriously to have the chiefs' sentences shortened, and when they were released they showed their gratitude by building a road for him partway between Apia and Vailima.

Stevenson took this as a great compliment—Samoans hated road making. In return for their pains he made them a speech, and it was an interesting one. He gave war no points at all, coming out in favor of peace and co-operation among chiefs and the rewards of industrious toil. The real defense of Samoa and Samoan interests was productivity, he said. "Who is the true champion of Samoa? It is not the man who blackens his face, and cuts down trees, and kills pigs and wounded men. It is the man who makes roads, who plants food trees, who gathers harvests, and is a profitable servant before the Lord . . . that is the brave soldier; that is the true champion." The Scottish Highlanders had not understood this. They were a fine people in the past, "brave, gay, faithful, and very much like Samoans, except in one particular, that they were much wiser and better at that business of fighting of which you think so much." But they had not developed their country, and so had lost it. The message for Samoan chiefs was clear. The day of the last great battle was at hand, "of the great and the last opportunity by which it shall be decided, whether you are to pass away like those other races of which I have been speaking, or to stand fast, and have your children living on and honouring your memory in the land you received of your fathers." Occupy and use your country, said Stevenson, or others will.

Stevenson meant all this seriously, just as in another part of himself he seriously meant to do great Gordonesque things and to rescue Mataafa from exile. He never did entirely put off his masks or grow altogether heavy and owlish. He was no real politician; there remained too much of the naughty boy or the impressionable romantic in him. Just the same, after he was dead it turned out that he had been as right as any politician about the situation in Samoa. It had been hard for him to get his analysis of events accepted as accurate in Europe. But when Germany and Great Britain came to make their own official investigations, they found nothing to contradict what Stevenson had said. He was right on the incompetence of the treaty officials, right on the idea that a three-power regime was unworkable, right in predicting that one nation would eventually rule (it turned out to be Germany, of which he would not have approved), and right on Mataafa, who was eventually brought back from exile by the Germans to be what all along he maintained he was, "king of the Samoans."

*   *   *

When Stevenson had the urge to ride those nine miles in wartime to Mataafa, become a general, seize the government, he let the moment go by, recognizing the temptation almost in the same breath as "childish." The fact of the matter was that in Samoa Stevenson, by whatever means and shifts, had come to identify himself as a grown-up man of substance— a family man with generations back and forward of him living at Vailima under the magnificent roof raised by his own labors. His place, he realized, not without regret but clearly, was at home, taking care of his family.

He was in a position which committed him to responsibilities stretching away beyond his own death, and he looked to discharging these responsibilities by providing for his dependents out of continuing royalties: once again, the author as householder. At the suggestion of Charles Baxter, who had been managing his finances for him in Edinburgh, he made arrangements for the publication of his collected works. A collected works—that he had come so far struck him as amazing when he looked back over his life. Half asleep one night aboard the *Casco*, somewhere between the Marquesas and the Tuamotus, he had suddenly thought of himself in his Edinburgh university days, pickling about drunk in the rain and the east wind: "how I feared that I should make a mere shipwreck, and yet timidly hoped not; how I feared I should never have a friend, far less a wife, and yet passionately hoped I might; how I hoped (if I did not take to drink) I should possibly write one little book, etc. etc." What a change between there and the South Seas. He had survived, he was married, he had written much and become wealthy and famous for it. "I feel somehow as if I should like the incident set upon a brass plate at the corner of that dreary thoroughfare, for all students to read, poor devils, when their hearts are down." And now, in 1894, six years on from the *Casco*, the better part of a million words on, writing to Baxter about his pleasure in the Edinburgh Edition, he recalled another night of drinking when the two of them were young, himself very drunk, maudlin, telling his friend about his yearnings for fame and his "intimations of early death." Preposterous then to think that "I should be well and strong at the age of forty-three in the island of Upolu, and that you should be at home bringing out the Edinburgh Edition." With gratitude and wonder he considered "the way in which I have been led."

Stevenson had somehow survived a fair amount of shipwreck. Among his friends of Edinburgh days he had seen youthful promise fail to mature, talent squandered, dissipation, and early death. And, of course, the Pacific was classic shipwreck country, literally and metaphorically. Stevenson could look out his windows to the sea beyond Apia harbor where the six men-of-war lay, to Apia itself which crawled with beached human wrecks, and look inside again to where Joe Strong had run his life on the rocks. And there sat Robert Louis Stevenson, RLS, somehow above it all now, a poor, sad, fantastic young man who had grown older, more stable, richer, happier, come into his kingdom in this great house on the mountain. He was fortunate.

The maps and charts that located Stevenson in his forties were not so very different from those by which Walter Murray Gibson had steered, when all was said and done. Like any number of people, Stevenson had a lost island in his mind, laid down on his personal chart when he was young. "There is scarce a family that can count four generations," he wrote once, "but lays a claim to some dormant title or some castle and estate: a claim not prosecutable in any court of law, but flattering to the fancy and a great alleviation of idle hours. . . . A paper might turn up (in proper story-book fashion) in the secret drawer of an old ebony secretary, and restore your family to its ancient honours, and reinstate mine on a certain West Indian islet (not far from St. Kitts, as beloved tradition hummed in my young ears) which was once ours, and is now unjustly some one else's."

This reference to phantom inheritances was part of an essay Stevenson wrote about his dreams and their relation to his creativity. He was fascinated by his ability to dream plots that could be written up as stories and sold for money. The idea for his first popular success, a boy's romance called *Treasure Island,* came out of a sort of daydream. Stevenson shared it with his young stepson Lloyd one rainy afternoon in Scotland. They talked and drew themselves a chart, Stevenson's father joined in enthusiastically, and so the story developed. In this case the treasure was not to be won by the mere finding of a piece of paper. There was a map, but along the way a young man had to challenge an older man, and go through bloody combat and trials of strength, and penetrate secret places by force to achieve the riches lying concealed in the earth.

Another story that he dreamed but never shaped into marketable fiction had Stevenson himself as the central figure, the son of a very rich and wicked man with much land and a violent temper. To get out from under his father's rages he went away and lived abroad. While he was gone his father took a new wife, a young woman. He came home, fell into the old kind of quarrel with his father, and in the course of it killed him. The crime went unsuspected. The son inherited the estate and lived under the same roof with his father's young widow. He began to suspect that she knew he was a murderer, a parricide, and finally he taxed her with it. Yes, she said, she knew, but she would never tell anyone, because—she loved him.

Now, Stevenson had discovered, as all little boys do, that his beloved mother belonged to his feared and envied father, and he had gone on (as not all boys do) to rebel comprehensively in adolescence against everything his father stood for, to the point where his father threatened to disinherit him. Actually Stevenson made it the work of decades to disinherit himself as best he could from his father's profession, from his own forced choice of a career in the law, from his family's Calvinism, from middle-class respectability altogether, from Edinburgh, then from England, then from Europe. All this took him as far as Samoa. And once there, he began reconstituting an inheritance in a way that suited him: the household at Vailima, patriarchy, property, political responsibilities, prayers in the great hall, collected works to go on the library shelves. His mother lived with him, and around the walls of the great hall were family faces—a portrait of his grandfather, a bust of his father, Stevenson and Fanny painted together by the American John Singer Sargent, Saint-Gaudens's bronze medallion. To symbolize the literary accomplishment that distinguished him among the old lighthouse builders from whom he was descended, Stevenson displayed two fancies from *Treasure Island,* Long John Silver's pistol and Blind Pew's knife. As a youth Stevenson had launched a life of his own by turning himself, with some effort, into a starving bohemian. If in middle age he continued to reject the bourgeois style, it was in favor of life as a self-made lord-in-a-distant-castle, with his family past exhibited all around.

So now at last he was prepared to come to terms with his family—on his own terms. With Vailima a fact, he began to take an interest in Stevenson family history, and this became a preoccupation that lasted the rest of his life. He wrote long letters to Scotland asking for genealogical information, and ruminated the results. Inevitably, he began by hoping to find romance among his forebears, descent from someone like, say, Rob Roy MacGregor, the celebrated Highland freebooter of the time before the '45. From there he went on to acceptance of the unglamorous truth that "we are a second-rate lot" or at least mixed in quality, including a "great party" in the wars of Edward the First and someone who died "£220. 10s to the bad, from drink." In between were tenant farmers, maltsters, "not very romantic," and gaps still to be filled. Thus far along, Stevenson lusted after completeness. "I wish to trace my ancestors a thousand years, if I trace them by gallowses. It is not love, not pride, not admiration; it is an expansion of the identity, intimately pleasing, and wholly uncritical; I can expand myself in the person of an inglorious ancestor with perfect comfort; or a disgraced, if I could find one." What he was after was just this sense of expansion, of the connections to be made between himself and all those others. That in itself turned out to be romance enough. "I have come so far; and the sights and thoughts of my youth pursue me; and I see like a vision the youth of my father, and of his father, and the whole stream of lives flowing down there far in the north, with the sound of laughter and tears, to cast me out in the end, as by a sudden freshet, on these ultimate islands. And I admire and bow my head before the romance of destiny."

Close to his own time, at least, there was nothing of great romance, or of ingloriousness and disgrace, just evidence of exceptional middle-class accomplishment. And in time Stevenson, the antibourgeois, was able— the ultimate in reconciliation—to appreciate that as well. For three generations before the birth of Robert Louis in 1850, Stevenson men had been consultants to the Commissioners of Northern Lights. Stevenson thought of *Northern Lights* as a name for his never-purchased trading vessel, called his Bournemouth coast house "Skerryvore," after a Stevenson construction, and perhaps generated from this lighthouse-building inheritance a taste for the metaphor of life as a sea journey with risk of shipwreck. Stevenson family work was solid, durable, worthy. Stevenson's grandfather Robert deserved and achieved recognition by a coat of arms. Robert's son Thomas, father of Robert Louis, made brilliant inventions in marine optics and never patented them, preferring to leave them in the public domain for the common good. That was what Stevenson had grown up with, what he had rejected and was now returning to. "What a singular thing," he wrote to his cousin Bob, "is this undistinguished perpetuation of a family throughout the centuries, and the sudden bursting forth of character and capacity that began with our grandfather!" Stevenson was going to write a book about it. This was another of the projects he never completed. But there was time enough for him to come to a mature and affectionate appreciation of his father, and, of course, time along the way to take meals with his mother at Vailima at the family table covered with the lighthouse tablecloth from Queen Victoria. Once, considering his own life, Stevenson said he should have been able to write novels and build lighthouses too.

There was another family for which Stevenson had a care, that of Scottish poets. After he turned forty he became intense about it: Robert Fergusson, Robert Burns, Robert Louis Stevenson, "three Robins who have touched the Scots lyre this last century." Burns had gone to his reward, the idol of Scotland forever. But Fergusson, the first of the three, born a hundred years before Stevenson, had suffered bad health, was forced to drudge in a law office, and died young in a madhouse. Stevenson felt a special affinity with the "poor, white-faced, drunken, vicious boy"— indeed even thought that Fergusson in some way lived on in him. He had seen himself headed in Fergusson's direction when he was young, but had managed to "outlive his greensickness," go on to outlive the second "greensickness of maturity," and achieve the living fame and reward that Fergusson never knew. Stevenson felt an injustice there and hoped to see restitution made. He wanted to pay for the refurbishing of the Fergusson monument in Edinburgh (originally put up by Burns); he wanted to see a life written; he even thought of dedicating the Edinburgh Edition of Stevenson to Fergusson (though he settled eventually on Fanny.)

Identification with those other Robins, with hundreds of years of Stevensons, the recognition that the best of the writing he did in Samoa was still—always—about Scotland . . . Like a king over the water, Stevenson was feeling his exile. When he was young, traveling Europe, sleeping in those two hundred ten towns one after another, he remarked on how un-Scottish people thought he looked, how he was taken as coming from any part of the globe other than the place where he originated. As late as the moment of choosing to live in Samoa, he was blithe enough about what he was forsaking at home. He missed all his old friends and was constantly inviting them to sail out (and recommending seasickness as good for the liver), but beyond that he was firm that he simply preferred Samoa. "I was never fond of towns, houses, society or (it seems) civilisation. Nor yet it seems was I ever very fond of (what is technically called) God's green earth. The sea, islands, the islanders, the island life and climate, make and keep me truly happier. . . . It is plain, then, that for me my exile to the place of schooners and islands can be in no sense regarded as a calamity." In retrospect he claimed that he chose Samoa rather than Honolulu because it was less civilized. "Can you not conceive that it is awful fun?"

But always he was given to visions of Scotland, flashes of stormy Edinburgh at night on board the *Casco*, whole Pacific landscapes at other times to take him suddenly home. He could look out at Vailima and see

Mt. Vaea as nothing but Scotland, and a rainy day would drench him in showers of remembered sensation so strong that he literally staggered: "highland huts, and peat smoke, and the brown swirling rivers, and wet clothes, and whisky, and the romance of the past, and that indescribable bite of the whole thing at a man's heart. . . ." A singular thing it was, he wrote to J. M. Barrie, "that I should live here in the South Seas under conditions so new and so striking, and yet my imagination so continually inhabit that cold old huddle of grey hills from which we come."

Finally, four years after he settled on Mt. Vaea, he admitted, almost casually, that he had had enough of the exotic. Samoa was certainly the place to absorb color, living color, but "I am used to it; I do not notice it, rather prefer my grey, freezing recollections of Scotland." When he opted for Samoa it was for reasons of health; he was there for life, in all senses. This inevitably raised the question of death away from Scotland, something Stevenson found a bitter thought. "I shall never set my foot again upon the heather. Here I am until I die, and here will I be buried. The word is out and the doom written."

* * *

There were stages along the way up the seven-hundred-thousand-word mountain of prose that Stevenson scaled in Samoa when he slowed, faltered, juggled subjects, abandoned one idea in favor of another, could not get started, could not go on, stopped writing altogether for short periods. At such times he saw himself, in his forties, as a tired old man. He spoke of a loss of skills—"even our proficiencies are deciduous and evanescent"—of "fiction-phobia," of having written too many books, of finding it hard to look ahead to the finishing of another one, of having sounded his top note, of being at the climacteric that came to all men who lived by their wits, of not wanting to see his work "senesce" and himself become "impotent and forgotten." At times he saw himself as talentless, merely industrious, as having done nothing but pile up words, and then he would ask himself what it was all for. "I wonder exceedingly if I have done anything at all good; and who can tell me? And why should I wish to know?" In this mood it seemed to him that not just the artist's skills were deciduous and evanescent, but the whole world he worked in. He spoke wistfully about wanting to leave an image upon men's minds for a few years, "for fun," and yet, "in so little a while, I, and the English language, and the bones of my descendants"—said Stevenson the childless—"will have ceased to be a memory."

Stevenson really hated getting older, and he fought it. Lloyd Osbourne thought he held on to exceptional youth until his mid-thirties, and certainly he did not greet with serenity the appearance of grey in his beard.

"O, it is bad to grow old," he wrote to Colvin at forty-three. "For me, it is practically hell. I do not like the consolations of age. I was born a young man; I have continued so; and before I end, a pantaloon, a driveller—enough. . . ." He was even capable of resenting the access of good health Samoa gave him if it meant that he would have to age further in order to die: "I was meant to die young, and the gods do not love me." Part of this horror may have had its origins in watching his father age and decay, go sadly through his sixties with what was evidently a series of outwardly imperceptible cerebral hemorrhages that left him uncertain in his physical movements, prone to terrible depression and debility, and, saddest of all (for he was a lover of language like his son), deprived of the joy of talk. Old Thomas would lose the line of his sentences; they would start well, and then the clinching word would be gone before he could speak it. Stevenson of all people did not want to be forced through anything like this slow, sad dissolution. Even in the maturity he cultivated and achieved at Vailima he stayed young, to the extent of fits and starts of infantility. He could talk about being ready to lie down with his fathers in honor, in thankfulness and fatigue, but then he would play toy soldiers; and he had days when he was nothing but a naughty child, pulling out his wife's hairpins, tangling his mother's knitting. His family, when these moods were upon him, called him "the Idiot Boy." Fanny, who saw him every day for years, remarked that at one moment he might look ancient, a man of eighty, the next "a pretty brown boy."

About all this he wrote, a middle-aged man, to his cousin Bob, with whom he had spent delightful years in his youth. "The mind runs ever in a thousand eddies like a river between cliffs. You (the ego) are always spinning around in it, east, west, north, and south. You are twenty years old, and forty, and five, and the next moment you are freezing at an imaginary eighty; you are never the plain forty-four that you should be by dates." Stevenson wrote this on learning that Bob had just had a child. Stevenson himself had none. Just after his forty-fourth birthday, death came to his mind once more and he drew back, because there was no one of his own to follow him. To another friend, the author Edmund Gosse, he wrote that the main difference between them was "that you have a family growing up around you, and I am a childless, rather bitter, very clear-eyed, blighted youth. I have, in fact, lost the path that makes it easy and natural for you to descend the hill. I am going at it straight. And where I have to go down it is a precipice."

At other times he talked freely about death, even of inviting it, wanting it. Ill health being intolerable and a Gordonesque end unavailable, he entertained the idea of killing himself. But he rejected suicide as unworthy or ungentlemanly or—once—ungenteel. He thought about suicide and Scotland together, about rewriting the doom of his death in Samoa. If he went back to where he had come from, he said, it would be "a voyage to a further goal, and in fact a suicide; which, however, if I could get my family all fixed up in the money way, I might perhaps, perform, or attempt." But it might not work out properly; and so "I believe I shall stay here until the end comes like a good boy, as I am."

Everything came back to family, which figured in Stevenson's last years both as millstone and bedrock. He talked of wanting to retire but being unable to because his family depended on him. Yet he depended on them, drew sustenance from them. He had a great mountain retreat that he rarely left because he loved it so much—"O my beautiful forest, O my beautiful shining, windy house"—and when he did ride out and was late coming back, the lamps of Vailima were always lit against his return. And the great house was filled with family. It was a real home. At Thanksgiving in 1894, not long after he turned forty-four, he celebrated the fact, proposing a toast to them all: his wife, to whom he owed happy years and life itself; his mother, who had forsaken all others to live with him; Lloyd and Belle, who graced his home and whom he regarded as son and daughter. And looking at young Austin Strong he was moved to say: "Vailima is blessed—there's a child in the house." He had made his emotional peace with Thomas Stevenson while the old man lived, and he managed finally to come to terms with his dead father's dying. The figure of the father still haunted the son, no longer as the failing old fellow who had lost his way with words, but most benignly and inspiritingly, in two remembrances— as a man of fifty, strong and well, lying on a hillside and carving mottoes on a stick, and younger again, stripped and running down the sands into the Scottish sea, beautiful in his small son's eyes.

With all this, and taking his consolations where he could, Stevenson was happy, in the way that people past their youth are happy. Samoa was at peace, and even if Mataafa was in exile it was possible to send him gifts of affection. Charles Baxter, a dear friend, was at last on his way to visit Vailima, bringing with him the first two volumes of the Edinburgh Edition of the collected works. And RLS was vigorously at work on a fine new novel, set in Scotland, peopled by powerful men and full-blooded women, all alive . . .

That is how death surprised him. On the morning of December 3 he wrote hard at his book, the story of a son condemned to death by a hanging-judge father and his escape across the seas with his true love. He left the lovers in an embrace, and in the afternoon sat down to answer the letters of distant friends. At sunset he came downstairs to play cards with his wife, and talked about how well he felt, how he was thinking of making a lecture tour in the United States. Then, hungry for dinner, he brought up a bottle of old burgundy from the cellar and set to work on the making of a salad, his specialty, with vegetables fresh from the Vailima garden. Suddenly he put his hands to his head, and just as suddenly collapsed. All his life he had lived in fear of his lungs, whose weakness he had inherited from his mother, but in the end he was struck down in an instant by the cerebral failure that had so slowly killed his father. The doctors were sent for; they rode up from Apia to Vailima as fast as they could. But they could do nothing. One of the physicians looked down at the negligible frame with all the nervous strength of its life ebbing away. The sticklike limbs lay still. "How can anybody write books with arms like these?" he asked. And Stevenson's mother said: "He has written *all* his books with arms like these."

*   *   *

Paul Gauguin

LOOKING AT THE TRANSFORMATION of Stevenson as he passed from youth to middle age, one of his literary contemporaries was struck by a kind of paradox. Nothing, he said, could be of more intense interest than the "madness" of Stevenson's "fall into respectability." Yet Stevenson came from the most respectable of backgrounds, and his ultimate acceptance of the householding life was wholehearted. He was content to have grown up into a failed bohemian.

A much more extreme case of the man at war with society (and with himself) was Paul Gauguin, and here there was real strangeness. Gauguin, in his early thirties was the model of a middle-class Frenchman, several years into married life with a woman of the utmost respectability who bore him children regularly—four sons and a daughter in all; and he was well set up in business, a stockbroker's agent dealing on the Paris exchange. Then, entering middle age, at the time of life when Stevenson declared himself a householder, Gauguin was seized by a need to declare himself an artist, and his way of making the declaration was to smash his connections with job, wife, family, home. In short, he tore his house down.

He did not stop with that. For the sake of his art—for the sake of his soul, as he would have said—he found himself driven to escape from Europe altogether. His need as a man wanting to live the artist's life in freedom was to slough off civilization. The project consumed the rest of his life. He was in his mid-thirties when he declared himself an artist, and it took him several years more to find the South Seas. At last, after a number of false starts, he set off in his forties to paint in Tahiti, becoming there the Gauguin the world knows.

But this was still not the last of the story. A decade and more later Gauguin ended his days beached in the Marquesas, with a bad heart and failing eyes, very likely morphine-addicted, possibly leprous, certainly syphilitic. That was the artist's life of Gauguin; he died of it.

*   *   *

It is a strange history. Yet in the perspective of his whole life, Gauguin the businessman and family man appears as a much more unlikely figure than Gauguin the mad artist. Given his real character, his underlying nature, it is surprising to find him making anything like a sustained attempt to live as a bourgeois.

In fact Gauguin was jailed in the middle class. One of his favorite stories—he put it on paper several times—was the fable of La Fontaine about the skinny wolf who wanders in from the wild woods to the edge of town and is attracted by the comfortable life of a plump domestic dog, until he sees that the well-fed neck has a collar on it. Gauguin was choking on his collar. When the chance came, he slipped it and ran.

The French economy was prosperous in the 1870s, and Gauguin the broker's runner profited from the rise in share prices. In 1878, the year of a great Universal Exposition in Paris, the government floated a three-billion-franc loan and got forty-two billion in subscriptions. This set the stage for a real boom at the end of the decade. Gauguin rode to and from work in a carriage, dressed expensively, collected paintings. Then in 1882 came the crash. Businesses failed all over Paris, a big banker or two went to jail for fraud, the national credit was shaken. Gauguin had changed employers at the height of the boom, and was now working as an insurance salesman. The slump meant that commissions were hard to come by, and in late 1883 Gauguin lost his job. His response—part push, part pull—was to strike out on his own: as an artist.

Gauguin seems to have wanted to persuade himself, at least to begin with, that he could make a go of things with his paintbrush. He had been a Sunday painter for years, since before his marriage. He painted for relaxation, as others might go to the races or pass a few hours in a boulevard café, but also because painting answered some need in him for self-assertion, self-definition. He studied the work of great men of the past, got to know practicing artists around Paris, talked theory with them, experimented with styles, found himself to be an instinctive enemy of the artistic establishment, and eventually got good enough to be hung—and noticed—in the exhibitions that the artistic rebels of the French capital, impressionists and neoimpressionists, organized in defiance of the official salon. In 1881 Gauguin showed a distinctive nude (of his maidservant—his wife Mette would never pose for him unclothed), and there was enough flattering critical comment to make him think he might really be a painter. But to paint for a living? If there was no money on the stock exchange any more, there was obviously going to be less than nothing in art, particularly in the risky, unconventional art that Gauguin favored.

Whatever else he might have been about with his artist's life, Gauguin was certainly wrecking his marriage. Mette took badly to hard times. As months of doing without showed signs of turning into years she became, understandably enough, bitter over what was being done to her. Nothing in her life had prepared her for poverty, and the fact that the poverty was colored bohemian did not help. Mette's background was Danish, safe and sound. She was the daughter of a civil servant. There was, as a matter of fact, a painter in her family, her brother-in-law, but he was a gentleman artist, painting conventionally and selling adequately. Mette had taken up married life with Gauguin on the clear understanding that he was dependable and aboveboard, a stockbroking Dr. Jekyll, so to speak. Now before her appalled eyes—there was something almost monstrous about it—he was turning into a demented Mr. Hyde with a paintbrush, who abused her for being herself, abused her in the end for existing. "Sale bourgeoise," filthy bourgeois, Gauguin called her; and his oldest son remembered him commandeering Mette's good linen tablecloths for canvas and tearing up her petticoats for paint rags. In 1884 Mette took the children north to live with her family in Copenhagen, and that was the beginning of the end of the Gauguin household.

The artist Gauguin actually did make some gestures in the direction of breadwinning, but they were all unconvincing. He took a job as a commission salesman for some textile makers, but left owing them money. One miserable winter he worked for a few weeks as a bill sticker. Somewhere along the line he seems to have gotten involved with some Spanish political exiles, and he may have made a clandestine trip into Spain and back, perhaps on a mercenary basis. He sold off some of his collection of impressionist art, cashed in his life insurance, and was eventually reduced to pawning clothes.

For years after he withdrew from Mette and her middle-class mind and body, Gauguin kept on talking as if he meant to go on taking responsibility for his family. He really did not. Still, when he set out to justify what he was doing, he at least began by using the language of the householder. He told Mette, for example, that he was not deliberately avoiding making money; it was just that money making took time. A man without any inheritance had to depend on the fruits of his labor, and, of course, hard times had to be expected initially. But Mette, without any taste for art, only for money, had merely to wait, because a successful artist was a money maker. So an artist's family was really no worse off than others to begin with, and in the long run had better things to look forward to: "Art is my business, my capital, the future of my children, it is the honor of the name I have given them, all things which one day will serve then well . . . an honorable father known everywhere can put himself forward and get them placed. . . . I am working at my art which is nothing (in money) for the present (times are hard) as a plan for the future."

On all counts this was unconvincing. There never was a man more sure of his talent than the artist Gauguin. With absolute certainty he knew he had genius in him. Yet just as surely he was aware that the nineteenth century was notorious for doing damage to artists, especially artists who took risks. In his day and age, genius of his sort would guarantee him nothing, not reward, not even proper recognition, and, therefore, not self-fulfillment. Stevenson had always envied what he took to be the great freedom of the artist in France. But Gauguin, his exact contemporary, living in what Stevenson regarded as a happy land, thought of himself as foredoomed. Not because his vocation as an artist was flawed, but because of the way society worked. Every man, so Gauguin asserted, had the right to live, and to live well in proportion to his labor. The artist—meaning Gauguin—could not live. He was a full-time artist who could sell nothing. His conclusion was that society was wrongly organized, a vast system of calculated unfairness, a monstrous and oppressive fraud. So Gauguin was consumed by a perpetual frightful rage against the world.

Actually, the rage had been in him all his life. It was what he knew best about himself. The only way he ever found of giving meaning to his rage was to declare himself an artist, live the artist's life. And for Gauguin the artist, living in society was like being confined to jail. To be free, to declare artistic freedom as a principle of life, was to be a criminal on the run. That is how Gauguin came to see himself, as a fugitive from the appalling, unjust punishments of European civilization, and his flight brought him at last to the South Seas.

* * *

It was easy to be impressed by the emerging artist Gauguin. A painter who knew him in the years before he departed for Tahiti described him as "the undisputed master" of the group in which he moved for a time. But to like Gauguin the man was next to impossible. Gauguin was aware of this, and he used to put it down to his looks. No matter what he did to compose his features, so he said, he ended up giving the impression that he was being disdainful; it was the way his face was made.

Certainly others saw Gauguin as heavily armored against his fellow man. Even among convivial artists he was solitary, distant, measured, calculating in his response to what was going on around him, never really spontaneous or even impulsive in what he said or did. One man who saw a good deal of him noted how unusually still he held himself, allowing perhaps a glance to left or right to follow a conversation but never moving his head or body. When he did speak—and at least he was ready to talk art at length—it was mostly to impose his views on others; he was a great maker of pronouncements. For the rest, he would sit, solidly built, short (only five feet four inches, though he liked to think of himself as tall), muscular, unrelentingly self-contained, so tightly packed that he seemed like something sculpted, with a hooked nose (aquiline to begin with, later broken in a fist fight), lips compressed so as not to give anything away, eyes heavy-lidded. The eyes were blue-green, and they were cold. Gauguin had his own saying about them: when he was young he went to sea, he had voyaged in cold parts, and his eyes had gotten frozen.

Everything about Gauguin broadcast the insistent message that he did not need people. His opinion was that he had good grounds for despising most of humanity. There were not many individuals who could be useful to him; he knew who they were and treated them appropriately. As for those who could harm him, it was his talent that offended them. All the rest he dismissed; there was nothing to be gained by paying court to imbeciles. One of his definitions of the good life, in fact, excluded human intimacy altogether. Good health, regular sex, independent work, and a man could pull through, he said. Nothing about love, or even companionability. He once wrote—and meant it—that to make him utter the words "I love you" it would be necessary to smash his teeth in. The truth is that Gauguin was incapable of caring about anyone other than himself.

His self-regard, though, was infinite. He was full of self-concern, self-love. Self-hate, too, which he turned outward against the world in the form of aggression and deliberate cruelty. He was a practical joker of the coldest and meanest sort, an unceremonious borrower of money (and ideas) who never acknowledged his creditors, and a remorseless sexual predator. He was determined to be cold-blooded, even in the presence of the literal shedding of blood. He was sharing a house and painting with Vincent van Gogh in the south of France when the unbalanced van Gogh, in the last distraught period of his life, made the famous gesture of cutting off part of his ear. Gauguin's response was to disengage, leave for Paris. And his first act there was to get up at dawn to watch a public execution, the guillotining of a murderer. He noted in great detail the horrible faultiness of the arrangements, the bad matching of the length of the board with the length of the condemned man's body, so that there was a struggle to get the neck in place under the knife. The blade fell, and in the crowd Gauguin pressed forward to get a close look at the severed head of society's victim.

All this deliberate deadening of tenderness Gauguin would have put under the heading of a long-term project of his. There were two parts to him, he once told his wife, the "sensitive" and what he called the "Indian," by which he meant a being capable of withstanding pain, emotional or physical, even torture, without flinching. He was engaged, so he said, in suppressing the sensitive side of his nature, closing off his heart, to allow the Indian to walk straight and strong. This was Gauguin doing his best to manage his bottomless rage against society, against the torture of having to be Paul Gauguin in France in the nineteenth century.

The sensitive survived. As part of the long exercise of transforming himself from a broker into an artist, Gauguin painted a number of self-portraits, and he wrote a great deal about himself, for the benefit of his wife and his fellow artists, though, of course, far more for his own benefit. There is no doubt that his first and most beloved creation as an artist was himself. Gauguin the bourgeois was dead; and this freed Gauguin the artist to identify himself, on canvas and on paper, as vagabond, unwilling provider, wicked child, lonely rebel, Ishmael figure, villain, criminal, savage, animal, wolf, inhuman monster, devil, fallen angel, potential suicide, lord of life reaching for the divine. Obviously Gauguin never did manage to kill off the sensitive in him; he remained open to great self-pity, to great surges of suffering in his own behalf. Indeed he came to conceive of his artist's life as a passion, and of himself as a kind of Christ on the cross.

Tahiti was a long time revealing itself to Gauguin. As early as 1886 he made a reference to an offer of "farming work in Oceania," whatever that might have meant, but nothing came of it; and not for another several years did he come to focus on the South Seas. In the meantime he cast about for places—any place—where he could be an artist. Some of his early years as a painter were passed in Brittany, in the northwest of France, where starving artists went for the picturesque backwardness of the province and its peasants and for the cheapness of bed and board. Gauguin felt a special affinity for the region: "I like Brittany. . . . When my sabots echo on that granite earth, I hear the dulled, muffled, powerful note I am looking for in painting." Granitic, muffled, powerful; this was how Gauguin wanted to present himself to the world. And he used two other words about Brittany that had special meaning for him: "I find there the savage, the primitive."

The savage was obviously the Indian into whom Gauguin was determined to transform himself, implacably restrained, unfathomable, but somehow powerfully expressive. The primitive came to mean something else. In his search for the true sources of art Gauguin kept going back and back, beyond his own society, beyond Brittany, beyond European civilization altogether, back to the childhood of the world. To him, civilized art was sterile; it was primitive art that was nourishing. Mother's milk, he called it. He was identifying the childhood of the world with his own infancy. As an artist, he once said, the horses in a Parthenon frieze did not interest him; what moved him to creativity was the wooden rocking horse of his babyhood. Putting together artistic impulse with childhood opened the way for Gauguin to arrive at an idea of primitivism that was all pleasure: a free self-expressive life in an unthreatening world of warmth and light, just as powerful and full of mystery as Brittany, but with nothing cold and somber about it. Where pleasure and plenty ruled, there was no need to be a savage impervious to pain. This was Gauguin's dream, a "dream before nature," as he called it, and it became a dream of islands.

No place in Europe met Gauguin's specifications—obviously—and civilization was oppressing him, exhausting him, so he said. He looked to the tropics. In 1887 he tried Panama, more specifically a tiny island called Taboga on the Pacific side of the isthmus, which he believed to be "almost uninhabited, free and fertile." There he would recoup his energies, "live like a savage," and paint.

It was a disaster. The Panama Canal was being dug; the Indians of Taboga had learned enough about civilization to charge staggering rents for worthless patches of land. Gauguin wound up doing laboring work for the canal company to feed himself. The whole place was disease-ridden, pestilential; Gauguin caught dysentery and what he called "yellow fever" (more likely hepatitis), and nearly died. He managed to get away to Martinique in the West Indies, which was much better: a warm climate, nature at its most luxuriant, seductive black and Creole women. There he painted well, but after some horrible times with recurrences of ill health that made him wish he was dead, he had to retreat to France. He never really recovered his former strength. Just the same, he decided that once he could raise the money he would be gone again. Gauguin was much impressed with a prediction made by Vincent van Gogh, that the future was with the painter of the tropics. The hot latitudes offered a whole new subject matter, and new motifs there must be, to please the "stupid buying public."

Gauguin was given any number of new tropical places to think about by a great event in Paris, the Universal Exposition of 1889. It was the latest of the enormous world fairs of the nineteenth century, a huge celebration of man's control over nature and Europe's domination of the globe, the triumph of bourgeois society, industrial capitalism, and Western imperialism. Thirty-two million people visited the sixty-one thousand exhibits laid out in the shadow of a new iron wonder of the world, the Eiffel Tower. The most extreme of the Parisian antibourgeois were rude about the vulgarity of all this supreme bourgeois display; one of them called the Eiffel Tower itself "a solitary suppository riddled with holes." Gauguin and some other avant-garde artists, not chosen to exhibit in the official salon, organized a show of their own in a restaurant opposite the pavilion where the academic painters were hung. For the rest, Gauguin just enjoyed himself. He wrote about the new art of architectural ironwork—the Eiffel Tower and the astonishing Galerie des Machines—and he got his notes published, his first art criticism in print. And he was attracted to the colonial exhibits. France and the other great powers were putting on display the exotica of their empires: a copy of the magnificent Cambodian temple of Angkor Wat, for example, and a Cairo street scene with belly dancers. The Javanese village had dancers who fascinated all Paris, and Gauguin went to watch them more than once. He picked up a "mulâtresse," a girl of mixed blood. And he watched Buffalo Bill's Wild West show with its Indians and their bows and arrows. (Later in Brittany he made arrows of his own and wandered along the beaches, playing at being an Indian savage.)

Gauguin sold nothing from his restaurant show, but the French colonial exhibits gave him the idea that his accursed homeland might be useful to him after all. There were jobs in the colonies, and if he could get away somewhere in the jungle on the government payroll he would have the best of all worlds; civilization would be behind him, he could save money, and he could paint. So he proposed himself to the colonial authorities as someone worth considering for a post in Tonkin. Months went by with no action, and when Gauguin presented himself again to see what was holding things up he was given a blunt rejection. He was outraged. And yet when he thought about it, everything fitted together. Society was rotten, and it exported its rottenness to the colonies, fools, men who had put their hand in the till or ruined themselves with women. Yet these caricatures were paid to run the Empire, while a painter like himself was debarred as being a subversive. Tonkin was out; his mind turned in other directions. Madagascar, for example. Five thousand francs, he calculated, and a man could live there as he pleased, build his own house, run a few cows and chickens, pick fruit, live the primitive life without effort. And the women were better than anything in France.

It was while Madagascar was in the air that the South Seas came under consideration. Part of Gauguin's grand primitive plan for abandoning civilization involved taking along a few free spirits who would found a society of artists, of the sort that France refused to tolerate, much less sustain. It is possible that the Australian impressionist painter John Peter Russell (who had talked to Stevenson about the South Seas) helped to direct Gauguin's mind toward the Pacific; Gauguin and Russell were acquainted, and Russell had been considered at one time for membership in the atelier that Vincent van Gogh planned for the south of France. Gauguin had several people in mind for companions, most of them younger painters easily led and dominated; and it was one of these, Émile Bernard, who finally came up with the idea of Tahiti.

Bernard was just as anxious as Gauguin to get away from Europe and Europeans—dolts, misers, fat swindlers, pestilential scum—and to taste the luscious liberties of primitivism, worship the sea, drink freedom to the full, as he put it. Madagascar might be all very well, but Bernard had just discovered the novels of Pierre Loti, a highly popular French writer who had been in Tahiti twenty years before, and Loti's Tahiti was clearly an earthly paradise.

It was not just Loti who said so. It was official. Bernard sent Gauguin a little brochure on Tahiti put out by the ministry of colonies, and there it all was in so many words, a land of no winter and no discontent, ripe fruit for the picking, a workless world where to live was to sing and to love. More marvelous yet for Gauguin the artist, the Tahitian woman was obviously the perfect model, dark-eyed, full-lipped, face unmarked by the stresses of civilization, sweet and innocently voluptuous. This was nothing less than the perfect primitive dream made flesh, if only in print, and Gauguin responded to the brochure as Bougainville and Commerson had responded more than a hundred years before to the island of Tahiti itself.

There had been a Tahitian exhibit at the 1889 Exposition. It had not

drawn Gauguin's attention, perhaps because the Polynesian women recruited to inhabit the huts were (by order, paradoxically, of the same
ministry of colonies that put out the seductive brochure) married and of
"impeccable morals." But now Gauguin's letters were all about the perfect place, full of overheated passages about the silence of beautiful tropical nights, the murmur of his own amorous heart beating in harmony with
the life of the Tahitians, a life of nothing but calm, ecstasy, art, joy.

Gauguin had once talked of the fascination of artistic discovery, of not
just going further with what he had already done, but of finding something else altogether, something more. He felt that possibility in himself
strongly, he said, but could not yet express it. What he wanted, he said,
was "a corner of myself still unknown." Now he was about to discover
Tahiti, and in that unknown corner of the world he would reveal himself
to himself.

So in this Tahitian mood he continued to talk about the rottenness of
Europe, and of how pleased he would be to be gone. For how long was
not clear. Sometimes the trip to Tahiti was to be just for a while, eighteen
months, perhaps as long as two or three years. But at other times he
would say he was leaving Europe for life, finished with civilization, uncar-
ing whether he was remembered or forgotten.

And in the same way he went back and forth on the question of companions. He had a specifically Polynesian version of the artist's colony,
dreamy to the point of fatuousness, in which a little hunting, fishing,
farming, and some offhand pearl diving would meet all costs. But each
candidate for membership dropped out or turned out to be unsuitable,
and, of course, in the end Gauguin went alone.

As for family, he wrote to Mette at one point that being on the other
side of the world bereft of wife and children was the worst thing he could
imagine, and that his plan was for them to join him. But then again he
wrote to her about all that harmony he was looking forward to in Tahiti,
and he talked about surrounding himself there with "a new family." His
last word, following a brief meeting with Mette, was that he felt reconciled with her, and that when he came back from the islands they would
"remarry," and they would grow old and white-haired in happiness,
among the children who were flesh of their flesh.

He was anxious, he said, that while he was gone Mette should not seek
out bad companions and fall into evil ways. Adultery, he once assured
her, was the only crime. As for his own ways, at the very moment when
he was promising future happiness all round for his family, he was busy
buying off a mistress he had acquired in Paris, a seamstress named Juliette Huet. She was pregnant by him, he was determined to leave the

country, and so that she could keep herself alive after the father of her baby was gone he paid for a sewing machine. The money came from an auction of his paintings. He did surprisingly well out of it, all things considered; beyond what he had to lay out on Juliette there was enough to get him to Tahiti and keep him alive for a time. So at last he was in a position to go. There was not enough money, though, to send an amount of any consequence to Mette. There never was.

When the sensitive surviving in Gauguin surfaced temporarily to overwhelm the savage—and this happened not long before he left for Tahiti—it was on Gauguin's own behalf. The young journalist and critic Charles Morice was congratulating him on being where he had always wanted to be, on the verge of fulfilling his destiny, when suddenly Gauguin broke down and began to weep. Morice was nonplused. Gauguin stammered out that he was a failure. He had given up his family for his art and then had failed in his art. And now that he was about to leave for Tahiti, he was tormented by the sacrifices he had made. (Not, it is to be noted, the sacrifices he had imposed on others, but the damage he had inflicted on himself.)

In avant-garde artistic circles, at least, self-exile seemed a grand gesture. Gauguin was seeing a good deal of the school of poets and writers who called themselves symbolists, and what he was doing with his art and his life amounted in their eyes to one great symbolic act, the ultimate artistic repudiation of Europe. In his honor the symbolist circle staged a banquet, dinner from a long menu with long speeches to follow. "Poems, toasts, and the warmest of compliments for me," wrote Gauguin to Mette, and it was true. The poet Stéphane Mallarmé spoke of Gauguin as a man superbly dedicated to his art, at the apogee of his skills, seeking a new strength in self-imposed exile. This was heady stuff, and in Gauguin's last weeks in Paris an immensely flattering article was published as well on his art, life, and aspirations. It said of him all that he would have wanted said of himself. He was leaving civilization and its overpowering noise to attend to his inner voices. Martinique had been one stop along the way in his journey back to the sources of himself, and now it was to be Tahiti, where "nature and his dreams are in better accord, where he hopes for tenderer caresses from the Pacific ocean, an old and faithful ancestral love rediscovered."

Gauguin took a clipping of this interview to Tahiti with him and pasted it into a little notebook in which he recorded his thoughts and feelings and copied down ideas that struck him. He did not want the whole text of the article to survive. Part of it he cut out and threw away, the paragraphs that had to do with his years as a stockbroker and his life as a married man with children. He was excising his bourgeois being, in favor of this dream before nature in which ancestral love was rediscovered.

The dream was by no means a simple one. In 1890, when Gauguin had already decided to leave Europe but did not yet know where he might go, or when or how, he painted an oil of Eve in a tropical paradise of his own imagining. In her hand she holds fruit from a tree, and she is reaching for more. Around the tree trunk the serpent coils, watching. The landscape lies in a kind of waking sleep, still, but vibrating with life. The figure of Eve is extraordinary. She is naked, obviously a woman, not big-breasted or curvaceous, but with her sex clearly marked. The body is unmistakably drawn from Javanese temple carvings that Gauguin had seen at the 1889 Exposition (and he carried photographs of these Buddhist friezes to Tahiti with him). The Javanese representation, though, was of a male. Gauguin in his painting left the physical outline and overall form unaltered, but imposed on it the genital sign of femaleness. And in place of the Javanese carved head from the temple he painted—equally unmistakably—the face of his mother.

*   *   *

"If I tell you," Gauguin wrote toward the end of his life, "that I am descended on my mother's side from a Borgia of Aragon, viceroy of Peru, you will say that it is not true and I am pretentious. But if I tell you that mine is a family of sewer-cleaners, you will scorn me. If I tell you that on my father's side they are all called Gauguin, you will say that this is absolutely naive; as I explain myself, meaning to say that I am not a bastard, you will smile skeptically."

Gauguin hardly knew his father. In the tangle of his feelings about his origins, it was his mother's line that gave him his sense of himself. His mother, whose name was Aline, and *her* mother, Flora Tristan, between them bequeathed him the life he ultimately lived. To all of them Peru was valuable, crucial; for Gauguin himself Tahiti was in many ways a version of Peru.

To begin at the beginning: Gauguin's grandmother, Flora Tristan, was born illegitimate, daughter of a nondescript Frenchwoman and a Spanish aristocrat with a Peruvian colonial background, Don Mariana Tristan y Moscoso. Her father died when she was young. Flora grew up poor, absorbing her mother's stories of the dead father who was a noble Aragonese, in whose veins ran the blood of the Borgias—and of the Incas too, god-kings. Disinheritance was a fact; Flora fed on fantasies of lost status and vanished wealth.

She matured with special powers of her own. When she was fourteen her first lover committed suicide over her. Married at seventeen to an artist-engraver named André Chazal, Flora had two children one after the other. She neglected them. When her husband impregnated her a third time she left him, and once the new baby was born, a girl who was given the name of Aline, Flora put her up with friends and sailed for Peru, chasing the Tristan inheritance she believed was her entitlement. At Lima her father's surviving brother, Don Pio, former viceroy of Peru and a wealthy man, gave her a cool welcome and not much more. Rebuffed, Flora went back to France and wrote a highly colored account of her life and sufferings, publishing it under her Tristan name and called it *Peregrinations of a Pariah*.

Flora's husband Chazal had deteriorated since she left him, to the verge of madness. He hunted for Aline, the daughter he had never seen, found her, kidnaped her, and attempted incest on her. He followed this up by stalking Flora with a pistol and shooting her, spectacularly but not fatally. At the trial Flora, a striking woman, made a great impression on the court. Chazal got twenty years.

Flora, continuing on her own singular way, turned herself into a propagandist for social reform. Not surprisingly, she spoke and wrote against marriage as it was constituted in bourgeois society, and against poverty as a curse. Eventually she came to think of herself as a messiah of the downtrodden, proclaiming a new law, the freedom of woman from man, of the poor from the rich, of the soul from sin. All over France she traveled, spreading the word, pariah turned prophet, a commanding presence, eventually attracting the worried notice of the police and the adoration of the working class. This, at least, was her own account of herself. A man who worked closely with her and was half smitten by her described her, feelingly, in other terms. Attractive, he called her, seductive, almost supernaturally so, but an emotional vampire, a Circe who secretly scorned the masses as stupid and brutish animals to be used, reserving her deepest love for herself, a superb personification of the most complete and implacable vaingloriousness.

When Flora died of a stroke in the midst of her mission, André Chazal was still in jail. Their daughter Aline, at twenty-one, married a journalist called Clovis Gauguin. The couple's first child was a daughter, the second a son, born in Paris during the revolution of 1848. They named him Eugène-Henri-Paul, and called him Paul. Clovis Gauguin, himself a left-winger, had no faith in the revolution. He saw reaction coming, repression of free speech, and decided to leave France ahead of it. In 1849 the Gauguins sailed for Lima, in the direction of the Peruvian inheritance of the Tristans. Clovis never arrived; he died at sea of a heart attack. Aline went on with little Paul and his sister, and in the never-ending family romance of the poor Tristan relatives this chapter at least had a happy ending. Don Pio Tristan y Moscoso survived, in his eighties now but still powerful, vigorous, and hugely wealthy, and he took a great liking to Aline. So the young mother and her little children were lifted up to luxury.

When Gauguin looked back from late middle age in the South Seas to his early life, the years he passed as a child in Lima glowed again for him with singular color and vibrated with memories of exceptional force and fascination. The white city was bathed in tropical sunshine under skies perpetually blue. In the streets there was tawdry brightness and squalor together, with carrion birds circling. By contrast the house where Gauguin lived was lavish, with servants, among them a Chinese laundry-man and a black girl to sleep in the children's room. There were interesting places to play and hide in so as to be found by a distraught mother, whose punishments were clearly more pleasurable than painful, a few slaps with "a little hand as supple as india-rubber," then tears, embraces, caresses. And there was a small girl cousin available for sexual games, with six-year-old Gauguin (as he recollected) the would-be rapist. One night, waking in his bedroom, Gauguin saw the unearthly figure of an es-caped lunatic descend a ladder from the roof, cross the courtyard, come right into the room, look at him tranquilly, and depart without a word into the silent moonlight. And another night an earth tremor rattled him out of sleep, and he lay in fear as the striking portrait of Don Pio on his bedroom wall shook and shook, and all the while the formidable old man's painted eyes stared fixedly down at him.

The child Paul had no real father to help his growing up, and there was something remote in Don Pio's magnificent existence. He was so rich and powerful he seemed more than human, so old he seemed immortal. (Gauguin said later, admiringly and inaccurately, that Don Pio fathered children in his eighties and lived to be one hundred thirteen.) And there was another and very different ever-present eye associated with Peru in the boy's mind—his mother's: "How beautiful my mother was in Lima dress, with the silk mantilla covering her face and leaving visible only one eye: that eye so sweet and imperious, so pure and caressing."

This enchanted life came to an end in 1854, when Gauguin's mother had to take her children back to Europe. Two years later Don Pio died, leaving Aline a very satisfactory bequest. But—according to the story Gauguin told later—the Tristan family cheated his mother, she got noth-ing, and all that remained of Peru in the Gauguin house was a little collec-tion of folk art work, silver pieces and figured pottery.

Aline put Paul in school in Orléans, where there were family connections, and went off to Paris to work as a dressmaker. Paul, uprooted from highly satisfactory Lima and set down in much less satisfactory Orléans, turned into an unsociable boy, withdrawn, refusing to show much of himself to others. What he saw about him struck him mainly as hypocrisy and false virtue, and he judged this severely. He was prone to judge himself harshly too. Perhaps, like many fatherless boys, he had a conscience about his condition, feeling childishly responsible for the disappearance of his father, aware of watching eyes that must surely know his criminality, and the intention behind the crime: Don Pio's eyes that remained unnervingly fixed while Paul lay in fear as the earth shook, and the ambiguously commanding and seductive eye of his mother, to be remembered all his life. At any rate, after his mother too went away and left him, his Orléans uncle would sometimes come across Paul stamping his foot in solitary rage and shouting, "Baby is wicked."

No one, child or adult, liked young Gauguin much, and he did not like anything about his situation. He daydreamed, and carved dream figures into knife handles, and played with the idea of running away. There was a picture in his uncle's house of a wanderer with his belongings on a stick over his shoulder. Paul filled a handkerchief with sand, tied it to a stick and set off, heading for the woods. The neighborhood butcher retrieved him.

When Gauguin finally left school his record was spotty and confusing. It was hard to know what to make of him. A cretin, said one of his teachers, or a genius. Gauguin's talents, whatever they might be, were as unfocused as his prospects. Speaking for himself, he said that when he grew up he wanted to be Marat—a frightening figure from the French Revolution, a ferocious guillotiner, death to the bourgeois, death even to radicals less extreme than himself. This was hardly a career.

Perhaps because his father had once been a sailor, Gauguin went to sea. Signing on for his maiden voyage as a *pilotin,* an apprentice on a merchant ship, he lost his virginity in a waterfront brothel at Le Havre, then had a month-long affair with a musical-comedy singer in Rio de Janeiro, and on the return trip bedded a plump Prussian lady passenger in the sail locker.

During the voyage an officer with whom he shared a night watch told him an interesting tale. This man had been a ship's boy on a Pacific voyage, and one day when he was scrubbing the deck he fell overboard. No one saw him go. He hit the water still clutching his broom, and it kept him afloat for forty-eight hours, and then miraculously another ship came by and picked him up. When they put in at an island he went ashore, stayed a little too long, and was left behind. The islanders were delighted to have him. He was fêted, petted, tickled, and relieved of his virginity, and he lived happily ever after for two years, till another ship put in and he found himself homesick for France. Since then he had cursed himself for coming back to civilization. "God, what a fool I was," he said to Gauguin, "now I have to work my way around the world. I was so happy!" Gauguin remembered this South Seas story all his life.

Gauguin left the merchant marine to do his national service in the crew of a French imperial yacht. In 1870 war broke out between France and Prussia, and the yacht joined the North Sea squadron and helped in the capture of some Prussian ships. Gauguin was serving at sea when he got the news that his mother had died. He came ashore after his last tour of duty to find that the place where Aline had passed her last months, Saint-Cloud, outside Paris, had been burned by the Prussians just before the armistice. Everything was gone, all his mother's belongings, family papers, the pieces of Peruvian art. Gauguin was twenty-three. He was alone in the world, and he had nothing.

His mother could bequeath him only solicitude. In her will she said that Paul had never endeared himself to her companions, that he would be someone who would find himself alone, abandoned. With this in mind she named a guardian for him, a friend of hers called Gustave Arosa, a talented photographer-printer who specialized in art reproductions and was a collector of paintings with excellent and adventurous taste. Arosa did Gauguin some kindnesses, substantial in themselves, that turned out to be momentous. He got Gauguin a job in a banking house that did business on the Paris stock exchange, and he got him interested in art to the point where he began putting paint on canvas for himself.

Within a year or two Gauguin had made enough money to be able to think about getting married. Within ten years he had had all he could take of married life and business life, enough to know that he did not want any more of either at whatever price. His real inheritance, passed on to him through his mother, was that of Flora Tristan. It amounted to a desperate trampling on ordinary middle-class convention, the wreckage of the bourgeois family: fantasies of aristocratic—even divine—origins, the fact of illegitimacy, incest in the shadows, crimes of passion acted out in public, and then a lonely, spectacular, attention-getting life of total self-absorption, self-conviction, staged in the costume of a messiah. All this Gauguin marshaled behind his declaration that he was an artist.

In one tangled assertion, put on paper in 1888, Gauguin described his beginnings and his end, where he came from and where he was going. He was fond of saying that the artist with his creative powers was a kind of divine figure; and at least one of the painters who knew him in those years before Tahiti agreed, considering him a genius, a giant of painting, "one of those who stormed the skies," coming close to godhood through his art. Gauguin's own version of this was to talk about risking everything in a flight from the civilized to the primitive, to the source of all life, all sensation, all power, the sun. "With wax wings the closer one gets to the sun the more in danger one is," he wrote. But "according to legend the Inca came straight from the sun and I shall return there." Gauguin was once again pushing beyond the classic or civilized tradition toward the triumph of the primitive. In Greek myth the boy Icarus with wax wings was destroyed by the sun. But it was the Incas, sun gods, invulnerable, immortal, from whom Gauguin liked to claim descent, with whom he identified himself. In fact Gauguin, like Walter Murray Gibson, was less an Icarus than another fatherless Phaeton, desperately at risk.

Vincent van Gogh once described Gauguin, with enigmatic rightness, as someone who came from afar and would go far away. For much the same reasons as Gibson, who never seriously pursued his claim to an estate in England, Gauguin as a grown man never made a serious attempt to get back to the actual Peru of his childhood. Instead, the artist Gauguin painted his mother as a naked Eve and set off for the South Seas.

* * *

Tahiti took Gauguin aback. Between Marseilles and Papeete he was more than two months at sea, and when finally he stepped ashore in his primitive paradise on earth it was to find that civilization was there ahead of him, and had been for more than a century. Papeete in 1891 was a grubby little port town of about three thousand people housed in a straggle of Western-style tin-roofed dwellings along the waterfront, with shabby shops that sold the worst of Western goods, a local market place of tawdry liveliness, and a polite white society of stupefying dullness enlivened only by chronic arguments between Catholic and Protestant, administrator and settler. This was no dream before nature.

Even so, Gauguin could glimpse what he had come for. The women of Tahiti thronged the dusty streets of the town, barefoot, undulant of walk, flimsily clad so that their nipples stood out like pointed seashells under their muslin dresses, passing by in a waft of animal odor and the perfume of sandalwood and the *tiare* flower. Gauguin became aware of a Tahitian word that stayed inextinguishably with him: *noanoa*, meaning fragrance.

Wanting to be where the fragrance was stronger, Gauguin set off for the rural districts. He took with him a Papeete town girl named Titi. She was young, of mixed blood, and she could be had for money. Whores were nothing new to Gauguin, and he tried to make the best of it by saying that all Tahitian women, even if they sold their bodies, had genuine love in them. But it was hard to make Titi conform to his dream of islands. She was a nonstop talker with a passion for ball gowns and fancy hats and a lust for presents—in fact she was altogether a false start, and Gauguin soon got rid of her.

The true country girls of Tahiti had a powerful effect on Gauguin, and interestingly it was not altogether a comfortable one. He had always been a sexual predator, and he was sure he was receiving a wordless sexual message from the village girls, a wish to be savagely taken, a "desire for rape." But along with this unspoken frankness they had a fearless dignity, and it intimidated Gauguin. Perhaps it was he who would be the sexual victim. So, having sent Titi back to town, he lived in a state of sexual suspense. Eventually he set out on a tour of the island, and at last, in the most remote of all the districts, he found his fate. A woman asked what he was doing there. He answered that he was looking for a girl, and the woman offered him her daughter.

Her name was Tehaamana, and Gauguin found her so beautiful that his heart leaped. She was silent, inward, there was pride in her serenity, and beneath her dress of pink muslin her skin glowed golden. Gauguin was captivated. He was a man well on in life, in his mid-forties—almost an old man, he remarked to himself—and Tehaamana was perhaps thirteen or fourteen, no more. Yet when they looked at each other it was Gauguin who was nervous. He had the feeling that he was being read like an open book, while to him Tehaamana was emotionally impenetrable. Was that slight movement of her lips tender? Or mocking? He could not tell. But she was willing to go with him to his hut by the sea, and that was enough.

With her he found contentment. More, through her he became young again, transported back, as he said, to a kind of childhood he had never known. Tehaamana opened herself to him, and he was enveloped in her fragrance, in the *noanoa* of Tahiti. He had learned to go barefoot like a native. Wearing only the native *pareu*, a wraparound that left the upper body bare, he felt himself absorbing the benign power of the sun. Even before Tehaamana, when he first settled in the country, he had fallen into the Tahitian way of going through the day without worry over the morrow, and now with Tehaamana day and night moved in a magical rhythm that seemed to stop time itself. Gauguin lost track of the hours, the days, and at last of good and evil. He saw in the stars the gold of Tehaamana's body, and in the morning at first light her face was radiant. They would go together at dawn, Gauguin wrote, to bathe in a stream, naturally, simply, as in paradise.

Tehaamana was no Titi. She knew instinctively when to speak and how to be silent. Gauguin told her something of Europe, and something of his universe. She had difficulty with the idea that the earth revolved around the sun, but eagerly learned the European names for the stars, and in turn told Gauguin how the Tahitian stars were born, and how shooting stars were really spirits of the dead, *tupapau*. Through her Gauguin penetrated the mysteries of the Tahitian mind; and stories of the old days, powerful myths of the goddess of the moon and tales of those sacred free lovers, the *arioi*, translated themselves into paintings full of light and mystery.

Of course, Gauguin painted Tehaamana. One night he came home very late and found his hut in darkness. He struck a match, and there was Tehaamana lying naked and fearful on the bed. Gauguin had an artistic illumination, and from it came a painted nude, showing, as he later explained, the native character, spirit, tradition. The way Tehaamana was lying could be seen as indecent—a bare-bodied brown girl ready for lovemaking, perhaps, or relaxed after having made love. Yet this was not what Gauguin wanted to convey. He was momentarily attracted, seduced as he often was by a form or a movement, and this was the impulse that helped him form a picture in his mind, but what he wanted to show was the fear in the naked girl, the fear of the spirits of the dead. So there in the background was the figure of an unearthly old woman, and the picture was strewn with sparks, like shooting stars, like *tupapau*, as the spirit of the dead stretched out its hand to seize the girl. Gauguin elaborated his inspiration until, as he said, the nude became subordinate. And the "music" of the composition—a favorite phrase of Gauguin's, coming from the symbolist idea that the arts had a unity in which one form of artistic expression could stand for another—was in the undulating harmonies of orange and blue linked by yellows and violets and strewn with greenish sparks. All this in what was otherwise simply a South Seas nude.

Gauguin, so it would seem from his own account, had achieved his deliverance. In Tahiti he was reborn. He had escaped from bourgeois civilization to primitivism, from Mette to Tehaamana. He no longer had to fight the war of the savage and the sensitive within himself. He drew strength from the sun of the islands, and from the mysteries of the islanders. He lived and loved and painted, and these were all the same thing. There was no reason why it should not go on forever, an eternal dream before nature.

* * *

Yet in not much more than two years after he sailed for Tahiti, Gauguin was back in France again. The fairy story of his life with Tehaamana was written down on his return to civilization in a little book he intended to publish under the title of *Noa Noa*, and what he said for publication was nothing like the whole story of his life in Tahiti. No more was it the whole truth about himself.

If Gauguin's first sight of Papeete took him aback, Papeete's first sight of him was equally startling. He arrived looking like an artist—hair down to his shoulders, brown velvet suit, broad-brimmed hat, purple shoes. There was nothing at all like him among the other whites, the administrators and settlers, and the Tahitians took him for a *taata vahine*, a man-woman, sexually ambiguous. Long hair and all, his first stop was the office of the governor. Gauguin had not been able to arrange any sort of paid job in the colonies, but he did manage before he left France to procure what was called an "unofficial mission," really not much more than a letter establishing that he was an artist coming to paint for a time in the islands. At least this guaranteed him a discount on his steamer fare, and he hoped as well that it would bring him commissions in Papeete; he would need the money. He cut his hair and started dressing in a white tropical suit, took a house in town close to the Catholic church, filled it with rented furniture, stuck photographs of Mette and his children on the walls, hung about for three months, did one portrait which appalled the client, a merchant, and the subject, his very plain and aging daughter, and then left for the country, settling for a time in the most urbanized rural district on the island, where he got lonely and sent for Titi.

He had brought a Winchester with him from France to hunt food with, but Tahiti had no wild animals except pigs in the mountains, and the mountains were inaccessible. The Tahitians still lived mainly off the land, but subsistence living in the islands, as anywhere, meant steady work, and if Gauguin had to work to stay alive he would have no time for his art. So he shopped at a Chinese store, eating mostly canned food and running through his money. He resurrected his old scheme of trying to get on the colonial payroll in some genuinely remote spot, and went to the governor to nominate himself for the post of magistrate in the Marquesas Islands. The governor laughed in his face.

So he was condemned to Tahiti. Slowly he learned something about the island, and he was beginning to get some interesting things on his sketching pad and on canvas. But after some months he was down to practically no money, and his health was uncertain. In his first weeks at Papeete he had a bad hemorrhage (the self-made, incomplete, and still very stressful savage very likely had a peptic ulcer). And his heart started to give him trouble. For a time he had to go into the hospital. On top of everything else, there was a deadline of sorts facing him. If, within twelve months of arriving in the islands, he applied to the governor for repatriation as an indigent, he could have his fare home paid; if he stayed beyond that time he would be considered a settler, entirely on his own. He did his financial sums, considered his health, and decided to ask for repatriation. All this in less than a year after his highly praised artist's farewell to Europe, and before he ever met Tehaamana.

It took months for his repatriation application to travel to France for processing and back to Papeete. This delay was really all that kept Gauguin in Tahiti. But while he waited he acquired Tehaamana for company, and he stumbled as well upon some interesting reading about ancient Tahiti, in the colony's official yearbook and in a book by a man named Jacques Antoine Moerenhout who had been a merchant and consul in Tahiti some decades earlier. (Moerenhout, in turn, had taken some of his information and ideas from the work of the Protestant missionary William Ellis, a contemporary of John Williams, but of course Gauguin did not know this.) Whatever caught his eye in Moerenhout's account Gauguin copied into a notebook, and he illustrated his reading with drawings of idols of his own imagining, magic landscapes, sexually charged mythical figures, a copulating couple cradled in the greenness of some great invented plant. He called the whole thing *Ancien Culte Mahorie*, the ancient native religion. "Mahorie" was an outstanding mis-hearing and misspelling. Gauguin's ear for Tahitian was not at all good. He took a few lessons in the language and then gave up, and many of the titles of his island paintings are so garbled as to be almost meaningless. Still, Moerenhout and his other reading enabled Gauguin to imagine that his life with Tehaamana had some connection with the traditional life of Tahiti. Tehaamana in fact knew next to nothing about the old days. She had none of the ancient culture except some of its vocabulary, its body language, and some of its superstitions. There had been more than a century of contact between Tahiti and the West, almost a century of missionary education. Tehaamana was a young girl of the 1890s; she knew only what she knew. It was Gauguin who insisted that Tahiti should provide him with ancient lore as well as a bedmate.

As for Tehaamana the bedmate, Gauguin did not even have her to himself. Like other Tahitian girls, missionary-educated or no, she took lovers when she felt like it. Gauguin taxed her with infidelity one night after he had come home from a fishing expedition. She admitted it because it was true, and wanted him to beat her because otherwise he would stay angry and make himself sick. But Gauguin looked at her, so he wrote in *Noa Noa,* at her resigned face and her superb body, saw a perfect pagan statue, and knew his artist's hands would be cursed forever if they struck such a "masterpiece of creation." She was a flower, naked, but clothed in golden purity, and Gauguin loved her as an artist and as a man. He

embraced her in the tropical night, and the new day—so he wrote—
dawned radiant.

The fact remained that Tehaamana was not his alone. When she got
pregnant, as she did, it may or may not have been by Gauguin. And in
any case she went off and had an abortion, village style, as Tahitian girls
often did so as not to be excluded from sexual sociability. Whatever
Gauguin put on paper about his relationship with Tehaamana, in fact he
was only one stop along the sexual way for her.

Still, Tehaamana was all he had in Tahiti. And even with this other
body to share his bed and bathe with him at dawn, Gauguin felt lonely.
He never learned to speak Tahitian fluently, and he had cut himself off
from white company. Before he found Tehaamana he had been close to
desperation, heavily dependent on the mail steamer for letters from
France, prone to feel lost and abandoned when there was nothing for
him, hungering for contact with his past as much as he hungered after
money.

He had been sending paintings to France, even some to Copenhagen,
where there was a chance that Mette could arrange to have them exhibited. But practically nothing sold, and the meager proceeds trickled back
to him across the world slowly and erratically. He worked until he ran out
of canvas, and still in eighteen months he had not seen a sou from his
work. "The conclusion is easy to draw," he wrote to Daniel De Monfreid,
an artist friend in France. "And as I have no big inheritance to look
forward to, what will I use to eat and even to buy paint with?" He was
thinking about coming home, and about giving up painting. He would
have a number of oils to carry back to France with him, and these were
his best work. But—he knew in advance—his homeland being what it
was, the better they were the less salable they would be.

Later, in the manuscript of his book *Noa Noa,* Gauguin talked about his
two years in Tahiti as a rejuvenation of twenty years. He was younger, so
he said, "savager too yet at the same time wiser." But to Mette he wrote
that his heart kept giving him trouble; as little as four or five minutes on
horseback and he was finished. He was not eating well, for the simple
reason that he was too poor to buy good food. Day after day he had
nothing but breadfruit and water; he could not even afford sugar for his
tea; he was losing weight, getting skinny and going gray. To Daniel De
Monfreid he wrote about a rapid aging, a feeling that he was stretching his
physical resources to breaking point. At times, when he had no money
and nothing in prospect, he wondered why he did not do away with himself. It was on will alone that he survived, he said, one day at a time.
Gauguin the Tahitian savage was still a starving painter at the mercy of

bourgeois society; his vocation, what he most profoundly insisted on doing with his life, would not keep him alive.

* * *

In *Noa Noa*, Gauguin wrote that his reason for going back to France was the call of "imperious family duty." Hardly. In his letters to Mette he made it clear that if he did come back to France, it would not be till his work in the islands was complete. This was no excursion, he told her; it was serious; it had to be got through before his roving life would be over. In other words Mette could wait. Gauguin would leave the islands for his own reasons—poverty, ill health, fatigue, a feeling that for the time being Tahiti as an artistic subject was worked out, or even that he as an artist was finished.

Mette, of course, remained a problem for him, one he could never resolve. He still wanted her to write to him, and was upset when she did not. But he was often just as upset with what she did write. One of the whites he met in Papeete noticed that Gauguin never wanted to talk about his family, even though he kept their photographs on his wall. When some Tahitians asked who the woman with the mannish, close-cropped hair was, he said it was his wife, but she was dead. This he put into a letter to Mette, adding that the natives were encouraging him to stay in the islands and take an island wife. Another time a Tahitian woman saw the reproduction of Manet's great female nude, *Olympia*, that Gauguin had brought with him; impressed by the beauty of the model, she asked if it was Gauguin's wife. Yes, said Gauguin. Just as he scissored Mette from the newspaper interview in favor of his rhapsodies on the Tahitian adventure to come, so he kept on using art and the islands to cancel her out. But Mette existed, just as France existed.

As for his children, they were more than ever Mette's children. It was years since he had seen them all together. Of the five he liked two best: Clovis, the son he had named after his own father, and above all Aline, his only daughter, who looked like him and who had been honored with the precious name of his mother. He kept insisting that Aline was his child rather than Mette's.

In Tahiti Gauguin kept a special notebook for Aline, dedicated to her because, in his mind, she was a savage like him and would understand him, because she had a "head and heart lofty enough not to be shocked or corrupted" by contact with the "demoniac brain" nature had given him. This, to be sure, was asking a lot of a carefully brought-up fifteen-year-old girl. The notebook was certainly savage enough in its own way. Along with Gauguin's constantly repeated insistence on the divine powers of the artist went denunciations of the accursed bourgeois who wanted to debase art to the material level. Society wanted to extinguish genius, and here Gauguin told again his favorite story about the bungled guillotining he had witnessed in Paris, his point being that society's workings produced criminals, society arranged for their condemnation, society clamped a cruel collar on the victim's neck to hold the head in place for severing, and then society bungled the execution, inflicting maximum frightfulness. Society's misfits were doomed. He was one of them, artist, criminal, victim; if he were to be saved, only his powerful will would do it.

All this was set down in the notebook for Aline disjointedly, as Gauguin acknowledged, out of sequence, like the stuff of dreams—or like life itself, which Gauguin perceived as being chopped into pieces. For him, the most systematic thing about life was its perversity. Why, he wondered, should God have destroyed Sodom for its sins and allowed Lesbos to survive?—perhaps God was a woman. On the subject of women—wrote Gauguin for his daughter who was growing up—they achieved individuality, even soul, only when they gave their love unconditionally to a man. If it was freedom that women wanted, it was not men who kept it from them; when a woman ceased to locate her honor "below her navel," she would be free. And as a father writing for a daughter whose love he wanted, Gauguin had this to say about the responsibilities of a parent: "Is it not bad policy to sacrifice everything to children, and does it not deprive the nation of the genius of its most active members? You sacrifice yourself for your child who in his turn grows up and sacrifices himself. And so on. There will be nothing but sacrifice. And the stupidity persists." Perhaps it was for the best that Aline never saw her father's notebook.

In Tahiti, in any case, they ordered all these things differently, and Gauguin had a personal reason for being glad about it—Tehaamana, at about the same age as his daughter, was pregnant. Gauguin was pleased to assume that the child was his. Five children by Mette in Denmark, a daughter by the seamstress Juliette Huet in Paris, and now this. Before Tehaamana decided to have an abortion Gauguin wrote to Daniel De Monfreid: "I must sow my seed everywhere. It is true there is nothing bad about it here, children are well received, and all the relatives put in a claim for them in advance. There is competition to bring them up." The finest present to give in Tahiti was a child. "So I am not worried about what will happen to this one."

By then Gauguin was committed to going back to France. All he was waiting for was repatriation free of charge. But his request was refused—a bad blow—and when he reapplied he was denied again, this time on the whim of the governor. (Writing up *Noa Noa* for publication in France,

Gauguin added a long postscript headed "After the work of art. The truth, the filthy truth," in which he set out in great detail his various betrayals by officialdom.) But he was saved when the mail steamer brought a remittance, blessed money from the sale of paintings, just enough to get him home. He moved from the country back to Papeete, rented a little house from an enterprising landlady (a Paris prostitute turned respectable colonial property holder), counted the days till sailing time, said good-by to Tehaamana in mid-June, 1893, went aboard ship, and disembarked at Marseilles on August 30 with sixty-six Tahitian canvases in his baggage and four francs in his pocket.

* * *

Arrived in Paris, Gauguin set about organizing a spectacular exhibition of his Tahitian work. In one of his South Seas moods he insisted that he cared nothing about society's opinion of him; in another mood, he could write that his Tahitian work was ugly, mad, terrifying even to himself, and how much more to the conventional public; but in yet another version of things, his sun was to shine ultimately not in Tahiti but in France. "My flight may be a defeat," he told Charles Morice before he sailed for Tahiti, "but my return will be a triumph." And now he wrote to Mette in Copenhagen that the exhibition would strike a great blow on which the future depended. To reinforce the impact of his art he was at work on a book—*Noa Noa*—"which will be very useful in making my painting comprehensible," and which would make money out of Tahiti as well, just as Pierre Loti's writing had done. Soon—at last—he would know if it was "madness" to have gone to the South Seas.

His opening day was widely publicized, well attended, and a disaster. The Tahitian oils glowing on the gallery walls, among them his nude of Tehaamana, *Manao Tupapau*, simply baffled the viewers—when they did not cause violent outrage. The bourgeois critics made loud, raucous fun of what they saw, and one art fancier, an Englishwoman, coming unexpectedly upon a red Gauguin dog on canvas, opened her mouth and screamed.

Gauguin smiled his way coolly through the horrible hours, taking his torture like an Indian, as Charles Morice said. But that night he broke down and wept like a child. Poverty, hardship, self-denial, years in the islands living his art like a sacrament, spilling his very lifeblood out on canvas, and the verdict of bourgeois society was what it had been before Tahiti—that in his chosen vocation he was a failure. And not even a noble failure, just a ghastly bad joke.

A few commentators were kind, and on the strength of this minority vote Gauguin reported to Mette that he had had a great artistic success—

to the point, characteristically, of "provoking rage and jealousy." The press, so he wrote with superb disregard for the facts, "has treated me as it has never treated anyone, reasonably and with praise. For the moment I am regarded by a good many people as the greatest of modern painters." But in truth he was reacting profoundly to the rout of his expectations. He had set his prices high with his hopes, but three out of four canvases failed to sell, and he lost rather than made money on the show. The blow to his pride was dreadful on all counts, and it made itself felt in his body. He wrote to Mette that he had somehow developed rheumatism in his right shoulder, and it had spread all the way down his arm to his hand, his painting hand. He had no funds coming in, he was in debt and could not meet his obligations, and all this was "paralyzing his arms." Mette must stop hectoring him about money; it would kill him.

News of a windfall cheered him considerably. A relative of his, the old uncle from Orléans in whose house he had lived as a child, died and left him thirteen thousand francs, enough to support him for months, longer if he was careful. In anticipation, Gauguin installed himself in a studio in Paris, painted the interior chrome yellow, lined the walls with his unsold canvases, added reproductions of works that he liked, dusted off the remnants of his old collection of originals, including some van Gogh sunflowers, filled any empty spaces with Tahitian curios and some of his own wood carvings done in the islands—"ultra-savage"—and brought in a piano and a big camera on a tripod. When the inheritance money actually came in, he treated himself to an extravagant wardrobe, more dashing than that of his stock-exchange days, topped it off with an imposing dark blue cloak with metal clasps and a big astrakhan cap, and strolled about the city flourishing a pearl-handled cane.

His old mistress, the seamstress Juliette Huet, was in Paris with their daughter, but as an experienced practicing savage Gauguin wanted something more exotic. It came his way in the shape of a "mulâtresse," a girl of mixed blood, reminiscent of the ones he had picked up at the 1889 Exposition and again at Papeete. This one was a part Ceylonese, part Malay who went by the inaccurate name of Anna the Javanese. Spiritually, Anna was not exactly a figure from a Buddhist temple frieze. She had been a Montmartre dancer, an artist's model, and the servant of an opera singer. Anna was willing to share Gauguin's bed, and even more his inheritance. She matched him flourish for flourish, with showy clothes and showy pets, a parrot for the studio and a monkey named Taoa who went for walks with her.

Anna was only thirteen years old, and this was an age Gauguin was greatly drawn to in females. It was Tehaamana's age when he met her, and whatever else Tehaamana stood for in Gauguin's South Seas dream before nature, she certainly represented a sexual straddling of childhood and womanhood. Now Gauguin had Anna. And this was not all. There was another thirteen-year-old girl around his studio. Gauguin's neighbor was William Molard, a failed composer married to a Scandinavian sculptress who had an illegitimate daughter fathered by an opera singer. Little Judith, on the edge of physical maturity, was infatuated with Gauguin, and he took advantage of this; he would cup her budding breasts in his hands and murmur breathily in her ear and reduce her to dizziness. Once, when Gauguin was away from Paris in Brittany, he wrote to Molard suggesting that Judith join him. He would look after her, he assured Molard, "like *a father.*" This was a loaded offer if ever there was one, and Molard did not respond to it. Gauguin had to content himself with painting his other thirteen year old, Anna, naked in his studio and giving the portrait a title in Tahitian that Molard would not be able to translate: "The child-woman Judith is not yet breached."

There is not much doubt that Judith brought to mind Gauguin's own daughter Aline, and through Aline all the women of his family who preoccupied him. Judith was illegitimate like Flora Tristan; she was pubescent as Gauguin's mother had been when her father André Chazal attempted incest on her; and Judith, like Gauguin's Aline, was the child of a Scandinavian mother. Behind this there was Gauguin's powerfully remembered childish infatuation with his mother Aline and her seductive eye and her sweet punishments; and then there was his fatherly attachment to his daughter Aline, who to his delight looked like him and who (so he convinced himself) shared his unshockable savagery. The young Aline was thirteen when Gauguin left France, a fact that he recalled to her in a fatherly note written three years later, reminding her that at this age she had naïvely said she wanted to marry him.

Over his studio door in Paris Gauguin hung a wood carving. *Te Faruru,* the inscription said, which was another one of Gauguin's Tahitian misspellings; it should have been *Te Faaruru.* But he was in no doubt about what he wanted the words to convey. The literal translation of the Tahitian was "to cause to shake," and the islanders used it to mean physically making love. Under this sign lived Gauguin, the man who in Tahiti copied down everything he could find out about the *arioi.* He obviously liked to think of himself, in fact, as a sort of *arioi,* artist and sexual entertainer in one, master of the revels. He amused himself doing private sexual theater of his own devising with little Judith Molard. He slept with Anna the Javanese and painted her naked. He had himself photographed in another artist's studio, seated on a music stool, hands on the keyboard, clad like a bourgeois down to the waist, but below that trouserless. And because isolation in Tahiti had given him an appetite for company, he held a weekly open house at his studio for artists and anyone else who was about. He would read passages newly written for *Noa Noa*, evoking the gold of Tehaamana's body. And he would dress up as a "cannibal chief" and dance the hipshaking *upaupa* of Tahiti, the great island representation of *te faaruru*, often an explicit invitation to love-making.

Gauguin's old fellow artists who dropped in at the studio were likely to find the goings-on a bit dismaying. Most of them were married now; they had grown away from the kind of wild things Gauguin kept on doing in his mid-forties; gradually they stopped coming.

Gauguin's revels, of course, had a precise relationship to his own marriage. He was financing his amusements out of his inheritance money, which he was not sharing fairly with his wife. He could afford to treat himself to a trip to Brussels to see an art exhibition, paying all expenses for a friend who went with him. But having gone that far, he did not go on to Copenhagen. It suited him to keep Mette at a distance.

In the spring of 1894 he went on another excursion, to Brittany, and ran into serious trouble. One day he was out walking in a little fishing town with some other artists, artistically dressed. Anna was with him, and she had brought Taoa the monkey, and the strange procession provoked some laughs from the village children. The artists remonstrated, the children's parents came out to argue, and blows were struck. Gauguin was good with his fists, but suddenly there were a lot of Breton fishermen to fight. He had the bad luck to put one foot into a hole in the ground and fell or was knocked over, and when he was down the fishermen kicked him where he lay. They were wearing sabots. Gauguin wound up barely conscious, with a leg broken so badly above the ankle that the bone showed through the skin.

The injury never healed properly. It kept Gauguin in agony for months. To dull the pain he took to drinking heavily, and to sleep at all he had to use morphine. (Some years before, when Mette was going through a bad fright about cancer and was getting severe migraine headaches, Gauguin, in the middle of training himself to be an Indian, wrote to her that drugs sapped moral strength; she should stay away from morphine and use tea as a tranquilizer. Now, of course, it was Gauguin who was in pain, and that was different.) When he was finally able to walk again it was only with the help of a stick, and there was no flourish in the way he got about. And then the assault case came to trial, and the Breton courts let his attackers off with a slap on the wrist and awarded Gauguin the victim only derisory damages. Gauguin had another lawsuit to go through. Years before, he had stored some paintings in a Breton boardinghouse. Now he wanted them back, and his old Breton landlady did not want to let him have them. This case was decided against him too. To add domestic insult to physical and legal injury, Anna deserted Gauguin, went back to Paris, stripped the studio of everything she put any value on, and disappeared— leaving only the paintings. As a last piece of tragicomedy, Taoa the monkey died. Anna had left the beast with Gauguin, and by bad luck it happened to eat a poisonous plant, and that was the end of it.

Gauguin was where he had been before and would be again, in ruins. Lying broken-legged in Brittany, less than a year after coming back to France, he thought about where his life had led him, and made the momentous decision to give up on Europe again, this time irrevocably. In an involved letter to a painter who knew him well he set down his thoughts, a mingling of rage and despair: "You know my life till now has been full of struggle, extreme suffering which most people would not have been able to stand." This Gauguin had endured, so he said, "without a word." (Of course he was hardly a silent savage. As much as anyone, more than most, Gauguin lived a life of noisy desperation; he just did not want anyone to think of him in that way.) He had accomplished great things, he went on, but still he had not realized his dreams, and this was hardest of all to take. At the same time glory was a vain word, a vain recompense. What he urgently needed now was surcease: "Ever since I came to know the simple life of Oceania, I have dreamed only of withdrawing far from the life of men, and consequently far from glory: as soon as possible I will go and bury my talent where the savages live and no one will ever hear of me again." It did not matter that Europeans found him incomprehensible—savages understood him. As for painting, very likely he would give it up. Perhaps a little for diversion, he told Daniel De Monfreid, but nothing more; he would live in a wood hut and carve imaginary figures into the trunks of trees.

To Mette, who always found herself at the center of the worst of his emotional storms, Gauguin wrote that the breaking of his leg had broken his health, reduced him to invalidism. He complained that his family cared nothing for him; he was all by himself; the summer of 1894 had turned to winter, and in the terrible cold weather he had caught a bronchitis that became chronic. There was no longer anything in Gauguin's self-expressiveness that brought to mind a powerful beating of wings in the air or a godlike creative ascent to the sun. He was earth-bound, immobilized, and now the heat of the sun was just curative, therapy for a desperately cold, sick man: "Literally I can only live on sunshine." Isolation and strength used to mean one and the same thing to him. Now that he was weak, shaky on his legs in every way, he was panicky that there was no one to support and sustain him. Equating physical and emotional collapse, he wrote that in order not to "fall" he had to surround himself with precautions. At forty-seven, he went on, "I do not WANT to fall into misery but I am close to it; once I am on the ground *no one* in the world will pick me up." Mette had evidently been telling him he must "shift for himself" (just as his mother in her will had predicted he would have to). The phrase, said Gauguin, was "profoundly wise. . . . I will be guided by it." Out of his inheritance of thirteen thousand francs he sent Mette only fifteen hundred. The rest he kept, to be spent on himself. And, getting ready to leave Europe, he told his wife nothing of his plans.

Leaving Europe—what Gauguin was proposing to do in 1895 was what he had already done once before, four years ago. Given the real hardships of his life in Tahiti, lack of food, lack of money, lack of companionship, the hemorrhages and the heart trouble, there was an eerie note in what he kept reiterating about the easeful life in paradise to which he would be returning. And for a man who was set on renouncing art in favor of obscurity, Gauguin continued to be publicly aggressive about what was true and beautiful on canvas. To his eye—and he said so, loudly—the Venuses exhibited in the salons of Paris were indecent, odiously lewd, but the Eves he painted, the Eves of Oceania, were animal yet chaste; they could walk naked without shame. So with the painter himself. Genuinely natural expression was everything. And this meant—as always—going back to the source, the childhood of man. Gauguin's need for a paradise on earth was absolute. In the face of all reason, all earthly evidence, the experience of his own life in Tahiti, he demanded that paradise exist and manifest itself to him.

Here his book *Noa Noa* was important to him. It had still not been published. He had decided to take on a collaborator, the writer Charles Morice, who was to polish the savage Gauguin prose and add some lyrical verses; but Morice was slow getting his part of the work done, and had not finished by the time Gauguin was ready to leave Europe. Gauguin did a set of woodcuts to be used as illustrations, a kind of life cycle of paradise. He named them one after the other to evoke the dream truths of the Tahiti he kept in his mind, *Noa Noa*, *Te Faruru*, and *Nave Nave Fenua*, this last meaning the land of sexual delight. And he made another copy of his manuscript in a notebook, together with what Morice had written so far, and took it with him to the islands. There he kept working on it, embellishing it, ornamenting it, for years.

To raise additional funds for his escape, Gauguin repeated what he had done in 1891 and organized an auction of his work. From his point of view the sale was another substantial failure. He had to bid in a good many of the paintings himself. Still, it was not a total washout; he did manage to net a little cash. When he wrote to his wife he falsified the accounts, making it look as if he had incurred a loss.

Gauguin also dusted off his old notion of an artist's colony. In one version of things the new destination was to be Samoa. (Gauguin had never been near the place, and no doubt this was one of its attractions. Of course, if he had read some Stevenson on Samoan politics he might have reconsidered; and now, in the mid-1890s with Stevenson not long dead, the powers were still bickering in Samoa, and German annexation was just a few years off.) His companions this time were to be two painters who had been with him on the awful day when he broke his leg. But, as in 1891, when it came to the point, there were no takers. One of the two thought Gauguin was too autocratic. The other found him generally offensive. Gauguin had written him a letter about sex, "details of the ideal position for intercourse"—*te faaruru* again—and he could not see himself going to the South Seas with "that character."

On the occasion of Gauguin's second lonely, long-distance leave-taking there was no symbolist banquet. This time Gauguin meant to go quietly, as befitted a man fleeing glory to bury his genius among savages. Actually he was forced to delay longer than he intended. Amusing himself in Paris, he had gone out to a dance hall; he picked up a woman, slept with her, and caught syphilis. It may not have been his first infection; whatever the case, it covered him with sores, and before he could leave for paradise he had to wait until they subsided somewhat.

When the time came to depart, he could not resist a final performance at his studio. He danced and sang like a Tahitian: "*Upaupa Tahiti, upaupa Faruru, e-e-e!*" The Molards, especially Judith, insisted on seeing him off on the train. There had been no farewell visit to Mette and his children. He never saw them again.

*   *   *

As soon as he set eyes on Tahiti, Gauguin started talking about leaving. Papeete was even more dire than he remembered: electric lights now, Tahitians wobbling along the streets on a new import, the bicycle, and from a spot near the old royal gardens the noisy phonograph music of a mechanical merry-go-round. He felt crowded, and to William Molard he wrote that in a month he would be off, gone to the Marquesas, to a ravishing small island without Europeans, where life would cost practically nothing. A well-arranged studio there, and he would be able to live on his small capital "like a lord."

Somehow he did not get around to sailing. Instead, he finished up paying for local workmen to build him a hut, Tahitian style, a few miles outside Papeete: "a big bamboo birdcage with a coconut-thatch roof, a shady open bedroom, and a studio full of light. On the floor, mats and my old Persian carpet, and everything decorated with fabrics, curios and drawings." He carved some coconut trunks in the shape of idols, and set about spending what was left of his inheritance on good times. Gauguin knew himself for a squanderer; he squandered anyway, trusting, as he said, to his talent to bail him out of crises. In the meantime he enjoyed himself. A great feature of his country place was a two-hundred-liter claret cask, emptied by his thirsty guests and refilled as long as his money lasted. And there were girls everywhere, "devilish" Tahitian girls invading his bed— three at a time one night, so he wrote back to France. Probably people would call him a criminal for leaving his family to live like this, but he admitted the charge cheerfully enough. He had thought it over repeatedly, and every time the conclusion was the same: get away from it all. A lifetime of "wiping babies' bottoms and arguing with a wife"—how could an ordinary man put up with it, much less an artist?

As things turned out, Gauguin had not meant what he said about giving up painting. He felt well, so he wrote to Daniel De Monfreid; he was sure there was better stuff in him now than on his first trip. What he intended to do next was to settle down and work steadily, give up the wild life, get himself a permanent woman. He looked for Tehaamana and found her. She was married now, but she came back to him anyway. ("I have been obliged to cuckold her husband," wrote Gauguin mock-regretfully.) But she could not be persuaded to stay more than a few days, and the permanent substitute that Gauguin found, a girl named Pauura, was less prepossessing on all counts. So was Gauguin, of course, especially when all his money was drunk away. He was older than he had been, his general emotional health was uncertain, and those sores on his body kept reappearing, especially on his legs, indeed getting worse all the time. Just as well Pauura was not overfastidious. If she was, indeed, "debauched"— Gauguin's word—it did not matter; there was no virtue to compare her with, he said. At least, like Tehaamana, she was young—fourteen and a half, a figure that Gauguin amended to make her thirteen when he met her.

Gauguin's good times lasted only a few months. His money ran out, and his health and self-confidence deserted him at the same time, as they so often seemed to do. With terrible suddenness he was back where he had been in the worst days of his life. Everything came to focus on his unhealed leg. The sores got worse all the time, till his ankle was just one big open sore. He was on pain-killing drugs again, and finally he had to go into the hospital. He could not paint vigorously for long stretches, the way he liked to do, finishing a canvas in one burst. He conceived of his pain and anguish as spreading over the canvas, and was reduced to hoping that this intensity of feeling would at least do something to offset the clumsiness of the execution. Once more he talked of his work as ugly, maladroit. And then, the old bourgeois question again: If his work would not sell, why paint at all? Obviously it did not matter where, or how often, Gauguin went looking for paradise; he carried his own hell with him.

He felt unmanned, beaten down by life, by the passage of time, by the encroachments of age. He worried about approaching fifty with nothing to show for his existence except wreckage of one sort or another. He talked about having been born under "a bad star." He talked about his life as a martyrdom. This went back to one of the woodcuts he had done for *Noa Noa*, in which he had represented himself as a distorted figure, with a hole in the ankle, a simultaneous reference to the pain in his leg and the crucifixion of Christ. And in 1896 he painted himself in white sacrificial robes and gave the canvas the title of *Self Portrait Nearing Golgotha*. And in the end Gauguin talked about suicide. Only a matter of a few months now, he wrote to France; a ridiculous act, he knew, but probably inevitable. And in any case, "what does the death of an artist matter."

Somehow, though, he struggled back to an imitation of health; and with a body that allowed him to work, and even the most modest sufficiency of money—some came in from France at the end of 1896—he could talk again of life as worth living, precarious but enjoyable. Pauura had become pregnant; when the child was born around Christmas, stillborn, Gauguin did not react badly. He painted one or two nativity pictures and settled down in the new year to an easy rhythm of work and relaxation. To a fellow artist in France—one of the painters who had refused to come to Tahiti with him—he wrote about the economics of contentment. "Just to sit here at the open door, smoking a cigarette and drinking a glass of absinthe, is an unmixed pleasure which I have every day. And then I have a fifteen-year-old wife who cooks my simple everyday fare and gets down on her back for me whenever I want, all for the modest reward of a frock, worth ten francs, a month. . . . You have no idea how far 125 francs will go here. . . . If I could sell 1,800 francs' worth of pictures I would stay here for the rest of my days. I want no other life, only this."

Artistically, Gauguin was capable once more of thinking on a grand scale. He made some notes on a big painting he was planning. It was the distillation of his old wish-dream of Tahiti, returning irresistibly, still potent, *Noa Noa* some years on. "The canvas is already stretched, prepared, carefully smoothed: not a knot, not a fold, not a mark. Think, this will be a masterpiece. . . . The principal figure will be a woman being transformed into a statue, retaining life, but becoming an idol. The figure will stand out against the background of a clump of trees that do not grow on earth but only in paradise." It would not be a Pygmalion statue becoming human, or the woman of Sodom turning into a pillar of salt. No—"woman becoming an idol." "Delightfully scented flowers grow everywhere, children play in this garden, young girls gather fruit; the fruits are heaped up in enormous baskets; strong young men carry them gracefully to the feet of the idol. The aspect of the picture should be grave, like a religious evocation, melancholy, and gay as children." Gauguin admitted to his notebook that it was easier to write about a masterpiece than paint one. His desire was greater than his powers, and the picture was far from being accomplished; but still . . .

Then the mail steamer of April, 1897, brought devastating news. Gauguin's daughter Aline was dead. She had gone out to a dance in the Danish winter and had caught pneumonia, and it had killed her. Gauguin's last letter to Aline, written in France, had talked about her going dancing: "Are you a good dancer? I hope you can gracefully say yes, and that young men talk to you a lot about me, your father. That is a way of courting you indirectly." Gauguin felt Aline to be very much part of himself, and for him this was coming as close to deep affection as was possible. Now a short and matter-of-fact letter from Mette told him Aline was gone. He shut himself off to emotion, and for a time felt nothing. But grief broke through. "I have lost my daughter, I no longer love God. Like my mother she was called Aline. Each one loves in his own fashion: for some love grows hot over the coffin, for others . . . I do not know. Her tomb far away, flowers, that is only appearances. Her grave is here by me; my tears are living flowers." Addressing himself to Mette, he was ferocious and final. She had cut him off from his children because he had no money. In return he would not say "God keep you," but—less falsely—"may your conscience sleep so that you do not have to await death as a deliverance." After this, Mette never wrote to him again, nor he to her. (And when toward the end of Gauguin's life his son Clovis died, his other favorite, he was not told.)

Once again Gauguin felt blackness rising to overwhelm him: "Ever since I was a child, bad luck has fed on me. Never a piece of good fortune, no joy. Everything always against me, and I cry to myself: God, if you exist, I accuse you of injustice, malice. . . . What use are virtue, work, courage, intelligence. The only thing logical and right is crime." His body was betraying him as God had done. His ankle gave him such pain that he could not put any weight on it. The "eruptions" on the injured leg spread; now it was both legs. He sprinkled arsenic powder on the sores to contain them, bandaged his limbs, and walked leaning on a stick. He was turning into a grotesque, and the Tahitians around his house spread the rumor that he had leprosy. Certainly Gauguin felt like a leper, an outcast; and it was very likely in this mood that he produced a statue of a leprous figure. There was something wrong with his eyes as well now. For months he did not put brush to canvas. His money was gone again, he could not walk into the mountains to get food for himself, he could not even get anyone to accept tubes of paint in payment for bread. "Head as empty as stomach, nothing clear ahead, and—hopeless," he saw no deliverance but death. The likelihood that his heart would kill him soon gave him grim satisfaction. If he should die suddenly, he wrote to De Monfreid, "keep in memory of me all the canvases stored with you: my family has too many."

Out of all this pain, turmoil, irresolution and rage came a fixed decision to kill himself, and an equal determination to leave a great painting behind him. He had no more artist's canvas, so he got hold of a length of jute sacking, almost as big as the imaginary studio-wide piece of canvas he had described for himself in a happier moment not long before. The huge painting he executed was a richer and bleaker version of his imaginary masterpiece. He worked on it day and night for a month, using the paints he could not barter for bread, laboring feverishly, without preparatory sketches or detailed studies, nothing like that, just his whole force, his whole passion, right off the brush onto the vast surface he set himself to cover before he left life. This at least was what he said. In fact he was assembling, in one culminating tableau, all the ruling images of his painter's career in the South Seas.

"At the bottom right," he wrote, tracing the outlines of his work in words, as he so often did, "a sleeping baby and three crouching women. Two figures dressed in purple confide their thoughts to one another; an enormous figure deliberately out of proportion crouches, raises its arms in the air and looks astonished at these two who dare to consider their destiny. The central figure is picking fruit. Two cats near a child. A white goat. The idol, its arms mysteriously and rhythmically raised, seems to point to the beyond. A crouching figure seems to listen to the idol; then, finally, an old woman near death seems to accept and resign herself to her thoughts and brings the legend to an end; at her feet, a strange white bird holding a lizard in its claw represents the uselessness of vain words. All this takes place on the banks of a wooded stream. In the background the sea, then the mountain of a neighboring island. . . ."

There was an Eve-figure in the painting, but not the magnificent animal chaste in nakedness that Gauguin spoke of before he came back the second time to Tahiti. Rather it was the figure of the crone in the lower left of the picture, doubled up at the end of her life, a fetus of old age about to be born into death. The old woman holds her head in her hands; her face is ugly and pained. This form in Gauguin's art goes back to a figure he had begun to paint even before he left Europe. When he first gave it a name he called it *Breton Eve,* certainly an Eve born into the knowledge that she must die, in pain and in sin. And the ultimate origin of the figure is something Gauguin came across in an ethnological museum in Paris, the preserved remains of a savage's corpse, huddled and bound for burial, from South America—a mummy, from Peru. This was the closure of the cycle in which Gauguin painted his mother as a naked Eve, then went looking in Tahiti for the garden innocence of his Peruvian childhood, half-knowing but desperately unwilling to concede that it was irrecoverable.

When Gauguin put a title to his great painting he used not the Tahitian language but French, to ask the eternal questions: *Where Do We Come From? What Are We? Where Are We Going?* The conclusion was there on canvas. Eve in the Garden of Eden, his own mother in Peru, the tropical Eve with the face of his mother, and his Tahitian Eves in turn, whose bodies he had possessed as a man and an artist, were all aspects of the Peruvian mummy, horrifying emblems of the transformation of life into death.

The life cycle may repeat itself endlessly, but man—even the painter, the artist-creator reaching through his work toward divinity—has only one life to live. One man's dream before nature cannot halt the cycle.

At the end of 1897 the mail steamer brought Gauguin, in unscheduled irony, the first published evidence of *Noa Noa,* the opening section of his old manuscript reworked by Charles Morice and printed in a Paris magazine. Gauguin was beyond being restored by a visitation from his Tahitian dream past, painted in the rosy colors of his old determined infatuation with the islands, varnished by Morice's prose. The steamer brought words but no money. He was finished.

He had no gun any more to kill himself, but he did have the arsenic powder that he used to keep the sores on his legs at bay. He limped up into the hills and swallowed his poison. The arsenic took effect. Gauguin lost consciousness. But he had swallowed too much, his stomach rejected the overdose, and he woke to find himself prostrate in his own vomit. Devastated, he lay out in the open all night, suffering. Next day he staggered back to his hut. For a month his temples throbbed, he was giddy, and eating nauseated him. He was not pleased with his failure to do away with himself, but he did not try suicide again. Later he spoke of being "condemned to life," and it took him years more to work out his sentence.

* * *

Gauguin's effort as a painter to comprehend all of existence and then his failure to end his own life left him, part of him anyway, reconciled to merely subsisting. It was as if for the time being Gauguin the artist ceased to struggle, even to assert himself. When an old acquaintance wrote to him from Paris inviting him to participate in a show which would mark the tenth anniversary of the exhibit Gauguin had arranged during the 1889 Exposition, he wrote back saying no, others had gone beyond him now; beside them he would look like a beginner; he was too old, his work was over. In time, though, he found himself able to enjoy small, beautiful things again, in a valedictory way. De Monfreid had sent him some flower seeds from France, and he liked watching them grow. Perhaps, he said, if he ever went back to painting he would do flower studies.

So Gauguin passed the next few years of his life in Tahiti as a nonartist, and it was a period that was curious in the extreme. He made an unlikely attempt to set himself up as a planter, on borrowed money. He built himself a new house, big and showy. But he defaulted on his loan payments. In order to survive, he had to take a job at a pittance as a draftsman in the colony's public works department. He fought with Pauura and impregnated her; the child was born in April, 1899, a son, and Gauguin named him Émile, as he had named his oldest son by Mette. And he started a disputatious little home-made newspaper—and then he was offered the editorship of a journal controlled by one of the colony's political factions, a group of antiadministration Catholics.

Gauguin was no Catholic; indeed the Church disgusted him. But for two years he did what his Catholic masters paid him to do, which was to maul their political opponents and flay the colonial administration. Gauguin was now giving an imitation of a householder, concerned settler, pillar of law and order, scourge of misgovernment. He had always been characterized at his meanest and least attractive by a sort of liverishness in his rage. Now he was directing this rage at local politics. Compared with Robert Louis Stevenson's householding enterprise at Vailima, what

Gauguin was up to reads like sick parody. It is hard to believe he meant any of it. As a man he never looked worse.

Still, on his regular salary as editor he was doing better financially than he had since his stockbroking days. His new prosperity allowed him to put on regular Sunday feasts at his country house, Tahitian meals of meat cooked in a ground oven, all sorts of canned foods, and liquor that lasted through the night. The meal itself might be orderly, one of his guests recalled; but later Gauguin the man of affairs was likely to turn back into the artist in his studio, the master of the revels and finally the cold joker of earlier days: "Gauguin amused himself by getting his guests to do all sorts of foolish things (getting the women to undress, etc. . . .), but though he had a good time himself, he never appeared drunk and always remained in control."

It was unlike Gauguin to apply himself steadily for any length of time to anything but his art, even when he was being paid to unload some of his rage on the world. Earlier, as a draftsman at six francs a day, writing miserably to De Monfreid on public-works letterhead paper, he said that if he could not paint—he, who loved nothing more than that—his heart was empty. There was no real satisfaction, he said, except in oneself, and at that moment he found himself disgusting. In this light, working as the editor of a political newspaper was really no more than acting out self-disgust at a higher daily rate. And in fact Gauguin was thinking seriously again about art and his artist's reputation. There was another great Paris world fair coming up in 1900, and if just the year before he had rejected the notion of exhibiting in France, now he was positively interested in the idea of showing some oils, drawings, and wood engravings. No matter what else became of him, Gauguin wanted fiercely to be justified in his artist's life. The great painting he had done before he took arsenic was described at length in a letter to De Monfreid as soon as he had recovered, and in time he packed the canvas up and shipped it off to France where people could see it. In fact, whatever else he told De Monfreid about his condition, in his monthly letters he always talked about painting: theory, practice, marketing strategy for his own work. He was proud of what he had done and wanted it well received, well understood.

Then in 1900 the opportunity came to immerse himself again in his life-long, death-deep artistic identity. A Paris art dealer, Ambroise Vollard—the man, incidentally, who had procured Anna the Javanese for Gauguin—offered him a business deal, so many francs per month for so many paintings per year. Vollard was distinctly not the noble patron Gauguin often wished for—an aristocrat by birth to be the benefactor of the aristocrat of art—but at least the proposition was a livable one, of the sort that Gauguin had been after for a long time. In 1901 Vollard sweetened the offer, and with this Gauguin got ready to take a step he had been talking about for years—leaving Tahiti for the Marquesas. The wolf was preparing to slip the collar again and head for the forest. Gauguin sold off his country place and left Pauura and little Émile to fend for themselves. Unencumbered and alone, he was once more an artist.

He was ready for a change, he said; in Tahiti his imagination had begun to cool. The Marquesas would offer him yet another chance to rejuvenate himself through exposure to savagery. (Enthusiastically but inaccurately, he spoke about cannibalism as if it still existed there on a considerable scale.) Now renewed strength would flow through his body onto his canvases. With new models, new landscapes, he would do fine things.

And there was something else to think about too: "the public has got used to Tahiti." On this vexed question of public acceptance Gauguin had never been single-minded, and certainly he had some involved things to say now: "People are so stupid that when they are shown canvases containing new and *terrifying* elements, Tahiti will become comprehensible and charming. My Brittany paintings turned to rose water because of Tahiti; Tahiti will turn to eau de cologne because of the Marquesas."

This might have been read to mean that Gauguin, by painting new savage things, hoped to domesticate his older works and thus get buyers interested in them. But it also sounded as though Gauguin the unregenerate artist, on a steady retainer for the first time in his artist's life, was determined to use this modest security to paint terrifyingly, meaning unsalably. (In the event, he was as likely to supply Vollard out of his backlog of paintings as he was to send new picutres. And, interestingly, the work he did in the Marquesas—indeed, most of what he did after his attempt at suicide—ceased to draw heavily on his version of Polynesian mythology. What "savagery" remained was mostly stylistic.)

As if these ambivalences were not enough, even before Gauguin left Tahiti for the Marquesas he was already planning—yet again—to put himself at maximum risk, by cutting himself off from the guarantee of his arrangement with Vollard. In the interest of getting away quickly he had sold his country place unnecessarily cheaply, and at the same time he was writing to De Monfreid, telling him to sell as many of his stored Gauguins as possible. When the proceeds added up to enough for two years' living, Gauguin said, he would cut loose from Vollard: the man was an exploiter. He was just waiting for the right moment to do it, and after that Vollard would have to meet Gauguin's demands or not get any more paintings.

The figure of two years weighed on Gauguin. To De Monfreid he wrote that if he could manage this much time in good health and free of money troubles, it should be sufficient for him to reach "a certain maturity" in his art. To Charles Morice he wrote rather differently, as if the Marquesas represented an end to the question of where he was going. He spoke not of maturity but of a "termination" to his work. And an end to life. Savagery and solitude, he said, "will give me one last flare-up of enthusiasm before I die." Gauguin had talked like this any number of times before. This time he prophesied truly. Feeling "prematurely aged" by sickness and misery, he was in and out of the Papeete hospital again before he left Tahiti, with the same old incurable ailments. When he sailed for the Marquesas he was fifty-three; and in less than the two years he wanted, he was dead.

*　*　*

In Gauguin's day France and the other great powers were colonizing the South Seas. Gauguin, in flight from civilization, was using the South Seas to decolonize himself. When he talked about going back to the sources of human existence to find inspiration for his art, and when he acted this out by going to live as a savage among savages, he really meant that he was responding to the struggle of his deeper self to assert itself against the repressiveness of civilized life. Gauguin believed that anything he could recover from the depths of his being—dreams, motifs for his painting, impulses to action—was valuable.

This was dangerous stuff. It ruined Melville, for one, and if Stevenson managed better it was because he was able to convince himself as well as others that he was only playing with those acceptable childhood toys.

Gauguin, for his part, was on the edge of awareness about what he was doing. Almost everything he wrote about his mother, for example, concerned his childhood years with her, when she appeared magically seductive; and clearly he placed his own daughter in the same sort of charged relationship with himself as parent. He desired his mother and he desired his daughter; he wanted to possess them, to make them part of himself.

Gauguin wanted not only to be free to embrace the women who were extensions of his own being, but free in himself to cross conventional sexual lines. The naked body he painted as his mother's was male in its original modeling; it was the artist's brush that imposed femaleness upon it. In the notebook he kept in Tahiti for his daughter, he wondered at length about Sodom and about Lesbos. And when, in his long description of the major painting he was preparing in his imagination, he was careful to say that the central female figure turning into an idol was not from Sodom, he made a verbal slip—meaning to say it was not Lot's wife, he actually wrote Lot's daughter. Twice, then, Gauguin openly linked thoughts of Sodom with thoughts of daughters.

This appetite for trespass across conventional sexual boundaries had surfaced in Gauguin's life before he came to the South Seas. There was, interestingly enough, something mannish about the woman he married; Mette had close-cropped hair, a broad-shouldered robustness in young maturity when Gauguin was courting her, a masculine hardness of feature as she got older, even an appetite for dressing in men's clothes. She used to go visiting in Paris wearing trousers and a soft felt hat and smoking a pipe. As a respectable lady getting on in years, long after she and Gauguin parted, she wore a man's cap to drive a car. And she was involved once in an odd incident on a railroad train, in the days when compartments were still sexually segregated. A guard tried to put out of the women's section a passenger with a cap, cravat, and cigar; it turned out to be Mette. In this as in all such matters in Gauguin's life, Flora Tristan made an appearance. One of her best stories about herself was how she became the first woman to watch both houses of the British parliament in session. Learning that females were forbidden entrance, she got a Turkish diplomat who had fallen under her charms to dress her as a man in Levantine costume so that she could satisfy her curiosity. In the Commons she passed inspection, but the Lords (like the noble savages of Tahiti with Commerson's servant Baré on Bougainville's voyage) were more sensitively attuned to sex, and they unmasked her. And then there was the curious circumstance that when Gauguin appeared at Papeete the Tahitians took him at first for a *taata vahine*, a man-woman.

Early in his first stay in Tahiti, after the regrettable Titi, before the miraculous Tehaamana, when Gauguin was living alone, intimidated by those village girls with their wordless invitations to rape and their silent, strong, unmanning dignity, he found a male friend, a young Tahitian. One day they went up into the mountains together to search for rosewood that Gauguin could use for carving. The occasion is described in *Noa Noa*. The youth walked ahead, bare-bodied except for a *pareu*. Gauguin followed, ax in hand, along an almost nonexistent path, winding past waterfalls, a mere fissure between mountains, up, up into impenetrable forest: "Complete silence, the only sound the murmur of water on rock, as monotonous as silence itself. And there we were, the two of us, two friends, he a young man, I almost old, body and soul, old in the vices of civilization and lost illusions."

Gauguin watched from behind the lithe animal body of his companion, enchanting in its youth, its beauty and harmony with nature giving off a special fragrance, the *noanoa* of the islands. Suddenly, Gauguin wrote, "love blossomed" in him. Then just as suddenly "a presentiment of crime, of unconscious passion, the awaking of evil." And, in another wave of feeling, "weariness of the male role, always having to be strong, protective. To be for a moment the weak being who loves and obeys." On the verge of overthrowing all the taboos of his life, he moved closer, temples throbbing. Then the youth turned to face him, and in an instant Gauguin was released from troubling sexual enchantment and he bent to refresh himself in the cold clear water of a stream. They found the rosewood they were looking for, and Gauguin wielded his ax, chanting,as he chopped about striking down desire and self-love. "Enraged and bloody-handed," he was felling his civilized self, so he said. When later he came to carve the wood, each cut of the chisel reminded him of "sweet silence, fragrance, a victory and a rejuvenation."

What caused the evil throbbing in Gauguin, the presentiment of crime and unconscious passion, was that he was on the verge of laying sexual hands on a man. But his first vision had not been of a male who aroused passion in him. Rather, he saw the figure of the Tahitian as animal, graceful, "without sex," "androgynous." And when he came to write about the mountain journey in his first *Noa Noa* notebook, he made some jottings in the margin, more thoughts to mull over."1. The androgynous aspect of the savage, the lack of sexual difference among animals. 2. The alluring purity of the sight of the nude and the easy relations between the two sexes. The unconsciousness of vice among savages. Desire for a moment to be weak, a woman." From the homosexual encounter and the surrender of his maleness he drew back. But the androgynous vision was to be pursued.

In *Noa Noa* soon after this androgynous vision is described, there is a cryptic passage in which Gauguin speaks of coming across a solitary Tahitian bending for a drink of water. The drinker senses the presence of a stranger and dives into a pool and disappears. It is a female; Gauguin says "she." The painting that is connected with this passage is based on a photograph, the work of a Papeete professional (who, incidentally, got an award for his island views in the Tahiti exhibit at the 1889 Paris exposition). The figure in the photograph might be either male or female. Bare back and side are visible; the front of the body is hidden; a *pareu* swathes the loins; sexuality is not clear. Gauguin's painting, *Papa Moe*, "Mysterious Waters," emphasized the musculature of upper arm and back, suggesting if anything maleness, even though he wrote about the Tahitian by the pool as "she." Those who have since described the figure in the painting (commentators male and female) simply cannot make up their minds about its sex.

Painting Tehaamana and all his other Tahitian Eves, Gauguin sometimes gave them the same body he had given his first tropical Eve, his mother. It was the male Buddhist body from the Javanese frieze of Borobudur, which in itself had an ambiguous maleness. As so often in Buddhist art, the physical form was soft and rounded, the musculature unstressed, with a certain sinuosity in the stance. It was easy and rewarding to transform this version of maleness on canvas into classic substantial Polynesian womanliness. Tahitian women were, in Gauguin's eye, indisputably superior in every way to the women of Europe. He thought of young white girls at a ball, in long gloves, skinny, pointy-elbowed, the forearm stronger than the upper arm, and compared them unfavorably with island women, who had a natural, graceful, dancing undulation in the body, and hands and wrists that were essentially aristocratic. Then he thought of European stage performers, women with enormous thighs and enormous knock-knees, and wrote admiringly of the contrast presented by the legs of island women, with the beautiful straight line from hip to foot that showed up so often in his paintings (and which could be seen in the Buddhist frieze figures). "The thighs are very strong, but not broad, which makes them rounded;" and there was nothing of that separation which gave European women's legs the look of pincers. The island woman overall was solid-footed, slim-hipped, broad-shouldered. It was these proportions that distinguished her from all other women—and, in Gauguin's words, often caused her "to be mistaken for a man." A natural androgyne.

Beyond this kind of thing, and most importantly for him, Gauguin was moving toward the idea of a blending and fusing of the sexes as an approach to the resolution of all the problems that plagued him, a solution to the riddle of existence. Ultimately this idea acquired for him an eternal character, something that transcended life and death. It was embodied for him in the word "androgyny."

Gauguin had been reaching for a long time toward this idea of the androgynous as divine, since before he went to the South Seas. In his Brittany days with the painter Émile Bernard he had become interested in Bernard's young and most attractive sister Madeleine. Bernard did a painting of her in reverie in the Bois d'Amour, the Forest of Love, chastely dressed and obviously innocent. Gauguin later did his own version of this, not from the life, at least not from Madeleine's life: he used his Paris mistress Juliette Huet for a model. In Gauguin's painting the girl lies nude, and the title is *The Loss of Virginity*. A fox, one of Gauguin's symbols of perversity, is held in the girl's arm and reaches out his paw to touch her breast, laying claim to her body—Gauguin appropriating Madeleine to his dream of young girls. He also did a ceramic sculpture for Madeleine, a savage head of himself. And he wrote her an enigmatic letter in which he pronounced that if she wished to amount to anything more than the common run of girls, she would have to rise above the body, not be a slave of the "material;" and for this "it is necessary firstly to consider yourself androgyne, without sex."

Again—inevitably—Flora Tristan appeared in Gauguin's notions of androgyny as they affected the spiritual. Gauguin recorded that Flora and a fellow reformer who went by the name of Père Enfantin, Father Childlike, had founded a new religion called MaPa, for Mother and Father, and that the two embodied the divine parental roles. Gauguin had his facts wrong; it was a sculptor named Ganneau who proclaimed the new faith. But the principle was the same: Ganneau's religion was called Évadisme, for Eve and Adam, and the two sexes were to be fused in religious affirmation. And Flora Tristan wrote a novel with a hermaphroditic theme, in which she asked the same fundamental question as Gauguin: "What are we?"

* * *

The cockroach-infested, copra-stinking little steamer that carried Gauguin away from Tahiti to savagery made its first Marquesan stop at the island of Nukuhiva, only a few miles along the coast from Herman Melville's valley of the Typee. Gauguin stayed aboard, disembarking eventually on the island of Hivaoa, where Robert Louis Stevenson had gone through his first Polynesian name-exchange ceremony. Gauguin never gave any indication that he had heard of either Melville or Stevenson.

The Marquesas were no longer the savage islands of Melville's time. Hivaoa had traders and priests and gendarmes of the colonial administration. As a people, the Marquesans of Gauguin's day were the saddest of nineteenth-century savages, reduced to ruin by their contact with civilization, on their way to near-extinction, and most of what they did in a savage way was drunken or drugged. They fled the realities of colonization in opium dreams; they took the moralizings of priests and turned them into chants to be sung while brewing palm toddy; they made orange wine in vast quantities, canoe hulls full of it, and drank it and sang and danced and made love all together in distant valleys where the gendarme could not hear them.

From the spot in the port village of Atuona where Gauguin had a house built for himself, he could see the church of the Catholic mission, the work of Brother Michel Blanc of the Sacred Hearts, a carpenter and self-taught architect who decorated his constructions with joyous naïve art (and carved a statue of the Virgin Mary into a soaring rock face above the anchorage at Hatiheu on Nukuhiva). Blanc was a Frenchman, a good country Catholic from Poitou, and interestingly he drew on the same peasant religious art of nearby Brittany that had fascinated Gauguin with its "savagery" and "primitivism" before he ever came to the South Seas. Blanc was still in the Marquesas when Gauguin arrived, but there is nothing to show that the two men ever met and talked, artist to artist.

Gauguin's only use for the Church in the Marquesas came from the circumstance that the Catholic mission controlled most of the land around Atuona, and he would need the good opinion of the bishop to locate himself there. So he smiled politely and went to Mass (and this would have given him a chance to see Brother Michel's work close up). Hypocrisy got him what he wanted, and he gleefully recorded in his notebook the success of his confidence trick.

The house he built was a Marquesan version of the Paris studio he called *Te Faruru*. This time he identified his home in big characters carved into a wood panel over his lintel: "Maison du Jouir," House of Pleasure, meaning sexual pleasure, perhaps a reference to the traditional sexual meeting houses of the old Polynesian culture, certainly a statement of personal appetite. On the walls were forty-five pornographic photographs bought at Port Said between France and the South Seas, a classic collection of filthy pictures. Downstairs he had a kitchen and a wood-carving shop, upstairs a small bedroom and a large studio, with some of his sexually loaded carved wood panels decorating the doorway. On working days in the studio he sipped at absinthe, and to keep his drinks cool he had a handy arrangement by which he dangled a water bottle in his well at the end of a string, reeling it in through the window of his top-floor studio with a fishing rod. He went about the house naked, leaning on his walking sticks, the heads of which were carved to represent a phallus and a couple in sexual embrace. He acquired a dog and named it Pego, a version of the abbreviated signature he sometimes used on his paintings, "PGo," which when said aloud sounded like sailor's slang for "penis." Every time Gauguin called his dog he was being outrageous, and he knew it.

Part of the attraction of the Marquesas for Gauguin was that models were supposed to be cheap there—or rather that women were cheap and could be used for models. Gauguin attracted women to Maison du Jouir by making a splash with his money, as he liked to do, giving parties as he had done at his country place in Tahiti. Any amount of wine was drunk, and he ran up a substantial liquor bill with the traders of Atuona. As an additional sexual lure he had brought with him from Tahiti a sackful of "bonbons." With these, and with food and clothes, Gauguin bought his women. And with tobacco—Marquesan girls were great pipe smokers, and had been at least since the days of Melville's Fayaway. For spur-of-the-moment sex, "an orange and a sidelong glance" seemed to work. Or else Maison du Jouir itself was sufficient, as when the young girl Vaituni was attracted by one of Gauguin's Port Said photographs, of a "bisexual" with round and charming breasts, the sight of which, Gauguin said, could rouse him from impotence. Gauguin followed her to a quiet stream, and they "threw aside their fig-leaves" and laughed together. Sometimes things simply got too much for him, as when an old woman moved in with him, ancient, skinny, repulsive, eleven times a mother, she said, by a hundred fathers. Gauguin could not rise to her, but she came back night after night, to his embarrassment, and when she gave up (Gauguin having successfully "defended his chastity" against her) she went around saying he had exhausted her, holding up all her fingers: "Yes . . . like that every night."

Gauguin did find at least one woman whom he liked to paint and who was willing to sit for him. Tohotaua was a strikingly unusual Polynesian, good-looking, brown-skinned but with red hair, offering physically the sort of visual play on nature that interested Gauguin the colorist. Perhaps Tohotaua was a descendant of one of those long-ago white sailors who mingled their blood with island blood and gave some Polynesians such attractiveness in the eyes of Westerners. Gauguin shared Tohotaua with her husband, and if there was nothing against this in traditional Marquesan culture, which was polyandrous, it outraged orthodox Catholic sensibilities in Atuona. (The husband, as it happened, was a Catholic, a strong defender of papal infallibility, but he was a Marquesan first. He held onto as much of the past as he could, was a great dancer and sorcerer as well, and considered the lending of a wife to be a friendly act.)

Gauguin even happened upon an authentic savage close to home. He had an elderly Marquesan neighbor, an emaciated old fellow, frighteningly tattooed. He had been a cannibal, imprisoned for it by the colonial authorities, then released before his sentence was up. He had got the idea that Gauguin had helped to free him. As a kindness in return—he had never been baptized a Christian and remained a sorcerer—he put a taboo on Gauguin and his property, magically warding off harm. Gauguin would give him tobacco, or a can of sardines which the old fellow would open with his teeth, and the two would sit and talk. "I used to ask him if human flesh was good to eat; then his face would light up with an infinite sweetness (a sweetness special to savages) and he would reveal his formidable fangs." This was the real nineteenth-century Marquesan savage, body tattooed, head full of sorcerer's spells and the emotion of cannibalism recollected in tranquillity. How good it was, he murmured.

* * *

Gauguin's filthy Port Said pictures were displayed at Maison du Jouir specifically to ward off respectability. "Men, women and children, almost everyone laughed at them, and after a moment did not think any more about them. The only people who did not come to my house were the self-styled respectables, and they were the only ones who thought about them all year long." The bishop heard about the photographs; the Catholic sisters grew pale, with rings around their eyes. "Meditate on that," wrote Gauguin, "and nail an indecency prominently over your door; from that time on you will be untroubled by respectable folk, the most insupportable people that God ever made."

The priests and sisters of the Marquesan mission had offended Gauguin, in general and in particular. They ran a convent school for girls, and according to them attendance was compulsory, which meant that Gauguin's supply of companions and models of the age he liked so much was severely curtailed. He found a way around the difficulty, and for once the law was on his side, at least the law on education. It turned out that the missionaries had been stretching things. Only if a child lived within two and a half miles of a school was attendance compulsory, beyond that not so. Gauguin came across a fourteen year old named Vaeoho from a country district outside the two-and-a-half mile mark; and, on the basis of a gift of a sewing machine and some cloth, he got her parents to take her out of school and let her live at Maison du Jouir. This was a satisfactory enough arrangement for Gauguin, along the lines of the one he had had with Pauura in Tahiti. But then a familiar thing happened. Vaeoho got pregnant and wanted to have the baby at home with her family, and she left Atuona for the country. Gauguin had trouble finding a replacement. The convent school closed up for the summer, not many girls were about, and those who were in evidence were being closely watched by the Catholic fathers and sisters. Gauguin was thwarted.

He took his revenge by doing some wood carvings which he displayed in front of his house. He had had practice at annoying Catholic missionaries in this way. At his country place in Tahiti—before his stint as a newspaper editor paid by Catholics—he had done a female nude in wax-covered clay and set it up in his garden, and when the village priest harangued him for his outrageousness, Gauguin called in the gendarme to secure him in his rights and freedoms. This time Gauguin carved several figures. One was of a homely missionary priest, shaped and titled to bring to mind an orangutan. This was bad enough, but there was worse. Gauguin carved a female nude, and titled it *Thérèse*. The Catholic bishop had a Marquesan housekeeper by that name. A companion statue was entitled *Père Paillard*, "Father Lascivious," and it had a lustful face and devilish horns. The gossip around Atuona was that the bishop had impregnated Thérèse and then for respectability's sake married her off to a Marquesan catechist. So, among those who would have enjoyed Gauguin's Port Said photographs, his statues provoked much laughter, and among the respectables much hostility. Gauguin followed this up by taking the bishop's second housemaid as a mistress.

In the Marquesas, more than in Tahiti, to be on the wrong side of the church was to be on the wrong side of the law. The resident gendarme at Atuona, a good Catholic, developed a jaundiced interest in Gauguin. Gauguin in turn broadened his criticisms of the Catholic mission and the administration. In time he got himself mixed up in some legal cases involving Marquesans accused of various crimes, all the way from noisy drunkenness to murder, and if here for once he was generally on the right side in terms of good law and ordinary good sense, still his style of attack was offensive in the extreme to the authorities who had ultimate power over him in the islands.

One of the reasons Gauguin gave for leaving Tahiti in favor of the Marquesas was that he would have peace and quiet, free from the cares of the world, out from under the heel of authority. Yet here he was again, putting himself at risk, living dangerously. It was a repetition of what had happened so many times before: in brief, Gauguin's health had failed again; he could not work as he wanted to, and his unfocused energies, such as they were, expressed themselves in the rage of despair. His eyes were giving him serious trouble; he was afraid he might go blind. His chronically bad leg was cripplingly painful. He needed both his carved sticks to walk at all. He was injecting himself with morphine all the time now, so much that he became afraid and asked one of the storekeepers to take his syringe away. For a while he tried laudanum, but then needed morphine again. Even on steady drugs and copious liquor he could not sleep. All his life he had been an insomniac, and never worse than now. He could not sleep and he could not work. So he raged. The artistic frenzy was a way for him to handle, to manage, to justify his rage. Without art—and this manifested itself whenever he was sick and could not work—he was nothing but a victim, a raging brain in a crucified carcass.

As he had the habit of doing, in his self-imposed isolation Gauguin began talking to himself on paper. What he set down grew to be a book-length manuscript, a kind of testament. Writing out of an awareness that very likely he did not have long to live, Gauguin proposed to account for himself on his own terms and in his own way: "childhood memories, the 'why' of my instincts, my intellectual development: also what I have seen and heard (criticisms on this subject of men and things), my art, that of others, my admirations, my hates too." It was being done for himself, but he presupposed an audience. His intention was to bare himself, and if his naked maleness was shocking, so be it. For him the only thing that mattered was the exercise of his will. He was able to "will himself to will," and this made him capable of daring anything. And it was the infinitely daring exercise of will that constituted for him the real meaning of life.

This was Gauguin talking yet again as if he were some kind of man-god, with nothing standing between him and his fantasies of omnipotence, able to wish himself, will himself, to the heights of creation, to the sun, where he would join the other gods. But Gauguin was human, therefore doomed not to achieve the sun, doomed in fact to kill himself by overreaching. He wanted everything, total conquest. Knowing he could not attain it, he invited total ruin.

There was no place for such a man in conventional society. Gauguin announced that in what he was writing he would have "terrible" things to say about the world he had been forced to live in, and in time the list of his "hates" on paper spread to cover all the larger families of man in the society that bred him, all the households of faith and law, church and state. Priests gave themselves to God and thus rendered themselves less than human, their vow of chastity a "sort of castration." These male virgins led along their female counterparts, the nuns, "grubby, unhealthy," revolting to the artist's eye for beauty, "brains inadequate to thought . . . with no real goal but blind obedience." The church that these grotesques served was a mockery.

Gendarmes and judges worked hand in hand with priests and were just as despicable. They would abuse Marquesan women and then have them fined in court, or they would get themselves infected by venereal disease, but none of this would stop them parading as enforcers of the moral law. And their wives, "covered head to foot in out-of-date fashions, vulgar-haunched . . . sham jewelry, elbows either menacing or sausage-like"—garbage in corsets, said Gauguin.

These were the representatives of civilization in the islands, and it was over the extinction of the islanders that they were presiding. The Polynesian child locked up in school, body always covered "for decency's sake," became delicate, unable to climb a coconut tree or go up into the mountains for bananas and stay out in the open all night. Feet in shoes turned tender, unable to take the rough paths and the rocks of streambeds. So the island race was enfeebled, and it was going down to ruin, in large part "tubercular, sterile of loins, ovaries destroyed by mercury." Gauguin in his hate was being, of course, holier-than-everyone. He himself was syphilitic, and he was a great sleeper with Polynesian women. And no doubt he had something to do with the ultimate "destruction of ovaries" by mercurials, the medicines used to treat venereal diseases.

His own first family, Mette and the children, survived in his life, if only as a sore he kept picking at. In the Marquesas, in the last period of his life, he wondered yet again what he had severed from himself when he renounced his family, and he referred to the self-toughening that kept the pain at bay as the forming of "scar tissue." His illegitimate children by island women he did not have to take responsibility for. He could be a savage, fathering babies on a brown female body, and that was that. But from his civilized family he could never free himself. His last view of Mette and the children was that even if they insisted on repudiating him totally, they still planned to attack and strip him and consume his substance. The way to deal with that, he said, was to do the pillaging himself, leaving nothing.

In Gauguin's view, a crazy war to the death over family, property, inheritance was central to civilization, and because he would not surrender to convention he was—in a phrase he liked—"an enemy of the people." He held that the savagery of civilization was worse than anything the islands produced in all their primitivism: "Civilized! You pride yourself on not eating human flesh . . . every day you eat the heart of your fellow man."

This baring of self was intended, as it turned out, for publication. There was, all in all, very little in Gauguin's life that was done without an audience in mind, himself first, as an all-important audience of one, but others too. He copied out his terminally enraged manuscript neatly (and this was an interesting thing about him—his physical agonies and spiritual miseries were always set down on the page in an orderly, well-managed hand, even in his private letters). He illustrated it with twenty-seven drawings, and proposed it to a Paris editor to whom he had once written from Tahiti about the condition of the suffering artist.

At the same time, Gauguin had been reworking an anti-Catholic essay he had written in Tahiti, making it more outrageous than ever. For this he had his audience ready-made. He sent it through an intermediary to the Catholic bishop (whose reputation he had held up to ridicule with the statue of Père Paillard). Without comment, the bishop sent back a book for Gauguin to read, a history of missionary Catholicism.

All this was Gauguin living dangerously, reaching out to conquer everything, battling the nullification of disease, ensuring that if he were to die he would die madly, that if his creative life was over, as he feared, he would at least go out wreaking ruin on paper. In 1903 he did legal battle with a gendarme whom he found particularly offensive, accusing him of taking bribes and of smuggling goods into the islands off American ships. He set out his case in elaborate detail and put it before the authorities. This was his final undoing. He was taken to court for libeling an officer in the course of his duties, convicted, fined five hundred francs, and sentenced to three months' jail. All his artist's life Gauguin had talked about society being criminal, about how crime in a crazy world was right and logical, about the artist being a criminal on the run. Now, in the islands that he had chosen for their savagery, society was sealing his claim to a criminal identity.

In a self-portrait done before he left Europe, Gauguin identified himself with Victor Hugo's famous criminal hero Jean Valjean, in every way the human equal of the police who hounded him. And he once said he would like to be the brother of Vautrin, from the novels of Balzac, a man of iron will and superior intelligence, a criminal on the loose, so formidable that the law finally surrendered to him and made him chief of the secret police. (Valjean and Vautrin, as it happened, were based on a single real-life figure.) A fine and ninety days for insulting a gendarme was something of a step down from the exploits of Valjean and Vautrin, but the sentence was worth fighting. Gauguin appealed. He would have to go to Tahiti to urge his case. In advance he wrote a long and closely reasoned defense, describing himself in the process as a protector of the Marquesan people. He spoke of the honor of his name, and proposed to challenge the offending gendarme to a duel. These were brave words, measure for measure those of the criminal under the Paris guillotine shouting, "Long live the murderer! Down with justice!"

At the same time Gauguin was writing to Charles Morice that he was downed, ruined. Yet still not vanquished: "Is the Indian who smiles under torture vanquished?" But to Daniel De Monfreid, who had his confidence if anyone ever did, Gauguin wrote that he could not afford to defend himself, that the sentence passed on him by the "bandit" judge was his "ruin."

All his life, he said, he had been falling, getting up again, falling, getting up, on and on. Now he was down once more and his energy was exhausted. Finishing his letter so as to catch the mail steamer, he wrote some last words: "All these anxieties *are killing me.*"

* * *

When Gauguin came to take seriously the thought of dying and being buried in the islands, he wrote to Daniel De Monfreid, asking him to send him a piece of sculpture, a statue, that he wanted for his grave marker. He had made it in France between his two Tahitian voyages, and it had never found a buyer. (Gauguin as potter, wood carver, and sculptor had the same problems with the buying public as Gauguin the painter; he was regarded as a "buffoon," his works "beyond all limits of insanity," a manufacturer of "pornographic images" with the "erotic-macabre temperament of a genius of lewdness, a dilettante of infamy who is haunted by vice.") For this particular piece Gauguin retained a special affection, and now he wanted it at his head in death.

It was called *Oviri*, meaning "Savage," it was in stoneware, and it was extraordinary. The head is modeled from a Marquesan mummified head, of a chief who became a god, and the body is Javanese, female with animal attributes. There is a striking ugliness and fierceness about it. It stands and stares; the arms clasp the body of an animal whose head and forepaws trail on the ground; there is a red stain at the figure's feet. Gauguin had a second name for the statue, *La Tueuse*, the (female) killer. But on the back of a drawing he made of it, he wrote enigmatically that the monster was embracing its own creation, fertilized by its sperm to engender "Seraphitus Seraphita." This refers to a novel by Balzac, a favorite of Gauguin's, about perfect androgyny, the transcendent union of male and female, in which a mysterious figure appears to men as a woman, to women as a man. If all the themes in *Oviri* are noted, there is a mummy, a head of one sex on the body of the other, a mingling of animal with male and female, a creature fertilized by the blood of its own creation, death engendering life—a life that through androgyny transcends anything earthly, anything human; a life that approaches divinity.

Oviri proposed that androgyny was divine, and *Oviri* was brought into being by Gauguin. One of his strongest convictions was that the creative artistic act was a version of divinity. God and Gauguin both worked with clay, God to create man, Gauguin to imitate God. As a potter Gauguin was much drawn to stoneware, which required powerful firing. *Oviri* was made this way. In the kiln the created work went through the burning that the artist had to endure in life, and perhaps in death.

So *Oviri* was meant to see Gauguin out of an artist's life into an artist's death, through creation, suffering, and purification to some kind of transcendence. But for Gauguin, transcendence was ultimately neither an escape out of time to the eternal childhood he fantasized with his mother, nor a fatherless flight to the sun to be with his god-ancestors the Incas. Rather it was a suffering climb up Calvary. All of which is to say that—of course—Gauguin never did make himself into a savage. He spoke of his art as a dream before nature, as if this would release the living savage in him and free him from Europe, from his European self. And yet when in the Marquesas he dreamed of death, an angel with wings came to him and illuminated God's mysteries for him. The savage dreamer, in other words, dreamed like a perplexed Christian craving reassurance. As far as art itself was concerned, Gauguin was finally forced to concede to himself that his artist's dreams were ideas recovered from the past, and that the originality of a painter lay in the way that he combined and transposed elements that were really links in a great chain of tradition. So he dreamed before nature and painted from photographs, called himself a savage and quoted Wagner, Poe, Swedenborg, Balzac, Mallarmé on art, rejected Europe passionately and just as passionately yearned after justification among his own people. His involvement with Europe was a torture, a passion. He gritted his teeth and smiled as he shouldered his cross, he said; but Calvary remained Calvary, and Gauguin remained nailed to the cross of his culture.

*   *   *

Not long before Gauguin died he wrote to De Monfreid saying that he was thinking of coming back to Europe, settling probably in Spain, and looking for a cure there. De Monfreid was firmly against the idea. It could do nothing, he said, but harm Gauguin as an artist—or rather as a figure in art. There was an "incubation" going on in public opinion about him, and it should be allowed to proceed undisturbed: "At this moment you are that extraordinary, legendary artist who from the depths of Oceania despatches his disconcerting, inimitable works. . . ." The particular quality of Gauguin's paintings was enhanced by the inaccessibility of the painter. As art Gauguin's paintings were remarkable enough. As exhibits, as evidence of a life, they were "definitive," the product of a great man "who has, so to speak, disappeared from the earth." Gauguin must not come back. It would break the spell. "You enjoy the immortality of the great dead, you have passed into the *history of art.*"

De Monfreid was sound in his perception that Gauguin was most valuably Gauguin because he had made the gesture of abandoning Europe for the South Seas. For these purposes Gauguin's death was as satisfactory to the interested world as that of John Williams. He could be talked of as having died in the right place in the right way, on his chosen stage, in the midst of his life's work, a man who suffered much to achieve much, who could be celebrated for having laid himself down for his vocation.

Gauguin never served his three-month jail term. On the morning of May 8, 1903, a Marquesan coming to visit him at Maison du Jouir found him lying lifeless across his bed, with some drug ampoules empty beside him. He may have taken an overdose. Or his battered heart may have given way. It did not much concern his enemies of church and state, who filled in the death certificate, burned some of his paintings and drawings of bare Marquesan flesh, and got rid of his carnally-carved walking sticks. The rest of his belongings were bundled up and shipped to Tahiti to be sold there at auction. For the third time since Gauguin committed himself to an artist's dream before nature, his vision was put up for public bid, and for the third time it was knocked down for next to nothing. At Atuona his enemy the bishop saw him buried and wrote home to France: "Nothing of note here except the sudden death of a sad case named Gauguin, known as a painter, but an enemy of God and everything decent."

* * *

THE BISHOP WASNT FAR WRONG -

Epilogue

GAUGUIN was a civilized man who wanted to be a savage. He said so, time and again. He enjoyed listening to cannibals talk about eating human flesh; but far from being a flesh eater, he thought of himself as being torn apart and consumed by the savagery of civilization. And he never got tattooed, sailor and beachcomber though he was. Herman Melville before him shuddered and shrank from the very sight of the tattooer's needle. Robert Louis Stevenson wrote nice descriptions of tattooed ladies, but the only needle he ever felt was the hypodermic. Walter Murray Gibson did not want islands to leave their mark on him; he wanted to leave *his* mark on islands. And for John Williams, a tattooed head was the sign and symbol of utter depravity.

The real white savage in the South Seas, if such a being existed, was the white man who jumped ship without telling anyone. He hid in the hills till his ship sailed, shed his clothes, got burned brown by the sun, took a brown woman or two, learned to speak like a savage, went under the tattooer's needle—and was never heard of again, never sending out so much as a message in a bottle, certainly not putting pen to paper or brush to canvas to justify himself to himself or to explain his desertion of the white world.

John Williams's message, when he came to the South Seas, was that Polynesians should be turned into brown Englishmen. None of the others wanted to be free of the West—obviously not. Not even Gauguin, and he only less obviously because he kept saying he wanted to turn himself into a Polynesian. To other Europeans, Gauguin's paintings might have seemed as savage as tattoos, but Europeans knew about him because he crated up his art and shipped it to Europe, wanting to show white men how savage he was. Europe obsessed him, tortured him—because he was a European . . .

One night at sunset Gauguin was sitting on a rock outside his house on Hivaoa, naked except for his *pareu*, smoking, thinking about not very much, when out of the gathering darkness came a blind old Marquesan woman, tapping along with a stick, completely naked, tattooed all over, hunched, tottering, dry-skinned, mummy-like. She became aware of Gauguin's presence and felt her way toward him. He sat in inexplicable fear, his breath held in. Without a word the old woman took his hand in hers, dusty-dry, cold, reptile-cold. Gauguin felt repulsion. Then, in silence, she ran her hand over his body, down to the navel, beyond. She pushed aside his *pareu* and reached for his penis. Marquesan men—savages—were all supercised, and the raised scarred flesh was one of their great prides as makers of love. Gauguin had no savage mark on his maleness. He was uncovered for what he was. The blind searching hand withdrew, and the eyeless tattooed mummy figure disappeared into the darkness with a single word. *"Pupa,"* she croaked—White Man.

Acknowledgments

I HAVE BEEN FORTUNATE to be able to draw on the resources of libraries, archives, and museums in Europe, the United States, and the Pacific. Everywhere my requests for assistance have been met with courtesy and efficiency. I thank the directors and staff of the British Museum, the Public Record Office, the Council on World Mission, the Courtauld Institute of Art, and the Tate Gallery, London; Lady Stair's House, the Edinburgh Public Library, and the National Library of Scotland; Archives Nationales, Bibliothèque Nationale, Musée de l'Art et de l'Archéologie, Salles du Jeu de Paume, and Musée de l'Art Moderne, Paris; Ny Carlsberg Glyptotek, Copenhagen; Stedelijkmuseum, Amsterdam; Nationalmuseum, Stockholm; Museum of Modern Art, Metropolitan Museum of Art, and New York Public Library, New York; Fogg Art Museum, Cambridge; Museum of Fine Arts, Boston; Massachusetts Historical Society; Houghton Library and Widener Library, Harvard; Beinecke Rare Book and Manuscript Library and Sterling Memorial Library, Yale; Berkshire Atheneum; National Gallery of Art, Washington, D.C.; Art Institute of Chicago; Fackenthal Library, Franklin and Marshall College, Lancaster, Pennsylvania; University of Virginia Library; Church Historian's Office, Church of Jesus Christ of Latter Day Saints, Salt Lake City; Newberry Library, Chicago; Huntington Library, San Marino; Archives of Hawaii, Bernice P. Bishop Museum, Hawaiian Mission Children's Society, and Academy of Arts, Honolulu; Alexander Turnbull Library, Wellington; Mitchell Library, Sydney; Australian National Library, Canberra; Musée Gauguin, Papeete.

For permission to reproduce paintings, photographs, and signatures in facsimile, I thank the Rex Nan Kivell Collection, National Library of Australia; Council on World Mission; Berkshire Atheneum; University of Virginia Library; Archives of Hawaii (Walter Murray Gibson); Edinburgh Public Library; National Library of Scotland; Musées Nationaux, Paris; the National Maritime Museum; the Whaling Museum, New Bedford,

Mass.; the Peabody Museum of Salem; the Central Library of Edinburgh; the A. Conger Goodyear Collection, Albright-Knox Art Gallery, Buffalo; Jiri Mucha; the Tomkins Collection, Museum of Fine Arts, Boston; Musée du Louvre, Paris.

For permission to quote from unpublished material, I thank the Council on World Mission (John Williams); Beinecke Rare Book and Manuscript Library, Huntington Library, Houghton Library (Robert Louis Stevenson); Archives of Hawaii, Church Historian's Office, Church of Jesus Christ of Latter Day Saints, and Hawaiian Mission Children's Society (Walter Murray Gibson); Mitchell Library (John Williams and Robert Louis Stevenson); National Library of Scotland (Robert Louis Stevenson); Alexander Turnbull Library (Robert Louis Stevenson).

I began work on this book with the help of the National Endowment for Humanities; continued it with the help of the Center for Cultural and Technical Interchange between East and West, Honolulu; and finished it at the Australian National University. My thanks to those who have made it possible for me to work in pleasant surroundings.

I am indebted to a great many people for useful services rendered and for favors generously offered. I thank them all for their kindness: Jacob Adler, Paul Binding, Fawn Brodie, Coral Coleman, Agnes Conrad, Geoff Cummins, Greg Dening, Ian Donaldson, Hank Driessen, Leon Edel, Andrew Field, James Field, Susan Gardner, John Garrett, Gerry Gibney, Lela Goodell, Niel Gunson, Rhoda Hackler, Renée Heyum, Ken Inglis, Maureen Krascum, Pierre Lagayette, Bob Langdon, Di Langmore, Elizabeth Larsen, Barrie Macdonald, Brian McFarlane, Ian Maddocks, Harry Maude, Paki Neves, Barry Nurcombe, Douglas Oliver, Judy Poulos, Deryck Scarr, Dorothy Shineberg, Barry Smith, Bernard Smith, Bob Sparks, Paul Theroux. The book's index has been prepared by Robert and Evelyne Chasse. Particular thanks indeed to Norah Forster and Robyn Walker. And special thanks—again—to my wife.

A Note on Sources

A BRIEF LISTING is given here of some sources that were useful in documenting this book. For anyone interested in detailed references, a complete set of footnotes is available on request from the Records Room, Department of Pacific and Southeast Asian History, Research School of Pacific Studies, Australian National University, P.O. Box 4, Canberra, A.C.T., Australia 2600.

A Dream Of Islands

For the opening of the Pacific, see J. C. Beaglehole, *The Exploration of the Pacific*, 3d ed. (Stanford: Stanford University Press, 1966); the introduction to Beaglehole's edition of *The Journals of Captain James Cook*, 3 vols. (London: Cambridge University Press for the Hakluyt Society, 1955–1967)—Vol. 4 is Beaglehole's *Life of Cook;* O. H. K. Spate, *The Pacific Since Magellan: 1. The Spanish Lake* (Canberra: Australian National University Press, 1979), and Spate's "The Pacific as an Artefact," in *The Changing Pacific: Essays in Honour of H. E. Maude*, Niel Gunson, ed., (Melbourne: Oxford University Press, 1978), pp. 32–45.

For the French, see John Dunmore, *French Explorers in the Pacific*, 2 vols. (Oxford: Oxford University Press, 1965, 1969); Louis Antoine de Bougainville, *Voyage autour du monde par le frégate du Roi la Boudeuse, et la Flûte L'Étoile; en 1766, 1767, 1768 et 1769* (Paris: Saillant & Nyon, 1771); Jean-Étienne Martin-Allanic, *Bougainville navigateur et les découvertes de son temps* (Paris: Presses Universitaires de France, 1964). A collection of documents on Bougainville and Tahiti is in a special issue of *Journal de la Société des Océanistes*, 24 (1968), entitled *Hommage à Bougainville*. A more complete collection is in Étienne Taillemite, ed., *Bougainville et ses compagnons autour du monde, 1766–1769*, 2 vols. (Paris: Imprimerie Nationale, 1978).

For the English, see John Hawkesworth, ed., *An Account of the Voyages . . . in the Southern Hemisphere . . . by Commodore Byron,*

Captain Wallis, Captain Carteret, and Captain Cook . . . , 3 vols. (London: W. Strahan and T. Cadell, 1773); J. C. Beaglehole, ed., *The Endeavour Journal of Joseph Banks*, 2 vols. (Sydney: Public Library of New South Wales and Angus and Robertson, 1962); Hugh Carrington, ed., *The Discovery of Tahiti: A Journal of the Second Voyage of H.M.S. Dolphin round the World by George Robertson, 1766–1768* (London: The Hakluyt Society, 1948).

For the Spanish, see Bolton Glanville Corney, ed., *The Quest and Occupation of Tahiti by Emissaries of Spain during the Years 1772–1776*, 3 vols. (London: The Hakluyt Society, 1913–1919).

On traditional Tahitian life, see Douglas L. Oliver, *Ancient Tahitian Society*, 3 vols. (Honolulu: University Press of Hawaii, 1974). On the encounter of Europeans and Tahitians: William Pearson, "European Intimidation and the Myth of Tahiti," *Journal of Pacific History*, 4 (1969): 199–217. On shipwrecked Spanish sailors: Robert Langdon, *The Lost Caravel* (Sydney: Pacific Publications, 1975). On Jeanne Baré and Ahutoru: Martin-Allanic, *Bougainville*. On Mai: E. H. McCormick, *Omai: Pacific Envoy* (Auckland: Auckland University Press, 1977). On Charlotte Hayes: *Les Sérails de Londres, ou Les amusements nocturnes* . . . (Brussels: Henry Kistemaeckers, 1801).

The following books, among many others, offer food for thought about the West's encounter with the Pacific: Henri Baudet, *Paradise on Earth: Some Thoughts on European Images of Non-European Man* (New Haven: Yale University Press, 1965); O. Mannoni, *Prospero and Caliban: The Psychology of Colonization* (New York: Praeger, 1956); Herbert Marcuse, *Eros and Civilization: A Philosophical Inquiry into Freud* (New York: Vintage, 1961); Edward Dudley and Maximillian E. Novak, *The Wild Man Within: An Image in Western Thought from the Renaissance to Romanticism* (Pittsburgh: University of Pittsburgh Press, 1972); W. H. Auden, *The Enchafèd Flood: or, The Romantic Iconography of the Sea* (New York: Random House, 1950); Bernard Smith, *European Vision and the South Pacific, 1768–1850: A Study in the History of Ideas* (Oxford University Press, 1960). See also Kerry Howe, "The Fate of the 'Savage' in Pacific Historiography," *New Zealand Journal of History*, 11 (1977): 137–154.

John Williams

The main manuscript sources for Williams' life are in London Missionary Society, South Seas Letters, South Seas Journals, and South Seas

Personal, in the archives of the Council for World Mission, held in the Library of the School of Oriental and African Studies, London.

Williams's own version of his work is in his *Narrative of Missionary Enterprise in the South-Sea Island . . .* (London: John Snow, [1858]). Note that the edition used here is one published after Williams's death; the book first appeared in 1837. Ebenezer Prout, *Memoirs of the Life of the Rev. John Williams, Missionary to Polynesia* (London: John Snow, 1843), is a biography by a contemporary and friend. A recent life is John Gutch, *Beyond the Reefs: The Life of John Williams, Missionary* (London: Macdonald, 1974). See also [John Campbell, comp.], *The Missionary's Farewell: Valedictory Services of the Rev. John Williams, with His Parting Dedicatory Address, to Which Is Now Added an Account of His Voyage to the South Seas, and of His Mournful Death at Erromanga* (London: John Snow, 1840).

A general context for missionary work is in Max Warren, *The Missionary Movement from Britain in Modern History* (London: SCM Press, 1965). On evangelism in the Pacific, see Neil Gunson, *Messengers of Grace : Evangelical Missionaries in the South Seas, 1797–1860* (Melbourne: Oxford University Press, 1978). For the LMS specifically: Richard Lovett, *The History of the London Missionary Society, 1795–1895* (London: Henry Frowde, 1899). See also Gunson's "John Williams and His Ship: The Bourgeois Aspirations of a Missionary Family," in *Questioning the Past: A Selection of Papers in History and Government*, ed. D. P. Crook (St. Lucia: University of Queensland Press, 1972), and his "Victorian Christianity in the South Seas: A Survey," *Journal of Religious History*, 8 (1974): 183–197.

Herman Melville

The principal collections of Melville manuscripts are the Melville family papers in Houghton Library, Harvard, and the Gansevoort-Lansing papers in the New York Public Library. Other collections are listed in Jay Leyda, ed., *The Melville Log: A Documentary Life of Herman Melville, 1819–1891*, rev. ed., 2 vols. (New York: Gordian Press, 1969).

Melville's collected works are being published in an authoritative edition, as yet incomplete, by Northwestern University and the Newberry Library. The edition of *Moby-Dick* by Harrison Hayford and Hershel Parker (New York: Norton, 1969) includes useful documents. See also Herman Melville, *Moby-Dick, or the Whale*, ed. Harrison Hayford and Hershel Parker (New York: Norton, 1976). For Melville's correspondence in published form see Merrell Davis and William H. Gilman, eds., *The Letters of Herman Melville* (New Haven: Yale University Press, 1960); Eleanor Melville Metcalf, *Herman Melville: Cycle and Epicycle* (Cambridge, Mass: Harvard University Press, 1953).

Biographical and other useful details have been drawn from Leyda, *Melville Log;* William H. Gilman, *Melville's Early Life and Redburn* (New York: Russell & Russell, 1972); Wilson L. Heflin, "Herman Melville's Whaling Years" (Ph.D. diss.; Vanderbilt University, 1952); Charles Roberts Anderson, *Melville in the South Seas* (New York: Columbia University Press, 1933); Leon Howard, *Herman Melville: A Biography* (Berkeley: University of California Press, 1951); Newton Arvin, *Herman Melville* (New York: William Sloane Associates, 1950); Hugh Hetherington, *Melville's Reviewers: British and American, 1846–1891* (Chapel Hill: University of North Carolina Press, 1961); Howard P. Vincent, *The Trying-Out of "Moby-Dick"* (Carbondale: Southern Illinois University Press, 1967).

See also Edwin Haviland Miller, *Melville: A Biography* (New York: Braziller, 1975); Leo Marx, *The Machine in the Garden: Technology and the Pastoral Ideal in America* (New York: Oxford University Press, 1964); G. J. Barker-Benfield, *The Horrors of the Half-Known Life: Male Attitudes toward Women and Sexuality in Nineteenth-Century America* (New York: Harper & Row, 1976); Charles J. Haberstroh, Jr., "Melville's Fathers: A Study of the Father Substitutes in Melville's Fiction" (Ph.D. diss., University of Pennsylvania, 1971); Henry A. Murray, "Dead to the World: The Passions of Herman Melville," in *Essays in Self-Destruction*, ed. Edwin S. Shneidman (New York: Science House, 1967), pp. 7–29, and Murray's introduction to Melville's *Pierre* (New York: Hendricks House, 1949); William Stanton, *The United States Exploring Expedition* (Berkeley: University of California Press, 1976); David Jaffé, "The Captain Who Sat for the Portrait of Ahab," *Boston University Studies in English*, 4 (1960): 1–22.

Walter Murray Gibson

There is no full-length biography of Gibson. (Professor Jacob Adler of the University of Hawaii is at work on one.) Aspects of Gibson's life are discussed in the following works: the introduction to Jacob Adler and Gwynn Barrett, eds., *The Diaries of Walter Murray Gibson, 1886, 1887* (Honolulu: University Press of Hawaii, 1973); Gibson's own *The Prison of Weltevreden: And a Glance at the East Indian Archipelago* (New York: J. C. Riker, 1855); United States, 34 Congress, 1 Session, House of Representatives, *Report*, No. 307, August 2, 1856; James Warren Gould, "The

Filibuster of Walter Murray Gibson," Hawaiian Historical Society *Report*, 68 (1960): 7–32; Frank W. McGhie, "The Life and Intrigues of Walter Murray Gibson" (M.Sc. thesis, Brigham Young University, 1958—contains a transcription of a Gibson diary); Gwynn Barrett, "Walter Murray Gibson: The Shepherd Saint of Lanai Revisited," *Utah Historical Quarterly*, 40 (1972): 142–162; R. Lanier Britsch, "Another Visit with Walter Murray Gibson," *Utah Historical Quarterly*, 46 (1978): 65–78; Britsch, "The Lanai Colony: A Hawaiian Extension of the Mormon Colonial Idea," *Hawaiian Journal of History*, 12 (1978): 68–83; Esther Leonore Sousa, "Walter Murray Gibson's Rise to Power in Hawaii" (M.A. thesis, University of Hawaii, 1942); Raymond Clyde Beck, "Palawai Basin: Hawaii's Mormon Zion" (M.A. thesis, University of Hawaii, 1972); Comfort Margaret Bock, "The Church of Jesus Christ of Latter Day Saints in Hawaii" (M.A. thesis, University of Hawaii, 1941).

Gibson's correspondence with Brigham Young and other Mormons is in the Church Historian's Office, Salt Lake City; photocopies are in the Archives of Hawaii, Honolulu.

The context of Gibson's political life in Hawaii is in Ralph S. Kuykendall, *The Hawaiian Kingdom: 3. 1874–1893, The Kalakaua Dynasty* (Honolulu: University of Hawaii Press, 1967); Gavan Daws, *Shoal of Time: A History of the Hawaiian Islands* (New York: Macmillan, 1968); Jacob Adler, *Claus Spreckels: The Sugar King in Hawaii* (Honolulu: University of Hawaii Press, 1966). The manuscript record of the Gibson regime is in the Archives of Hawaii, especially in the Foreign Office & Executive file. Gibson published three newspapers in Honolulu: *Nuhou, Elele Poakolu,* and *Pacific Commercial Advertiser.*

See also for general context on Gibson as a person and a politician Lucille Iremonger, *The Fiery Chariot: A Study of British Prime Ministers and the Search for Love* (London: Secker & Warburg, 1970); and Maryse Choisy, "Le Complexe de Phaéton," *Psyché,* 5 (1950): 715–731.

Robert Louis Stevenson

Stevenson manuscript materials in the following repositories were useful in writing this chapter: Harvard University (Vailima Letters, Widener MSS, Houghton Library); National Library of Scotland (Advocates MSS; Stevenson-Colvin Letters; Balfour Papers; Rosebery Papers); University of Hawaii (Catton Papers); British Museum; Mitchell Library, Sydney; Alexander Turnbull Library, Wellington, New Zealand. The collection of Stevenson material in the Beinecke Rare Book and Manuscript Library, Yale, is described in George L. McKay, comp., *A Stevenson Library:*

Catalogue of a Collection of Writings by and about Robert Louis Steven-son Formed by Edwin J. Beinecke, 6 vols. (New Haven: Yale University Library, 1951–1964).

The Vailima Edition of the *Works of Robert Louis Stevenson*, ed. Lloyd Osbourne, with prefatory notes by Fanny Van de Grift Stevenson, 26 vols. (New York: Scribner's, 1922–1923), has been used. *The Letters of Robert Louis Stevenson*, ed. Sidney Colvin, 4 vols., comprise Vols. XX–XXIII of the Vailima Edition. Other useful published collections of letters are: Delancey Ferguson and Marshall Waingrow, eds., *R.L.S.: Steven-son's Letters to Charles Baxter* (New Haven: Yale University Press, 1956); and Janet Adam Smith, *Henry James and Robert Louis Stevenson: A Record of Friendship and Criticism* (London: Rupert Hart-Davis, 1948).

Biographical detail has been drawn from J. C. Furnas, *Voyage to Wind-ward: The Life of Robert Louis Stevenson* (New York: William Sloane As-sociates, 1948); Graham Balfour, *The Life of Robert Louis Stevenson*, 2 vols. (New York: Scribner's, 1901); and Margaret Mackay, *The Violent Friend: The Story of Mrs. Robert Louis Stevenson* (Garden City, N.Y.: Doubleday, 1968).

See also Kenneth Starr Mackenzie, "Robert Louis Stevenson and Samoa, 1889–1894" (Ph.D. diss., Dalhousie University, 1974), and Mack-enzie's "The Lost Opportunity: Robert Louis Stevenson and Samoa, 1889–1894," in *More Pacific Islands Portraits*, ed. Deryck Scarr (Can-berra: Australian National University Press, 1979), pp. 221–247; Robert Kiely, *Robert Louis Stevenson and the Fiction of Adventure* (Cambridge, Mass.: Harvard University Press, 1964); Isabel Proudfit, "The Big Round World: A Psychiatric Study of Robert Louis Stevenson," *Psychoanalytic Review*, 23 (1936): 121–148; Mark Kanzer, "The Self-Analytic Literature of Robert Louis Stevenson," in *Psychoanalysis and Culture: Essays in Honor of Géza Róheim*, ed. George Wilbur and Werner Muensterberger (New York: International Universities Press, 1951), pp. 425–435.

Paul Gauguin

For a guide to Gauguin's paintings, see Georges Wildenstein, *Paul Gauguin: 1. Catalogue* (Paris: Editions les Beaux-Arts, 1964). Gauguin's papers are scattered. There is no collected edition; see the discussion in Pierre Leprohon, *Paul Gauguin* (Paris: Grund, 1975), pp. 403–412. The principal published collections of letters are Maurice Malingue, ed., *Lettres de Gauguin à sa femme et à ses amis*, rev. ed. (Paris: Bernard Grasset, 1949); and Mme. A Joly-Segalen, *Lettres de Gauguin à Daniel de Monfreid* (Paris: Georges Falaize, 1950). Two works by Gauguin frequently referred to are: *Cahier pour Aline,* ed. Suzanne Damiron (Paris: Société des Amis de la Bibliothèque d'Art et d'Archéologie de l'Université de Paris, 1963); and *Avant et après* (Paris: G. Crès et Cie, 1923). The edition of *Noa Noa* used is by Jean Loize (Paris: André Balland, 1966); it has a useful bibliography. A selection of Gauguin's writings is in Daniel Guérin, ed., *Paul Gauguin: Oviri: Ecrits d'un sauvage* (Paris: Gallimard, 1974). The American edition of *Oviri,* entitled *The Writings of a Savage, Paul Gauguin* (New York: Viking, 1978) has an introduction by Wayne Andersen.

Biographical and other useful detail is from Henri Perruchot, *Gauguin* (Cleveland: World, 1963); Bengt Danielsson, *Gauguin in the South Seas* (Garden City, N.Y.: Doubleday, 1966), which looks at its subject from close range—a revised French edition is Bengt and Marie-Therésè Danielsson, *Gauguin à Tahiti et aux Îles Marquises* (Papeete: Éditions du Pacifique, 1975); John Rewald, *Post-Impressionism: From Van Gogh to Gauguin,* rev. ed. (New York: Museum of Modern Art, 1962); Ursula Frances Marks-Vandenbroucke, "Gauguin: ses origines et sa formation artistique," *Gazette des Beaux-Arts,* 47 (1956): 1–61; Jean Baelen, *La Vie de Flora Tristan: Socialisme et feminisme au XIXe siècle* (Paris: Éditions du Seuil, 1972); Merete Bodelsen, "Gauguin, the Collector," *Burlington Magazine,* 112 (1970): 590–615.

See also Wayne Andersen, *Gauguin's Paradise Lost* (New York: Viking, 1971); Ruth Deborah Rothschild, "A Study in the Problems of Self-Portraiture: The Self-Portraits of Paul Gauguin" (Ph.D. diss., Columbia University, 1961); Christopher Gray, *Sculpture and Ceramics of Paul Gauguin* (Baltimore: The John Hopkins Press, 1963); Merete Bodelsen, *Gauguin's Ceramics* (London: Faber and Faber, 1964); Henri Dorra, "The First Eves in Gauguin's Eden," *Gazette des Beaux-Arts,* 41 (March, 1953): 187–202; Barbara Landy, "The Meaning of Gauguin's 'Oviri' Ceramic," *Burlington Magazine,* 109 (1967): 242–246.

Index